HADRIAN AND THE CITY OF ROME

MARY TALIAFERRO BOATWRIGHT

# HADRIAN AND THE CITY OF ROME

PRINCETON, NEW JERSEY

PRINCETON UNIVERSITY PRESS

MCM · LXXXVII

COPYRIGHT © 1987 BY PRINCETON UNIVERSITY PRESS
PUBLISHED BY PRINCETON UNIVERSITY PRESS, 41 WILLIAM STREET
PRINCETON, NEW JERSEY 08540
IN THE UNITED KINGDOM:
PRINCETON UNIVERSITY PRESS, GUILDFORD, SURREY

LIBRARY OF CONGRESS CATALOGING IN PUBLICATION
DATA WILL BE FOUND ON THE LAST PRINTED PAGE OF THIS BOOK

ISBN 0–691–03588–1

PUBLICATION OF THIS BOOK HAS BEEN AIDED BY THE
PUBLICATIONS PROGRAM OF THE NATIONAL ENDOWMENT FOR THE
HUMANITIES AN INDEPENDENT FEDERAL AGENCY

THIS BOOK HAS BEEN COMPOSED IN LINOTRON BEMBO

CLOTHBOUND EDITIONS OF
PRINCETON UNIVERSITY PRESS BOOKS
ARE PRINTED ON ACID-FREE PAPER, AND
BINDING MATERIALS ARE CHOSEN FOR
STRENGTH AND DURABILITY. PAPER-
BACKS, ALTHOUGH SATISFACTORY FOR
PERSONAL COLLECTIONS, ARE NOT
USUALLY SUITABLE FOR
LIBRARY REBINDING

★

PRINTED IN THE UNITED STATES OF
AMERICA BY PRINCETON UNIVERSITY PRESS
PRINCETON, NEW JERSEY

*To Paul*

# CONTENTS

# ILLUSTRATIONS

# ACKNOWLEDGMENTS

IT IS WITH a deep love for the city of Rome and fascination with Roman imperial history that I have written this book. It is, however, a work of synthesis and interpretation, for although I have lived and studied in Rome over a period of years, I have not yet had the chance to excavate there. My information is based on the published work of others, as well as on the generous communications of scholars currently investigating the ancient city of Rome.

The book would not have been possible without the support of the American Philosophical Society, in the form of a travel grant in 1984, and that of Duke University, in the form of research grants from the University Research Council in 1984 and 1985, and a funded leave of absence in spring 1982, when I began the project. Only the generosity of these two institutions enabled me to visit Rome in 1982 and 1984 for research in situ to supplement work in the United States, and I am most grateful to both.

In Rome and the United States I have benefited immensely from the assistance of many colleagues. Rome's excavators and topographers have been unfailingly helpful, discussing their current and previous work and allowing me access to monuments and collections otherwise unavailable. I have cited specific debts to these individuals throughout the footnotes, but would like to acknowledge them here as well. The list includes: C. Buzzetti, F. Castagnoli, F. Coarelli, C. Coletti, L. Cozza, G. Crifó, E. Gatti, I. Jacopi, C. Krause, E. La Rocca, G. Martines, S. Panciera, S. Panella, R. L. Rakob, E. Rodriguez-Almeida, M. Steinby, M. Torelli, P. Zanker, and F. Zevi. Others in Rome whose time and suggestions aided me include R. T. Scott, L. La Follette, J. T. Peña, and J. Poe. Here at Duke and in America I am grateful to G. W. Houston, G. M. Koeppel, J. Packer, K. J. Rigsby, O. S. Wintermute, and J. G. Younger, all of whom critiqued portions of my manuscript; to B. Frischer and W. L. MacDonald for discussion and correspondence; to C. I. Rine, who helped with the seemingly endless job of checking footnotes; to W. E. Lee, who helped with some of the maps; and to D. A. Conner, who drafted Illustrations 1, 11, 22, 31, and 35. My father, V. T. Boatwright, provided expert editorial advice. Any errors in the book, of course, are my own and not attributable to the individuals mentioned above.

E. Buchner and K. de Fine Licht generously gave me permission to use some of their illustrations. I also thank the responsive audiences of the American Philological Association meetings of 1983 and 1984, the Classical Association of the Atlantic States fall meeting of 1984, Duke's Erasmus Club meeting of October 1983, and the Archaeological Institute of America, North Carolina Society meeting of September 1985, at which I presented portions of my work. Special gratitude is due as well to the library and staff of the American Academy in Rome, to the editors of the *American Journal of Archaeology* for suggestions regarding "The '*Ara Ditis–Ustrinum* of Hadrian' in the Western Campus Martius and Other Problematic Roman *Ustrina*," now a part of Chapter 7, and to Joanna Hitchcock, my editor at Princeton University Press.

Finally, I am most grateful to my colleague Lawrence Richardson, Jr., who urged me to this topic and has helped me unstintingly at every stage of the book; and to my husband, Paul J. Feldblum, who has encouraged and advised me throughout the project. This is a better book because of them and indeed, without them, might never have been written.

*March* 1986

# ABBREVIATIONS

Abbreviations used for periodicals, standard references, and the more unusual ancient references throughout the notes and bibliography are explained here. More common ancient authors and works are abbreviated according to the conventions of the *Archaeological Journal of America* and the *Oxford Classical Dictionary*.   All translations are by the author.

| | |
|---|---|
| *AA* | *Archäologischer Anzeiger* |
| *AE* | *L'Année épigraphique* |
| *AJA* | *American Journal of Archaeology* |
| *AJP* | *American Journal of Philology* |
| *AnalDan* | *Analecta Danici* |
| *ANSNS* | *American Numismatic Society, Numismatic Studies* |
| *AntCl* | *L'Antiquité classique* |
| *AntK* | *Antike Kunst* |
| *ANRW* | Temporini, H., ed. *Aufstieg und Niedergang der römischen Welt.* Berlin 1972– |
| *ArchCl* | *Archeologia Classica* |
| Aur. Vict. *Caes.* | Sextus Aurelius Victor. *De Caesaribus.* Ed. F. Pichlmayr and R. Gruendel. 2nd ed. Leipzig 1970 |
| *BdA* | *Bollettino d'Arte* |
| Beaujeu | Beaujeu, J. *La Religion romaine à l'apogée de l'empire.* 1: *La Politique religieuse des Antonins.* Paris 1955 |
| BEFAR | Bibliothèque des Ecoles françaises d'Athènes et de Rome |
| *BGU* | Aegyptische Urkunden aus d. Kgl. Museen zu Berlin. Griechische Urkunden. Berlin 1895–1926 |
| *BJb* | *Bonner Jahrbücher* |
| Blake, I | Blake, M. E. *Ancient Roman Construction in Italy from the Prehistoric Period to Augustus.* Carnegie Institution of Washington. Publications 570. Washington, D.C. 1947 |
| Blake, II | Blake, M. E. *Roman Construction in Italy from Tiberius through the Flavians.* Washington, D.C. 1959 |
| Blake/Bishop | Blake, M. E., D. T. Bishop, and J. D. Bishop. *Roman Construction in Italy from Nerva through the Antonines.* Memoirs of the American Philosophical Society 96. Philadelphia 1973 |

Bloch, *Bolli*  Bloch, H. *I bolli laterizi e la storia edilizia romana. Contributi all'archeologia e alla storia romana.* Restamped from *BullComm* 64 (1936)–66 (1938), with analytical indices published in 1947. Rome 1968

*BMC, Emp.*  Mattingly, H. *Coins of the Roman Empire in the British Museum.* I– . London 1923–

Buecheler, *Carm. Epig.*  Buecheler, F. *Carmina Latina Epigraphica.* 2 vols. with supplement by E. Lommatzsch. Leipzig 1895–1926

*BullComm*  *Bullettino della Commissione Archeologica Comunale di Roma*

*BullInst*  *Bullettino dell'Istituto di Corrispondenza Archeologica.* Rome 1829–85

*CAR*  *Carta Archeologica di Roma,* I–III. Florence 1962–77

Castagnoli, *TRA*  Castagnoli, F. *Topografia di Roma antica.* Turin 1980

*CIG*  *Corpus Inscriptionum Graecarum*

*CIL*  *Corpus Inscriptionum Latinarum*

*Città e architettura*  *Città e architettura nella Roma imperiale. AnalDan,* Supplement 10. Copenhagen 1983

Clem. Al. *Protr.*  Clemens Alexandrinus. *Protrepticus*

Coarelli, *Roma* (1974)  Coarelli, F. *Guida archeologica di Roma.* Verona 1974

Coarelli, *Roma* (1980)  Coarelli, F. *Roma.* Guide archeologiche Laterza 6. Bari 1980

*CP*  *Classical Philology*

*CPCA*  *University of California Publications in Classical Archaeology*

*CQ*  *Classical Quarterly*

*CRAI*  *Comptes rendus de l'Académie des inscriptions et belles lettres*

Crema  Crema, L. *L'architettura romana.* Enciclopedia Classica III.12.1. Turin 1959

*DarSag*  Daremberg, C. and E. Saglio. *Dictionnaire des antiquités grecques et romaines.* Graz 1877–1919

*DialArch*  *Dialoghi di Archeologia*

*Dig.*  *Digesta*

Dio Cass.  Dio Cassius. *Roman History.* Ed. E. W. Cary. London and New York 1914–27

*DizEpig*  De Ruggiero, E. *Dizionario epigrafico di antichità romane,* I– . Rome 1895–

*Doxa*  *Doxa. Rassegna critica di antichità classica,* I–IV. Rome 1948–51

| | |
|---|---|
| *Empereurs d'Espagne* | *Empereurs romains d'Espagne.* Colloques internationaux du centre national de la recherche scientifique. Sciences humaines. Organized by A. Piganiol and H. Terrasse. Paris 1965 |
| *Epit. de Caes.* | *Epitome de Caesaribus.* Ed. F. Pichlmayr and R. Gruendel. 2nd ed. Leipzig 1970 |
| EPRO | *Etudes préliminaires aux religions orientales dans l'empire romain* |
| Eutrop. | Eutropius |
| *FGrHist* | Jacoby, F. *Die Fragmente der griechischen Historiker.* Berlin and Leiden 1923– |
| *FIRA* | *Fontes Iuris Romani Anteiustiniani.* Ed. S. Riccobono, J. Baviera, C. Ferrini, J. Furlani, and V. Arangio Ruiz. 2nd ed. Florence 1940–43 |
| *Forma Urbis* | Carettoni, G., A. M. Colini, L. Cozza, and G. Gatti. *La pianta marmorea di Roma antica.* Rome 1960 |
| *G&R* | *Greece and Rome* |
| Garzetti | Garzetti, A. *From Tiberius to the Antonines. A History of the Roman Empire, AD 14–192.* Trans. J. R. Foster. London 1974 |
| Gnecchi | Gnecchi, F. *I medaglioni romani.* 3 vols. Milan 1912 |
| *HA* | *Scriptores Historiae Augustae.* Ed. E. Hohn. 2 vols. Second Teubner edition corrected by C. Samberger and W. Seyfarth. Leipzig 1971 |
| *HAC* | *Bonner Historia Augusta Colloquium* |
| Helbig | Helbig, W. *Führer durch die öffentlichen Sammlungen klassischer Altertümer in Rom.* 4th ed. Tübinger 1963–72 |
| *Hellenismus in Mittelitalien* | *Hellenismus in Mittelitalien.* Ed. P. Zanker. Abhandlungen der Akademie der Wissenschaften in Göttingen III.97. Göttingen 1976 |
| Henzen, *AFA* | Henzen, G. *Acta Fratrum Arvalium quae supersunt.* Berlin 1874 |
| *HJ* | Jordan, H. *Topographie der Stadt Rom in Alterthum.* I.3. Rev. C. Hülsen. Berlin 1907 |
| *HSCP* | *Harvard Studies in Classical Philology* |
| *HThR* | *Harvard Theological Review* |
| *IG* | *Inscriptiones Graecae* |
| *IGRR* | *Inscriptiones Graecae ad Res Romanas Pertinentes* |
| *IGUR* | Moretti, L., ed. *Inscriptiones Graecae urbis Romae.* Studi pubblicati del Istituto italiano per la storia antica. Fasc. 17, 22, 24, –. Rome 1968– |
| *II* | *Inscriptiones Italiae.* Rome 1931– |

| | |
|---|---|
| *ILS* | Dessau, H. *Inscriptiones Latinae Selectae.* Berlin 1892–1916 |
| Inst. Neg. | Istituto Archeologico Germanico, Rome (Deutsches Archäologisches Institut, Römische Abteilung), Negative |
| *JdI* | *Jahrbuch des (k.) deutschen archäologischen Instituts* |
| Jerome, *Chron.* H. | Helm, R. *Eusebius Werke. Siebenter Band. Die Chronik des Hieronymus. Hieronymi Chronicon.* Die griechischen christlichen Schriftsteller der ersten Jahrhunderte 47. Berlin 1956 |
| Jordan | Jordan, H. *Topographie der Stadt Rom in Alterthum.* 1.1 and 1.2, II. Berlin 1878, 1885, 1871 |
| *JRS* | *Journal of Roman Studies* |
| *JSAH* | *Journal of the Society of Architectural Historians* |
| Lanciani, *FUR* | Lanciani, R. *Forma Urbis Romae.* Milan 1893–1901 |
| *Le Culte des souverains dans l'empire romain* | *Le Culte des souverains dans l'empire romain.* Ed. W. den Boer. Entretiens sur l'antiquité classique 19. Vandouvres-Geneva 1973 |
| Lugli, *Centro* | Lugli, G. *Roma antica. Il centro monumentale.* Rome 1946 |
| Lugli, *Fontes* | Lugli, G. *Fontes ad topographiam veteris urbis Romae pertinentes.* I– . Rome 1952– |
| Lugli, *MAR* | Lugli, G. *I monumenti antichi di Roma e suburbio,* I–III, e supplemento. Rome 1931–40 |
| Lugli, *StudMin* | Lugli, G. *Studi minori di topografia antica.* Rome 1965 |
| Lydus *de Mens.* | Lydus, *de Mensibus* |
| *MAAR* | *Memoirs of the American Academy in Rome* |
| Magnaguti | Magnaguti, A. *Ex nummis historia,* I–III. Rome 1950 |
| Mazzini | Mazzini, G. *Catalogo della collezione Mazzini,* I–III. Rome 1955 |
| *MélRome* | *Mélanges d'archéologie et d'histoire de l'Ecole française de Rome* |
| *MemLinc* | *Memorie della R. Accademia Nazionale dei Lincei* |
| *MemPontAcc* | *Atti della Pontificia Accademia Romana di Archeologia, Memorie* |
| Mommsen, *Chron. Min.* | Mommsen, R. *Monumenta Germaniae Historica.* Vols. 9, 11, 13: *Chronica minora saec. IV, V, VI, VII.* 3 vols. Berlin 1892–98 |
| *MonAnt* | *Monumenti Antichi* |
| Nash | Nash, E. *Pictorial Dictionary of Ancient Rome.* 2 vols. New York 1961–62 |
| *NC* | *Numismatic Chronicle* |
| *NSc* | *Notizie degli Scavi di Antichità* |
| *NumCirc* | Spink and Son, *Numismatic Circular* |
| *ÖJh* | *Jahreshefte des österreichischen archäologischen Instituts* |

| | |
|---|---|
| *OpusArch* | *Opus Archaeologica* |
| *OpusRom* | *Opuscula Romana* |
| Origen *C. Celsus* | Origen, *Contra Celsum* |
| *PBSR* | *Papers of the British School at Rome* |
| *PdP* | *La Parola del Passato* |
| P. Giss. | *Griechische Papyri im Museum des oberhessischen Geschichtsvereins zu Giessen.* Ed. O. Eger, E. Kornemann, and P. M. Meyer. Leipzig and Berlin 1910–22 |
| Philostr. *VS* | Philostratus. *Vitae Sophistarum* |
| *PIR* | *Prosopographia Imperii Romani* |
| *PL* | Migne, P. *Patrologiae Cursus, series Latina* |
| Platner-Ashby | Platner, S. B. and T. Ashby. *A Topographical Dictionary of Ancient Rome.* Oxford 1929 |
| P. Lond. | *Greek Papyri in the British Museum.* London 1893– |
| PMAAR | American Academy in Rome, Papers and Monographs |
| Pol. Silv. | *Polemii Silvii Laterculus.* In Mommsen, *Chron. Min.* i |
| P. Oxy. | *The Oxyrhynchus Papryi.* Published by the Egypt Exploration Society in *Graeco-Roman Memoirs.* London 1898– |
| *ProcBritAc* | *Proceedings of the British Academy* |
| *PropKg* | *Das römische Weltreich.* Ed. T. Kraus. Propyläen Kunstgeschichte 2. Berlin 1967 |
| *QuadAEI* | *Quaderni del Centro di Studio per l'archeologia etrusco-italica* |
| *QuadIstTopAnt* | *Quaderni dell'Istituto di topografia antica* |
| *RA* | *Revue archéologique* |
| *RACrist* | *Rivista di Archeologia Cristiana* |
| *RE* | Pauly-Wissowa. *Real-Encyclopädie der klassischen Altertumswissenschaft* |
| *REA* | *Revue des études anciennes* |
| *REL* | *Revue des études latines* |
| *RendLinc* | *Rendiconti della R. Accademia dei Lincei* |
| *RendPontAcc* | *Atti della Pontificia Accademia Romana di Archeologia, Rendiconti* |
| *RG* | *Res Gestae divi Augusti (Monumentum Ancyranum)* |
| *RHR* | *Revue de l'histoire des religions* |
| *RIC* | Mattingly, H. and E. A. Sydenham. *The Roman Imperial Coinage.* London 1923–81 |
| *RIN* | *Rivista Italiana di Numismatica* |
| *RivFil* | *Rivista di Filologia e d'Istruzione Classica* |

| | |
|---|---|
| *RömMitt* | *Mitteilungen des deutschen archäologischen Instituts, Römische Abteilung* |
| Roullet | Roullet, A. *The Egyptian and Egyptianizing Monuments of Imperial Rome.* EPRO 20. Leiden 1972 |
| *SIG* | Dittenberger. *Sylloge Inscriptionum Graecarum* |
| Smallwood | Smallwood, E. M. *Documents Illustrating the Principates of Nerva, Trajan and Hadrian.* Cambridge 1966 |
| Steinby, "CronFig" | Steinby, M. "La cronologia delle *figlinae* doliari urbane dalla fine dell'età repubblicana fino all'inizio del III secolo." *BullComm* 94 (1974–75) [1977] 7–132 |
| Strack, I | Strack, P. L. *Untersuchungen zur römischen Reichsprägung des zweiten Jahrhunderts.* I: *Die Reichsprägung zur Zeit des Traian.* Stuttgart 1931 |
| Strack, *Hadrian* | Strack, P. L. *Untersuchungen zur römischen Reichsprägung des zweiten Jahrhunderts.* II: *Die Reichsprägung zur Zeit des Hadrian.* Stuttgart 1933 |
| *Studies in Roman Property* | *Studies in Roman Property.* Ed. M. I. Finley. Cambridge 1976 |
| *Suda* | Greek lexicon formerly known as Suidas |
| *TAPA* | *Transactions of the American Philological Association* |
| *Valentini and Zucchetti* | Valentini, R. and G. Zucchetti. *Codice topografico della città di Roma.* Vols. I–IV. Fonti per la storia d'Italia 81, 88, 90, 91. Rome 1940–53 |
| Weber | Weber, W. *Untersuchungen zur Geschichte der Kaiser Hadrianus.* Leipzig 1907 |
| *YCS* | *Yale Classical Studies* |
| Zos. | Zosimus |
| *ZPE* | *Zeitschrift für Papyrologie und Epigraphik* |

HADRIAN AND THE CITY OF ROME

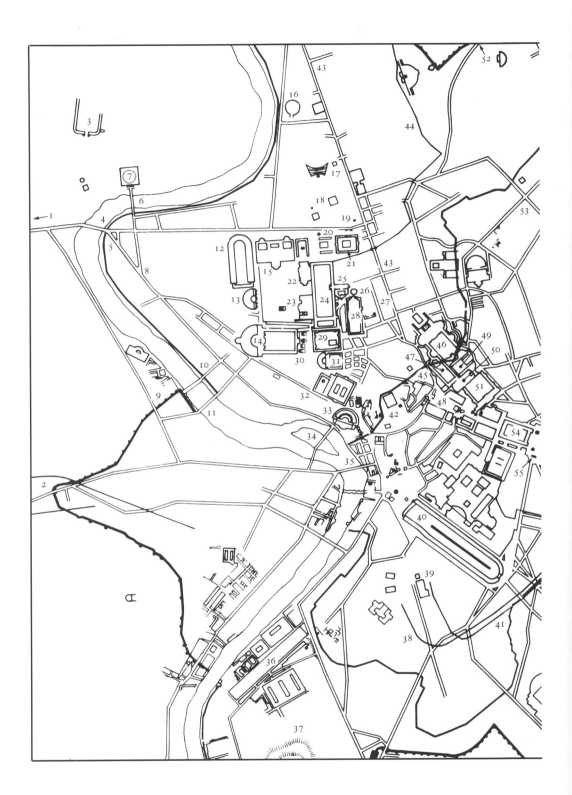

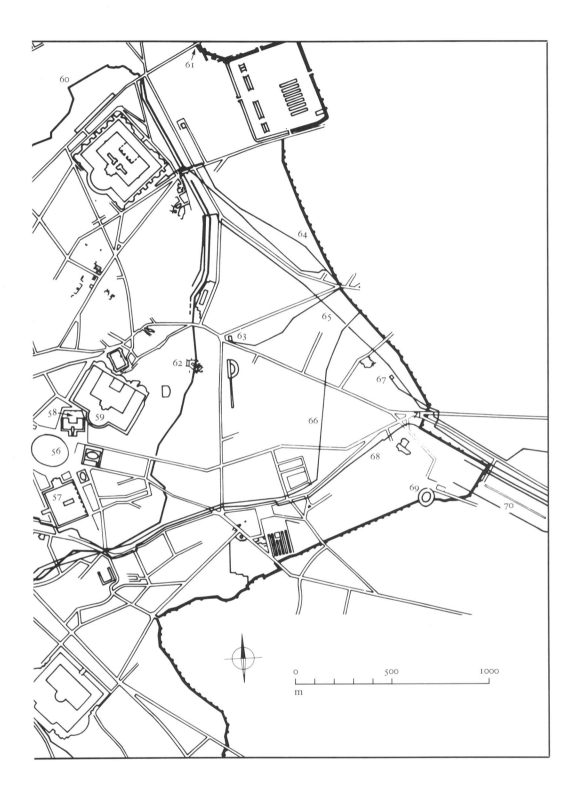

## Key to Map of Imperial Rome

# INTRODUCTION

As princeps from A.D. 117 to 138, Hadrian left an indelible mark on the city of Rome and the Roman empire, and even today many of the best-known buildings of ancient Rome are Hadrianic. The enigmatic Pantheon, the looming mass of the Temple of Venus and Roma, Hadrian's enormous Mausoleum transformed into Castel Sant'Angelo, and his extensive villa close to Rome at Tivoli, which is said to have been named in its varied parts for places throughout Rome's dominion, epitomize for many the power and resources of Rome at its zenith. Because other urban changes in the capital city during Hadrian's principate have left less visible traces, however, few people realize how powerfully Hadrian transformed the face and life of the capital city not only by these and other monumental edifices, but by renovating buildings and even entire districts, and by reorganizing the building industry and neighborhood life. The full significance of Hadrian's constructions and sociopolitical urban changes remains elusive, and no comprehensive catalogue of them yet exists.[1] This study has a twofold purpose: to bring together and to discuss in urban and historical context Hadrian's constructions and administrative changes in Rome.

Lewis Mumford has observed that a city is at one and the same time a "collection of architectural forms in space" *and* the container and transmitter of culture, that is, of history.[2] Similarly, this book aims at both a detailed topographical examination of Hadrianic Rome—in order to establish the physical constructions and changes that occurred during Hadrian's rule—and a deeper understanding of Hadrian's principate. Ancient and modern historians

---

[1] Lists of Hadrian's works in Rome, many of which are now outdated, usually include only new buildings and renovations: see Platner-Ashby, 597; Blake/Bishop, 40–65; G. Lugli, *La tecnica edilizia dei romani con particolare riguardo a Roma e Lazio* (Rome 1957) I.331, 438–40, 604–606 (hereafter Lugli, *Edilizia*); Bloch, *Bolli* 348–49; B. d'Orgeval, *L'Empereur Hadrien, oeuvre législative et admi-*

*nistrative* (Paris 1950) 270–71; and T. Frank, *Economic Survey of Ancient Rome,* v (Baltimore 1940) 71–72. Information on urban administration and changes in the economy of the city during his rule is scattered.

[2] L. Mumford, "City. Forms and Functions," in *International Encyclopedia of the Social Sciences,* 2, ed. by D. L. Sills (New York 1968) 447–48.

mark this as a time of great transition, almost a watershed in Roman history, yet it is an era for which the evidence is particularly poor.[3] Although new evidence and painstaking review of known material is proving some claims for the period to have been exaggerated,[4] no one denies that Hadrian was responsible for important and wide-ranging achievements during a principate that lasted twenty-one years, the longest since Tiberius. His accomplishments are all the more remarkable in light of the resentment and suspicion infecting his earliest and latest years as princeps, to which we shall return in the course of the book.

The starting point and focus of this book is the topography of Hadrianic Rome: the buildings and changes in the city's life that can be assigned to Hadrian's reign. This relatively unexplored body of evidence in turn illuminates Hadrian's principate. Thus, for example, the discussion of Hadrianic changes in the Campus Martius will turn to the wider questions of Hadrian's conception of the principate and his emulation of Augustus; similarly, the evaluations of the Temple of the Deified Trajan and Plotina and the Temple of Venus and Roma involve consideration of traditional and innovative aspects of Roman religion during Hadrian's rule, and the investigation of the Athenaeum sheds light on the development of the Roman empire as a Greco-Roman world. Detailed research on the topography of Rome is set against the more general history of Hadrian's principate, although the present undertaking is by no means a full-scale history of the era. The book is intended not only for scholars specializing in Roman topography, but for anyone interested in the politics, culture, and religion of Rome in the first half of the second century A.D.

Although Hadrian built extensively throughout the Roman world (cf., e.g., *HA, Hadr.* 19.2; *Epit. de Caes.* 14.4–5), this book focuses on his work in Rome. The detailed knowledge of Hadrian's effect on the capital of Roman power and culture[5] is a prerequisite to understanding the multifaceted phenomenon of Hadrianic urbanism in the Roman empire, a subject to which I

[3] For example, P. Petit, "Le II<sup>e</sup> siècle après J.-C. Etat des questions et problèmes," *ANRW* II.2 (1975) 354–80, esp. 354–65.
[4] Such as Hadrian's elevation of equestrians at the expense of senators, alleged by *HA, Hadr.* 7.5 and Aur. Vict. *Caes.* 13.5 (cf. P. A. Brunt, "Princeps and Equites," *JRS* 73 [1983] 44, 70); his reorganization of the *consilium principis* (cf. J. Crook, *Consilium Principis*

[Cambridge 1955; reprinted New York 1975] 56–65); and his dramatic break with Trajan's traditionally expansionistic policy cited by, e.g., *HA, Hadr.* 9.1 (cf. Garzetti, 371–82).
[5] For specific reference to Rome's merited supremacy, see, e.g., Aristid. *Or.* 26.6–9; Amm. Marc. 16.10.14–16; and Dion. Hal. *Ant. Rom.* 3.67.5; and see the other citations collected in Lugli, *Fontes* I, 102–12.

hope to return at a later date. During the principate the ancient city of Rome was restricted in physical extent, some 1373 hectares in the inhabited area later surrounded by the walls of Aurelian (about 3391 acres, or 5.30 square miles); within this area, much of which was taken up by public buildings and parks, the people were densely packed, with a population estimated as high as one million by the beginning of the second century A.D.[6] Traditionally, Rome was the main seat of the emperor, who was at once the political, military, and religious head of the state; Hadrian's prolonged absences from the city will be discussed in Chapter 5. The city was also the seat of the Roman senate, the chief magistrates and officials, and the central archives of the state, as well as the principal site of foreign diplomats and ambassadors. The buildings serving the political needs of Rome—the curiae and temples in which meetings of the senate were convoked, the fora and basilicae in which oratory resonated, the residences of the princeps and notables in which men made valuable social contacts and fostered cultural and artistic accomplishment and learning—reflected glory and prestige on the Roman ruling elite, and also shaped their image of themselves and their princeps, their society, culture, and religion (cf. Vitruv. *De Arch.* 1. *praef.* 2, 3).

The great majority of the Roman people had neither wealth nor political power, but as the inhabitants of the capital city they felt entitled to distributions and entertainment provided by the princeps. Although the masses' aesthetic sensibilities are rarely mentioned in the sources,[7] the populace of Rome must have benefited from the opportunities for employment offered through building programs and also from improvements in the city's hygiene, communications, and habitable space. Even less well documented are the effect on the tenor of life made by shrines, temples, public buildings such as baths and theaters, and the atmosphere of a constant succession of processions and affairs of state, all of which must have shaped perceptions of religion, social order, and power in Rome.

[6] K. Hopkins, *Conquerors and Slaves* (Cambridge 1978) 96–98; cf. P. A. Brunt, *Italian Manpower 225 B.C.–A.D. 14* (Oxford 1971) 376–88, esp. 387; and L. Homo, *Roma imperiale e l'urbanesimo nell'antichità*, trans. A. Friedemann and M. Leva (Milan 1976) 81 (hereafter Homo, *Urbanesimo*). J. E. Packer, "Housing and Population in Imperial Ostia and Rome," *JRS* 57 (1967) 80–95, says the figures are impossible to calculate.

[7] An anecdote preserved by Pliny the Elder sheds some light on the Roman populace's reactions to artistic (and presumably topographical) changes in Rome: when Tiberius removed the Apoxyomenos of Lysippus from the public baths of Agrippa to his own residence, the populace raised such an outcry that he was forced to return it (*HN* 34.62). Even if the story is apocryphal, it attests to the tradition that the populace was intimately concerned with the appearance with their city.

Knowledge of the physical city during Hadrian's principate elucidates certain broader questions of the political, religious, economic, social, and intellectual history of the time. The discovery of Hadrianic Rome is no easy task, for the same general difficulties of too little and too ambiguous evidence hamper this as other investigations into Hadrian's period. Only the combined testimony of archaeology, epigraphy, art and architectural history, numismatics, and the literary record makes possible a definitive catalogue of Hadrianic buildings and improvements. Parts of the literary record, moreover, help in evaluating the effect such constructions and changes had, and this in turn must be viewed in the context of the topography and history of Rome leading up to it, especially the Rome of the early principate and of the time of Trajan. This approach owes much to the excellent work in recent years of F. Castagnoli, F. Coarelli, P. Gros, L. Richardson, Jr., P. Zanker, and other modern topographers and classicists who turn directly to the physical remains of the ancient capital city to discover the values and perceptions of the Romans; indeed, many of their works have been indispensable to the present study and will be frequently cited.[8]

Such an approach to Hadrianic Rome, however, is relatively new, at least in its concentrated application. Because of the problems associated with the evidence for Hadrian's constructions and principate, and because of the magnificence and brilliance of Hadrianic architecture, previous scholarship on Hadrianic Rome has focused on specific buildings or questions, or on aesthetics and engineering. Thus, for example, there are many provocative studies on the Pantheon and on Hadrian's Mausoleum,[9] yet we lack an overall assessment of the relationship of these two buildings to one another and to the city as a whole. In fact, consideration of the effect any building had on the fabric of the city is generally lacking in evaluations of Hadrianic architectural style and construction. To my knowledge, only D. Kienast has preceded me in investigating both the actual changes effected by Hadrian in the city and their intent and consequences. Yet his discussion in *Chiron* 1980 includes only

---

[8] F. Castagnoli and F. Coarelli are particularly important, the former with *TRA* and his numerous articles encompassing many different aspects of the ancient city, the latter with his editions of archeological guides of Rome and more detailed articles on the topography of republican Rome. See also, e.g., P. Gros, *Aurea Templa* (Rome 1976); P. Zanker, "Das Trajansforum in Rom," *AA* 85.4 (1970) 499–544; and L. Richardson, Jr., "The Villa Publica and the Divorum," in *Essays in Honor . . . O. J. Brendel*, ed. L. Bonfante and H. von Heintze (Mainz 1976) 159–63 (hereafter Richardson, "Divorum").

[9] See Chapters 2 and 6.

the extant Pantheon, Temple of Venus and Roma, and Mausoleum, with the reorganization of the building industry.[10]

Any investigation into the topography of Rome relies heavily on archaeological evidence, which can at best furnish unequivocal information on the date and appearance of a structure. Interpretation of one primary source for our knowledge of ancient Rome, the fragmentary marble plan of Severan Rome (*Forma Urbis*), has been aided by a magisterial publication of it by a team of scholars in 1960 and by subsequent refinement in our ability to place the still unlocated fragments.[11] The three fascicles that have appeared so far of the *Carta archeologica di Roma* prove the immense value of this project, which locates archaeological discoveries on the map of the modern city and gives an outline of the ancient one.[12] Dedicatory inscriptions, inscriptions on utilitarian objects such as water pipes, and notations for three years in the Fasti Ostienses provide firsthand evidence for such Hadrianic constructions as the Auguratorium, which Hadrian restored in 136. Here, in addition to the standard comprehensive compilations such as that in the *CIL*, I have been able to make use of E. M. Smallwood's more convenient collection of Hadrianic documents.[13]

Some monuments, when uncovered, have dated themselves by their construction technique. The vast diffusion of brickstamping in the Hadrianic period has made relatively easy the chronology of the brick-faced buildings of the time. H. Bloch's fundamental studies on brick stamps furnish a chronological catalogue of brick stamps and prove that during the Hadrianic period such stamps give not only a terminus post quem for a building, but a date thereafter of not more than three to five years. His main conclusions have been reaffirmed by M. Steinby's recent reinvestigations of the stamped bricks of Rome and its surroundings.[14] G. Lugli and M. E. Blake, the latter with the

[10] D. Kienast, "Zur Baupolitik Hadrians in Rom," *Chiron* 10 (1980) 391–412.

[11] In this book references to the marble plan are to the 1960 publication, called *Forma Urbis*, reviewed and summarized by H. Bloch, "A New Edition of the Marble Plan of Ancient Rome," *JRS* 51 (1961) 143–52. See in addition to the refinements published by L. Cozza, in *QuadIstTopAnt* 5 (1968) 9–22, the new work by E. Rodriguez-Almeida, *Forma urbis marmorea, aggiornamento generale 1980* (Rome 1981) (hereafter Rodriguez-Almeida, *FUM*); and n.18 below.

[12] Abbreviated in the text as *CAR*.

[13] In the text all possible references to this publication are made as Smallwood, followed by the number of the document.

[14] Bloch, *Bolli*; and idem, "The Serapeum of Ostia and the Brick Stamps of 123 A.D.: A New Landmark in the History of Roman Architecture," *AJA* 63 (1959) 225–40; M. Steinby, "Ziegelstempel von Rom und Umgebung," *RE, Suppl.* 15 (1978) 1489–1531; idem, "CronFig"; and for further refinements, A.C.G. Smith, "The Date of the 'Grandi Terme' of Hadrian's Villa at Tivoli,"

collaboration of D. T. Bishop in her volume covering the Hadrianic period, have established the chronology of other materials for Roman construction.[15]

Other useful determinants for Hadrianic building are supplied by architectural history. Here F. L. Rakob's work on Roman domes is fundamental, and the increasingly sophisticated investigations of W. L. MacDonald, C. F. Giuliani, and others act as a corrective to unfounded speculation excited by the virtuosity of Hadrianic engineering.[16] Yet only occasionally does enough of a Hadrianic building remain for us to be able to apply such criteria. Rome's continuous habitation and the constant reuse of ancient structures have caused many to disappear, although sometimes they lie hidden behind stucco, and in places vestiges can still be discerned in the city plan. But large-scale excavation is virtually impossible, and archaeological discoveries have tended to be sporadic.

Important finds of the Renaissance and Baroque periods were often recorded by antiquarians and artists. Sometimes important evidence is jotted on a drawing, like the remarks of Antonio da Sangallo the Younger about the location of the Obelisk of Antinoos. At other times fact and fantasy mingle, as when Ligorio "typically" and "syncretically" reconstructed ancient buildings and ornaments. Despite such problems, which modern art historians and topographers are now revealing and unraveling,[17] the drawings and plans

---

PBSR 46 (1978) 73–93 (hereafter Smith, "Grandi Terme"). As a rule references for adjusted dating and figlinae chronology will be to Steinby and not to Bloch, so as to avoid double references. In conversation, Dr. Steinby has communicated to me her suspicions, based on her extensive work with Roman brick stamps and brick-faced buildings, that in a period of intense construction bricks would be used even within a year of their manufacture if needed.

[15] Lugli, Edilizia; Blake, I and II; and Blake/Bishop. Although in the absence of brick stamps it is tempting to date brick-faced edifices by the dimensions of bricks and mortar levels (cf., e.g., Lugli), recent work by Steinby is now revealing the many variations in construction technique among contemporaneous brick-faced buildings ("I bolli laterizi e i criteri tecnici nella datazione delle cortine laterizie. Esame su un gruppo di edifici ostiensi dei primi anni di Adriano," in Miscelà-

nea Arqueologica II [Ampurias] [Barcelona 1974] 389–405; cf. idem, "Edilizia" 219). She convincingly attributes the inconsistencies to the differences in contractors and commissions.

[16] F. L. Rakob, "Litus beatae Veneris aureum," RömMitt 68 (1961) 114–69 (hereafter Rakob, "Litus aureum"); for W. L. MacDonald, see, e.g., his work with B. M. Boyle, "The Small Baths at Hadrian's Villa," JSAH 39.1 (1980) 5–27; and for C. F. Giuliani see, e.g., "Domus Flavia: una nuova lettura," RömMitt 84 (1977) 91–106; idem, "Il lato nord-ovest della Piazza d'Oro," QuadIst-TopAnt 8 (1975) 51–52; and idem, "Volte e cupole a doppia calotta in età adrianea," RömMitt 82 (1975) 329–42. Also useful for the architectural background is G. Gullini, "Apollodoro e Adriano," BdA 53 (1968) [1971] 63–80.

[17] See, e.g., E. Mandowsky and C. Mitchell, eds., Pirro Ligorio's Roman Antiquities

of Marten van Heemskerck, G. A. Dosio, and others are sometimes our primary or solitary record of a building, as in the case of the Tempio di Siepe, usually considered Hadrianic on the strength of the three sketches depicting it.

"Scientific" archaeology came relatively late to the discovery of ancient Rome, and the concomitant advent of photography has been of inestimable value. As we will see in the case of Hadrian's "*Ustrinum,*" a conjectural monument at or on which members of his imperial family are supposed to have been cremated, archaeological reports predating the common use of photography, even those of the *Bulletino Comunale* and *Notizie degli Scavi*, must be scrutinized with particular care. Nevertheless, the care and insight of the early topographers of Rome are always admirable: G. Boni, R. Lanciani, C. Hülsen, and others often comprehended from scrappy and lacunose evidence relationships that have subsequently been confirmed.[18]

The difficulties in evaluating the evidence of artists, antiquarians, and unsystematic excavators are slight in comparison to those involved in the interpretation of the monuments that appear on the reverses of coins. When topographers and archaeologists try to reconstruct a building from its depiction on a coin, as B. L. Trell has acutely noted, not only do all the variations in a type have to be accounted for, but also the conventions (or lack thereof) of the individual die-cutters.[19] Although Hadrianic coinage poses particular problems due to the lack of unequivocal internal means of dating individual issues, P. V. Hill has clarified its chronology through stylistic analyses, and M. Pensa's recent investigation of Hadrianic coins with building types is exemplary in its thoroughness.[20] Nevertheless, problems remain, especially

(London 1963) 35–51, and G. A. Dosio, *Roma Antica e i disegni di architettura agli Uffizi*, ed. by F. Borsi et al. (Rome 1976).

[18] For example, Boni's suspicion that the fragment of the marble plan depicting the Lacus Juturnae is from a map of the city predating the Severan one is now confirmed by the Finnish School's recent excavations in the area. I thank M. Steinby for this information, which will soon be published. Castagnoli, *TRA* 1–7, 33–47 (with copious bibliography), discusses the general history of topographical work in Rome, a subject also explored in a recent series of shows in Rome ("Roma Capitale, 1870–1911"). In addition to the archaeological reports in *Bullettino*

*Comunale* and *Notizie degli Scavi*, one should also consult *AA*, *Studi Romani*, and *Fasti Archeologici* for new archaeological finds.

[19] B. L. Trell, "Architectura Numismatica," *NC*, ser. 7, 12 (1972) 45–59, esp. 46–47.

[20] Chronological problems are caused by Hadrian's constant omission of numeration of his tribunician power (*tribunicia potestas*) on coins and its frequent lack in official inscriptions as well, and by the fact that he held the consulship only twice while princeps, in 118 and 119, after which he simply repeated *cos. III*. The addition of *Pater Patriae* to his titulature in 128 is of some help. See P. V. Hill, *The Dating and Arrangement of the Undated Coins of Rome*, A.D. *98–148* (London 1970) (hereafter

concerning issues that lack an identifying legend but are our only evidence of a building, such as the Trajanic type traditionally associated with the Temple of the Deified Trajan and Plotina. Furthermore, there is still dispute as to the overall significance of such coin types.[21] On the other hand, numismatic evidence for buildings, however controversial, can clarify the appearance of an edifice, and it is disappointing that the Hadrianic coins depicting monuments are so few in comparison to the number of new buildings known for his rule, quite apart from the still greater number he restored.[22]

Historical reliefs and sculpture are another frustrating type of evidence for the Hadrianic city. On the basis of inscriptions or historical identifications, only a few historical reliefs are clearly identifiable as Hadrianic: G. Koeppel's recent survey, for example, lists only three major pieces.[23] Stylistic consid-

---

Hill, *D&A*); idem, "The Dating and Arrangement of Hadrian's Cos III Coins of the Mint of Rome," in *Mints, Dies and Currency*, ed. by R.A.G. Carson (London 1971) 39–56; and M. Pensa, "Rappresentazioni di monumenti sulle monete di Adriano," *RIN* 80 (1978) 27–78 (hereafter Pensa, "Adriano"), although her knowledge of the topography and archaeology of Rome is not as keen as her knowledge of numismatics. (See n. 22 below.) The most important catalogues of Hadrianic coins are those of Strack, *Hadrian*; *BMC, Emp.* III; *RIC* II; and J.M.C. Toynbee, *The Hadrianic School* (Cambridge 1934). In general, references in this text are to *BMC, Emp.* III.

[21] See, e.g., Trell, "Architectura Numismatica" 47, who expresses specific dissatisfaction with Brown's thesis that architectural types appeared in the empire to: (1) represent actual building activity of an emperor; (2) commemorate some event important to the empire; (3) "picturize" a religious ceremony; or (4) commemorate an essentially political event (as proposed in D. F. Brown, *Temples as Coin Types* [New York 1940], and reported by her). F. Panvini Rosati, "Osservazioni sui tipi monetali romani figuranti monumenti di Roma," *RIN* 3, ser. 5, 57 (1955) 74–78, also notes the difficulty of placing all such coins in these four categories. Nor is Trell convinced that such types were chosen as the best means for Romans to show their piety toward their

ancestors (as proposed by G. Fuchs, *Architekturdarstellungen auf römischen Münzen der Republik und der frühen Kaiserzeit* [Berlin 1969]). The propaganda value of coin types is discussed most recently by M. H. Crawford, "Roman Imperial Coin Types and the Formation of Public Opinion," in *Studies in Numismatic Method Presented to Philip Grierson*, ed. by C.N.L. Brooke et al. (Cambridge 1983) 47–64, with earlier bibliography on the debate; Crawford concludes (overly skeptically) "that the pictorial types of the imperial coinage were little noticed and often misunderstood."

[22] Cf. Pensa, "Adriano" 69–71, who suggests unconvincingly that the relative rarity of this type of issue is due both to Hadrian's reluctance to strike coins showing restorations (because he did not wish to take for his own the glory due to the original builder and he assumed such renovations to be a state duty: *HA, Hadr.* 19.10), and to the paucity of new buildings attributable to him. We should note that one new edifice she ascribes to Hadrian, the Hadrianeum, was built by Antoninus Pius.

[23] G. Koeppel, "Official State Reliefs of the City of Rome in the Imperial Age," *ANRW* II.12.1 (1982) 496–98 (B-D: the Tondi, the Vota Vicennalia relief, and the Chatsworth relief, all discussed in Chapter 7), with earlier bibliography, and see his comments on p. 479. Toynbee's excellent work on Hadrianic

erations are not very useful: the controversy surrounding the Anaglypha Traiani/Hadriani, expounded in Chapter 7, is a good example of the current uncertainties involved in distinguishing Hadrianic style from Trajanic. Although D. E. Strong's article on late Hadrianic architectural ornament in Rome satisfactorily defined its elements and syntax some thirty years ago,[24] early Hadrianic ornament is not so easily classified. C. F. Leon's and H.-D. Heilmeyer's compilations and analyses of architectural ornament have shown that the new principate did not break sharply with the techniques and tastes of Trajan's; this very ambiguity, however, seems to have led Heilmeyer to identify the Pantheon as a Trajanic building, quite implausibly.[25]

The collection of the various types of archaeological evidence mentioned above has been greatly facilitated by E. Nash's *Pictorial Dictionary of Ancient Rome*, which also includes references to the ancient literary sources for the buildings its photographs illustrate so well. Another essential aid for the Roman topographer is Lugli's *Fontes ad topographiam veteris urbis Romae pertinentes*, although unfortunately this compendium is not yet complete.[26] For the purposes of the present study, however, we turn to literary references for help in interpretation.[27] Here we may distinguish two categories: specific mention of Hadrianic buildings, and indirect testimony about life in Hadrianic Rome. Neither category, lamentably, is very large, nor does either contain very explicit information.

There is no satisfying history of Hadrian's rule from antiquity. The historical narrative of Dio Cassius survives for Hadrian's reign in the excerpts of Xiphilinus, a jurist, monk, and ultimately patriarch of Trapezus (Trebizond) in the eleventh century. Little topographical information is found in the remnants of Dio's work. Xiphilinus' rather erratic selection of Dio's material was determined by his own interests, which do not seem to have embraced detailed information about the city of Rome so far removed in time and space

---

style, *Hadrianic School*, unfortunately was of little direct use to this book due to the difference in our focuses.

[24] D. E. Strong, "Late Hadrianic Architectural Ornament in Rome," *PBSR* 21 (1953) 118–51.

[25] C. F. Leon, *Die Bauornamentik des Trajansforum und ihre Stellung in der früh- und mittelkaiserzeitlichen Architekturdekoration Roms* (Vienna-Cologne-Graz 1971); W.-D. Heilmeyer, *Korinthische Normalkapitelle* (Heidelberg 1970); for the redating of the Pantheon,

see his "Apollodorus von Damaskus, der Architekt des Pantheon," *JdI* 90 (1975) 316–47.

[26] Vol. VI, 2, on the Capitoline, the most recent fascicle of this series beginning in 1952, appeared in 1969 under the care of F. Castagnoli after Lugli's death.

[27] For the difficulties encountered when evaluating the meaning of Roman architecture, see, e.g., H. Drerup, "Architektur als Symbol. Zur zeitgenössischen Bewertung der römischen Architektur," *Gymnasium* 73 (1966) 181–96.

from his own life.²⁸ Furthermore, such information as is included incidentally has to be evaluated carefully, because some of it is obviously wrong.

Much of Dio's work was composed in Rome at the end of the second century and beginning of the third, and he was personally familiar with many of the buildings he mentions. Yet his interest in them seems not to have gone far beyond that of a sightseer: for example, when he describes the Pantheon in the course of his history of the Augustan principate, he apparently never realizes that the building he knows was constructed under Hadrian and not Agrippa (Dio Cass. 53.27.2–4). In most cases, his topographical descriptions are those of a sharp-eyed but naive tourist.²⁹

Another problem with Dio's information about Hadrian is that, as F. Millar has pointed out, it reflects a senatorial bias against the princeps. The notice that Hadrian personally designed the Temple of Venus and Roma, for instance, comes in an anecdote intended to show Hadrian as a despot whose jealousy of others' accomplishments led him to kill Apollodorus, Trajan's architect (Dio Cass. 69.4.1–5).³⁰ Other motives Dio ascribes to Hadrian in his buildings may be equally untrustworthy.

Our other considerable historical source for Hadrian's reign is the biography of Hadrian that forms the first of the series known collectively as the *Historia Augusta*. The *HA* includes information about building activities as proper to a biography, as had Suetonius:³¹ a section in the middle of Hadrian's

---

²⁸ F. Millar, *A Study of Cassius Dio* (Oxford 1964) 2–3 (hereafter Millar, *Dio*). Zonarus, another epitomator of Dio who wrote a half century later, apparently used only Xiphilinus' excerpts and not Dio himself for the period after Nerva. Recently P. A. Brunt, "On Historical Fragments and Epitomes," *CQ* 30 (1980) 488–92, has underlined Xiphilinus' indifference to administrative changes and his "usual failure" to make clear Dio's interpretation of events.

²⁹ Similarly, Dio's explanation of the Forum and Column of Trajan seems to be based on his own reading of the inscription on the Column's base: 68.16.3. For Dio's life, see Millar, *Dio* 5–27; the main scheme is accepted, although some points are still debated (e.g., G. W. Bowersock, in *Gnomon* 37 [1965] 473, doubts Millar's belief in Dio's respect toward Septimius Severus).

³⁰ Millar, *Dio* 60–72, on Dio's general account of Hadrian; he notes the "hostile and critical spirit" prevailing in Dio's book. For the topographical information of the anecdote, see Chapter 4. Hadrian's responsibility for the death of Apollodorus should be doubted: *HA, Hadr.*, which includes many such passages designed to defame Hadrian (cf., e.g., 15.10, 16; 23.2–9), notes Hadrian's planned collaboration with Apollodorus for the statue of Luna that was to be erected near the Temple of Venus and Roma (19.13), but has no hint of the events described by Dio (cf., in general, R. P. Saller, "Anecdotes as Historical Evidence for the Principate," *G&R* 27 [1980] 69–83).

³¹ On the topographical information of Suetonius, see A. Wallace-Hadrill, *Suetonius* (New Haven and London 1983) 18, 119–29, esp. 119–20; he elsewhere remarks that the

biography that lists Hadrian's buildings in and outside Rome serves to illustrate the princeps' character,[32] which is also the apparent purpose of a later discussion of Hadrian's villa at Tivoli (HA, Hadr. 19, 26.5). Yet the HA is notoriously riddled with problems and inaccuracies.[33] At the height of the controversy over its authorship, A. von Domaszewski argued that the work had been composed in sixth-century Nimes by a man with no independent knowledge of Rome; thus, most of the topographical information was untrustworthy.[34] This thesis has been refuted in detail by D. M. Robathan,[35] and more recent work on the sources of the HA specifically substantiates the credibility of Hadrian's biography.

R. Syme and T. D. Barnes have maintained that for the second century the author of the Historia Augusta relied chiefly on two sources—Marius Maximus and an unidentified author, whom Syme calls "Ignotus"—and that the biography of Hadrian is among the best and most veracious of the collection.[36] For our purposes we may note that although Marius Maximus was hostile to Hadrian, offering scandalous and gossipy anecdotes, he was a consular who had had a rapid and brilliant career at the end of the second century and beginning of the third. Among other posts, he held the urban prefecture,[37] which would have given him access to the city records and a good knowledge of the city. Moreover, the other source, Ignotus, actually provides more information for Hadrian's biography. He seems to have written in Rome, witnessing firsthand the tumultuous events of 193, and to have been an equestrian rather than a senator. Calling Ignotus "accurate and sober, with a liking for facts and dates," Syme credits him with the topographical details

"imitation [by the HA] of Suetonius is acknowledged by all, but oddly there is no satisfactory study of their debt" (p. 9 n. 14).

[32] Note the "good" attribute of his reluctance to put his own name on restorations, HA, Hadr. 19.10 (cf. E. W. Merten, Bäder und Badegepflogenheiten in der Darstellung der Historia Augusta [Bonn 1983] 16–20). This forebearance was later regulated by law: Dig. 50.10.7.

[33] See, in brief, the introduction in H. W. Benario, A Commentary on the "vita Hadriani" in the "Historia Augusta" (Chico, Calif. 1980) 1–14, with reference to earlier discussion, and further in this chapter.

[34] A. von Domaszewski, Die Topografie Roms bei den "Scriptores Historiae Augustae,"

Sitzungsberichte der Heidelberger Akademie der Wissenschaften, Philosophisch-historische Klasse 7 (Heidelberg 1916) 11.

[35] D. M. Robathan, "A Reconsideration of Roman Topography in the Historia Augusta," TAPA 70 (1939) 515–34; detailed vindication of the topographical information for the Severan lives is provided by H. W. Benario, "Rome of the Severi," Latomus 17 (1958) 712–22.

[36] R. Syme, Emperors and Biography (Oxford 1971); idem, Ammianus and the "Historia Augusta" (Oxford 1968); T. D. Barnes, The Sources of the "Historia Augusta" (Brussels 1978).

[37] See, e.g., Syme, Emperors and Biography 113–45.

about the city.[38] There is no reason to doubt a priori topographical information found in Hadrian's biography.

There is some other textual evidence for buildings dating to Hadrian's reign, but it is of a predominantly documentary nature. The Regionary Catalogues of Rome, the *Notitia urbis Romae regionum XIIII* and the *Curiosum urbis Romae regionum XIIII* derived from an original catalogue of the city's regions and framed in the late third and early fourth centuries, occasionally identify Hadrianic buildings, as do the chronicles and breviaria compiled in the fourth century and later.[39] The accuracy of the topographical information in such works is now increasingly substantiated.[40] Overall, however, the topographical information provided by such sources for Hadrian's rule is meager and often simply unadorned fact. Seldom can we discern the intent of Hadrian's changes and constructions, and in the few instances in which motivations are supplied, we must weigh the evidence carefully. For a better understanding of the causes and effects of Hadrian's changes in Rome, we must turn to both the second category of literary evidence, contemporary literature, and the general history of Hadrian's principate.

The extant works of Hadrian's contemporaries and near contemporaries, although containing little specific information on the topography of the capital city, help to fill in the background necessary for real comprehension of Hadrianic Rome. Syme was the first to explore an author of this period as a means of illuminating the political and cultural atmosphere, which he did so well in his monumental *Tacitus* of 1958; A. N. Sherwin-White's commentary on Pliny's letters has been equally useful; and now we have A. Wallace-Hadrill's monograph on Suetonius, E. Champlin's on Fronto, and P. A. Stad-

---

[38] Syme, *Emperors and Biography* 30–53, esp. 43; and *Ammianus* 92–93.

[39] For the Regionary Catalogues, composed originally in the time of Diocletian, see Castagnoli, *TRA* 12–14, with bibliography; the texts are found most conveniently in A. Nordh, *Libellus de regionibus urbis*, Acta Instituti Romani Regni Sueciae, ser. 8, 3 (1949), and in Valentini and Zucchetti, 1.63–188. A. Momigliano provides an excellent discussion of the late chronicles and breviaria, "Pagan and Christian Historiography in the Fourth Century A.D.," first published in *The Conflict between Paganism and Christianity in the*

*Fourth Century*, ed. by A. Momigliano (Oxford 1963) 79–99, and republished in his *Essays in Ancient and Modern Historiography* (Middletown, Conn. 1977) 107–26.

[40] For a reevaluation and confirmation of the tradition of topograpical information in the chronicles, see J. C. Anderson, Jr., "A Topographical Tradition in Fourth Century Chronicles: Domitian's Building Program," *Historia* 32 (1983) 93–105, who pleads for further use of such sources. See also H. Braunert's work, cited in Chapter 7, for the Athenaeum, known primarily from the breviaria and other late texts.

ter's on Arrian of Nicomedia. The earlier works of G. W. Bowersock on the Second Sophistic and J. H. Oliver on Aelius Aristides' *Ode to Rome* are also essential to an understanding of the Hadrianic period.[41] The common premise of these works, and one that is explicitly and cogently argued in such books as Millar's and R. Saller's recent investigations into the emperor's political position in Rome, is that the emperor personally engaged in much of the varied business of running Rome and the empire; further, he was expected to be, and in fact usually was, accessible to everyone in the Roman world, especially the elite. An additional point made by Millar and Saller, both of whom depend heavily on the ancient literary and epigraphical sources, is that continuity characterized the first two centuries of the principate.[42]

Many of the specific events and trends in Hadrian's rule, such as the increasingly paternalistic policies of the emperor and the abandonment of expansionism, are well established in A. Garzetti's, M. Hammond's, and W. Weber's histories of Hadrian's principate.[43] The religious history of the time, which emerges from examination of textual and archaeological

---

[41] See the Bibliography and the List of Abbreviations. We still lack detailed investigations of other important literary figures such as Aulus Gellius. Plutarch seems to have died before or at the beginning of Hadrian's reign, and in any case was out of Rome for the last thirty years of his life: C. P. Jones, *Plutarch and Rome* (Oxford 1971) 28–29. Juvenal's allusions are quite difficult to assess specifically, despite the provocative (but somewhat contrived) work of J. Gérard, *Juvénal et la réalité contemporaine* (Paris 1976). The earlier tendency (embodied by Syme) to associate strictly authors' remarks with specific events in Hadrian's reign is being checked: see, e.g., K. R. Bradley, "Imperial Virtues in Suetonius' *Caesares*," *Journal of Indo-European Studies* 4 (1976) 245–53; and Wallace-Hadrill, *Suetonius* 198–200.

[42] The continuity extends past the second century, although Saller's work stops there. See F. Millar, *The Emperor in the Roman World* (Ithaca, N.Y. 1977) (hereafter Millar, *ERW*); R. P. Saller, *Personal Patronage under the Early Empire* (Cambridge 1982); cf. W. Williams,

"Individuality in the Imperial Constitutions: Hadrian and the Antonines," *JRS* 66 (1976) 67–83. The fictitious *Sententiae Hadriani*, for example, seem to have been designed in antiquity primarily to show the emperor personally involved in judicial work (cf. Millar, *ERW* 532).

[43] See the List of Abbreviations. For a recent brief overview of Hadrian's principate, see M. K. Thorton, "Hadrian and His Reign," *ANRW* II.2 (1975) 432–76. I have not cited B. W. Henderson, *The Life and Principate of the Emperor Hadrian*, A.D. *76–138* (London 1923), however, because he lacks references and much new material has appeared in the last half century. S. Perowne, *Hadrian* (New York 1960), and W. Weber's chapter on Hadrian, in the *Cambridge Ancient History* IX (Cambridge 1936) 294–324, are both too imprecise and sentimental to have been of advantage; similarly, I have not used as scholarly references the interesting works of M. Yourcenar, *Mémoires d'Hadrien* (Paris 1974), or R. Lambert, *Beloved and God: The Story of Hadrian and Antinous* (New York 1984).

sources,[44] has been admirably investigated by J. Beaujeu, with valuable contributions offered by J.-C. Richard, J. Gagé, Oliver, and others.[45]

Since this study endeavors to determine the imprint left on Rome by Hadrianic buildings and urban changes, the material is divided by location as far as possible, treating natural geographical rather than administrative regions. Each chapter focuses on a different area of the city, and the chapters are arranged in roughly chronological order. The three exceptions are the first chapter, dealing with Hadrian's personal interest in the city and his administrative and organizational changes; the seventh chapter, which collects the "missing" and misidentified buildings attributed to all periods of Hadrian's rule; and the eighth, concluding, chapter. An appendix on the Obeliscus Antinoi and a comprehensive catalogue follow the text.

[44] G. W. Bowersock, "The Imperial Cult: Perceptions and Persistence," in *Jewish and Christian Self-definition,* III: Self-definition in *the Greco-Roman World*, ed. by B. F. Meyer and E. P. Sanders (Philadelphia 1982) 171–82, for example, notes that the literary sources (written by the elite) only rarely mention the imperial cult.

[45] See the List of Abbreviations and the Bibliography.

# CHAPTER ONE

# THE PRINCEPS AND THE CITY

H ADRIAN was directly and personally interested in the workings and welfare of the city of Rome. Augustus had established the principle that the improvement and embellishment of the capital city was the responsibility of the princeps, and should not be left, as it had been under the republic, to the whims and fortunes of Rome's political elite.[1] Yet one must not assume without corroboration that Hadrian followed that precedent as had most of the intervening emperors, particularly given the facts that he spent more than half his rule in travels outside of Rome, that he moved the imperial (summer) residence out of the city, and that he is alleged to have died hated by the people of Rome (e.g., Dio Cass. 69.23.2; *HA, Hadr.* 25.7, 24.3–5, 27.2, *Pii* 2.4–6).[2] We lack for Hadrian's rule any document such as the *Res Gestae* of Augustus, in which he proclaims his personal responsibility for and pride in the renovation of Rome.[3] Nor do Hadrian's biography, the later epitomes, or Dio's

[1] Although G. Bodei Giglioni (in *Lavori pubblici e occupazione nell'antichità classica* [Bologna 1974] 137–39) stresses that during the triumviral period and later Octavian had pressed his peers to undertake financial responsibility for the execution of public works (cf. Suet. *Aug.* 29.4), Gros, *Aurea Templa* 37–38, rightly notes that the works he delegated to them were never as important as the ones Augustus undertook himself. After Augustus monumental building in Rome was generally left to the imperial family (cf. Tac. *Ann.* 3.72.1–2). For the "beneficent princeps" principle, see, e.g., Z. Yavetz, *Plebs and Princeps* (Oxford 1969) 131–39; and H. Kloft, *Liberalitas Principis* (Cologne 1970) 115–18, 166–70, with particular regard to building in Rome. P. A. Brunt, "Free Labour and Public Works at Rome," *JRS* 70 (1980) 85, articulates the skeptical view that although "[e]mperors like Augustus frequently take credit for the erection of new buildings . . .

[i]t seems improbable, and is certainly not recorded, that they engaged in personal supervision of the work." For public building and maintenance during the republic, see D. E. Strong, "The Administration of Public Building during the Late Republic and Early Empire," *Bulletin of the Institute of Classical Studies of the University of London* 15 (1968) 97–103.

[2] For the journeys and Rome's reaction to them, see Chapter 5; for the early and late years of the reign, see Chapters 3 and 6.

[3] Gros, *Aurea Templa* 15–52, esp. 44, uses this and the contemporary evidence of poets and others to establish Augustus' primary concern with the physical and moral renewal of Rome, a theme brilliantly elaborated by P. Zanker in the Jerome Lectures of 1984, "A Cultural Program for the Roman Empire: Art and Architecture in the Augustan Age" (publication forthcoming).

abbreviated history contain the kind of detail that Suetonius occasionally reports, such as Vespasian's shouldering of the first hod of earth for the reconstruction of the Temple of Jupiter Optimus Maximus and his rejection of a labor-saving building device on the grounds that it would deprive the Roman populace of work (Suet. *Vesp.* 8.5, 18).[4] Nevertheless, the evidence for Hadrian's principate, as disparate and deficient as it is, supports the proposition that Hadrian's personal involvement with Rome was broad in its scope and an intense and continuing commitment.

Hadrian's extensive building programs created work for tens of thousands of free men in Rome, although we cannot prove that this was high among his motivations.[5] After the completion of Trajan's Forum in 113 and Trajan's departure for the Parthian campaigns in 114, monumental building virtually ceased in the city.[6] Hadrian's projects, some of the largest of which were begun soon after his accession, reemployed huge work forces of both skilled craftsmen responsible for architectural decoration, and unskilled laborers who transported materials, dug foundations, poured concrete, and laid bricks.[7] Hadrian's individual recognition of the significant role building

[4] Wallace-Hadrill, *Suetonius* 119–41, esp. 137, illuminates the unsystematic way in which Suetonius includes material on the imperial administration; his criteria include the relevance of the incident to the individuality of the emperor, and the impact it made on common life.

[5] See Brunt, "Public Works" 81–100, with comparative figures for work forces in other preindustrial cities during building expansion (pp. 92–93). He convincingly substantiates the traditional view of public works in Rome as a means of securing popular support (and refutes the recent doubts both of L. Casson, in "Unemployment, the Building Trade, and Suetonius, *Vesp.* 18," *Bulletin of the American Society of Papyrologists* 15 [1978] 43–51, who assumes that slaves did most of the building, and of Bodei Giglioni, who considers Vespasian's expressed policy, noted at the beginning of this chapter, to be an atypical and conscious attempt at economic development: *Lavori pubblici* 175–84). For some detailed evidence substantiating Brunt's conclusions, see M. Steinby, "L'edilizia come industria pubblica e privata," in *Città e architettura* 219–21,

and for a more cautious view of the topic, see J. E. Skydsgaard, "Public Building and Society in Ancient Rome," in *Città e architettura* 223–27.

[6] Smith, "Grandi Terme" 73–77: during these years Rome lacked both the "Imperial impetus" for more building and money (probably diverted to the war), and Apollodorus also may have been in the east. For stockpiling bricks during this period, see Bloch, *Bolli* 316–20, 113; idem, "Serapeum" 236. In "Apollodorus" 327–30, Heilmeyer's arguments to the contrary are not convincing.

[7] Leon, *Bauornamentik* 22–25, gives an important and concise overview of the various skilled workers, architects, and contractors involved in imperial projects, as well as discusses the organization of such works (though without figures). Brunt, "Public Works" 83–92, surveys the entire process, including the unskilled labor force. He considers, however, that Hadrian's paramilitary staff of construction workers (see n.8) was only for projects outside of Rome: its notice follows a statement of Hadrian's provincial

played in the economy of Rome is implied by the note of the *Epitome de Cae-saribus* crediting him with organizing the workers in the building trades on paramilitary lines (*Epit. de Caes.* 14.5).[8]

The similarities of early Hadrianic decorative work to Trajanic ornament have been used most recently by Leon and Heilmeyer as evidence that Hadrian reemployed already existing schools of sculptors, if not Apollodorus himself, in such buildings as the Pantheon.[9] Strong and Leon have further tied the notable Asiatic style of later Hadrianic ornament in Rome to the migration west of groups of craftsmen, perhaps from Pergamum.[10] Yet overall in Rome the architectural decoration of Hadrian's buildings is less ornate and less pervasive than that of Domitian's and Trajan's. In part the large scale of many Hadrianic buildings made careful detailing superfluous; there was also a predilection for colored marble rather than fluted columns.[11] Furthermore, Hadrianic monuments and remains as preserved in Rome, without ever being at all plain, do not exhibit the extravagant use of sculpture and relief that characterizes Trajan's Forum and the Forum Transitorium.

It seems significant that Hadrian's earliest building projects in the capital made extensive use of concrete with brick facing. The reconstructions of Julio-Claudian buildings and other work in the Campus Martius are almost entirely of this characteristically Roman construction, with the Pantheon the most conspicuous example. Certainly concrete is better suited to the flood-prone Campus Martius than are travertine and tufa (cf. Vitruv. *De Arch.* 2.6.1; Pliny *HN* 35.166); but, as Rakob has said, concrete also requires a mini-

---

activities. Kienast, "Baupolitik" 399, briefly notes the possibilities for employment Hadrian's programs ensured.

[8] *Namque ad specimen legionum militarium fabros perpendiculatores architectos genusque cunctum exstruendorum moenium seu decorandorum in cohortes centuriaverat* (for on a military model he arranged in cohorts carpenters, surveyors, architects, and every type of person used in constructing or decorating buildings), noted by, e.g., Bloch, "Serapeum" 237, and Brunt, "Public Works" 83 (who suggests that *perpendiculatores* should be understood as *mensores*).

[9] Leon, *Bauornamentik*, e.g., 210–32, 236–38, 284; Heilmeyer, *Normalkapitelle* 157–61, 177, 181; idem, "Apollodorus," esp. 330; and see Strong, "Late Ornament" 119–22, who

does not, however, postulate Apollodorus' participation.

[10] Strong, "Late Ornament" 133–40; Leon, *Bauornamentik* 238–43, 284; these and other scholars note the similarity of the architraves of Venus and Roma to those of the Hadrianic Traianeum in Pergamum. See Chapter 4, n. 102.

[11] Just before his death, J. B. Ward-Perkins suggested provocatively that in A.D. 132 there was "an official stock-taking in order to determine precisely how much marble was already available in the imperial marble yards of the capital," and that it "would have shown large surpluses of many of the commoner marbles [like Numidian]": "Nicomedia and the Marble Trade," *PBSR* 48 (1980) 26.

mum degree of skill on the part of laborers.[12] Thus, a great number of workers could be employed in projects launched at the onset of Hadrian's rule.

The reorganization of the brick industry must be considered in the light of the enormous increase in building activity that occurred at the beginning of Hadrian's principate. Roman brickmakers habitually stamped bricks and tiles, while still fresh and unfired, with "factory marks" usually containing the name of the *officinator*, or that of the proprietor of the yard, or both. Beginning in Nero's time, consular dating, designation of the year by the eponymous consuls' names, was added to the marks on bricks made outside Rome, but it did not appear on those of Rome until the bricks of M. Rutilius Lupus began to carry it in 110. For more than ten years he seems to have been the only proprietor to use this system, but then in 123 there was a sudden widespread use of consular dating in the products of almost all the *figlinae* (brickyards) of Rome. The practice, however, was sporadic in the next years, until it became more common again in 134. Subsequently, it remained in only intermittent use, until it was abandoned in 164.[13]

Bloch, followed by most scholars, has plausibly suggested that these changes in brick stamping reflect an interest on the part of the imperial government in 123 or slightly earlier.[14] Although we still have no real understanding of how the brick stamps functioned in the brickmaking industry, they probably served as a regulatory measure.[15] The intervention seems to have been confined to 123, for the universal use of consular dating was abandoned after that year (despite the mysterious semiresurgence eleven years later). Hadrian's absence from Rome in 123 does not preclude his involvement. Such a widespread occurrence must have been planned well in advance.

Hadrian's interest in the building industry can also be seen in the notice transmitted in the biography that he prohibited throughout the empire dem-

[12] F. L. Rakob, "Hellenismus in Mittelitalien. Bautypen und Bautechnik," in *Hellenismus in Mittelitalien* 372; for the strength of concrete, see, e.g., Lugli, *Edilizia* I.392–402.

[13] Bloch, *Bolli* I, 316–34. The resurgence of consular dating in 134 should not be overemphasized, however: in 123, 240 stamps carried such dating; in 134, 40; and in 135, only 10: M. Steinby, "Ziegelstempel von Rom und Umgebung," *RE, Suppl.* 15 (1978) 1503.

[14] Bloch, *Bolli* 320–27; Steinby, "Ziegelstempel" 1503–1504, and "CronFig" 22; and

Castagnoli, *TRA* 27. Bloch's hypothesis that the intervention was suggested by one of the great "latifondisti" of figlinae, M. Annius Verus, *praefectus urbi* from 121 to 125, has been slightly reinforced by Steinby's work ("CronFig" 80). The merely partial resumption of the practice in 134 argues that this resurgence was not imperially ordered.

[15] Bloch, *Bolli* 324–25; Steinby, "Ziegelstempel" 1504, 1514. Bloch, "Serapeum" 237, suggests that it may well have been associated with a grant of fiscal privileges aimed at intensifying brick production.

olition of houses for the purpose of transferring their materials to another city (*HA, Hadr.* 18.2).[16] More doubtful is his connection with the *SC Acilianum* of 122 (*Dig.* 30.1.41, 43; cf. *Dig.* 18.1.52), which amended and tightened earlier laws against demolishing buildings. Beginning in the late republic, a series of poorly known laws was passed in Italy and in Rome against dismantling buildings, including some that explicitly prohibited demolition for the sake of profit. Until the *SC Acilianum* was passed in 122, the most complete of the laws, the so-called *SC Hosidianum* of about A.D. 44–46 and the *SC Volusianum* of 56, contained a major loophole that made it possible for a testator to benefit his heirs by bequeathing them elements of a building (such as columns or beams) or by leaving instructions in his will for the demolition of buildings he owned.[17] The *senatus consultum* of 122 takes its name from M. Acilius Aviola, one of the consuls of the year. Hadrian was away from the capital at the time, but the biography's note of a similar law passed by him, since it is not corroborated by any other source, may reflect his interest in the better documented *senatus consultum*.

Hadrian himself addressed a letter on 1 March 127 to the citizens of Stratonicaeia-Hadrianopolis (Lycia), in which he ordered that a Ti. Claudius Socrates either repair his house there or surrender it to his fellow citizens so that it might not become dilapidated from age and neglect (*FIRA* 1.80 = Smallwood, #453).[18] P. Garnsey sees the laws against demolition and Hadrian's letter as motivated primarily by a concern for the physical aspect of cities,[19] but

[16] Benario, *Commentary* 112, remarks that the costs of transport would make demolition for transportation of the materials to another city uneconomical. We should note, however, that such costs are often overestimated, and that the value of dressed marbles and good building timber must have been high.

[17] For these laws: P. Garnsey, "Urban Property Investment," in *Studies in Roman Property* 133–36; E. J. Phillips, "The Roman Law on the Demolition of Buildings," *Latomus* 32 (1973) 86–95 (p. 95 for the "loophole"); and M. Sargenti, "Due senatoconsulti—politica edilizia nel primo secolo dell'Impero e tecnica normativa," in *Studi in onore di C. Sanfilippo* (Milan 1984) 639–55. Such laws seem to have been applicable in Rome itself only after the end of the republic: E. Gabba, "Considerazioni politiche ed economiche sullo sviluppo urbano in Italia nei se-

coli II e I a.C.," in *Hellenismus in Mittelitalien* 320–21. The *SC Acilianum* is discussed specifically by J. L. Murga, "Sobre una Nueva Calificación del *aedificium* por Obra de la Legislación Urbanistica Impérial," *Iura* 26 (1975) 67ff., which I was unable to obtain; I thank Dr. E. Crifó, however, for calling it to my attention.

[18] Also published in *IGRR* 4.1156a; *SIG* 3rd ed., 2.837; and by L. Robert, in *Hellenica* 6 (1948) 80–84.

[19] Garnsey, "Urban Investment" 133–36; and see J. L. Murga, *Protección a la estética en la Legislación Urbanística del Alto Imperio* (Seville 1976) 36–46. For a reaffirmation of a socioeconomic aim of the legislation, that of preserving social peace in times of intense building activity, see Sargenti, "Politica edilizia" 646–47.

even if this were the main inspiration, the laws aided the building industry by encouraging the importation and elaboration of material in cities, including Rome.

In connection with the question of demolition we should note that most Hadrianic construction in Rome did not necessitate any clearing away of existing domestic buildings. The Temple of Matidia and other new buildings in the Campus Martius (see Chapter 2) rose on open public land, and Hadrian's Mausoleum, as we shall see in Chapter 6, was built in imperial gardens. So was the new imperial triclinium in the Horti Sallustiani (see Chapter 5).[20] The Temple of Venus and Roma replaced the *vestibulum*, the ceremonial court, of Nero's Golden House (Chapter 4). The only new edifice that may have dislodged Roman households was the Temple of the Deified Trajan and Plotina at the edge of the Campus Martius, but as Chapter 3 shows, even this was probably built on vacant land.[21]

The use of Rome's land for housing seems to have been respected: Hadrian did not sacrifice residential areas for the projects that employed so many of Rome's inhabitants.[22] Indeed, the retracing and marking of Rome's *pomerium* (sacred boundary) in 121, which Hadrian initiated (see Chapter 2), seems to have involved the creation of a dike in the Campus Martius that rendered usable for housing and storage buildings land along the Via Lata formerly subject to flooding.

Thus Hadrian's building programs and interventions in Rome had a clear socioeconomic pattern, and it improved life for the unskilled masses of the city. There is other evidence of Hadrian's active concern for Rome's masses. The biography, for example, notes that Hadrian always boasted of his love of the plebs (*fuit et plebis iactantissimus amator, HA, Hadr.* 17.8), and he provided the customary games and spectacles for Rome.[23] In a less conventional move, Hadrian apparently involved himself in the religious and social administration of Rome's neighborhoods.

[20] For the confusion of public land and imperial property in Rome, see Millar, *ERW* 621–22: there may have been little or no distinction. Homo, *Urbanesimo* 278–89, discusses the restraints the availability of land imposed on monumental building in Rome. In the third century at least some land in the Campus Martius was in private hands: *HA, SevAlex.* 25.

[21] Even if this land southeast of the Via Lata were not pomerial (i.e., public) land, it could have been acquired for the fiscus when Trajan bought the land for the Forum and Markets.

[22] See, e.g., Garnsey, "Urban Investment" 135, on "wasteful and grandiose building projects" in imperial Rome.

[23] For example, Garzetti, 432–33; cf. Dio Cass. 69.6.1, 8.2, 10.1, 16.3; and *HA, Hadr.* 7.12, 19.4 (noting that Hadrian was careful never to take actors or gladiators from Rome), and 23.12.

Since the time of Augustus, the emperor had left the day-to-day control of Rome to others, and the administration of the city had become a source of prestige and pride for the senatorial and equestrian orders. Augustus' reorganization of Rome's urban administration had created numerous senatorial and lower positions that were autonomous or only nominally under the supervision of the consuls. In the clearest example, when in 7 B.C. the city was divided into fourteen regions, the praetors, aediles, and plebian tribunes drew lots for individual regions, which they supervised with equal powers.[24] Similarly, consulars became the *curatores aedium sacrarum locorumque publicorum, curatores viarum,* and after Tiberius, *curatores alvei Tiberis* (who were to help prevent flooding in Rome).[25] The urban prefect, whose duties included supervising the Roman city police, was of the senatorial class, but somewhat paradoxically, he seems to have always had less independence from the princeps than the others. Other important new magistracies in the city—the prefectures of the praetorians, the grain supply, and the *vigiles*—were equestrian offices and closely dependent on the princeps.[26]

The varied new magistracies, along with those traditionally concerned with the appearance and upkeep of the city, such as the aedilate, conferred status if not great power on their holders even while Augustus set about adorning and renovating Rome. He and subsequent principes paid out of their private funds for most of the public building in Rome, often inscribing the formula *sua impensa* or *sua pecunia* on their constructions or restorations,[27] but

[24] See S. Panciera, "Tra epigrafia e topografia," *ArchCl* 22 (1970) 146–48, with earlier bibliography; and R.E.A. Palmer, "The *excusatio magisteri* and the Administration of Rome under Commodus," *Athenaeum* 52 (1974) 278 (the second part of this article is published in *Athenaeum* 53 [1975]; reference to the two sections will be by author's name and year). For the close relationship of senate and princeps that was fostered by Augustus, see P. A. Brunt, "The Role of the Senate in the Augustan Regime," *CQ* 34 (1984) 423–44.

[25] Most recently, A. E. Gordon, "Q. Veranius, Consul A.D. 49," *CPCA* II.5 (1952) 257, 279–83, and G. Molisani, "Una dedica a Giove Dolicheno nell'Isola Tiberina," *RendLinc,* ser. 8, 26 (1971) [1972] 808–11, discuss the curatores aedium. For the curatores viarum, alvei Tiberis, and aedium, see O. Hirshfeld, *Die kaiserliche Verwaltungsbeamten*

*bis auf Diocletian* (Berlin 1905) 205–11, 258–72; and in general for curatores in imperial Rome, *DizEpig,* II.2, s.v. Curator, 1326–29. For the Augustan period: Brunt, "Role of the Senate" 439–40.

[26] See, e.g., Brunt, "Princeps and Equites" *JRS* 73 (1983) 59–61, on the creation of equestrian prefects in Rome; and in general, see G. Vitucci, *Ricerche sulla praefectura urbi in età imperiale* (Rome 1956); A. Passerini, *Le coorti pretorie* (Rome 1939); H. Pavis d'Escurac, *La Préfecture de l'annone. Service administratif impérial d'Auguste à Constantin* (Rome 1976); and P.K.B. Reynolds, *The Vigiles of Imperial Rome* (London 1926).

[27] Gros, *Aurea Templa* 16, citing Wilcken, "Zu den impensae der *Res Gestae,*" *Sitzungsberichte Berliner Akad. Wissenschaft,* 1931, 772f.: Augustus paid from his *patrimonium* (inheritance) and *manubiae* (money obtained

senators had administrative authority over lesser projects. The consular *curatores aedium sacrarum locorumque publicorum*, for example, oversaw the upkeep
of temples and the safeguarding of temple property, and also assigned public
land for private dedications.[28] The praetors, aediles, and tribunes in charge of
the city's regions supervised the building or rebuilding of shrines to the *Lares
Augusti compitales* (e.g., *CIL* 6.452: A.D. 109).

An inscription, recently published by S. Panciera, indicates that under
Hadrian the emperor himself assumed responsibility for permission to restore
compital shrines of the ruler cult in the city's fourteen regions. He was assisted in his task by the prefect of the vigiles, who in turn had two subalterns
for each region, a *curator* and a *denuntiator*, both freedmen. This change, which
at first sight may seem trivial, was a significant increase in the emperor's involvement in urban administration, albeit relatively short-lived. By the mid-
third and possibly as early as the mid-second century, the urban prefect had
assumed primary authority over the regions.[29] The Hadrianic change seems
due to a personal interest on Hadrian's part in neighborhood life rather than
to increasing administrative centralization or the concern for the city's beauty
and welfare, of which there is evidence in Hadrianic legislation against heavy
wheeled traffic and increased penalties against burial of the dead within city
limits.[30]

---

from the sale of booty). This was not the rule,
of course; Nero's Golden House cost the state
enormously (Suet. *Nero* 31). Despite the
claims of emperors to have built or restored
buildings and parts of Rome *sua impensa*, the
distinction between their moneys and the
state's could not have been very clear: P. A.
Brunt, "The 'Fiscus' and Its Development,"
*JRS* 56 (1966) 75–91; Millar, *ERW* 189–201.

[28] Gordon, "Veranius" 280–83, suggests
that the two curatores may have split these
duties. An excellent example of their supervision, which incidentially underscores Hadrian's interest in the city and its beautifica-
tion, is the statue base inscribed to Sabina,
dedicated by the African city of Sabratha, and
found in the Forum of Caesar in Rome:
(front) *Divae Sabinae A[ug(ustae)] Sa-
brathe[nses] ex Af[rica]*; (side) *Iussu imp. Cae-
saris Traiani/ Hadriani Aug. p. p./ locus adsi-
gnat. a Valerio Urbico et/ Aemilio Papo cur.
operum locor./ public. ded. Idib. Dec./ P. Cassio
Secundo et Nonio Muciano cos.* ([front] To the

deified Sabina Augusta, the people of Sabratha, Africa. [side] By order of [the emperor
Hadrian], father of his country: the place assigned by Valerius Urbicus and Aemilius Pa-
pus, the supervisors of public works and
places, was publicly dedicated on the Ides of
December in the consular year of P. Cassius
Secundus and Nonius Mucianus: 13 Dec. 138;
*NSc*, 1933, 432–34 = *AE* 1934, 146 = Smallwood, #145b).

[29] Panciera, "Topografia" 138–51; Palmer
(1975) 62–63, 79, 82. For the role of the urban
prefect: Palmer (1974) 277–78. Palmer also
discusses Hadrian's personal excuse to certain
*magistri vicorum* from paying the cost of wild
beast hunts: (1974) 285–88; (1975) 57–59 and
passim.

[30] Centralization: the urban prefect, for instance, has duties of the urban praetor and aediles at least as early as Hadrian's reign: Palmer (1974) 275; and Vitucci, *Praefectura urbi*
69–71. Brunt, "Role of the Senate" 436 n. 68,
notes that by Hadrian's period the emperor

Other evidence corroborates Hadrian's concern with Rome's populace. The biography notes that Hadrian frequently went among the public and even bathed at the public baths (*HA, Hadr.* 17.5). More important, his trusted freedman P. Aelius Phlegon wrote, among other works, a topographical study of the city.[31] Nothing remains of this "On the Places in Rome, and the Names by Which They Are Called" (*Suda,* s.v. Phlegon, IV, 745 Adler), but it may have been similar to earlier antiquarian studies of the city's regional history, such as that of Varro. Gros has argued that Varro's antiquarian research was essential to Augustus' building program in Rome;[32] such information illuminated Rome's past and the traditions of its neighborhoods, enabling the princeps to build and restore edifices and monuments of high popular appeal. It complemented the drier data on the population and neighborhoods of Rome available in records for grain distribution and similar archives.[33]

A fragmentary monument of 136, the Capitoline Base, seems to affirm Rome's reciprocal appreciation. The base, found on the Capitoline in the fifteenth century and now in the Museo dei Conservatori, must have been part of a larger monument. It now carries on its front a dedication to Hadrian by the *magistri vicorum urbis regionum XIIII*; on the right side it lists each *vicus* (neighborhood) and the names of its freedmen curatores, denuntiatores, and four magistri vicorum (chief officers of the urban neighborhoods) for regions I, X, and XIII, and on the left, each vicus and the names of the corresponding officials in regions XII and XIIII (*CIL* 6.975, cf. 31218 = *ILS* 6073 = Smallwood, #146). There is no trace of writing on the back, and no companion piece has ever been found listing officials of other regions. The reason for the dedication is not given; nevertheless, in its list by name of the regions' vici, and its annotation of their magistrates' names and status, it is one of our most important documents of Rome's neighborhood life,[34] and its date in Hadrian's principate is suggestive.

had assumed formal control of public finance. Legislation: *HA, Hadr.* 22.6 (against wagons) and *Dig.* 47.12.3.5 (strict fines against burying cadavers); cf. Garzetti, 410–11.

[31] E. Frank, "Phlegon (2)," *RE* 20.1 (1941) 261–64; and *FGrHist* II B, #257, pp. 1159–96. There were many other antiquarians writing at this time, such as Suetonius, who wrote the books *On Rome and Its Customs* and *On Games.* Phlegon and Hadrian were thought to be so close that Hadrian's biography alleges

Phlegon's books were actually written by Hadrian, and that the princeps had Phlegon publish under his own name Hadrian's autobiography: *HA, Hadr.* 16.1.

[32] Gros, *Aurea Templa* 23–24, who notes Augustus' reliance on other antiquarians as well.

[33] For such records, see, e.g., Brunt, "Fiscus," 89–90.

[34] A better edition of the dedication and names of the *vici,* as well as a photograph of

Except for his administrative reform (which may incidentally account for Hadrian's reputation for meddlesomeness: Dio Cass. 69.5.1; cf. *HA, Hadr.* 11.4), Hadrian seems to have taken care to respect the political and social prerogatives of the senate while making the government more efficient (cf. Dio Cass. 69.7).[35] Indeed, Hadrian's building activity in the capital city involved large segments of the upper classes, without whom Rome and the empire could not function. The senatorial and equestrian ranks benefited indirectly by means of their possession as rentiers of the figlinae around Rome from which bricks and tiles were made.[36] They certainly also profited from the quarrying and transport of marble and other materials to Rome, from engineering contracts, and from their control of mines and foundries. Yet the traditional scorn evinced by the upper classes toward commerce (affirmed even in the laws against demolition cited above) makes it unlikely that these benefits were ever explicitly spelled out.[37]

Hadrian's building programs also directly involved the senatorial class in a distinctly honorable way. The construction of temples and public buildings in Rome was traditionally within the purview of the senate: although a rebulican general or a princeps might vow an edifice, customarily approval by the senate had to be decreed before anything could be constructed or restored (cf. Suet. *Tib.* 30.1). The senate's power in this sphere was grounded in its control of the finances of the republican state, and whereas as a rule Augustus and his successors financed their buildings from the imperial fiscus, the senate continued to exercise its right to approve such construction.[38] Thus, for ex-

---

the right side, is produced by Valentini and Zucchetti, 1.37–47, who also discuss its findspot on the Capitoline. Palmer (1975) 82, suggests that "Hadrian was honored [by the dedicants of the base] because he had partially lifted from the magistri vicorum the contribution toward *venationes* [combats of wild beasts], which had become a heavier burden when the superintendence of the regions was transferred from aristocratic magistrates to the lowborn curatores"; this assumes his earlier argument that venationes given at the Ludi Augustales were to be at least partially financed by the magistratus vicorum: (1974) 286–88; (1975) 78.

[35] For example, Garzetti, 402–403.

[36] Steinby, "Ziegelstempel" 1514–15; P. Setälä, *Private Domini in Roman Brick Stamps of the Empire* (Helsinki 1977) 210–29, 242–44;

T. Helen, *Organization of Roman Brick Production in the First and Second Centuries* A.D.: *An Interpretation of Roman Brick Stamps* (Helsinki 1975) 22–23; and E. Champlin, "Figlinae Marcianae," *Athenaeum* 71 (1983) 258. See also Steinby, "Edilizia" 220–21.

[37] J. H. D'Arms, *Commerce and Social Standing in Ancient Rome* (Cambridge, Mass. and London 1981) 149–71, citing for upper class involvement in profitable commerce, e.g., J. B. Ward-Perkins, "The Marble Trade and Its Organization: Evidence from Nicomedia," in *The Seaborne Commerce of Ancient Rome*, ed. by J. H. D'Arms and E. C. Kopff (Rome 1980) 325–36.

[38] F. J. Hassel, *Der Trajansbogen in Benevent* (Mainz 1966) 2 nn. 6, 7, lists the imperial monuments and statues, erected with senatorial approval, that are known from inscrip-

ample, the senate's participation in the Temple of Venus and Roma is marked by the presence of both *SPQR* and *(Ex) S.C.* on coins showing the *aedes* (see Chapter 4), and the dedicatory inscription of the Temple of the Deified Trajan and Plotina erected by Hadrian begins *Ex S.C.* (*CIL* 6.31215 and 966; cf. *HA, Hadr.* 6.1, and Chapter 3).

In other ways as well the senate's involvement with almost every aspect of Roman religion committed it to involvement in Hadrian's building programs in the city. A prerequisite for the Temple of the Deified Trajan and Plotina and for the Temple of the Deified Matidia was official deification. This could be obtained only by senatorial decree.[39] The Hadrianic restoration of Vespasian's pomerium was also undertaken by senatorial decree, although, as we shall see in Chapter 2, one that came on Hadrian's initiative.

Such religious responsibilities of the senate, often overlooked in histories of the principate, demanded the collaboration of this body with Hadrian. In this light, it may be significant tht most surviving Hadrianic buildings in Rome are religious rather than secular. Some of these, the Temples of Venus and Roma and of the Bona Dea and the Auguratorium, the last of which Hadrian restored *sua pecunia* (*CIL* 6.976; cf. Chapter 7), evoked Rome's beginnings and probably appealed to the sentimental traditionalism of the senate; the selection may have been determined through Phlegon's antiquarian researches. Other new or restored buildings, such as the Pantheon, Saepta, Divorum, Temple of the Deified Trajan and Plotina, and Temple of the Deified Matidia, appealed to the senate's reverence of earlier "good" emperors. Although senatorial approval of such constructions strengthened the imperial cult, and thus ultimately the princeps himself, in no case can we discern that Hadrian had to force or attempted to force the senate's hand.

This final group of buildings suggests another motivation for Hadrian's work in the capital: emulation of Trajan. Hadrian's adoptive father had en-

---

tions; his main argument, however, that *SC* on a dedicatory inscription implies financing by the senate, has been corrected by Leon, *Bauornamentik*, 234. For senatorial cooperation, see, too, H. Bardon, "La Naissance d'un temple," *REL* 33 (1955) 166–82; and J. Stambaugh, "The Functions of Roman Temples," *ANRW* II.16.1 (1978) 558, 564–66. Hirschfeld, *Verwaltungsbeamten* 265–66, less convincingly holds that the senate was consulted only exceptionally. For the vexing question of whether only the imperial family could

erect or renew public buildings from the Augustan period to the fourth century (cf. Tac. *Hist.* 4.9), see P. Veyne, *Le Pain et le cirque* (Paris 1976) 686–89 (although Leon supersedes Veyne's note 405); and n. 39 below.

[39] See M. Hammond, *The Antonine Monarchy* (Rome 1959) 203–209 (hereafter Hammond, *AntMon*); for the senate's general supervision over religious matters, including religious buildings, see Brunt, "Role of the Senate" 437–39.

deared himself to the Romans by the magnificence of the complexes for
which he took credit, although much of the work was really the completion
of enterprises initiated by Domitian.[40] In part, Trajan's fame as a builder is
tied to the survival of contemporary or later praises, such as those of Pliny for
his work (cf., e.g., *Pan.* 51.3). Yet the Baths of Trajan, his Forum, and his
Markets were splendid and highly useful additions to the city, as was the
completed restoration of the Temple of Venus Genetrix and of the Circus
Maximus, for example.[41]

Many of these constructions and restorations were heavily publicized: we
have records of them on Trajanic coinage, in the Fasti Ostienses, and in other
inscriptions. Numerous coins showing architecture carry the legend SPQR OP-
TIMO PRINCIPI, apparently indicating that all of Rome felt it participated in or
benefited from the work.[42] The constructions seem carefully calculated to
win and maintain popularity for Trajan in Rome. The Baths and the Circus
were aimed to please the population as a whole. The Forum was closely associated with both the military and the civic life of Rome, and with the praetorian prefects in particular. The Markets, with space apparently reserved for
the prefect of the *annona* (grain supply) and other administrators, housed central offices for much of the commerce of Rome.[43]

Trajan's popularity emphasized the importance of imperial building at
Rome, and Hadrian followed his lead. Hadrian, too, was interested in more
than providing employment, for his villa at Tivoli could and did engage vast
numbers of construction workers and artisans. In Rome, however, among
his first works were his Temples of the Deified Trajan and of the Deified Matidia, Trajan's niece. Hadrian was also responsible for the basilicae named for
Matidia and Marciana, Trajan's sister. The buildings showed that Hadrian
was assuming his father's roles, a theme adumbrated by the early Hadrianic
coins depicting a phoenix.[44]

More private reasons also impelled Hadrian in his programs in Rome. The
sources unanimously agree on Hadrian's passionate fascination with architec-

[40] In brief, see Garzetti, 330. Blake/Bishop, 10–39, discuss Trajan's buildings in Rome in more detail.

[41] Gullini, "Adriano" 63–80, stresses the urban benefits of Trajan's Forum, Markets, and Baths, though giving much of the credit to Apollodorus.

[42] Mattingly, *BMC, Emp.* III, pp. lxx–lxxi, for the general honorific significance of this legend on coins struck in Rome ca. 104–111.

[43] For example, Blake/Bishop, 28–29, and J. C. Anderson, Jr., *The Historical Topography of the Roman Imperial Fora* (Brussels 1984) 160–67 (hereafter Anderson, *HistTop*).

[44] See, e.g., J. P. Martin, "Hadrien et le phénix. Propagande numismatique," in *Mélanges . . . W. Seston* (Paris 1974) 327–37; Mattingly, *BMC, Emp.* III, p. cxxvii.

ture and other fine arts,[45] and Dio even attributes the plan of the Temple of Venus and Roma to him, and mentions Hadrian's designs of "pumpkin domes" (69.4.2–6; see Chapter 4). Although we should not use Dio's anecdote as evidence that Hadrian necessarily designed the Pantheon and all the brilliant pavilions and courts of the villa at Tibur and other contemporaneous buildings with segmental domes, the story does affirm Hadrian's taste for such things.[46]

The concern in itself is not at all unusual; Cicero's and Pliny's letters and Pliny the Elder's remarks on the growth of luxury, for example, reveal the interest of the Roman upper classes in the planning and decoration of their houses and of the public buildings they financed and oversaw.[47] On a larger scale, Vitruvius' address to Augustus is an unequivocal plea for the princeps' personal interest in and respect for the work of a professional architect, whom Vitruvius portrays as a man of liberal education and high ideals rather than simply a builder. A century later, during Trajan's principate, Apollodorus of Damascus commanded supreme respect both in the field, as a military architect, and in Rome, as Trajan's adviser for architectural matters and as a member of the imperial court.[48] The literary tradition, however, affirms that Hadrian surpassed all his predecessors in his partiality to architecture, sculpture, and painting, for he is said to have practiced these arts actively (e.g., *HA, Hadr.* 14.8; Dio Cass. 69.3.2).[49]

Although some have argued that Apollodorus must have continued working under Hadrian, we have clear evidence for only one *architectus* who worked in association with the princeps, the Decianus who was commis-

---

[45] Besides the references in the text, see *HA, Hadr.* 16.10 and *Epit. de Caes.* 14.2. The evidence is sensitively treated by Toynbee, *Hadrianic School* xxiii. Hadrian's interests in literature will be discussed in Chapter 7.

[46] For example, W. L. MacDonald, *The Pantheon* (Cambridge, Mass. 1976) 12, states: "The architect of the Pantheon . . .[a]lmost certainly . . . was not Hadrian himself . . . [but] there can be no doubt that the conception of the building and the motivating personality behind its creation were Hadrian's." A similar conceptual framework is employed by H. Kähler, in *Hadrian und seine Villa bei Tivoli* (Berlin 1950), hereafter Kähler, *Villa.*

[47] Some outstanding instances: on the eve of crossing the Rubicon, Caesar studying

plans for a gladiatorial school he was going to build (Suet. *Jul.* 31.1); Cornelius Fronto personally choosing one plan from many submitted to him for a bath (Aul. Gell. *NA* 19.10.2–3). Gros, *Aurea Templa* 53–77, thoroughly examines the building and decoration of monumental structures in Augustan Rome, and discusses the possible extent of upper-class involvement.

[48] Vitruvius: P. Gros, "Vitruve, l'architecture et sa théorie, à la lumière des études récentes," *ANRW* II.30.1 (1982) 659–95; and F. E. Brown, "Vitruvius and the Liberal Art of Architecture," *Bucknell Review* 11.4 (1963) 99–107. For Apollodorus, see Leon, *Bauornamentik* 26, with references.

[49] The recent article of J. Beaujeu, "A-t-il

sioned with the task of moving the colossal statue of Nero (*HA, Hadr.* 19.12).
In contrast to Trajan, whose reliance on Apollodorus in his building programs is well known, Hadrian has no real collaborators. This unusual singu-
larity, differing so sharply from the harmonious association of princeps, senate, and court in most activities in the early principate, may account for the
silence that shrouds or clouds much of Hadrian's building program for
Rome.

Nevertheless, it is clear that for many different reasons and in many ways
Hadrian directly participated in the transformation of Rome during his principate. In consideration of the complexities of urban administration today,
this conclusion may seem preposterous, but the Roman world is not always
analogous to the modern one. The decidedly more personal involvement of
the Roman principes in the tasks of governing the Roman world has been
mentioned in the introduction. Hadrian was aided in his many bureaucratic
tasks by his individual characteristics of organizational skill, which enabled
him to create a more efficient and honest bureaucracy, and indefatigable en-
ergy, combined with a limitless thirst for knowledge (cf. Tert. *Apol.* 5.7). Yet
even Hadrian could never have managed Rome and the empire alone: he
needed the cooperation and trust of the senatorial and equestrian classes, and
the allegiance of the Roman populace. His building programs in Rome were
one way by which he achieved these goals and became one of the most effective emperors of Roman history.

---

existé une direction des musées dans la Rome
impériale?" *CRAI*, 1985, 671–88 (which I
read after this book went to press), strengthens my arguments for Hadrian's deep-seated
interest in the arts and in the appearance of
Rome. From *CIL* 6.10324 (= *ILS* 7213) and
other evidence, Beaujeu convincingly suggests that Hadrian appointed a *procurator a pi-*
*nacothecis* in a temporary position to inven-
tory and rearrange the public collection of
works of art in the Campus Martius, in temples, and in the imperial house. Beaujeu associates this Hadrianic work in the Campus
Martius with the earlier initiatives of Agrippa
and Augustus there.

# CHAPTER TWO

# THE CAMPUS MARTIUS

THE BIOGRAPHY of Hadrian includes in its brief, dateless list of his buildings in Rome the Pantheon, Saepta, Basilica Neptuni, and *lavacrum Agrippae* (Baths of Agrippa), grouping these with "many sacred buildings" and the Forum of Augustus, all of which the princeps restored or rebuilt and reconsecrated in the names of their original builders (*Romae instauravit Pantheum, Saepta, Basilicam Neptuni, sacras aedes plurimas, Forum Augusti, Lavacrum Agrippae; eaque omnia propriis auctorum nominibus consecravit* [at Rome he restored the Pantheon, the Saepta, the Basilica of Neptune, many sacred temples, the Forum of Augustus, the Baths of Agrippa; and he consecrated all of these in the names of their original builders]: *HA, Hadr.* 19.10). It does not mention that the Pantheon and Saepta, at least, were works of Hadrian's earliest years as princeps, and that together with the Baths of Agrippa they formed a tightly knit complex in the central Campus Martius (*see Ill. 1*).

The biography also fails to mention many other constructions and alterations in the Campus Martius that can be assigned to Hadrian. Behind the Pantheon he built a basilican structure, the "South Building," and to the northeast of the Pantheon, the Temple of the Deified Matidia with the Basilicae of Matidia and Marciana. To the Saepta he added a monumental portal leading to the precinct of Isis and Serapis, and in 126 he dedicated a restoration of the Divorum southeast of the Isaeum Campense. In addition to these works, attested to by good evidence, three other constructions in the immediate vicinity indicate Hadrianic interest in the area. Some 150 meters south of the Ara Pacis, along the east side of the Via Lata/Flaminia, there is a group of at least three uniformly planned and solidly built *insulae* (blocks of apartments) of Hadrianic date. About 150 meters farther south on the west side of the street a first-century porticus was rebuilt in part and extended by additions in brick-faced concrete, dated to Hadrian's rule by a brick stamp as well as by style. Architectural style has led some scholars to date a third building to Hadrian's reign: the Tempio di Siepe, which once stood just north of the

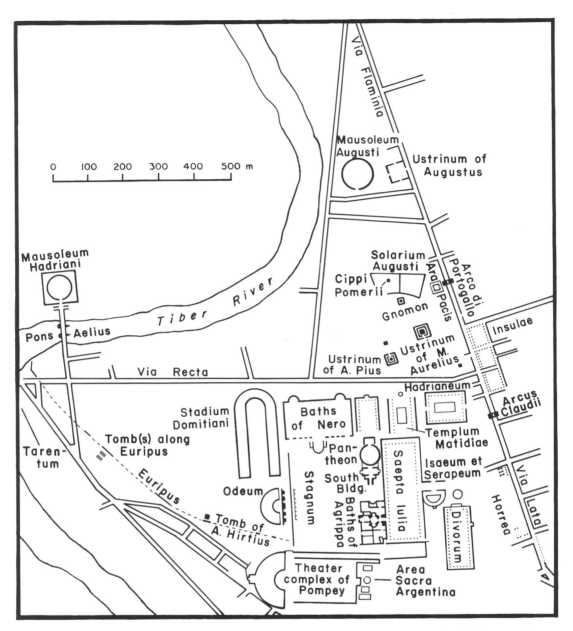

1. *The central, western-central, and northern Campus Martius in the second half of the second century* A.D. *The circular structure just north of the Templum Matidiae is the Tempio di Siepe; that just north of the Divorum, the Temple of Minerva Chalcidica.*

Temple of the Deified Matidia but has now vanished. Finally, in the northern part of the plain, around Augustus' Solarium and Ara Pacis, Hadrian raised the ground level some 1.80 to 2.90 meters, probably in connection with the restoration of the pomerium in that area. In sum, the Campus Martius is the area of the most numerous changes in the city in the Hadrianic period.

The evidence, predominately brick stamps, shows that most of this building activity took place in the first decade of Hadrian's principate, continuing through his absence from Rome from 121 to 125. His work in the Campus Martius is divided between the northern and the central Campus Martius, areas separated by the ancient paved street now known as the Via Recta in the absence of an ancient name (*see Ill. 1*). Stretches of basalt paving stones lying 1.5 to 2.0 meters below the modern Via del Curato, Via dei Coronari, Via di S. Agostino, Via delle Coppelle, and Via del Collegio Capranica trace it. It ran almost due west from the Via Lata/Flaminia to the Pons Neronianus and gave access to the Baths of Nero along its course, and so has been presumed to have been a Neronian creation.[1] The street, like all the buildings in the central portion of the Campus Martius, is oriented to the cardinal compass points.[2] To the north of this street Hadrian seems to have been primarily concerned with raising the ground level and modifying existing structures to accord with this; in the central part he erected new buildings and restored old ones. The two operations, however, were apparently contemporary.

To understand the extent and direction of Hadrian's work in these two areas, we must first consider this part of the Campus Martius at his accession. In the early Augustan period, with the monumentalizing of parts of the central and northern Campus Martius, the area became closely associated with Augustus and the Augustan ideology.[3] Before this the low-lying plain, al-

[1] R. Lanciani, *NSc*, 1881, sect. XII; *NSc*, 1883, 81; *NSc*, 1885, 251; and more recently, S. Quilici Gigli, "Estremo Campo Marzio. Alcune osservazioni sulla topografia," in *Città e architettura* 51–52. For the name of the road, see *HJ*, 503 n. 78 and 504, who associate the street with Hadrian, as does K. de Fine Licht, *The Rotunda in Rome* (Copenhagen 1968) 230 (hereafter de Fine Licht).

[2] F. Castagnoli, "Il Campo Marzio nell'antichità," *MemLinc*, ser. 8, 1 (1946) 148, suggests that this orientation was determined by the original Saepta (later enlarged in the Saepta Julia), which as an inaugurated *tem-*

*plum* was oriented to the cardinal points.

[3] For the Augustan central Campus Martius, see the early but still fundamental work of F. W. Shipley, *Agrippa's Building Activities in Rome* (St. Louis 1933); F. Coarelli, "Il Pantheon, l'apoteosi di Augusto e l'apoteosi di Romolo," in *Città e architettura* 41–42; and J.-M. Roddaz, *Marcus Agrippa* (Rome 1984), esp. 252–91. De Fine Licht, 227–34, provides a thorough survey of the central Campus Martius. For Augustus in the northern Campus Martius, see E. Buchner, "Solarium Augusti und Ara Pacis," *RömMitt* 83 (1976) 319–65; idem, "Horologium Solarium Augusti.

ways subject to flooding, seems to have been free of large permanent structures, while eminent individuals and *triumphatores* built up the southern Campus Martius with temples, squares, and porticoes, works culminating in the
vast theater complex of Pompey.[4] Agrippa took on the land around what
Caesar had intended for the Saepta Julia, and here carried out a huge building
program. To drain the area, which included the Capreae Palus and the lowest
land in Rome, he constructed deep sewers and built the Stagnum Agrippa and
the Euripus, which may have functioned as a collecting tank and runoff.[5]
Here he built his Baths and finished the Diribitorium and the Saepta Julia. The
latter, begun by Julius Caesar and continued by M. Lepidus, replaced the old
Ovile as the voting place of Rome, but its encircling porticoes also served as
a promenade and market for luxury goods. Its long flanks, the Poseidonion
(also referred to as the Porticus Argonautarum and Stoa of Poseidon) and the
Porticus Meleagri, were named for the paintings embellishing them. Just
west of the north end of the Saepta, in the lowest area of all, Agrippa built the
Pantheon, associated with the cult of the gens Julia. South of the Pantheon
and adjacent to the Stagnum, Agrippa's Baths and Horti made up the first
great public bath and park complex of Rome. Not surprisingly, these projects
required more than twenty years, from 29 to 7 B.C., to complete.[6] If Agrip-

Bericht über die Ausgrabungen 1979/80,"
*RömMitt* 87 (1980) 355–73; both published together with a "Nachtrag" (pp. 78–80), in *Die
Sonnenuhr des Augustus* (Mainz 1982); these
works hereafter cited as Buchner (1976),
(1980), and "Nachtrag," respectively. Augustus' Mausoleum is discussed in more detail in Chapter 6.

[4] For the character of the west, south, and
south-central Campus Martius, built up during the republican period by various temples
and propagandistic complexes of families in
the republican period, see F. Coarelli, "Il
Campo Marzio occidentale. Storia e topografia," *MélRome* 89 (1977) 807–46; Gros, *Aurea
Templa* 80; and cf. Quilici Gigli, "Estremo
Campo Marzio" 47–57, L. Quilici, "Il
Campo Marzio occidentale," in *Città e architettura* 59–85.

[5] R. B. Lloyd, "The Aqua Virgo, Euripus
and Pons Agrippa," *AJA* 83 (1979) 195–200,
discussed further in Chapter 7; de Fine Licht,
232; P. Narducci, *Sulla fognatura della città di*

*Roma* (Rome 1889) 16–39, 63–64; and Blake,
1.128, 159. For the swampy nature of the Capreae Palus, see *HJ*, 473–74; and for its symbolic importance as the spot of Romulus'
apotheosis, Coarelli, "L'apoteosi" 41–46.

[6] For the Saepta Julia and Diribitorium, see
nn. 17 and 71 below; E. Sjöqvist, "Kaisa-
reion. A Study in Architectural Iconography,"
*OpusRom* 18 (1954) 86–108; and Cozza's iden-
tification of a fragment of the *Forma Urbis*, pl.
31 (text, pp. 97–102), as the Diribitorium.
For the Agrippan Pantheon, see Coarelli,
"L'apoteosi" 41–46; W. Loerke, "Georges
Chédanne and the Pantheon. A Beaux-Arts
Contribution to the History of Roman Ar-
chitecture," *Modulus*, 1982, 40–55; de Fine
Licht, 172–76, 191–94, and fig. 194 on p. 177;
MacDonald, *Pantheon* 77–84; and below. For
the Baths of Agrippa, still partly visible in the
Via dell'Arco della Ciambella: A. M. Colini,
"La sala rotonda delle Terme di Agrippa,"
*Capitolium* 32.9 (1957) 6–14; C. Hülsen, *Die
Thermen des Agrippa. Ein Beitrag zur Topogra-*

pa's Pantheon had a monumental northern facade as the northernmost front of the Agrippan complex, it may have had a visual axis with Augustus' Mausoleum, a somewhat earlier manifestation of Augustus' ambitions.[7]

This visual connection would reflect a close ideological one between the Augustan buildings in the northern and central Campus Martius. In the north stood Augustus' Mausoleum, his Ustrinum, the Solarium, and the Ara Pacis. The area around these splendid monuments was a public park described as *silvae atque ambulationes*, groves and promenades (cf. Suet. *Aug.* 100.4).[8] This relative isolation set off the individual monuments (*cf. Ill. 2*), which had a thematic unity, according to a recent investigator of this area, E. Buchner. They celebrated the mortal Augustus as almost divine, the bringer of peace and order to Rome and the cosmos.[9]

Between the death of Augustus and Hadrian's accession, however, the central Campus Martius changed character. Caligula was probably responsible for the large temenos dedicated to the Egyptian deities Isis and Serapis and situated just east of the Saepta.[10] At the Via Lata/Flaminia Claudius trans-

---

*phie des Marsfeldes in Rom* (Rome 1910); and below. We are not certain of the Baths' eastern wall, now completely obliterated (de Fine Licht, 26), and the Baths' location may have been determined by Agrippa's Stagnum to their south. A battered column recently found under the Via di S. Chiara, about 45 meters from the corner of Via dei Cestari, has been attributed to the Baths: *BullComm* 83 (1972–73) [1976] 86.

[7] Loerke, "Chédanne" 51, hypothesizes from the siting of the Baths of Nero a northern forecourt for the Agrippan Pantheon, but his evidence for this forecourt is not as compelling as are his arguments for the columnar northern facade of the Agrippan Pantheon.

[8] For this aspect of the (northern) Campus Martius, see Castagnoli, "Campo Marzio" 127–40, with references to the ancient literature. Note, too, that the travertine cippus *CIL* 6.874, found in the Via del Seminario, is often interpreted as signifying that in the Augustan period the area north of it was not built up (e.g., de Fine Licht, 228; Coarelli, "L'apoteosi" 41).

[9] Buchner (1976) 363–65. Augustus' Mausoleum and Ustrinum are discussed later, in

Chapters 6 and 7, and his Solarium in this chapter. For more on the Ara Pacis, see G. Moretti, *Ara Pacis Augustae* (Rome 1948) (hereafter Moretti); E. Simon, *Ara Pacis Augustae* (Tübingen 1967); M. Torelli, *Typology and Structure of Roman Historical Reliefs* (Ann Arbor, Mich. 1982) 27–61, who offers new interpretations of the friezes on pp. 35–55; and E. La Rocca, *Ara Pacis Augustae* (Rome 1983). For other, less controversial, interpretations of the friezes, see especially Simon, *Ara Pacis* 15–30.

[10] Augustus banned worship of the Egyptian deities from the pomerium of Rome (Dio Cass. 53.2.4), and Tiberius later ordered to be dismantled a sanctuary to Isis established in the Campus Martius outside the pomerium (Jos. *AJ* 18.3.4): see Platner-Ashby, s.v. Isis, Aedes, pp. 283–85. The plan of the Isaeum before its Domitianic restoration is unknown. For the Domitianic rebuilding, see G. Gatti, "Topografia dell'Iseo Campense," *RendPontAcc* 20 (1943–44) [1945] 117–63, with earlier bibliography; de Fine Licht, 310 n. 74, with additional bibliography; M. Malaise, *Inventaire préliminaire des documents égyptiens découverts en Italie* (Leiden 1972) 187–214;

formed the crossing of the Aqua Virgo into a triumphal arch celebrating his conquest of Britain, and a vast porticus complex faced with rusticated blocks of travertine, just south of this, has been given a Claudian date on grounds of style.[11] In 62 or 64 Nero, who had used the Agrippan monuments first for pleasure and later as a refuge for those made homeless by the fire of 64 (e.g., Tac. *Ann.* 15.37, 39), built a second large bath complex northeast of the Pantheon. His innovative Baths came in for criticism for their "Greekness": they were the first public baths in Rome to include athletic facilities (Tac. *Ann.* 14.47.2, cf. 14.20).[12]

The catastrophic fire in 80 during the reign of Titus brought further changes, and Domitian's restorations left his characteristic imprint on the devastated area.[13] Part of the Villa Publica, a public park originally extensive but now much reduced in size by the encroachment of other monuments, was transformed into the magnificent Divorum, an elegant and ornate precinct of about 75 by 190 meters, enclosing temples to the Deified Vespasian and Titus. Just to the north of this Domitian added a temple of unusual circular plan in honor of his patroness divinity, Minerva, here given the epithet Chalcidica.[14]

and Roullet, 23–35, and her fig. 352. For recently discovered remains of part of the central exedra, see *BullComm* 83 (1972–73) [1976] 84–85.

[11] For Claudius' arch, see *CIL* 6.920, 31203; H. P. Laubscher, "Arcus Novus und Arcus Claudii, zwei Triumphbogen an der Via Lata im Rom," *Nachrichten Akad. Göttingen,* 1976, 65–108; and most recently, E. Rodriguez-Almeida, "Il Campo Marzio settentrionale: *Solarium* e *Pomerium,*" *RendPontAcc* 51–52 (1978–79/1979–80) [1982] 200–202. The porticus has been identified as the Porticus Minucia Frumentaria by, e.g., Castagnoli, "Campo Marzio" 180 (with reservations), and now G. Rickman, "Porticus Minucia," in *Città e architettura* 105–108. Yet the Claudian Porticus Minucia Frumentaria is now plausibly identified as the porticus of the Via delle Botteghe Oscure east of the Largo Argentina: F. Coarelli, *L'area sacra di Largo Argentina* (Rome 1981) 35–36; and C. Nicolet, "Le Temple des Nymphes et les distributions frumentaires à Rome à l'époque républicaine," *CRAI,* 1976, 30–37.

[12] B. Tamm, *Neros Gymnasium in Rom* (Stockholm 1970); W. Heinz, *Römische Thermen. Badewesen und Badeluxus im römischen Reich* (Munich 1983) 68–71. The Baths were later renovated by Severus Alexander. For the Baths' original character, see also Dio Cass. 61.21.1; Platner-Ashby, s.v. Thermae Neronianae, 531–32; and A. M. Colini, *Stadium Domitiani* (Rome 1943) 22–24. Recent finds from the area are noted in *BullComm* 83 (1972–73) [1976] 86.

[13] For the ancient testimony for the fire, conspicuously Dio Cass. 66.24.2, see P. Werner, *De incendiis urbis Romae aetate imperatorum* (Leipzig 1906) 30–32. For Domitian's extensive restorations, see Blake, II.100–105; G. Lugli, "La Roma di Domiziano nei versi di Marziale e di Stazio," *Studi Romani* 9 (1961) 3–17; cf. Anderson, "Topographical Tradition" 93–105.

[14] For the Divorum, see Richardson, "Divorum" 159–63; cf. *NSc,* 1925, 236–42; *BullComm* 83 (1972–73) [1976] 85. The Villa Publica is investigated by F. Coarelli, "Il Tempio di Bellona," *BullComm* 80 (1965–67) [1968] 61–66; and by M. G. Morgan, "Villa Publica and Magna Mater," *Klio* 55 (1973)

West of this he rebuilt the Isaeum and Serapeum very splendidly, adding obelisks and ornamentation befitting gods who were given credit for preserving him during the civil war of 69. The hieroglyphs on one obelisk (now in Piazza Navona) echo the dynastic message of the Divorum, for they proclaim Domitian the ever-living pharaoh, the son and brother of the gods Vespasian and Titus.[15] (This precinct will be mentioned later in the chapter.) Finally, along the west side of the Agrippan complex he constructed his Stadium and Odeum, buildings for athletic and musical contests of Greek type, erected in conjunction with his new Capitoline Games, the Ludi Capitolini or Capitolia of 86.[16]

Other changes, too, had occurred in the Campus in the course of the first century. After Tiberius transferred elections from the Comitia Centuriata, the Saepta had ceased to be used as a voting place and became simply a porticus and bazaar.[17] Caligula destroyed some arches of the Aqua Virgo for his unrealized project of building an amphitheater near the Saepta (Suet. *Calig.* 21), but Claudius restored these (*CIL* 6.1252). Trajan is said to have built a theater in the Campus, but nothing more is known about it.[18] In sum, at Ha-

---

216–22 (for differing views: T. P. Wiseman, "The Circus Flaminius," *PBSR* 42 [1974] 19–20). For the temple to Minerva, see Cozza's correct identification of the "Lavacrum Agrippae" fragment of the marble plan, *Forma Urbis*, pp. 97–102, pl. 31; and F. Castagnoli, "Minerva Calcidica," *ArchCl* 12 (1960) 91–95. Coarelli, *Roma* (1980) 297–98, suggests that the epithet Chalcidica may be interpreted as "she who guards the door," alluding to the physical relationship of the adjacent temples Domitian built for his and his family's glorification. K. Scott, *The Imperial Cult under the Flavians* (Stuttgart and Berlin 1936) 61–82, 166–88, discusses in detail Domitian's devotion to Minerva, as does J.-L. Girard, "Domitien et Minerve: une prédilection impériale," *ANRW* II.17.1 (1981) 233–45, esp. 235–36.

[15] See above, n. 10. For the obelisk and inscription, see Malaise, *Inventaire* 203–7, based on A. Erman, "Römische Obelisken," *Abhandlungen der königlich preussischen Akademie der Wissenschaften* 4 (1917) 18–28 (hereafter Erman [1917]). Domitian's temple of Fortuna Redux, near the Porta Triumphalis, which he

restored, has been conjectured to have been near the Isaeum Campense, but is convincingly relocated by F. Coarelli in the S. Omobono area ("La Porta Trionfale e la Via dei Trionfi," *DialArch* 2 [1968] 66–93).

[16] Colini, *Stadium Domitiani*; when I last visited Rome (1984), the stadium was under excavation and restoration. For the ludi themselves, see L. Robert, "Deux concours grecs à Rome," *CRAI*, 1970, 7–8; I. Lana, "I ludi capitolini di Domiziano," *RivFil*, n.s. 29 (1951) 147–60; and the section on the Athenaeum in Chapter 7 below. The evidence for the location of the Odeum is very slight, consisting only of some finds to the south of the Piazza Navona (*BullComm* 66 [1938] {1939} 264–66, summarized by Colini, *Stadium Domitiani*, 37).

[17] G. Gatti, "I Saepta Iulia nel Campo Marzio," *L'Urbe* 2.9 (1937) 8–23; Platner-Ashby, s.v. Saepta Julia, 460–61.

[18] Nero built a temporary wooden amphitheater to replace the stone one of Statilius Taurus, probably in the southern Campus Martius: Platner-Ashby, s.vv. Amphitheatrum Neronis, Amphitheatrum Statilii Tauri,

drian's accession the central Campus Martius was much more densely built up than in Augustus' day,[19] and the monuments were especially buildings that glorified individual principes and their families.

Alterations in the northern Campus Martius had not been so drastic, consisting mainly of modifications in the level and paving around the Ara Pacis and the Solarium. The Augustan Ara Pacis was originally surrounded by a travertine pavement laid on two levels probably due to a slope in the terrain, since the Augustan level of the Ara Pacis seems to have been higher than the Augustan level of the Solarium.[20] On the east side, toward the Via Lata/Flaminia, the pavement was level with the eastern entrance; on the other three sides, however, it was approximately 1.28 meters lower, and a flight of shallow stairs led up to the western entrance.[21] (These steps have been reproduced in the modern reconstruction.) The difference in the two levels was left as a straight drop (*see Ill. 2*). At some time before Hadrian the area around the Ara Pacis was leveled, a new pavement being laid on the north, west, and south sides. This buried the western stairway running up to the threshold of the western entrance. Two of Buchner's core samples taken in 1980, about 5 meters south of the Ara Pacis, indicate that this new unilevel pavement did not extend even that far south.[22] The date of the repaving is still uncertain: although Tiberius, Nero, and Domitian issued coins depicting the Ara Pacis, their coinage had other motivations and did not show the detail. Indeed, Domitian's issue of 86 depicts the western staircase.[23]

---

11. Evidence for the theater of Trajan is confused; see Chapter 7, n. 95.

[19] De Fine Licht, 230, remarks that by the end of Hadrian's reign the buildings east of the Pantheon were predominantly temples and sacred monuments, whereas south and west lay establishments mainly for recreation and amusement. He considers the character of the area "sumptuous" and of a "possibly somewhat obtrusive and ostentatious grandeur."

[20] Buchner (1980) 356, notes that the modern street level is 8.00 meters above the Augustan paving at the Horologium Solarium, but only 7.45 meters above at the Ara Pacis.

[21] Moretti, 94–96.

[22] Buchner (1980) 369–70, reports evidence only for the Augustan paving discovered by his cores nos. 8 and 9.

[23] S. Weinstock, "Pax and the Ara Pacis," *JRS* 50 (1960) 51–54, with illustrations of all three coin types, claims that the two later issues do not represent the Augustan Ara Pacis in Rome; he is convincingly refuted by J.M.C. Toynbee, "The 'Ara Pacis Augustae,'" *JRS* 51 (1961) 154. Eadem, in "The Ara Pacis Reconsidered: Historical Art in Roman Italy," *ProcBritAc* 39 (1953) 70 nn. 2, 3, suggests that Nero's issue of sestertii was struck to commemorate the end of the Parthian war in 66, and that Domitian's issue of sestertii in 86 was an anniversary issue designed to mark the altar's centenary. Torelli, *Roman Historical Reliefs* 32, associates the two later issues with issues representing Ianus Quirinus, and interprets them as announcements of *pax*. The coins are also represented by M. Grant, *Aspects of the Principate of Tiberius* (New York 1950) pl. 2, no. 3, and pp. 78–79 (coin of Tiberius); *BMC, Emp.* 1, pp. 271–

2. *G. Gatti's reconstruction of the Ara Pacis during the Augustan period, from the southeast. Note the change in the levels of the eastern and western entrances.*

The first century apparently brought almost no change in the northern Campus Martius, and at Hadrian's accession this area had the parklike character it was given under Augustus. In 75 Vespasian and Titus had traced a new line for the pomerium through at least part of the Campus Martius and crossing this area, but this would have been marked only by cippi at intervals.[24] As we shall see below, Domitian was probably responsible for raising the *platea* of the Solarium some 1.60 meters, but this change only reproduced the Augustan Solarium at the new level.

72, nos. 360–65, pl. 47.2 (coin of Nero); *BMC, Emp.* II, p. 384, no. 391†, pl. 74.6 (coin of Domitian).

[24] P. Romanelli, "II.—Roma," *NSc*, 1933, 241 (hereafter Romanelli), first reported the Vespasianic cippus from the area of the Solarium. According to tradition a clear space was to be left to either side of the pomerium: Liv. 1.44.4; cf. J. H. Oliver, "The Augustan Pomerium," *MAAR* 10 (1932) 145–47. Recent reevaluation of discoveries made while building Palazzo Montecitorio indicates buildings in the area predating the "Ustrinum" of Marcus Aurelius, but we have no knowledge of date, type, or function: R. Paris and A. Danti, in *Dagli scavi al museo* (Rome 1984) 43–48.

Castagnoli proposes the attractive theory that the northern Campus Martius was left open because it was the Campus Martius proper, sacred and dedicated to the cult of Mars,[25] but there is a more pragmatic and obvious reason the area should have remained *silvae atque ambulationes*: it was low and subject to flooding. Within some sixty years of the Solarium's construction the sun clock was no longer accurate, and among the possible reasons for this listed by Pliny the Elder is that inundations of the Tiber may have caused the substructures of its obelisk gnomon to settle (Pliny *HN* 36.73).[26] He may have been thinking of such floods as the sudden great and destructive one during Otho's short rule, which was regarded as a portent of disaster as the inundation blocked the Via Lata/Flaminia in the Campus Martius along which Otho intended to take his army out to war (Tac. *Hist.* 1.86; cf. Suet. *Otho* 8.3 and Plut. *Otho* 4.5). At least one major inundation occurred under Trajan (ca. 107: Pliny *Ep.* 8.17; *Epit. de Caes.* 13.12),[27] and Hadrian's biography lists a flood among the disasters of his reign (*HA, Hadr.* 21.6). Only the construction of the Tiber embankment and regular dredging in comparatively recent times have checked the periodic floods of the district,[28] although as we shall see, Hadrian apparently attempted a certain measure of flood control. First, however, we turn to his much better attested work in the central Campus Martius.

In the central Campus Martius Hadrian built on a grand scale.[29] The key

[25] Castagnoli, "Campo Marzio" 146. Though his definitions of Campus Martius are not universally accepted, the objections are minor. E. Welin, "Ara Pacis in Campo," *OpusRom* 18 (1954) 168–69, 189–90, e.g., proposes that the Campus Martius proper is north of the Stadium Domitiani, thus slightly west of the location fixed by Castagnoli.

[26] Other possible reasons he lists are a change in the sun's course; one in the heavens'; and earthquakes in Rome. Buchner favors the theory that an earthquake of 51 was responsible for the clock's inaccuracy ([1980] 362 n. 1).

[27] A. N. Sherwin-White, *The Letters of Pliny* (Oxford 1966) 467, for the date. For the ditch, see *ILS* 5797a; R. Meiggs, *Roman Ostia*, 2nd ed. (Oxford 1973), App. iii, pp. 488–89; and J. Le Gall, *Le Tibre, fleuve de Rome dans l'antiquité* (Paris 1953) 132. Pliny's silence about any damage to the city has led Sherwin-White to conclude that the ditch succeeded in

keeping the city dry. The passage in the *Epitome*, however, indicates a devastating flood in the Trajanic city, and strongly implies an earlier one under Nerva, although the Trajanic flood may not be that which Pliny records.

[28] For a list of the floods known from antiquity, see Le Gall, *Tibre* 29–30; for a general discussion of the floods of the Tiber and their effect on Rome, see G. Lugli, "Come si è trasformato nei secoli il suolo di Roma," *RendLinc*, ser. 8, 6 (1951) 477–91, republished in his *StudMin*, 229–45.

[29] The scholars who have noted the extent of Hadrian's renovation of the area are hard put to explain it: Heilmeyer, "Apollodorus" 326–28, assumes that the entire central Campus Martius—rather than the Pantheon only—was burnt in 110; and Coarelli, "Campo Marzio occidentale" 844, postulates a calamity, perhaps a devastating fire, prior to Hadrian's reign. The extent of the Hadrianic

to understanding his extensive rehandling of the central plain is the Pantheon, which survives almost intact, and provides a dated contrast for construction, design, and ornament in other buildings. The biography of Hadrian lists it first in the enumeration of his buildings, and brick stamps document its construction as beginning in 118, almost as soon as he arrived in Rome as princeps.[30] Of all Hadrian's restorations known from various sources, only this one has a clear history: its immediate predecessor was struck by lightning and burned down in 110 (*concrematum*: P. Orosius, *Historiae adversum paganos* 7.12.5; cf. Jerome, *Chron.* p. 195 H.). Similarly, this is one of the few Hadrianic edifices the use of which is explicitly attested to: Cassius Dio tells us that Hadrian used to hold court there (69.7). The remarkable preservation of the building with so much of its decoration gives a notion of what the entire area must have looked like under Hadrian; it also underscores the audacious innovation of Hadrianic architecture and engineering. On the other hand, its simple inscription on the epistyle of the pronaos, *M. Agrippa L. f. cos. III fecit* (Marcus [Vipsanius] Agrippa, son of Lucius, consul for the third time, had [this building] made: *CIL* 6.896 = *ILS* 129), shows Hadrian's respect for his predecessors and corroborates the biography's statement that he customarily restored buildings in the names of their original builders (*HA, Hadr.* 19.10).

The Hadrianic Pantheon has excited discussion of its architectural brilliance and of its symbolism since the time of Dio (53.27), with recent outstanding contributions by K. de Fine Licht and MacDonald. It was much larger than and apparently of a completely different plan from its Augustan predecessor (and presumably from the Domitianic rebuilding as well). In the place of Agrippa's rectangular building, which was about 19.82 by 43.76 me-

---

work makes such a hypothesis attractive, although confirmation must await new evidence. Blake/Bishop, 42, 50–51, consider that Hadrian restored the central Campus Martius and raised the level in an attempt to control flooding, but cite no evidence, and the layer of bluish alluvial soil they claim as visible over the Domitianic phase of the Pantheon is actually below the Agrippan building.

[30] Bloch, *Bolli* 102–17, analyzes the stamps (as do, with erroneous conclusions, G. Cozzo, in *MemLinc*, ser. 6, 5 [1936] 327–43, and J. Guey, "Devrait-on dire: le Panthéon de Septime-Sévère?" *MélRome* 53 [1936] 198–249). Heilmeyer's recent attempt in "Apollodorus" to redate the Pantheon to the period A.D. 113–125 is surely erroneous: aside from his overly refined stylistic arguments that the Pantheon's design and ornamentation resemble known Apollodoran structures so closely that the building can have been planned only by this architect (pp. 330–43), he stresses that of the datable brick stamps (collected on pp. 327–29), at least one-sixth come from the period more than ten years before the accepted beginning of the building in 117. But these brick stamps cannot be used to prove that the building was begun before 117. See Chapter 1, n. 6. In addition to the references cited below for the Pantheon, see K. Ziegler, "Pantheion," *RE* 18.3 (1949) 729–42.

bers in the attic. Originally an equally wide (33.10 meters) facade of eight monolithic gray granite columns with Pentelic marble capitals and bases (total height, 13.96 meters), with four pairs of similarly ornamented rose granite columns, led back 15.5 meters toward the intermediary block. The rose granite columns, in line with the first, third, sixth, and eighth columns of the facade, make three aisles: a large central one leading to the vaulted entranceway into the rotunda, and narrower lateral ones terminating in large half-domed niches in the intermediate block.[37] Dio's description of the Pantheon has led to the supposition that statues of Augustus and Agrippa filled the niches (Dio Cass. 53.27.3), although there is no trace of a statue base in either one.

The boldness of this design was softened in antiquity. The sculptural program evoked both the Augustan tradition and the concept of peace. The dedicatory inscription of Agrippa was emblazoned across the pronaos, and above it, to judge from the pattern of attachment holes, the pediment carried an eagle within a wreath, presumably a *corona civica*.[38] The civic crown placed over Augustus' door in 27 B.C. was one of his proudest honors (*RG* 34.2; Dio Cass. 53.16.4; Pliny *HN* 16.3–4).[39] This symbol in Hadrian's pediment would have linked the new building to the spirit of the original one. The friezes at the central vaulted entranceway and the sides of the intermediate block depict sacrificial instruments and looped garlands. Although this may have been a common decorative motif by the second century, it could not but evoke the similar decoration on Augustus' Ara Pacis, and perhaps also the frieze of the Temple of the Deified Vespasian and Titus.[40]

Architecturally as well, there seems to have been an effort to disguise from the front the unconventionality of Hadrian's new building. The approach to the temple seems typical of its period. A rectangular forecourt, about 60 me-

[37] Capitals (derivative from those in the Forum of Trajan): Heilmeyer, *Normalkapitelle* 158–59; Leon, *Bauornamentik* 212–13; and W. L. MacDonald, *The Architecture of the Roman Empire*, rev. ed. (New Haven and London 1982) 98 (hereafter MacDonald, *ARE*). The framing of the porch's roof is controversial: A. Frazer, *AJA* 73 (1969) 489. The unfluted granite shafts are 11.79 meters tall.

[38] De Fine Licht, 45–46; Heilmeyer, "Apollodorus" 345. Both refer to L. Cozza, who also stresses the relief's similarity to a relief from Trajan's Forum (now in the wall of SS. Apostoli, Rome).

[39] Heilmeyer, "Apollodorus" 345, emphasizes the obvious Augustan connection and

notes that Trajan wears the corona civica in portraits, and Trajanic coins of ca. 100 carry the legend OB CIV(ES) SER(VATOS) in an oak wreath (cf. *BMC, Emp.* III, pp. xcvii, xcii). De Fine Licht, 292 n. 12, notes the importance of the eagle in the iconography of Trajan's Column and stresses the symbolism of the oak wreath in literature and art. Yet I cannot agree with his conclusion that the Agrippan pediment was like the Hadrianic one.

[40] De Fine Licht discusses and illustrates these friezes, listing similar ones, although he cautions that "no definite cases of close connection between a group of objects and a definite cult, or the building they decorate, can be proved" (pp. 80–82).

ters wide and perhaps 100 meters deep, extended from the pronaos at a level 1.30 meters below its floor. The forecourt, paved in travertine, was framed by colonnades 5 to 6 meters deep, reached by six steps of giallo antico; their gray granite columns echoed on a smaller scale those along the facade of the pronaos.[41] Nothing has been found to show how the forecourt's eastern and western porticoes adjoined the Pantheon itself. The most plausible theory is that stairs led to a door or opening in the southern walls of the two elevated porticoes; thus people coming from the south either could enter the pronaos directly by a narrow lateral stair cut into the porch on both east and west, or could pass along one of the porticoes to the forecourt.[42] An arch—the Arcus Pietatis, known only from medieval documents—may have stood in the forecourt, but both its situation and its date are uncertain.[43] We are equally uncertain about the forecourt's northern side, the entrance front.[44] From within the forecourt, however, the visitor would have seen only the massive, more or less traditional architecture of the pronaos with the intermediate block looming behind it. These would have hidden the rotunda, and the effect of the dome would have been confined entirely to the interior.[45]

[41] De Fine Licht, 26–30; note that Lanciani considered the pavement (which he identifies as of "granitello") of the forecourt's porticoes to be Severan: R. Lanciani, *NSc*, 1881, 270; cf. *NSc*, 1882, 347. De Fine Licht, 26, cites various theories of scholars on the length of the forecourt as extending from about 60 to 150 meters north. His own hypothetical reconstruction (p. 29) of a forecourt 60 meters wide, 100 meters deep, divided midway by a wall or open colonnade that runs east-west and incorporates the Arcus Pietatis, cannot be correct. For recent finds of pavement and drainage systems in the area of and around the forecourt, see *BullComm* 83 (1972–73) [1976] 92–93, s.vv. Piazza della Rotonda, Via dei Coronari, and Piazza della Maddalena: the find of a wall and a large sewer at a depth of 4 meters under the modern Piazza della Maddalena excludes Lanciani's design of a paved area here, and suggests a relatively short forecourt.

[42] De Fine Licht, 32. Blake/Bishop, 48, suggest that twin arches were placed to either side of the podium (resembling the arrangement at the east end of Augustus' Forum).

[43] De Fine Licht, 26, who notes that in the house opposite the pronaos of the Pantheon are found remains of masonry that may belong to this arch. Heilmeyer, "Apollodorus" 345–46, considers this ("Trajanic") Arcus Pietatis to be convincing proof that the whole complex, including the Pantheon, was designed by Apollodorus. Most topographers assume, probably correctly, that there was indeed an arch in the temenos in antiquity, but the meager evidence does not permit us to determine either its date or its location. De Fine Licht, 26, argues on ideological grounds that it was Hadrianic, and A. L. Frothingham, Jr., "A Revised List of Roman Memorial and Triumphal Arches," *AJA* 8 (1904) 34, dubiously attributes it to Antoninus Pius. The medieval sources for the arch, *Mirabilia* 23 and *Anon. Magliab.* 10, Merckl, are conveniently collected and discussed by *HJ*, 590 nn. 86–87; and Heilmeyer, "Apollodorus" 346, who quotes Dante, *Purgatorio*, 10.73ff., a description of an arch thought to be the Arcus Pietatis.

[44] De Fine Licht, 25; and see n. 41 above.

[45] This almost deceptive setup has been noted by MacDonald and others, including H. Kähler, "The Pantheon as Sacral Art,"

The excavation on the Pantheon's west side has not reached far enough to reveal how this area was treated, but the attempt to disguise the cylinder and dome from the exterior is obvious on the Pantheon's south and east sides.[46] On the south the Pantheon backed onto a large building that has never been fully explained or even convincingly identified. Although this building is commonly called the Basilica Neptuni (after Gatti so identified it in 1938), this identity cannot be proved and we may do well to refer to it simply as the "South Building" (following de Fine Licht).

Only the north and the northern parts of the east and west walls of the South Building have been freed today, but its brick stamps, construction, details of planning, and what little remains of its architectural decoration prove this structure to be contemporary with the Pantheon[47] (*see Ill. 4*). The basilican structure was 48.55 meters wide externally and 45 meters internally, giving it almost the same external and internal widths as the Pantheon. The north wall is 20 meters from the Pantheon at its east and west ends, but the back of its central apsidal niche came within 1.75 meters of a shallow rectangular projection behind the Pantheon's central niche. The two niches are on axis and mirror images of one another. Renaissance drawings and plans show that the South Building's original depth was 19 meters.[48] Its height may have approached that of the second cornice of the Pantheon, for the top of the hall's internal cornice stands 14.50 meters above the floor, and there seem to have been three concrete groin vaults springing at this level from imposts set over two corner columns (slightly inset in the corners) and the two columns flanking the central niche. The unusual thickness of the walls (1.75 meters) may be

---

*Bucknell Review* 15.2 (1967) 43–44. In this context it may be significant that Dio's remarks about the physical aspects of the building are concerned primarily with the impression made by its interior (53.27.2).

[46] De Fine Licht, 32; I arrived independently at conclusions similar to his (p. 236) regarding the restrictions other buildings imposed on the view of the Pantheon.

[47] Details from de Fine Licht, 108, 147–56, and Blake/Bishop, 48–50. For the frieze, see Tedeschi Grisanti, who has identified an ancient frieze of Proconnesian marble reused in Pisa in a twelfth-century screen as one part of the decoration for one of the short walls of the South Building ("Il fregio con delfini e con-

chiglie della Basilica Neptuni: uno spoglio romano al Camposanto Monumentale di Pisa," *RendLinc*, ser. 8, 35 [1980] 181–92). For the conformity of the capitals, cornices, and other decoration with Hadrianic work, see Leon, *Bauornamentik* 211, 226–27, 258–60.

[48] Those who sketched the building during its clearing under Pope Paul III (1542) include the following: B. Peruzzi (Uffizi, *Arch.* 456); Pirro Ligorio (*Cod. Taurin.*, vol. xiii); G. A. Dosio (Uffizi, *Arch.* 2023, 2038: de Fine Licht, p. 153, fig. 168); G. and C. Alberti (*Cod. Borgo S. Sepolcro*, f. 11, 12); and Palladio (many reproduced in Hülsen, *Thermen des Agrippa*).

evidence for the reconstruction of vaulting. The Proconnesian marble frieze under the interior Luna cornice (total height, 2.38 meters) was decorated with shells and dolphins, and the internal order was Corinthian. Internally the hall was symmetrical around its north-south axis and possibly around its east-west one as well, and a recent investigator of the frieze, G. Tedeschi Grisanti, notes that the spacing of the decorative elements on the frieze varies according to the original placement of parts of the frieze, with tighter spacing on the short sides of the basilica.[49] Overall, the South Building is a basilica hall of the type of the great central hall in the Thermae Traiani.

The purpose of this hall is uncertain. From the literary references to the Saepta and the maritime motifs in the South Building's decorative program, Gatti concluded that this is the Basilica Neptuni, a new building erected by Hadrian in conjunction with the Poseidonion (the Porticus Argonautarum) of the Saepta Julia in his reconstruction of this.[50] But the decorative use of dolphins was fairly common in many contexts from the late first century (it is found, for example, in Domitian's palace on the Palatine), and Gatti's identification cannot be proved. De Fine Licht suggests instead that the building we now see may have housed the library *en Pantheio* mentioned by Julius Africanus as being furnished by him for Severus Alexander (P. Oxy. III.412, lines 63–68),[51] but again there is no proof. What is certain, however, is that the building screened the view of the rotunda's curved back at the same time it visually extended the Pantheon toward the south.

Near the end of Hadrian's reign, six heavy walls parallel to one another were added between the South Building and the Pantheon. Although not bonded to either structure, the 1.47 meters thick outermost walls are flush with the east and west facades of the South Building and run to the Pantheon's curved walls. Vertical grooves near their north and south ends indicate that they originally supported a pitched roof. The four inner walls, each 1.18 meters, also are not bonded to either structure, and are symmetrically arranged although not identical in construction. Arches make a roughly continuous

[49] Tedeschi Grisanti, "Fregio" 187–92, with measurements and analysis of the marbles.

[50] In this he is following a suggestion of C. Hülsen, *ÖJh* 15 (1912) 133. See G. Gatti, "Il portico degli argonauti e la basilica di Nettuno," *Atti del III° convegno nazionale di storia dell'architettura* (Rome 1940) 61–73, esp. 68 (hereafter "Basilica di Nettuno").

[51] De Fine Licht, 156, 231, cf. 306 n. 43; we should note, however, that there are no niches or other architectural features of a library. On p. 279 n. 18, de Fine Licht lists other examples of the dolphin motif in decoration; see also P. Pensabene, "Fregio in marmo nero da Villa Adriana," *ArchCl* 28 (1976) [1978] 126–27, 148.

passageway running east-west, and inner walls and vaults divide this block between the South Building and the Pantheon into a series of irregular vaulted rooms. Buttressing added to both the outside wall of the South Building's north exedra and the rectangular projection behind the central niche of the Pantheon made the main transverse passageway only 1.31 meters wide at its midpoint. These six walls, which serve no apparent purpose, make the Pantheon and the South Building appear physically continuous without connecting them.[52] The resulting plan and impression of the Pantheon and its annexes is that of an essentially longitudinal building arranged to either side of a circular hall; on plan, the South Building basically echoes the pronaos of the Pantheon.

Yet there was little room in the immediate area to gain even this impression, for the Saepta Julia blocked the view from the east. All along the eastern side of the rotunda, at its closest point only 42 centimeters away, runs a brick-faced concrete wall, dated by brick stamps contemporaneous with the Pantheon (see Ill. 3). A superficially similar wall to the west of the Pantheon, 1.18 meters thick at its base, about 20 meters long and 1 meter high, is Severan.[53] The long stretch of wall on the east of the Pantheon, much reworked but preserved in places to a height of 7 meters, originally had a maximum thickness of 2.09 meters, and in its better preserved portion is broken by a series of rectangular niches on its east front (see Ill. 3). This must be the back wall of a colonnade at least 10 meters high, the west portico of the Saepta as rebuilt by Hadrian.[54] From other evidence we can reconstruct the Saepta itself as 310 meters long on a north-south axis, and 120 meters wide.[55]

The Saepta's proximity and height would have prevented any clear view of the rotunda from the east. Yet the Saepta was designed to harmonize with the Pantheon. De Fine Licht tentatively assigns to the Saepta Julia a Corinthian capital, discovered in 1910 below the Via dei Cestari and now set up in the South Building, that is stylistically close to the decoration of the Pantheon. Although the capital may well belong to the South Building itself,[56]

[52] De Fine Licht, 157–62, for details. Blake/Bishop, 50, see these eight (sic) walls as "[reflecting] concern for the stability of the vaulting [of the basilica]."

[53] De Fine Licht, 163, 290 n. 46.1.

[54] De Fine Licht, 163–66, 170. The inscription CIL 6.31269, ]AGRIPP[ , found in 1662 built into the west wall of the Saepta, seems to have come from the Saepta: F. Castagnoli, "Note di topografia romana," BullComm 74

(1951–52) [1954] 53. Roddaz, Marcus Agrippa 280, more implausibly associates the inscription with the Baths of Agrippa.

[55] Coarelli, Roma (1980) 296; Gatti, "Saepta Iulia nel Campo Marzio" 8–23.

[56] De Fine Licht, 278 n. 6, fig. 271. Leon, Bauornamentik 211 and fig. 83.2, however, associates the capital with the "Basilica Neptuni" (the South Building), as have we above.

other elements of the Saepta accord with the Pantheon. The niches of the Saepta Julia were framed by pilasters, now mostly stripped of their marble veneer, whose spacing corresponds to the intercolumniations of the Pantheon's forecourt portico. Judging from the proportions of the niches, the Saepta once had a cornice corresponding to the height of the pronaos.[57] Furthermore, the wall's construction indicates that there was communication between the Saepta's northwestern corner and a small paved courtyard to the east of the Pantheon's pronaos; a second communication, between the Saepta and the area of the chambers between the Pantheon and the South Building, is less certain. The east-west walls between the Saepta's west wall and the rotunda, and the walls between the rotunda and the South Building, are Hadrianic as well, but later than the Pantheon.[58] The north front of the Saepta was aligned with the facade of Hadrian's Pantheon and must have always kept to that line, for this is where the Aqua Virgo ran along the Saepta on its way from the Lucullan gardens into the Campus Martius (Frontin. *Aq.* 1.22.2).

Finally, there was a close thematic connection and counterpoint between the Saepta and the Pantheon. Agrippa had been responsible for the original construction of both, and the Saepta, like the Pantheon, had a close association with Augustan ideology and the Julian house. The senate had convened in the Saepta in 17 B.C. to decree the Ludi Saeculares (*CIL* 6.32323, lines 50–53); in 7 B.C. games in memory of Agrippa were held there (Dio Cass. 55.8.5); and in 2 B.C. gladiatorial games were offered in the Saepta to celebrate the dedication of Mars Ultor in the Forum Augustum (Dio Cass. 55.10.6–7). It was here that Tiberius met Augustus, the senate, and the people of Rome on his victorious return from Germany in A.D. 9 (Dio Cass. 56.1.1; Suet. *Tib.* 17).[59] The Augustan connection may have been reaffirmed by the simultaneous renovation of both.

If it were not for the listing in the *Curiosum* and *Notitia* of both a "basilicam Neptuni" and a "Porticum Argonautarum,"[60] it would be tempting to identify the "Basilica Neptuni" restored by Hadrian with the Porticus Argonautarum. Gatti has convincingly identified this latter building with the "Stoa of Poseidon," known from Dio to have been one of the porticoes of the original Saepta (Dio Cass. 53.27.1). The Porticus Argonautarum was almost certainly

[57] Blake/Bishop, 50; Gatti, "Basilica di Nettuno" 69, who also notes that the niches correspond with the intercolumniations of the Pantheon's portico.

[58] De Fine Licht, 164–71, esp. 165.

[59] See Gatti, "Saepta Iulia nel Campo Marzio" 11–12. According to Suet. *Tib.* 17 (cf.

Dio Cass. 56.1), a tribunal was sometimes set up in the Saepta.

[60] Nordh, *Libellus* 87.16–17, 100.9; cf. Valentini and Zucchetti, 1.125, 126, 153, 177. For the distinction of the "Basilica Neptuni" and the "Porticus Argonautarum" in the *Curiosum*, see Gatti, "Basilica di Nettuno" 68.

the western porticus, for another of the four porticoes, known as the Porticus Meleagri, is proved by fragments of the *Forma Urbis* as the eastern colonnade of the huge complex.[61] The Basilica Neptuni is known only from the biography of Hadrian and the summary lists of the *Curiosum* and *Notitia* (cf. Pol. Sil. 545); it looks like a simple translation of the "Stoa of Poseidon" (see below on the Basilicae of Marciana and Matidia). If this is so, the biography would designate here the west portico of the Saepta, which brick stamps prove to be Hadrianic.[62] As we shall see, Hadrian effected a great change in the eastern porticus by building an imposing gateway to the Isaeum there; this would account for the biography's distinction of Saepta and Basilica. Lacking new evidence, however, we cannot make these identifications; all we can say is that the name and presumable theme of the Basilica Neptuni probably evoked the Agrippan Porticus Argonautarum. The Augustan character of Hadrian's restorations would be emphatic.

The biography mentions a fourth Agrippan building in the Campus Martius that was restored by Hadrian, the Lavacrum Agrippae (Baths of Agrippa). This building is known from literary references, a fragment of the *Forma Urbis*, Renaissance drawings, and remains of Roman brick-faced concrete still visible about 145 meters due south of the Pantheon, although the Hadrianic rebuilding is ascertained only from Hadrian's biography. The remains now extant date from the Severan or perhaps even Constantinian period (cf. *CIL* 6.1165), and Palladio's sketches of the building and his restored plan of it are largely fanciful. By investigation of the meager evidence, Hülsen reconstructed the imperial bath complex as laid out according to an architectural scheme in favor much earlier, small more or less rectangular rooms, irregularly placed, surrounding a circular hall (*see Ill. 5*). The rooms are oriented according to the cardinal points of the compass, and the circular hall, still visible in part in the Via dell'Arco della Ciambella, had an internal diameter of about 25 meters. The plan is familiar from the early imperial bath complexes, particularly in its irregularity.[63]

[61] *Forma Urbis*, pl. 31; *HJ*, 574–75; Valentini and Zucchetti, 1.177 (*Notitia*); and Gatti, "Basilica di Nettuno" 61–65.

[62] In this passage the biography lists restorations rather than new buildings, and the South Building was a new structure. Polemio Silvio's notice is found most conveniently in Valentini and Zucchetti, 1.309.

[63] E. Sjöqvist, "Studi archeologici e topografici intorno alla Piazza del Collegio Romano," *OpusArch* 4 (1946) 99–121, proposed that the Lavacrum Agrippae was the round building depicted on the *Forma Urbis*, pl. 32, frag. m, but this is now identified as the Temple of Minerva Chalcidica. Hülsen, *Thermen Agrippa*, reproduces the most important plans and drawings of the Baths. See, in addition to the works cited above in n. 6: D. Krencker, *Die Trierer Kaiserthermen* (Augsburg 1929) 263; Heinz, *Thermen* 60–67; and de Fine Licht,

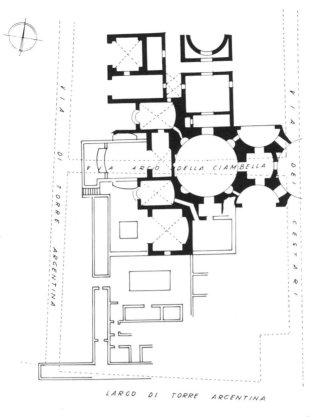

5. *C. Hülsen's reconstruction of the remains of the Baths of Agrippa in their latest phase.*

Although the extant dome, with its ribbed construction, is third-century at the earliest,[64] the layout of the whole may reflect previous restorations and the original plan of Agrippa. If so, the conservatism of Hadrian's restoration is striking when compared to the radical modifications he made to the Agrippan Pantheon, although this aspect might have been the result of practical

232, who gives the dimensions of the whole as 85–100 meters east-west (between the Via di Tor Argentina and the Via dei Cestari), and 100–120 meters north-south (with the southern boundary a little north of the Corso Vittorio Emanuele; cf. Coarelli, *Roma* [1980] 292). In an overly subtle philological discussion, Merten, *Bäder* 16–17, doubts that Hadrian ever restored the baths. F. Coarelli, *Il Foro Romano. Periodo arcaico* (Rome 1983) 252–53 (hereafter Coarelli, *ForArc*), has recently resuscitated Boni's proposal that the fragment of a marble plan (and that showing

the area of the Lacus Juturnae) is not from the Severan marble plan, but from a Flavian one; if so, we have no evidence for the Hadrianic restoration other than the notice of the biography. The juxtaposition of this bath complex and the Pantheon subtly suggests one of the possible inspirations for the form of the Pantheon as the round bath hall. For the derivation and difference of the Pantheon from such structures, see MacDonald, *Pantheon* 49–54; and de Fine Licht, 214–18.

[64] De Fine Licht, 232.

considerations of space. The Saepta to the east of the Baths did not leave room to expand in that direction, and to their west lay the Stagnum Agrippae. People approaching the central Campus Martius from the south could have passed along the eastern portico of the precinct of the Largo Argentina temples and continued just east of the Agrippan Baths; the buildings would have appeared antique. Thus the transition into Hadrian's imperial quarter, featuring the startling new design of the Pantheon, would have been a calculated progression in terms of chronology as well as space.

The Baths are too far south to have been connected with Hadrian's South Building, about 75 meters distant, and perhaps the intervening area was part of Agrippa's Horti. Nothing remains to identify the area, nor can we recreate a link, if there was one, between this and the Saepta.[65]

In the Saepta's east colonnade, however, was a monumental quadrifrons gateway connecting it to the central courtyard of the Isaeum Campense. The remains of this portal were sketched in the Renaissance by Antonio da Sangallo the Younger and identified as "Giano accanto alla Minerva" (Uffizi, Arch. 1152). The core of the arch was sturdy brick-faced concrete, later incorporated into the adjacent structures. Only in 1872 was it finally demolished, at which time were recorded some marble architectural fragments, including four cipollino column fragments (three with diameters of about 1 meter, the fourth with a diameter of 0.80 meter), a travertine base, and twenty-three brick stamps. The majority of the brick stamps date to 123. Gatti has plausibly reconstructed the gateway with wide central arches flanked by narrower arches in two stories (*see Ill. 6*). Overall 26.24 by 21.34 meters, the Giano accanto alla Minerva is the largest arch known in Rome, twice the size of the Arch of Titus, for example.[66]

On the opposite side of the Isaeum forecourt, in line with the Giano, another large gateway, known as the "Arco di Camigliano" or "Camillo," led in from an open area north of the Divorum and Minerva Chalcidica. Although the two-story, triple-arched gateway, already denuded of decoration, was demolished almost completely in the 1500s and 1600s, in 1944 Gatti was able to reconstruct its basic form from plans of the area, and recently a trav-

[65] Gatti, "Basilica di Nettuno" 70; de Fine Licht, 232, 308 n. 62.

[66] Blake/Bishop, 50; Gatti, "Iseo Campense" 137–50 and figs. 11–18 (cf. idem, "Un ignoto monumento adrianeo nel Campo Marzio," *L'Urbe* 7.1 [1942] 2–14); de Fine Licht, 234; Malaise, *Inventaire* 192. Of the

twenty-three brick stamps listed by Gatti ("Iseo Campense" 144 n. 38), fifteen are in Steinby, "CronFig," and carry consular dating of 123: *CIL* 15.76, 80, 89, 227, 265, 267, 270, 272, 359, 373, 393, 454, 607, 1113, 1384 (cf. Bloch, *Bolli* 103 n. 91).

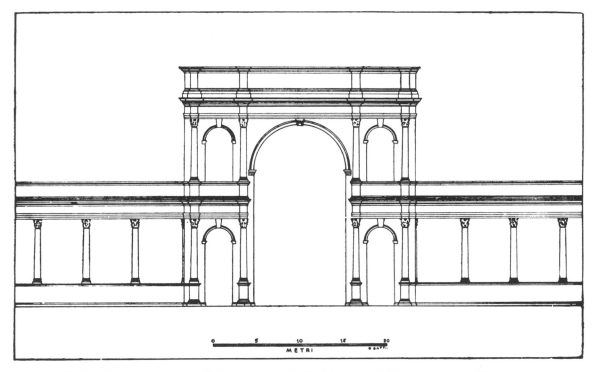

6. *G. Gatti's reconstruction of the monumental Hadrianic quadrifrons gateway, Giano accanto alla Minerva, which led east from the Saepta Julia into the Isaeum Campense.*

ertine pier at least 11 meters high and rising from a platea of travertine blocks has been uncovered in and below the lower story of one of the buildings on the Piazza Collegio Romano. The Arco di Camigliano, almost certainly the "Arcus ad Isis" depicted and inscribed on the relief of the Tomb of the Haterii, is Flavian at the latest.[67] The Hadrianic Giano accanto alla Minerva is carefully aligned with this earlier arch.

[67] Gatti, "Iseo Campense" 124–37, figs. 4–10; Nash, s.v. Arcus ad Isis, I.118–19; C. Hülsen, "Porticus Divorum und Serapeum im Marsfelde," *RömMitt* 18 (1903) 54–57; F. Castagnoli, "Gli edifici rappresentati in un rilievo del sepolcro degli Haterii," *BullComm* 69 (1941) 65–66; Malaise, *Inventaire* 189–91; B. Sesler, "Arco di Domiziano all'Iseo Campense in Roma," *RivNum*, ser. 5, 3 (1955) 88–93; and C. Roncaioli, "L'Arco di 'Camilliano' e il 'Cacco' di S. Stefano nell'Iseo e Serapeo del Campo Marzio," *Giornale Italiano di Filologia* 66 (1979) 81–96. The new discoveries, which indicate that the main opening of the arch was 2.90 meters wide, the lateral openings each 2.40, are reported by M. Concetta Laurenti, "Nuova luce sull'Iseo Campense: l'Arco di Camilliano," in *Dagli scavi al museo* (Rome 1984) 41–42.

Any interest of Hadrian in Egyptian things in Rome has to be dated after 130,[68] but the arch connecting the Serapeum and Saepta had a practical function in the traffic pattern through the central Campus Martius, facilitating east-west traffic through the now densely built-up area (*see Ill. 7*). This is particularly important in light of Hadrian's restoration of the Domitianic Divorum. In 126 he rededicated this with an exhibition of 1,835 pairs of gladiators.[69] This restoration of the Divorum, the area of the Campus Martius closely associated with the Flavian dynasty, was contemporaneous with Hadrian's work on the Agrippan and Augustan buildings west and northwest of it. The date of the Giano accanto alla Minerva fits with the rest.[70]

The Giano's function in connection with a passageway through the central Campus Martius is also significant in light of the vast utilitarian building east of the Divorum along the west side of the Via Lata/Flaminia (*see Ill. 1*). The best remains are under the church S. Maria in Via Lata, but the building was at least 230 meters long, extending under Palazzo Simonetti (now the Banco di Roma) and Palazzo Doria.[71] Under S. Maria in Via Lata are remains of a once-porticoed building opening to the Via Lata/Flaminia with piers of heavy rusticated travertine blocks, an indication of Claudian date. After severe damage by fire, the building was reconstructed to a somewhat different plan: most of the internal piers were walled up with brick masonry, and a series of rectangular cellae opened to a central courtyard, with a single major

---

[68] Beaujeu, 238–40, discusses manifestations in Rome of Hadrian's Egyptianizing tastes in this period, but apparently did not know of the "Giano." See Appendix.

[69] *II*, 13.1, 202–203, 233. Although on p. 233 Degrassi says that the gladiatorial games should be disassociated from the rededication of the temple, on p. 203 he reconstructs the text so that the two events are linked: *[. . . Imp. Caesar Traianus Hadri]anus Aug(ustus) munu[s]/ [edidit . . . t]emplum Divoru[m]/ [. . . dedicavit, ob quam] causam in circo/ [. . . munus editu]m et consumm[at(um)]/ [. . . (paribus)] MDCCCXXXV* ([The emperor Hadrian] produced a show of gladiators . . . the Temple Divorum . . . he dedicated, for which reason in the circus . . . the [a?] show of gladiators was produced and brought to perfection with 1835 pairs of gladiators: = Smallwood, #24, lines 1–5; A.D. 126).

[70] It may have taken the place of an earlier passageway: Blake/Bishop, 50, and de Fine Licht, 234.

[71] These structures were identified as the Saepta (e.g., by Platner-Ashby, s.v. Saepta Iulia, 460–61) until G. Gatti located the Saepta as framed by the Via dei Cestari, Via del Seminario, and Corso Vittorio: G. Gatti, "*Saepta Iulia e Porticus Aemilia* nella *Forma* Severiana," *BullComm* 62 (1934) 123–49, and above. For other early bibliography: de Fine Licht, 311 n. 86. E. Rodriguez-Almeida, "*Forma Urbis Marmorea*: nuovi elementi di analisi e nuove ipotesi di lavoro," *MélRome* 89 (1977) 243–46, would identify pl. 47, frag. 376, as this portico, but personal inspection of the piece, assisted by discussion with Dr. L. Cozza, convinces me that the identification is implausible.

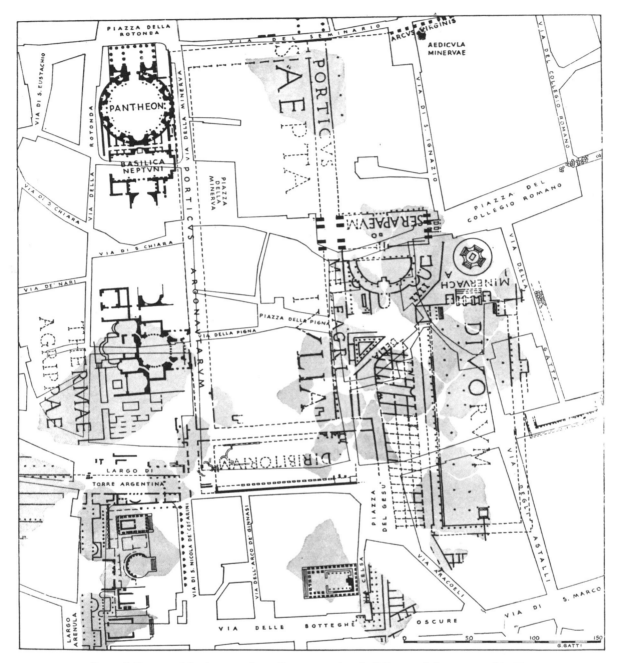

7. *Central Campus Martius: overlay of known ancient buildings and fragments of the* Forma Urbis *on modern street plan. Note alignment of the Giano accanto alla Minerva and the Arco di Camigliano at the Serapeum.*

entrance leading in from the Via Lata/Flaminia to the central court. A *taberna* near the entrance in the northeast was larger than the rest, and may have been a guardroom. At this corner the Diocletianic Arcus Novus later spanned the Via Lata/Flaminia (*see Ills. 7 and 17*).

This new plan strongly resembles those of *horrea* (storehouses) of the second century, and the construction and one recorded brick stamp (A.D. 123, from a *bipedalis*, a square tile 2 Roman feet, or 0.59 meter, a side) show that it was built in middle to late Hadrianic times. Other remains to the north and south of this are similar to it in construction, but a road under the modern Via Lata (perpendicular to the Via del Corso) separated the main building from its annex to the north.[72] This series of utilitarian buildings apparently bordered the Via Lata/Flaminia from the Arch of Claudius south to a point some 200 meters below the later Arcus Novus of Diocletian.

These horrea also framed the eastern side of an open square, unencumbered except for the Temple of Minerva Chalcidica, lying north of the Divorum. Thus, prosaic as they may have appeared in comparison to the magnificent structures to the west, the brick-faced horrea were an integral part of the central Campus Martius. The most direct access from the Via Lata/Flaminia into the monumental heart of the central Campus was the street under the modern Via Lata that passed between two parts of the Hadrianic horrea. This was on axis with the Arco di Camigliano and the Giano accanto alla Minerva, the splendid gateways to monuments farther west; to the south was the newly restored Divorum (*see Ill. 1*).

In addition to these restorations and elaborations, Hadrian also erected an important new complex in the area, the Temple of the Deified Matidia with the Basilicae of Matidia and Marciana, and possibly the Tempio di Siepe as well. Another new construction was a residential quarter east of the Via Lata/Flaminia at the head of the Via Recta.

The Temple of the Deified Matidia, named for Hadrian's mother-in-law, who was deified by the senate around 23 December 119,[73] was situated north

[72] Sjöqvist, "Collegio Romano" 77–95, esp. 84–85, 93–94; Blake/Bishop, 51–53, argue from the thinness of the bricks that the building is late Hadrianic. Coarelli, *Roma* (1980) 261–62, associates it with the insulae east of the Via Lata.

[73] The date of Matidia's consecration is uncertain: H. Temporini, *Die Frauen am Hofe Trajans* (Berlin and New York 1978) 229–30 (referring to Henzen, *AFA*, CLVIII, 4). There

were also games for the Deified Matidia (*HA, Hadr.* 9.9, 19.5), presented together with the games given on Hadrian's own birthday on 24 January 119, which M. Buonocuore attributes to Hadrian's endeavors to win popular favor (Dio Cass. 69.8.2; "Munera et venationes Adrianei nel 119 d.C.," *Latomus* 44 [1985] 173–77). Coins: (aurei) *BMC, Emp.* III, p. 281, nos. 328–31, pl. 53.2–3; *RIC* II, p. 476, no. 1554, pl. 89.5. He also built an altar of the Saepta and east of the Pantheon's forecourt. The evidence for the Temple and associated buildings is scrappy and enigmatic.[74] Two badly struck examples of a medallion of 120–121 show on the reverse a temple with flanking porticoes (and two aediculae?) and the legend DIVAE MATIDIAE SOCRUI. The example in Vienna, which we illustrate, also has the letters S C on the sides (*see Ill. 8*). A lead pipe found leading west on the Via del Seminario near S. Ignazio is inscribed *Templo Matidiae* (*CIL* 15.7248), and the entries "basilicam Neptuni. Matidies. Marcianes" (*Curiosum*) and "basilicam Matidies et Marcianes" (*Notitia*) appear in the Regionary Catalogues for Regio IX. Sporadic archaeological finds from the seventeenth century through 1966, including five column stumps of cipollino found in and near the Vicolo dello Spado d'Orlando, only one of which is still visible, prove that a monumental structure of great magnificence stood in the vicinity of modern Piazza Capranica.

8. *Medallion* (120/121) *illustrating the Temple of the Deified Matidia. The two lateral porticoes coming toward the viewer are possibly to be identified as the Basilicae of Matidia and Marciana.*

for her: *CIL* 6.31893.b, lines 10–11: *Bull-Comm*, 1891, 343, 356 (cf. Temporini, 174–75, 258).

[74] H. Dressel, "Der Matidiatempel auf einem Medaillon des Hadrianus," in *Corolla Numismatica in Honour of Barclay Head* (Oxford 1906) 16–28, was the first to establish the authenticity of the medallion discussed in the text; see also Pensa, "Adrianei" 59–65; and

C. Hülsen, "Trajanische und hadrianische Bauten im Marsfelde in Rom," *ÖJh* 15 (1912) 124–42, although his reconstruction of the ancient buildings is implausible (see n. 75). The obverse shows a laureate bust of Hadrian with the legend IMP CAESAR TRAIAN HADRIANUS AUG P M TR P COS III, thus dating the issue to 119–121. The Regionaries' notices are reproduced in Nordh, *Libellus* 87.16–17; and

This meager evidence has been assembled and rearranged in many different ways, with at least three distinct plans for its reconstruction.[75] It makes
most sense to suppose that the Temple of the Deified Matidia had the same
orientation, with its main entrance to the north, as do the Pantheon to its west
and the Saepta to its south. This would also be the most convenient arrangement, since the main access would then open to the Via Recta, the major east-
west artery of the region (*see Ill. 1*).

On the other hand, the evidence is unequivocal on other points. Parts of
the temple complex must have been very large: the one cipollino column
stump still visible in the Vicolo dello Spado d'Orlando has a diameter of 1.70,
which would suggest a column height 13.7 to 17 meters. Such height, appropriate to the dimensions of a temple rather than a portico, is greater than that
of the Pantheon's granite columns and that of the columns of the Hadrianeum
to the east.[76] Excavations in 1745 uncovered travertine paving blocks, and in

Valentini and Zucchetti, I.125, 153, 176, 184–
85, and see 233 and 254. R. Lanciani, "La Basilica Matidies et Marcianes dei Cataloghi,"
*BullComm* 11 (1883) 5–16, argues that there
was only one temple in the area, the Templum Matidiae constructed by Hadrian for
both Matidia and Marciana, rather than two
distinct buildings as previously thought. He
collects much of the Renaissance and Baroque
testimonia for the finds of the area, showing
them schematically in his Plans I-II. The
"arco antico magnifico, composto di smisu-
rati travertini" found in the Via del Seminario
"appresso al" Palazzo Serlupi in 1703 and recorded by Valesio must have been either part
of the Saepta's northern facade (the Aqua
Virgo), or perhaps a southern entrance into
the Templum Matidiae opposite the Aqua
Virgo. Much of this information is reproduced in brief by E. Lissi Caronna, "Roma.
Rinvenimenti in Piazza Capranica 78," *NSc*,
ser. 8, 26 (1972) [1973] 398–403, in which she
reports results of the excavations of 1966, and
see Blake/Bishop, 51. The ancient brick wall
that now immures the one visible cipollino
stump must be medieval.

[75] For example, Hülsen, working from
Dressel's interpretation of the medallion, hypothesizes that the Temple faced north,
flanked by an aedicula to either side of its stair

of approach, these in turn flanked by twin
porticoes (which he identified as the Basilicae
of Matidia and Marciana); he places the Tempio di Siepe axially and north of the eastern
"basilica," and conjectures a corresponding
structure to the north of the western one
("Bauten im Marsfelde"). Lugli, *MAR*
III.229–31 and pl. 4, proposes an east-west
orientation for the buildings; embellishing
this, Nash, s.v. Matidia, Templum, II.36, and
Blake/Bishop, pl. VIII, p. 52, reconstruct a
layout unparalleled (to my knowledge) in
Roman architecture: the two flanking aediculae are aligned with the eastern front of the
Temple, and the two basilicae extend east
from the outer forward corners of the aediculae. Lugli, in the *Forma Urbis Romae*, shows
a temple within an incomplete porticus on an
east-west orientation; he is followed by Coarelli, *Roma* (1980) 265, and this design has been
generally reaffirmed by Rodriguez-Almeida,
*FUM* 127–29.

[76] Both Coarelli, *Roma* (1980) 298, and
Rodriguez-Almeida, *FUM* 127, postulate a
height of 17 meters, but the proportions of
the contemporary Pantheon are not so large.
The granite columns of the Pantheon's pronaos have a diameter of about 1.48 meters,
and a height of 11.79, approximately eight
times the lower diameter (de Fine Licht, 40);

the most recent excavation, undertaken in 1966, a large fragment of a column of a material identified as "granito verde" (green granite) by the excavator E. Lissi Caronna came to light.[77] Its diameter (about 1.10 meters), smaller than that of the cipollino column fragments, suggests that it came from the Temple's temenos. The Temple of the Deified Matidia apparently partook of the same coloristic richness as the Pantheon to its west.

The Basilicae of Matidia and Marciana have not survived, but the medallion's representation of the Temple of the Deified Matidia (*see Ill. 8*), together with comparison with other second-century temple complexes and the use of the term "basilica" in this period, suggests that these structures were two-story porticoes along the long sides of the Temple's temenos.[78] If so, they would be somewhat analogous to the Poseidonion, or Porticus Argonautarum, and the Porticus Meleagri, although different in that the two porticoes of the Saepta received their epithets from the works of art exhibited within them, whereas Hadrian's two "Basilicae" were named to honor his deified mother-in-law, Matidia, and her deified mother, Marciana, consecrated in 112.

Buildings in Rome had not been named for women of the imperial family since the Julio-Claudian period. In a similar reversion to Julio-Claudian practice Hadrian also delivered a public eulogy for Matidia (*CIL* 14.3579 = Smallwood, #114 = *II*, 4.1.77).[79] His honors to his mother-in-law were

only the later Hadrianeum has columns of a height equal to or more than ten times the lower diameter, with a diameter of 1.44 meters, and a height of 15 meters.

[77] Lissi Caronna, "Piazza Capranica" 403. For unverifiable reports of granite columns associated with the temenos, see Lanciani, "Basilica Matidies" 8.

[78] No definitive study has yet been made of the large porticoed temple complexes that proliferated during the first and second centuries A.D. For the use of "basilica," see *DizEpig* I, s.v. Basilica, 976; some parallels supporting my interpretation of the basilicae as two-story porticoes on the lateral sides of a temenos are *CIL* 8.12006, *Ephemeris Epigraphica* 8.371, and the Basilica Alexandrina, which was to be a porticus "100 (Roman) feet wide, 1000 (Roman) feet long between the Campus Martius and the Saepta Agrippiana [*sic*]" (*HA, SerAlex.* 26.7).

[79] W. Kierdorf, *"Laudatio funebris": Interpretationen und Untersuchungen zur Entwicklung der römischen Leichenrede* (Meisenheim am Glan 1980) 137–48, provides a list of *laudationes* to both men and women; and see Temporini, *Frauen* 168–73. Funeral *laudes* were rare in general, and for women even rarer, with only the following women known to have been so honored during the imperial period: Octavia, died 11 B.C; pseudo-Turia, d. 8–2 B.C.; Murdia, d. Augustan period; Marcia-Junia, d. A.D. 22; Livia, d. A.D. 29; Julia Drusilla, d. A.D. 38; Poppaea, d. A.D. 66; and Plotina, d. A.D. 121(?). Kierdorf, discussing Hadrian's eulogy for Matidia (pp. 112–13), gives earlier bibliography, and notes that *dignemini rogo*, on line 34, shows it as a public oration. From 117 both Matidia and Plotina received the unusual honor of coinage (cf. *BMC, Emp.* III, p. cxxviii, and Temporini, *Frauen* 174–75).

more than extraordinary. The Temple of the Deified Matidia is the first temple in Rome known to have been dedicated from the outset to a deified
woman.[80]

The Tempio di Siepe, another construction possibly of Hadrianic date,
was adjacent to the Temple of the Deified Matidia. This octagonal building,
once incorporated in the Palazzo Capranica, had disappeared so completely
by 1650 that it is known to us only from an engraving of A. Giovannoli (see
Ill. 9) and two sketches from the early seventeenth century, now in the Uffizi
and Windsor Castle.[81] Its plan, however, presents such similarities with
known Hadrianic buildings that it is commonly attributed to Hadrian's time.
It was square in plan, made an octagon by curvilinear niches fitted into the
angles; the main entrance was through a shallow vestibule with a small bowed
niche to either side, and an elongated apselike projection opposite the main
entrance was furnished with similar bowed niches to either side. The segmental dome had a diameter of 9.37 meters, with its oculus 1.90 meters in diameter; and the eight internal columns that carried a massive entablature (about
1.20 meters high?) under the imposts of the vaulting were perhaps 5 to 5.30
meters high, if one can trust the Florentine sketch.[82] The purpose of the Tempio di Siepe is unknown. Blake and others have suggested that its plan would
be suitable for a nymphaeum,[83] but there is nothing else to support this.

Yet the Tempio di Siepe is reminiscent of another small building nearby

[80] J. H. Oliver, "The Divi of the Hadrianic
Period," *HThR* 42 (1949) 36–40, maintains
implausibly that Matidia and Marciana were
the first women to be officially deified
(cf. Hammond, *AntMon* 205–208, and
G. Grether, "Livia and the Roman Imperial
Cult," *AJP* 67 [1946] 222–52), and he further
dates Marciana's deification to the Hadrianic
period rather than to the period of her consecration in 112 (contra, Temporini, *Frauen*
174–75, 258–59, and E. J. Bickerman, "Diva
Augusta Marciana," *AJP* 95 [1974] 362–76).
Nevertheless, Oliver's indubitably correct
emphasis (p. 38) on the importance of Matidia's and Marciana's consecrations for legiti-
mizing and consolidating Hadrian's power at
the beginning of his reign effectively refutes
the suggestion that the Basilica of Marciana
should be dated to Trajan's time (as proposed
by, e.g., R. Paribeni, *Optimus Princeps* [Mes-
sina 1926–27] II.58 [hereafter Paribeni, *OP*]).
Temporini, *Frauen* 138–39, 175, 258–59,

seems undecided on the date of Marciana's
basilica.
[81] A. Giovannoli, *Veduti degli antichi vestigi
di Roma* (Rome 1619) fol. 39; Uffizi, *Arch.*
2976 (ascribed to Ciro Ferri), and Windsor,
no. 12138. The Windsor sketch shows most
clearly the internal Corinthian order, and that
the columns are unfluted (thus cipollino or
granite?).
[82] The fundamental discussion of the evidence for its plan, dimensions and location is
that of Hülsen, "Bauten im Marsfelde" 124–
32, who suggests that the "round building" is
Hadrianic, as does Rakob, "Litus Aureum"
141. Lugli, *MAR* III.231–33, dates it to the
third century. I know no earlier parallels for
the bull's-eye windows in the dome.
[83] Blake/Bishop, 51, with bibliography including N. Neuerburg, *L'architettura delle fontane e dei ninfei nell'Italia antica* (Naples 1965)
71 (hereafter Neuerburg, *Fontane*).

9. *Tempio di Siepe, as depicted in 1619 by A. Giovannoli.*

that was also long considered a nymphaeum: Domitian's Temple of Minerva Chalcidica.[84] If we assume that the Temple of the Deified Matidia faced north, the Tempio di Siepe stands in the same relationship to it as the Temple of Minerva Chalcidica does to the Divorum (*see Ills. 1, 7*).

Northeast of the Temple of the Deified Matidia and the Tempio di Siepe was the large Hadrianic residential complex under Galleria Colonna. Although outside Regio IX, Circus Flaminius, because it lies on the east side of the Via Lata/Flaminia, it is at the head of Via Recta, the main east/west artery through the central Campus, and really belongs with the central plain (*see Ill. 1*). The plan of this complex is relatively clear, although the remains are no longer visible. In 1955 Gatti's excavations for the underpass at Largo Chigi brought to light the remains of at least three insulae in brick-faced concrete. The construction was homogeneous throughout, and is dated by brick stamps from 123 through to the death of Hadrian. The insulae were laid out together with a regular grid of streets to the east of the Via Lata/Flaminia. The entire complex filled an area extending 220 meters north-south and 120 meters east-west, with each insula measuring about 62.40 meters north-south and 48.50 meters east-west. Each had thirteen brick-faced piers with travertine bases on each of its longer sides (thus twelve rooms), and ten similar ones

[84] See n. 63 above. For more bibliography: de Fine Licht, 311 n. 87.

on the shorter. At least one insula, and probably all three, had a portico along the Via Lata/Flaminia, and the upper stories are believed to have been divided into residential apartments[85] (*see Ill. 10*).

Gatti concludes from the absence of pre-Hadrianic artifacts and from the regularity of the plan that there was no earlier construction on the site, and he notes the perfect analogy of the plan of the whole with Hadrian's work along the Decumanus Maximus in Ostia.[86] The absence of earlier buildings here seems odd; not only is the area close to the heart of the city, but it also is at the intersection of two important streets. The large scale and dense planning of the Hadrianic insulae contrast strikingly with the earlier lack of exploitation of the site. We may perhaps see here the consequences of Hadrian's work in the northern Campus Martius, to which we now turn.

Important evidence of Hadrian's work in the northern Campus Martius came to light in 1930 and was reported by P. Romanelli in *NSc*, 1933. During the demolition of a house at the corner of the Vicolo della Torretta and the Via di Campo Marzio, two cippi of the pomerium were found in situ, superimposed, their tops at depths of 3.10 and 6 meters below the present street level. Both were inscribed on their eastern faces, which were smoothed for a depth of 1.10 meters on the Vespasianic cippus and 1.05 meters on the Hadrianic one. Thus the Hadrianic ground level was about 4.15 meters below the modern street level, and the Vespasianic level about 2.95 meters below that, some 7.10 meters under the modern street level.[87] On both cippi the worked eastern faces were slightly deeper than the worked faces of the other three sides, possibly indicating that the ground sloped a little from west to east.[88]

The lower cippus is identified by its inscription as the 158th cippus of the pomerium extended by Vespasian and Titus as censors in A.D. 75 after the territory of the Roman people had been enlarged. The cippus above it was set up in 121 by the college of augurs on decree of the senate, but at the instance of Hadrian. This cippus, like the Vespasianic one below it, was marked as the 158th, thus confirming the inscription's statement that the augurs had overseen a restoration of the pomerium.[89]

---

[85] G. Gatti, "Caratteristiche edilizie di un quartiere di Roma del II secolo d.Cr.," in *Saggi di storia dell'architettura in onore del prof. Vincenzo Fasolo* (Rome 1961) 49–66; Blake/Bishop, 53.

[86] Gatti, "Caratteristiche" 54–56. J. Packer, "La casa di Via Giulio Romano," *BullComm* 81 (1968–69) [1972] 132, compares these Ro-

man insulae to others in the capital city and in Ostia.

[87] Romanelli, 240–44; the evidence is reassessed, with new photographs of the cippi, by Rodriguez-Almeida, "Solarium" 197–200.

[88] Rodriguez-Almeida, "Solarium" 208.

[89] Romanelli reproduces the inscriptions on p. 241. The Vespasianic inscription reads:

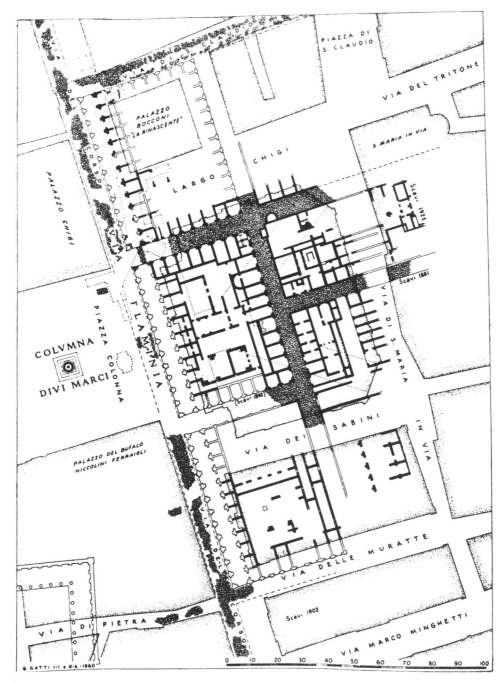

10. *Insulae on the east side of the Via Lata/Flaminia at the head of the Via Recta, as reconstructed by G. Gatti.*

The two cippi, found in situ, reveal a dramatic change in the ground level of almost 3 meters in less than fifty years. Two and nine-tenths meters of earth is too much to have been due to floods between 75 and 121; in the same place the ground level rose only some 4 meters from the Hadrianic period to the present day. Moreover, evidence from the environs of the Ara Pacis indicates that Hadrian raised the ground level artificially.

Brick stamps of 123 and later have been found in a retaining wall around the Ara Pacis built when the ground level surrounding it was raised 1.80 to 1.88 meters on all sides, making the encircling area approximately level with the meander band separating the upper figured friezes of the outer screen wall from the lower scrolled panels. This elevation of the ground level necessitated the creation of two descending staircases, the eastern one of eight travertine steps 3.20 meters wide, the western, 2.80, leading to the east and west entrances of the altar.[90]

The Hadrianic retaining wall, crowned along its edge by a travertine pulvinus-shaped curb 0.50 meter high and 0.90 meter wide, was not equally dis-

*[i]mp Cae[sar/ Vepasianu[s (sic)/ Aug. pont. ma[x./ trib. pot. VI imp. XI[V/ p. p. censor/ cos. VI desig. VII/ T. Caesar Aug. [f./ Vespasianus imp. VI/ pont. trib. pot. IV/ censor cos. IV desig. V/ auctis p. R. finibus/ pomerium ampliaverunt/ terminaveruntque.* On the left side: CLVIII. The Hadrianic: *[ex s.]c. co[llegium]/ [au]gurum auctore/ [imp.] Caesare divi/ T]raiani Parthici f./ d]ivi Nervae nepote/ T]raiano Hadriano/ Aug. pontif. max. trib./ potest. V cos. III procos./ terminos pomerii/ restituendos curavit.* On the left side: CLIIX, on the right, P CCXI. ([The emperor Vespasian], pontifex maximus, with tribunician power for the sixth time, [acclaimed] imperator for the fourteenth time, father of his country, censor, consul for the sixth time, consul designate for the seventh time, [and] [Titus], son of [Vespasian], [acclaimed] imperator for the sixth time, pontifex, with tribunician power for the fourth time, censor, consul for the fourth time, consul designate for the fifth time, enlarged and marked off by boundaries the pomerium, since the territory of the Roman people had been increased. On the left side: 158). The Hadrianic: In accordance with a decree of the senate: the college of augurs at the instance of

[the emperor Hadrian], son of [the deified Trajan], grandson of the deified Nerva, pontifex maximus, with tribunician power for the fifth time, consul for the third time, proconsul, had the boundary lines of the pomerium restored. On the left side: 158; on the right side: 211 feet). Rodriguez-Almeida, "Solarium" 197 n. 9, notes that the cippus of Vespasian also carried on its right side the inscription of the distance *inter cippos* (between boundary stones), although the inscription is incomplete (CCX[ ). For reconstructions of these two pomerial lines, see Rodriguez-Almeida, "Solarium" 209–12; M. Labrousse, "Le *pomerium* de la Rome impériale. Notes de topographie romaine," *MélRome* 54 (1937) 168–72, comes to different conclusions using the same evidence. The evidence for the two pomerial lines is collected most conveniently in Lugli, *Fontes* I.2, pp. 129–31.

[90] Moretti, 94–98; see also *CAR* II-G, no. 85, iv–v, pp. 166–68. The dating to ca. 123 and later of the reported brick stamps is confirmed by Steinby, "CronFig" (*CIL* 15.244, 361, 465 b or variant, 482 d–e, 482 a–f or 484 a–b).

tant from the four sides of the Ara Pacis. On the altar's north, south, and east sides, the retaining wall stood 2.80 meters from the altar wall. At the main approach on the west, however, the retaining wall was 2.50 meters distant, reduced to only 0.55 meter distant at the outer corners. The travertine curb seems to have once held a grille.[91] Basalt paving on the Hadrianic level, about 4 meters below the modern street, led from the Via Lata/Flaminia to the eastern staircase.[92]

The Hadrianic level around the Ara Pacis seems to have extended across the Via Lata/Flaminia, for the Via Lata/Flaminia itself in the immediate area is also about 4 meters below the modern surface. Recent excavations under S. Lorenzo in Lucina, undertaken by the Soprintendenza Archeologica and the Deutsches Archäologische Institut, show that the ground there was raised some 2.35 meters between the Flavian and late Hadrianic periods.[93] The depth of the ancient Via Lata at Galleria Colonna 200 meters farther south (5.35 meters below the modern street level) indicates that the Hadrianic fill did not extend that far in that direction.[94]

Hadrian's raising of the ground around the Ara Pacis must be associated with the change in level attested by the two cippi found in situ some 170 meters west of this. Both belong in the first half of Hadrian's reign: the cippus is dated to 121 and the 3-meter earthwork beneath it must have been begun somewhat earlier; the brick stamps of the retaining wall give it a probable terminus post quem of 123.

Between these two points is the platea of the Solarium Augusti, whose axe-head shape Buchner has calculated covered 160 by 75 meters in its origi-

[91] The measurements come from Moretti, 94–98. Gatti, "Caratteristiche" 57, reports that he studied the wall in 1937, and that it had on its external part a level of bipedales, almost a sidewalk.

[92] CAR II-G, no. 85, iv, pp. 166–67.

[93] The excavations were undertaken in late 1982 and early 1983 under the direction of Dr. M. Bertoldi and Dr. F. L. Rakob; I am grateful to Dr. Rakob for discussing them with me.

[94] The level of the Via Lata/Flaminia here is judged from the level of the road connecting it and the new (eastern) entrance to the Ara Pacis (see n. 92 above); the even higher level of the thoroughfare at the Arco di Portogallo, only 2.90 meters below the modern one (cf.

CAR II-G, no. 64, p. 160), is one reasons Stucchi assigns the arch a fifth-century date; see "L'arco detto di Portogallo sulla via Flaminia," BullComm 73 (1949–50) [1953] 121. For the level of the Via Lata/Flaminia at the Galleria Colonna about 200 meters farther south, CAR II-G, no. 197, p. 191. Gatti, "Caratteristiche" 57, dates the wall around the Ara Pacis contemporaneous with the three insulae under the Galleria Colonna, and hypothesizes that the rise in the level of the central plain (in both region IX and VII) was undertaken for flood control and to raise the level to that of the imperial fora. He also here suggests that the earth came from Domitian's excavation for the Forum later completed by Trajan.

nal layout.[95] Investigations of this monument have revealed two important post-Augustan rehandlings: (1) when the graph of the clock, set into travertine or marble, was removed and reset 1.60 meters above its original level; and (2) when a water basin, about 6 meters wide with walls over 1.1 meters high, was built along the meridian line. The basin covered the meridian line, and the excavated walls show that along and outside the basin earth was piled almost to the top of the walls, and that a coping capped the walls themselves.[96] The earlier of these phases has to be later than 77, when Pliny commented that the Solarium had been inaccurate for thirty years (*HN* 36.73).[97] Buchner has demonstrated how the elevation by 1.60 meters of the earthen platea and pavement bearing the graph of the clock compensated for the inaccuracy caused by the dislocation of the gnomon's shadow. At the same time, a bench around the obelisk gnomon was also raised 1.60 meters.[98] These elevations are attested to only by beddings for paving blocks, except where the month line approaches the gnomon, and by some drawings of the bench.[99]

Although there is little solid evidence for dating the two post-Augustan phases, Buchner suggests a Domitianic date for the second phase and a Hadrianic, or possibly third-century, one for the last. He cites as support for a Domitianic date that princeps' extensive building program in the Campus Martius after the great fire of 80, and his interest in obelisks, attested to (according to Buchner) not only in the Isaeum and Serapeum, but also possibly by the two obelisks erected at the entrance to the Mausoleum of Augustus.[100]

[95] Buchner (1980) 358, 372–73. His figure includes, however, the area under the pomerial line, where there was no paving. In the 1980 article (p. 364), he estimates the overall extent of the Augustan clock diagram as 75 meters north-south, that of the "Domitianic" one, 72 meters north-south.

[96] Buchner (1980) 357–59, 369–73, and passim; "Nachtrag" 79. For the rough state of the wall, see his ill. 131.1.

[97] Buchner (1976) 322–23; idem (1980) 362 n. 1.

[98] Buchner (1976) 325, 355–65; idem (1980) 362–64.

[99] Buchner (1980) 369–73, where he also discusses the irregular appearance of the Solarium in its two earliest phases; idem, "Nachtrag" 79. The paving blocks themselves (rather than beddings) were found only along the beginning of the meridian line, and in his cores nos. 8 and 9, which were both about 5 meters south of the Ara Pacis. The two-level paving these two cores revealed is to be connected with the Ara Pacis rather than the Solarium.

[100] Buchner (1980) 362, 372. Although the two obelisks at the Mausoleum are post-Augustan (cf. Amm. Marc. 17.4.16), there is no conclusive evidence that they were imported or erected by Domitian: Platner-Ashby, s.v. Obelisci Mausolei Augusti, 370; Nash, s.v. Obelisci Mausolei Augusti, II.155–56. E. Iversen, *Obelisks in Exile*, I: *The Obelisks of Rome* (Copenhagen 1968) 47 n. 5, calls pure conjecture the attribution to Domitian of the obelisks of Augustus' Mausoleum.

Referring to the ambiguous archaeological remains from the third phase, Buchner notes that the creation of a type of Euripus (water basin) accords well with our knowledge of Hadrianic architecture, but that in any case the canal is third-century at the latest.[101]

The excavations of 1982–83 in the area of the Solarium, mentioned above, tend to confirm Buchner's hypotheses and his favoring a Hadrianic date for the third phase. Under S. Lorenzo in Lucina, in the presumed northeast corner of the Augustan platea, remains of a private house of Flavian date have come to light. And above that are the remains of a market building of brick-faced concrete, believed to be late Hadrianic work.[102] These discoveries, although still unpublished, fit with our other information about the area of the Solarium, and permit a tentative reconstruction of its history.

Romanelli reported that the superimposed pomerial cippi discovered in 1933 were found in virgin earth.[103] Their location within the platea hypothesized for the Augustan Solarium has never been satisfactorily explained.[104] Nor has the relationship of the ground levels they represent to the levels of the Augustan and post-Augustan sundials revealed only some 15 meters west and 9 meters south of the cippi by Buchner's drilling in the Vicolo della Torretta, about 50 meters west of the meridian line. Here Buchner found the remains of the beddings for the Augustan and later paved networks of the Solarium[105] (see Ill. 11).

In lieu of further excavation in the area, I propose the following reconstruction of its topographical history. The earth below both cippi must be fill. Buchner's findings indicate that most of the platea of the Augustan sundial was of earth; only the major lines and the most southern band between the

[101] Buchner (1980) 372 nn. 11, 12; idem, "Nachtrag" 79.

[102] I am grateful to Dr. Rakob for generously discussing with me his findings. A. M. Colini, *BullComm* 66 (1938) [1939] 277–78, reports the discovery of a "rather vast and noble construction of the beginning of the second century A.D." above the commonly accepted site of the crematory of Augustus, which leads him to relocate that ustrinum farther south. The building with marble columns and bases was oriented to the Via Flaminia, like the newly discovered market building farther south at S. Lorenzo. Together they seem to attest to a secularization of the area.

[103] Romanelli, 240; and see n. 87 above.

[104] The findspot of the cippi led Rodriguez-Almeida, writing "Solarium" in 1978–79, to conclude that the platea was paved only on the eastern side; Buchner's 1980 findings indicate instead that the clock network was in stone on the west, although not as completely delineated as it was east of the meridian line ([1980] 371–72).

[105] Buchner (1980) 370, with his core no. 13; its distance from the findspot of the pomerial cippi is calculated from his fig. 1. The beddings are apparently about 6.80 and 8.57 meters below the street (pp. 357, 373), but we cannot make any inferences from such rough calculations.

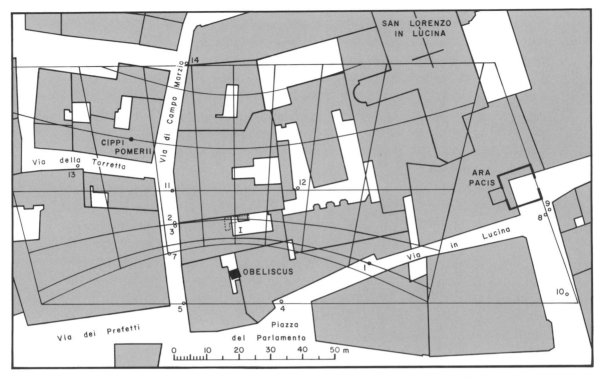

11. *Plan of the Horologium Solarium Augusti indicating E. Buchner's 1979/1980 excavation (I) and 1980 core samples (arabic numerals), and the approximate location of Vespasianic and superimposed Hadrianic pomerial cippi.*

first and second hour lines were of stone, with the network less complete on the west than on the east, toward the Ara Pacis.[106] As Pliny attests, by his day the Augustan sundial had long been unserviceable; apparently Vespasian and Titus felt no compunction about running their new pomerial line, probably raised on an earthen ridge, across a corner of Augustus' largely earthen platea.

When Domitian later raised the entire area by 1.60 meters of fill, he seems to have reconstructed at this higher level only the most essential lines, and only in the immediate vicinity of the gnomon and meridian line.[107] The elevated platea may have coincided more closely with the raised demarcation of the pomerial line as newly drawn by his father and brother. The curtailment by the earth fill of the sundial's full extent may then have permitted the building of a private house over the platea's northeast corner. Finally, it is also logical to assign the elevation of the paving immediately north, south, and west of the Ara Pacis to Domitian, who would thus have accentuated the Augustan monument. This last point, however, must remain controversial, because the

[106] Buchner (1980) 371–72.    [107] Ibid.

Domitianic coin issue in 86, mentioned earlier, shows the western side of the Ara Pacis with its entrance staircase.

The Hadrianic elevation of the Flavian pomerium by 2.95 meters and the addition of about 1.85 meters of earth fill around the Ara Pacis raised the areas west and east of the Solarium above the Domitianic platea.[108] At this time, it seems, more fill was added over the platea to diminish the discrepancies with the higher Hadrianic levels of the pomerial line and of the area around the Ara Pacis. The water basin was installed above the meridian line, and the clock was maintained only at the basin.[109] The Domitianic curtailment of the platea had already restricted the sundial's use as a calendar, and in the interval, the finely calibrated graph may have again become unserviceable. The whole area must now have been a park surrounding the Augustan obelisk gnomon and Ara Pacis. A little north of the Ara Pacis and over the private house of the Flavian period a new market building was constructed by the end of Hadrian's reign.

Hadrian, therefore, raised the ground level all across the northern Campus Martius. We may imagine this as a broad dike or ridge, higher on the west than the east and extending for at least 170 meters between the pomerial cippi and the Via Lata/Flaminia. His reasons for the undertaking must have included a wish to control the repeated inundations of the region mentioned earlier. One of the flood paths in Rome led from the modern Ponte Cavour over to the Corso at Via Condotti;[110] the Hadrianic ridge would have been parallel to and south of that, protection for the areas around the Solarium and farther south, including the monumentalized central Campus. Inscribed embankment cippi from 121–124 further attest to Hadrianic interest in regulating the Tiber.[111]

Consideration of the visual effect of such a dike prompts further specula-

[108] To an approximate height of 3.45 meters above the original Augustan pavement.

[109] Buchner, "Nachtrag" 79; in conversation Dr. Rakob has suggested that the western wall was adapted for use as a sundial by additions on its coping.

[110] This flood plain extended from the Aqua Sallustiana, running between the Pincian and Quirinal hills, almost due west through the Campus Martius: U. Ventriglia, *La geologia della città di Roma* (Rome 1971) 88; and see Rodriguez-Almeida, "Solarium" 207–208 and fig. 4.

[111] *CIL* 6.31552 (five examples), 11.3364, 2.6084(?), *NSc*, ser. 5, 13 (1916) 318–20, and *NSc*, ser. 8, 10 (1956) 50–51, attest to work on the Tiber's banks, which Le Gall, *Tibre* 141–42, 161, characterizes as simply a restoration of the embankments established under Trajan. For a purported Hadrianic systemization of the river banks into three stepped levels for flood control, see Chapter 6, n. 54. Hadrian also worked on embankments of the Cephisos River in Athens, there adding a bridge as well: P. Graindor, *Athènes sous Hadrien* (Cairo 1934) 35; and A. Kokkou, *Archaiologikon deltion* 25 (1970) [1971] 171–73.

tion about Hadrian's motivations. In this substantial elevation in the northern plain Hadrian was considerate of the Augustan monuments already there. The Ara Pacis was framed and isolated; the retaining wall extended only as far as the division between the upper and lower zones of decorative relief. Thus the figured friezes, depicting the blessings of peace gained and maintained by military success, were, if anything, more conspicuous than they had been.[112] The new passage around the altar was broader toward the Via Lata/Flaminia on the east, so that passers-by on that side, certainly more numerous than visitors from the west, had an optimal view of the monument accessible to them via the little paved street, possibly Hadrianic, that led from the Via Lata/Flaminia to the eastern entrance to the altar. Furthermore, the Hadrianic landscaping of this area as a park was a restatement of the parklike character Augustus had given the whole northern Campus Martius around his Mausoleum, which early visitors found so impressive. We may associate with Hadrian's work in this area the series of silver quinarii struck around 126 with Augustus' conception sign of Capricorn. These have been said to be Hadrian's claim to having begun a second Augustan age on the occasion of his own decennalia (the festival of the tenth anniversary of his reign),[113] but they might refer more specifically to Hadrian's interest in and restoration of Augustus' Solarium and Ara Pacis.

By restoring and emphasizing the Augustan character of the northern Campus Martius, Hadrian paid homage to the first princeps and proclaimed his adherence to the Augustan policy of peace supported by imperial strength. The reinstatement of the pomerium is dated to 121, and work must have begun earlier to raise the dike on which part of it ran. Brick stamps date the construction around the Ara Pacis a few years later, as we might expect from the scope of the project. Hadrian's statement came at a crucial point in his principate, for by 121 no war was being waged on any frontier, and Hadrian was unjustly criticized for abandoning Trajan's imperialistic policies (cf. *HA, Hadr.* 9.1; Eutrop. 8.6).[114] It is in the mid-120s that Hadrian seems most vigorously to promote an "Augustan" ideology. Starting in 125, when he returned to Rome from his first great journey, coins began to be issued with the full title HADRIANUS AUGUSTUS, occasionally AUGUSTUS HADRIANUS, rather

---

[112] In this interpretation of the altar's iconography, I agree with Simon, *Ara Pacis* 15–30; and Weinstock, "Ara Pacis" 47–49. P. A. Brunt, *JRS* 53 (1963) 170–76, cogently argues that even late in his reign Augustus made much of his continuing military successes.

[113] Silver quinarii, from the Cos III series that Mattingly dates to after 125, Hill to 126: *BMC, Emp.* III, pp. cxxxvi, 294, no. 440, pl. 55.4; and Hill, *D&A* 59.

[114] Garzetti, 380–86.

than with the titulature Hadrian used earlier in conjunction with an abbreviation of "Augustus."[115]

By the end of his life Hadrian had modified almost the entire central and northern Campus Martius, with the most monumental work in the central plain dating from his earliest years. This urban renewal must have been the result of a comprehensive and far-reaching plan, for it affected many buildings that had been built or renovated only some forty years or so earlier by Domitian, while a subsequent calamity is documented for only one building, the Pantheon. Hadrian's restorations, embellishments, and additions in the area created a well-organized area that expressed a number of different concepts important in his early principate. Roads and gateways piercing the tightly built central Campus Martius gave easy access to the individual monuments and brought unity to the whole, and symbolize Hadrian's unifying and organizing vision. More obviously, his restoration of the Pantheon and other Agrippan and Augustan buildings closely associated him with Augustus and the imperial cult, much as his work in the northern Campus Martius was doing. By reproducing Agrippa's original dedicatory inscription, Hadrian made certain that this connection was not overlooked. Additionally, by the time of his first decennalia, Hadrian had renovated the complex dedicated to the deified Vespasian and Titus, the founders of Rome's second dynasty.

Along with these marks of traditional respect for previous imperial dynasties, Hadrian was responsible for a completely innovative building, the Temple of the Deified Matidia. With this and the Basilicae of Matidia and Marciana, Hadrian turned back to, but surpassed, the Julio-Claudian precedents of buildings erected in the names of imperial women. He thus established his own family as the third dynasty of Rome, equal in dignity to the other two; he enhanced the message of the Temple of the Deified Trajan he built to complete Trajan's Forum (discussed in the following chapter). The buildings dedicated to the three dynasties can be seen as parts of an ongoing tradition.

[115] *BMC, Emp.* III, pp. cxxxiv, cxvi, 282–304, nos. 334–512 (some with the addition of P P on the obverse), pp. 449–64, nos. 1382–1475 and passim; Strack, *Hadrian* 12–15; cf. F. R. Walton, "Religious Thought in the Age of Hadrian," *Numen* 4 (1957) 167. P. Kneissl, *Die Siegestitulatur der römischen Kaiser* (Göttingen 1969) 94, notes the new legend as marking Hadrian's break with the policies of Trajan; earlier, Hadrian had dropped first Trajan's military titles, and then his filiation. See, e.g., Mannsperger, "Rom. et Aug.," *ANRW* II.1 (1974) 970. The year 125 is also the date of the eastern cistophorus with the controversial legend "AUGUSTUS REN(ATUS)": *BMC, Emp.* III, pp. clxi, 395, no. 1094, pl. 75.5; idem, "Some Historical Coins of Hadrian," *JRS* 15 (1925) 219–20; and D. Kienast, "Hadrian, Augustus und die eleusinischen Mysterien," *Jahrbuch für Numismatik und Geldgeschichte* 10 (1959/60) 61–69; contested by Mannsperger, "Rom. et Aug." 971 n. 124; and W. E. Metcalf, *The Cistophori of Hadrian* (New York 1980) 89–90.

CHAPTER THREE

# THE IMPERIAL FORA

ANOTHER FOCAL point of Hadrianic building, the imperial fora, is closely linked to Hadrian's work in the Campus Martius. As we saw above, the biography includes the Forum Augustum (Forum of Augustus) in a brief list that seems to center on Hadrian's restoration of Augustan buildings in the Campus Martius (*HA, Hadr.* 19.10). The preceding sentence in the biography notes Hadrian's temple to his father, Trajan, as the sole instance in which Hadrian inscribed his own name on one of his buildings: *cum opera ubique infinita fecisset, numquam ipse nisi in Traiani patris templo nomen suum scripsit* (although he had built innumerable works everywhere, he himself never inscribed his own name on anything except the temple of his father, Trajan: *HA, Hadr.* 19.9). Another connection between Hadrian's work in the Campus Martius and this work in the imperial fora is the emphasis on the new imperial dynasty. Duplicate inscriptions found northwest of Trajan's Forum testify that Hadrian honored both of his deified parents in the temple: *[E]x S.C. divi[s Tr]aiano Parthico et [Plotinae/ im]p. Caes[ar di]vi Traiani Parthici [f.] divi N[ervae nepos Traia]nus Hadrianus Aug./ pont. m[ax. trib. pot. —] cos. III/ parentibus sui[s]* (In accordance with a decree of the senate: to the deified [emperor Trajan] and Plotina, [the emperor Hadrian], son of the deified [emperor Trajan] and grandson of the deified Nerva . . . to his parents: *CIL* 6.966 and 31215 = *ILS* 306 = Smallwood, #141a). This temple, therefore, may be Hadrian's temple to Plotina that the epitome of Dio mentions (69.10.3.1).

The documentation of Hadrian's work in the imperial fora, however, is complicated by deficiencies in the evidence. Scanty archaeological remains and ambiguous numismatic material for the Temple of the Deified Trajan and Plotina have lent themselves to controversy, with scholars recently asserting ever more loudly that the Temple must have been planned, if not built, under Trajan, though that goes against all that we know about Roman religion. And on the other hand, the architectural fragments from the Forum of Augustus identified as Hadrianic by T. Kraus and others are too few and of too uncertain a character to be used to evaluate separately the biography's statement that Hadrian restored that Forum.[1] But the veracity of the statement can be assessed independently in light of Hadrian's work in the Forum of Trajan, directly to its north, so we turn first to the Temple of the Deified Trajan and Plotina.

The archaeological evidence for the Temple of the Deified Trajan and Plotina is disappointing. Its location north of Trajan's Forum, between Trajan's Column and the Via Lata/Flaminia, and its size and magnificence are known from the find spots of the two inscriptions mentioned above, from architectural fragments, and from indications on the *Forma Urbis*. Fragments of gray granite and rose granite columns have been found in this area: huge diameters indicate an original height of 50 Roman feet (14.785 meters) for some of them, for others slightly less.[2] An enormous Corinthian capital (height: 2.12 meters), bigger than those assigned to the Basilica Ulpia and the Forum of Trajan, although stylistically similar, stands next to the Column of Trajan[3] (*see Ill. 12*). Some correspondingly large fragments of a cornice, again stylistically close to the ornament in Trajan's Forum[4] (*see Ill. 13*), and some richly ornamented bases, which were sketched by Ligorio,[5] have been identified as

[1] T. Kraus, "Ornamentfriese vom Augustusforum," *Mitteilungen des deutschen archäologischen Instituts* (Munich and Berlin) 6 (1953) 52–54; for the stylistic debate, see nn. 59–61 below.

[2] In 1765 a fragmentary gray granite column eight and a half palms in diameter (1.897 meters), part of a cornice, and five smaller gray granite columns were seen by Winckelmann *al posto* under the Palazzo Valentini, and he persuaded Cardinal Albani to acquire the large column fragment and cornice piece for the Villa Albani (ref. to *Storia delle arti* [Prato 1832] vol. XI, 3). Two columns of rose granite were found in the courtyard of the Palazzo Colonna (ref. to Richter-Grifi, *Restauro del Foro Traiano* 21), and there are rumors of cipollino fragments as well: Paribeni, *OP* II.91; Leon, *Bauornamentik* 35 n. 59; Jordan, I.2, 464. The partial gray granite column still at the site of Trajan's Column was apparently quarried at the Mons Claudianus, as were the Pantheon columns: T. Kraus and J. Röder, *AA* 77 (1962) 743–44; and J. B. Ward-Perkins, "Columna divi Antonini," in *Mélanges*

. . . *P. Collart* (Lausanne 1976) 347–48, 351. I cannot accept the latter's argument that the diameter of this column fragment, equal to the diameter of the column later used in the memorial to Antoninus Pius, which is inscribed on its base with a date of 105–106, can mean only that the column found in the vicinity of the Temple of the Deified Trajan was also quarried in 105–106.

[3] This capital, found in 1869 (R. Lanciani, *BullInst* 1869, 237) is one of the largest capitals ever found in Rome: Heilmeyer, *Normalkapitelle* 151–54, pls. 52.4, 53.3–5; Leon, *Bauornamentik* 35, 56, 94, 210, ill. 3.1–2.

[4] The fragment in the Villa Albani and other fragments are discussed and illustrated by M. E. Bertoldi, *Ricerche sulla decorazione architettonica del Foro Traiano* (Rome 1962) 18, pl. 17.3–4, and by Leon, *Bauornamentik* 64, 75, pl. 21.2; the height of the cornice is about 1.54 meters.

[5] T. Ashby, "The Bodleian Ms. of Pirro Ligorio," *JRS* 9 (1919) 192: on 88v Ligorio gives the diameter of the base he illustrates as "3 palmi, 2 once," and elsewhere gives the di-

12. *Corinthian capital from the Temple of the Deified Trajan and Plotina, 2.12 meters high. (Capital now near the base of the Column of Trajan, Rome.)*

13. *Cornice fragment (approximately 1.54 meters high) from the Temple of the Deified Trajan and Plotina. (Fragment now in the Villa Albani, Rome.)*

belonging to an exterior and interior orders of the Temple. The *Forma Urbis* shows the beginning of a colonnaded portico running north from the eastern library of Trajan's Forum[6] (*see Ill. 14*), and marble paving slabs, found in excavations in the 1930s at the Piazza Venezia reused in a fifth-century context, may well have come from this portico or its counterpart connecting the libraries and the Temple.[7] These porticoes might have been the source of the smaller granite columns (diameter: 1.80 meters) of which fragments were discovered in the vicinity. In short, the scant archaeological evidence for the Temple of the Deified Trajan and the Plotina cannot be used to date its construction.

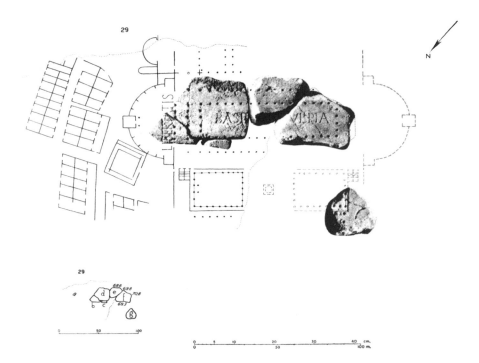

14. *Area of the Basilica Ulpia, libraries, and Column of Trajan, as depicted on the* Forma Urbis *(plate 28, fragment 29).*

---

ameter of the columns of the Temple as 6 feet; the bases must be from the interior of the Temple.

    [6] *Forma Urbis*, pl. 28, frag. 29g.
    [7] The white marble slabs were found while building the Palazzo delle Assicurazioni Generali at the corner of the Via dei Fornari and the Via Nazionale (*NSc*, 1904, 153–54; *BullComm*, 1904, 141), and are now exhibited on the walls of the Palazzo's cortile.

A prevalent recent interpretation of the archaeological evidence maintains that it supports a Trajanic, rather than Hadrianic, date. The unusual plan of the Forum of Trajan, the last of the imperial fora of Rome, has led J. B. Ward-Perkins, Zanker, and others to attribute to Trajan or his architect, Apollodorus of Damascus, the design of the Temple that makes this Forum conform to the pattern of its predecessors.[8] Noting that all the earlier imperial fora— the Forum of Julius Caesar, that of Augustus, the Templum or Forum Pacis, and the Forum Transitorium—are dominated by a temple placed axially at the far end of each complex, these scholars conclude that the original design of Trajan's Forum must have included the temple that is commonly represented as the climactic element of the plan[9] (see Ill. 15).

The evidence in support of this is Trajanic coins issued in bronze of all denominations and in silver during Trajan's fifth consulate (103–111). The reverses show an octastyle temple holding a seated female(?) figure, with monumental porticoes extending forward to either side. This is sometimes varied on the sestertii by the additions of an altar before the steps and of two statues

---

[8] Ward-Perkins, "Columna divi Antonini" 348–52; Zanker, "Trajansforum" 503–504, 537–39; Blake/Bishop, 17; C. Ricci, A. M. Colini, and V. Mariani, *Via dell'Impero* (Rome 1933) 126. P. H. von Blanckenhagen, "The Imperial Fora," *JSAH* 13.4 (1954), strongly suggests this on pp. 23, 25–26. Contra, Carla Maria Amici, *Foro di Traiano: Basilica Ulpia e Biblioteche* (Rome 1982) 76 n. 2. Usually the knowledge of Trajan is assumed, though W. Gauer attributes the plan to Apollodorus alone (*Untersuchungen zur Trajanssäule. Erster Teil* [Berlin 1977] 74–75). Leon, *Bauornamentik* 29, considers the question insoluble. There were indeed some buildings in this area begun by Trajan but finished by Hadrian: some work under the Villa Aldobrandini on the Quirinal, and on the slopes of the Capitoline (suggested by G. Lugli, "I mercati Traianei," *Dedalo* 10.3 [Feb. 1930] 537; see Chapter 7, n. 122); a wall between the Temple of Venus Genetrix and the Forum of Trajan (Blake/Bishop, 41), and the "director's suite" in the Markets (Blake/Bishop, 27). Similarly, Domitian began but Trajan finished most of the work of the Forum of Trajan: cf. Aur. Vict. *Caes.* 13.5; G. Lugli,

"Date de la fondation du Forum de Trajan," *CRAI*, 1965, 233–38; and Leon, *Bauornamentik* 42–43. The first report on the modern excavations of the region was in Ricci, *Via dell'Impero* 122–30.

[9] For convenience sake I am treating the Templum Pacis as one of the imperial fora, although it was not a forum and did not acquire that name until the fourth century. For a comparison of it to the imperial fora see, e.g., A. M. Colini, "Forum Pacis," *BullComm* 65 (1937) [1938] 9; J. C. Anderson, Jr., "Domitian, the Argiletum and the Temple of Peace," *AJA* 86 (1982) 105–106; idem, *HistTop* passim; and von Blanckenhagen, "Imperial Fora," although I do not agree with all of the latter's conclusions. Crema, 271, 274–75, distinguishes it from the other imperial fora. R. Martin, "Agora et Forum," *MélRome* 84.2 (1972) 912–22, points out that the imperial fora were not a spontaneous and unified creation, but evolved in progression combining political and urban considerations; nevertheless, he treats them together as a building type. We should note that the Temple of Venus Genetrix may be an addition to Caesar's original plans for his Forum.

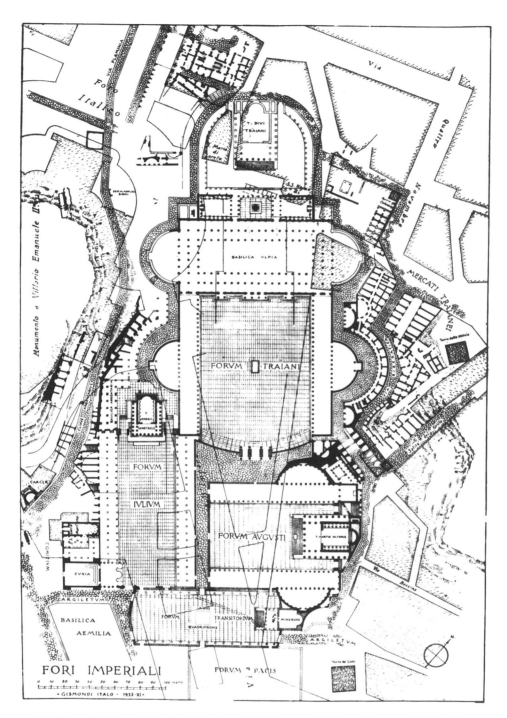

15. *Archetypal but partially fanciful plan of the Forum of Trajan, Forum of Julius Caesar, Forum of Augustus, and Forum Transitorium, as drawn by I. Gismondi in 1933. Unknown and uncertain elements have been schematized in an axial and unified plan.*

on the podium before the end columns of the pronaos[10] (*see Ill. 16*). There is
no explanatory legend, and on pictorial and iconographical grounds the temple cannot be identified securely with any other of the temples, new or restored, that are attributable to Trajan.

The complete design of Trajan's Forum is still imperfectly known, and no
detailed account of the excavations that exposed much of it in the 1930s has
yet been published, although J. Packer is now assembling and studying the
scattered evidence for the Basilica Ulpia.[11] The forum shows signal differences from its predecessors (*see Ill. 15*): first, that the *area Fori*, an open square
of about 108 meters by 89 meters with a curving(?) entrance wall and two
large, symmetrically placed hemicycles opening off the lateral porticoes, has

16. *Unidentified octastyle temple with
flanking porticoes on reverse of Trajanic
sestertius from ca. 105–106.*

[10] *BMC, Emp.* III, pp. 182–83, nos. 863–66,
pl. 32.8–9; p. 193, no. 913 †; p. 202, no. 958,
pl. 37.8; and see below, n. 32.

[11] J. Packer, K. L. Sarring, and R. M. Shel-
don, "A New Excavation in Trajan's
Forum," *AJA* 87 (1983) 165–67, give exten-
sive bibliography on the earlier excavations.
And Ricci, *Via dell'Impero* 122–25; Bertoldi,
*Foro Traiano* 4–8; and Amici, *Basilica Ulpia e
Biblioteche* 1–4, give good reviews of the For-
um's history down to the present. The his-

tory of the site before Trajan's time was first
published by G. Boni, "Esplorazione del
Forum Ulpium," *NSc*, ser. 5, 4 (1907) 361–
427, especially 389–414, 426–47. M. Pensa,
"L'architettura traianea attraverso le emissioni edilizie coeve," in *Atti Centro Studi e Documentazione sull'Italia romana* 2 (Milan 1969–
70) [1971] 275–96, provides the most thorough recent treatment of the coinage associated with the Forum. Her work is referred to
hereafter as Pensa, "Architettura traianea."

a strong central cross axis rather than the dominant longitudinal axis of the other fora;[12] second, that the axis of its monumental entrance arch terminates in the triple-arched entrance of the Basilica Ulpia, a sumptuous secular building sweeping across the width of the square, rather than in a prominently placed temple.[13]

Moreover, instead of being a spatially united experience clearly defined by enclosing walls, as the earlier fora were, the Forum of Trajan included what on plan looks like a second smaller complex.[14] North of the Basilica in the

[12] Leon, *Bauornamentik* 33, underlines this distinction of the Forum Traiani from the others. Gullini, "Adriano" 65, and von Blanckenhagen, "Imperial Fora" 22, note that the cross axis established by the hemicycles of the Forum Augustum would not have been perceptible to a visitor to the site. Although none of the Fora has yet been excavated completely, apparently no other one had a monumental axial entrance: the main entrance to the Forum of Caesar seems to have been from the Forum Romanum, via the Chalcidicum and other secondary buildings set perpendicular to the axis of the Forum itself (see Chapter 4); the close proximity of the Forum Augustum, which was perpendicular to the Forum of Caesar, speaks against a monumental entrance; and the two entrances to the Forum Transitorium from the Forum Romanum seem to have been off axis (H. Bauer, "Il Foro Transitorio e il Tempio di Giano," *RendPontAcc* 49 [1976–77] {1978} 142–48). Colini, "Forum Pacis" 34, hypothesized a monumental entrance in the center of the north side of the temenos of the Templum Pacis, but so far we have no evidence for this. For the prominence of the aedes in this complex, ibid., 36–39, and Anderson, "Temple of Peace" 105–106. G. Rodenwaldt, "Römische Staatsarchitektur," in H. Berve, ed., *Das neue Bild der Antike* II (Leipzig 1942) 364, stresses three cross axes for Trajan's Forum established by the hemicycles of the main square, by the Basilica, and by the two libraries. The equestrian statue of Trajan at the intersection of the main cross axis (Amm. Marc. 16.10.15–16) may be depicted on a sestertius from Trajan's sixth consulate (A.D. 112):

*BMC, Emp.* III, p. 206, nos. 969–70, pl. 38.2; Pensa, "Architettura traianea" 275.

[13] Entrance to the Forum: *BMC, Emp.* III, p. 99, no. 492, pl. 17.15; pp. 207–208, nos. 982–83, pl. 38.8. Although the date of this arch has been debated, it is now agreed that it was in place at the dedication of the Forum in 112, since "Parthicus" is not part of Trajan's titulature on the coins. The arch on the coin should not be identified with that mentioned by Dio (68.29.3) and described by Gellius (*NA* 13.25.1) as decorated with *simulacra equorum atque signorum militarium* (statues of horses and representations of military standards). Leon, *Bauornamentik* 29–31, understands Gellius as referring to the entrance of the Basilica Ulpia. See Pensa, "Architettura traianea" 275–77. J. Packer considers the south facade of the Basilica to have been an open colonnade: "Trajan's Basilica Ulpia," *AJA* 86 (1982) 280; idem, "Numismatic Evidence for the Southeast (Forum) Facade of the Basilica Ulpia," in L. Casson and M. Price, eds., *Coins, Culture and History in the Ancient World. Numismatic and Other Studies in Honor of B. L. Trell* (Detroit 1981) 57–67; and idem, review of *Foro di Traiano,* by C. M. Amici, in *AJA* 87 (1983) 570 (cf. Pensa, "Architettura traianea" 279–81).

[14] The original Forum of Caesar was not as self-contained as the later fora: tabernae, built into the Capitoline hill, opened on the northwest side, and the southwest side was closely connected with the Forum Romanum through the Chalcidium and Curia. See G. Fiorani, "Problemi architettonici del Foro di Cesare," *QuadIstTopAnt* 5 (1968) 91–103.

direction of the Temple of the Deified Trajan were the Column of Trajan and the two libraries. Two doors led from the Basilica to a small rectangular colonnaded courtyard between the libraries, which was dominated by the Column at its center. The libraries, contiguous with the Basilica, are attributed by Dio to Trajan (68.16.3); brick stamps found in situ can be used to confirm his date.[15]

Between the twin facing libraries rose the great Column. Although after Trajan's death in 117 it became famous as the princeps' tomb (cf. Dio Cass. 68.16.3), this may not have been its original purpose.[16] Its puzzling dedicatory inscription commemorates the work undertaken for the Forum: *Senatus populusque Romanus/ Imp. Caesari divi Nervae f. Nervae/ Traiano Aug. Germ. Dacico pontif./ maximo trib. pot. XVII imp. VI cos. VI p. p./ ad declarandum quantae altitudinis/ mons et locus tant[is oper]ibus sit egestus* (The senate and people of

[15] The libraries were called either the "Bibliotheca Ulpia" or the "Bibliotheca Templi Traiani" (references collected in Jordan, 1.2, 463–64). L. Richardson, Jr., "The Architecture of the Forum of Trajan," *Archaeological News* 6 (1977) 106–107, has suggested from evaluation of the brick stamps found in and around the libraries (fifty-five of which are Hadrianic, forty-three Trajanic), of the names for the libraries of the area attested to in antiquity, and of the plan of the whole, Hadrian was responsible for the entire area northwest of the Basilica Ulpia: he erected the Templum and the libraries, and moved the Column from an original location in the northeast hemicycle of the Forum of Trajan (cf. Anderson, *HistTop* 152–59). Yet the three brick stamps found in situ in the wall of the western library indicate a date shortly after ca. 110 for these buildings (Bloch, *Bolli* 57–61; Leon, *Bauornamentik* 43–44). For the puzzling legend [LI]BERTAT[IS] inscribed in the northern apse of the Basilica as depicted on the marble plan (pl. 28, frags. 29b, d; our *Ill. 14*), see Richardson, and Zanker, "Trajansforum" 522–23. See also for the libraries: O. Brendel, "Rom, Kaiserfora," in *AA* 48 (1933) 613–15; C. Callmer, "Antike Bibliotheken," *OpusArch* 3 (1944) 162–64; and B. Götze, "Antike Bibliotheken," *JdI* 52 (1937) 238–40, cf. 245–46. The recent reconstruction of the libraries with two high stories by Amici, *Basilica Ulpia e Biblioteche* 71–87, has been justly criticized by Packer in his review, pp. 570–71 (see n. 13 above); her reconstruction of a deep portico north of the Column is equally untenable. For the colonnade around the Column, exposed in the excavations of the French in 1810–14, see both the measured design made at the time by A. De Romanis (published in Packer et al., "New Excavation" pl. 22, fig. 5, cf. p. 167), and Amici, 52–69.

[16] Zanker maintains that the Column was planned from its inception to be Trajan's funerary monument ("Trajansforum" 534–36), as do Gauer, *Trajanssäule* 74–75, and Leon, *Bauornamentik* 34–35. Although the chamber in the base certainly was planned at the time of the monument's design, it may have been intended for another purpose. Their theory also discounts the obvious discrepancy between an original funerary purpose for the Column and its inscription and decoration: G. Becatti, "La Colonna Traiana, espressione somma del rilievo storico romano," *ANRW* II.12.1 (1982) 540–44; cf. G. Lugli, "La tomba di Traiano," in *StudMin* 295. Koeppel, "Official State Reliefs" 491–94 B, has a thorough bibliography on the monument; add now P. M. Monti, *La Colonna Traiana* (Rome 1980); and *L'esame storico-artistico della Colonna Traiana* (Rome 1982).

Rome, to [the Emperor Trajan], pontifex maximus, with tribunician power for the seventeenth time, [acclaimed] Imperator for the sixth time, consul for the sixth time, father of his country, to declare how high a hill and area was removed for [or by] such great works: *CIL* 6.960 = *ILS* 294 = Smallwood, #378).[17] It is turned toward the Basilica and the Forum of Trajan, two of the great works to which it alludes, and its orientation indicates that the Column is to be considered together with these. Its spiral frieze has been likened to a gigantic book roll, associating the commemorative Column in program with the libraries to either side.[18]

The unity of this anomalous collection of buildings is confirmed by literary references identifying the Column, libraries and Basilica as belonging to the Forum of Trajan,[19] by the brief space of only nine years, ca. 104–113, for the construction of these varied and magnificent works,[20] and by their unifying theme, the glorification of Trajan as a leader whose military brilliance and success guaranteed the smooth political functioning of Rome.

This theme, most obvious in the sculptural program of the Forum and the Column,[21] helps explain the lack of a temple. G. Rodenwaldt has proposed

[17] I interpret *tantis operibus* as dative. For the supplement, see Mommsen on *CIL* 6.960, and for the controversial and often implausible interpretations of the inscription after Boni's excavations, see M. Raoss, in *Seconda Miscellanea greca e romana* (Rome 1968) 399–416. Although Dio says that Trajan built the Column for his own tomb and to show the amount of work undertaken for the Forum (68.16.3), he is clearly reading this into the monument (cf. his attribution of the work to Trajan himself). The various coin issues associated with the Column are discussed by Pensa, "Architettura traianea" 281–91, and by Becatti, "Colonna Traiana" 544–46.

[18] For example, Becatti, "Colonna Traiana" 546–47, with earlier bibliography.

[19] Dio Cass. 68.16.3: ". . . and he (Trajan) also built libraries. And he placed in his Forum the great Column . . ."; Eutrop. 8.5.2: *ossa conlata in urnam auream in foro, quod aedificavit (Traianus), sub columna sita sunt, cuius altitudo CXLIV pedes habet* (His bones, collected in a golden urn in the Forum that he [Trajan] built, are placed under the Column,

whose height is 144 feet); *Exposito totius mundi et gentium*, 55 (Valentini and Zucchetti, 1.264): † *sicut et quae dicitur forum Traianum, good habet basilicam praecipuam et nominatam* (likewise just as that which is called the Forum of Trajan, which contains the extraordinary basilica that is name for him [Trajan]); *Chronicon Gallense* of 511 (Mommsen, *Chron. Min.* i, p. 640, line 349): *Traianus obiens intra urbem in foro (suo) sepelitur solus omnium* (At his death, Trajan, unique among all, is buried within the boundaries of the city in his Forum). Some of these literary references are topographically incorrect.

[20] The Forum and the Basilica Ulpia were dedicated at the beginning of January 112, the Column and the Temple of Venus Genetrix, 12 May 113: *II*, 13.1, pp. 200–203, 231–32 = Smallwood, #22. For the fullest and most recent discussion of the date of Trajan's Forum, see Leon, *Bauornamentik* 38–50, who notes *CIL* 6.959 (= Smallwood, #97), a dedication to Trajan set up in 112 probably in the *area Fori*.

[21] The Column itself is now the most strik-

that the inspiration for the Forum came more from the plan of a military camp than from earlier imperial fora. In *principia*, the central squares of military camps, a basilica similarly closed one side of the open area; behind it were the rooms for the storage of military archives, and between these was the sanctuary for the legion's standards and the image of the emperor. This arrangement corresponds to the general layout of Trajan's Forum, and it appears that Apollodorus of Damascus, Trajan's architect for military as well as civic projects, wished to commemorate Trajan's military glory by evoking such associations in the plan of the Forum.[22] The plan did not need the focus of a temple, for the Column served that purpose.

Practical considerations support this theory. The Basilica was at least 50 meters high.[23] For one entering or standing in the *area Fori*, the great mass of the Basilica would have blocked the view of everything beyond. Its roof of bronze tiles, so admired by Pausanias (5.12.6; cf. 10.5.11), indicates the dominance of the Basilica. Despite the clearly enormous size of the Temple of the Deified Trajan and Plotina, calculated to have risen some 40 meters from the ground to the peak of the tympanum,[24] from the platea of the Forum the

ing reminder of this theme: e.g., Becatti, "Colonna Traiana," esp. 544. For the military note once pervasive in these Trajanic works, see Zanker, "Trajansforum" 520–31; Leon, *Bauornamentik* 34–35; Paribeni, *OP* II.65–100. For the great military frieze, part of which is now on the Arch of Constantine and which is thought to have come from the Forum of Trajan: H. Plommer, "Trajan's Forum," *Antiquity* 48 (1974) 129; Koeppel, "Official State Reliefs" 494–95C. W. Gauer, "Ein Dakerdenkmal Domitians. Die Trajanssäule und das sogenannte grosse trajanische Relief," *JdI* 88 (1973) 318–50, implausibly attributes the frieze to Domitian. The Forum also housed imperial and other statues: see Zanker, "Trajansforum" 518; H.-G. Pflaum, "La Carrière de C. Aufidius Victorinus, condisciple de Marc Aurèle," *CRAI*, 1956, 189–200. Crema, 358–63, discusses other architectural and thematic reminiscences of the complex.

[22] Among others, Becatti, "Colonna Traiana" 543; Leon, *Bauornamentik* 33–34; Coarelli, *Roma* (1980) 112; and Anderson, *HistTop* 160–61, endorse this theory first pro-

posed by G. Rodenwaldt, in his review of *Das Römerlager Vetera*, by H. Lehner, in *Gnomon* 2 (1926) 338–39, and elaborated in "Röm. Staatsarchitektur" 364–65 (contra, e.g., Plommer, "Trajan's Forum," 129–30; and Martin, "Agora et Forum" 922.) Zanker, "Trajansforum" 506, concedes the similarity of the plan of Trajan's Forum to that of *principia*, but wonders how many contemporaries would have recognized the allusion.

[23] Ricci, *Via dell'Impero* 128, gives the ground dimensions of the basilica as about 55 meters wide, 159 meters long. For differing reconstructions of the Forum's interior, see Leon, *Bauornamentik* 31–32, and Packer (n. 13 above).

[24] Ricci, *Via dell'Impero* 126, gives (without evidence) the following dimensions for the Temple of the Deified Trajan and Plotina: height (stylobate to top of tympanum), 40 meters; depth, 100 meters; width, 50 meters. Dr. Packer has generously shown me his calculations of 32.65,4 meters for the height of the Temple, which would make the Temple impossible to see from Trajan's Forum.

Temple would not have been visible and the view even of the top of the Column would have been obstructed.[25] A legion's *sacrarium* would have been similarly hidden from the open central square in legionary camps.[26]

Yet the Column's location can be explained in other ways as well. Trajan's Forum united the political center of Rome and the Campus Martius.[27] The slender 100–foot Column marks this connection between the two areas more obviously than do the transversely placed Basilica and libraries, for the libraries faced one another across a small forecourt, and only relatively minor doorways of the Basilica Ulpia opened toward the Via Lata/Flaminia. Architecturally, the Column functions to draw attention to Trajan's change of the urban landscape.

The placement of the Column north of the Basilica seems also motivated by the desire to have it fully visible from the Via Lata/Flaminia, the main road into Rome from the north. The course of the Via Lata/Flaminia through the Campus Martius was more or less level, perhaps rising slightly at its southern end where it joined the Vicus Jugarius, which must have sloped gently upward.[28] No building between the road and the Column is known to have existed prior to the construction of the Temple of the Deified Trajan. In 1902–1904, demolition of the Palazzo Torlonia at the Piazza Venezia (where the Palazzo delle Assicurazioni Generali di Venezia now stands) brought to light a road bordered by five cippi on its west (under the southern end of the Corso), a brick insula with marble decorative elements and a courtyard paved with colored marble, and numerous sepulchral inscriptions of imperial date that do not seem to have been in situ when found. Excavations in 1932 in Piazza Venezia, 12 meters west of, but parallel to, the facade of the Assicurazioni Generali, exposed a wall with shop doors and mezzanine windows that Colini associated with the brick insula under the Assicurazioni Generali. On the basis of construction he dated this to the third century. Of the twenty different

[25] Rodenwaldt, *Gnomon* 2 (1926) 338–39, asserts that everything north of the Basilica would have been hidden by that building, as does Packer (personal communication, 28 May 1984).

[26] The Column was, however, probably quite visible from the north side of the Basilica. Behind each library was a stair ramp giving access to the roofs of these from the Basilica Ulpia, and possibly to galleries over their entrance porticoes, from which the Column could be viewed: Ricci, *Via dell'Impero* 127.

[27] Gullini, "Adriano" 64; Fiorani, "Foro di Cesare" 100–101, seems to suggest that Trajan's porticus in the northwest part of Caesar's Forum and behind the Temple of Venus Genetrix connected Caesar's Forum with the southern hemicycle of Trajan's Forum.

[28] See the orographic map of Lugli, "Date du Forum de Trajan" 237, and Boni's altimetric diagram showing the changes in level from the top of the Quirinal to the base of the Capitoline ("Forum Ulpium" 363, fig. 1).

examples of brick stamps recorded from the excavations of 1902–1904, although none is reported to have been found in situ, only three definitely antedate Hadrian's period. Twelve are Hadrianic, with the others of uncertain or later date.[29] Excavations of 1980 under the northwest corner of the Palazzo Valentini (the modern Prefettura), just northeast of the insula described above, exposed a private bath structure dated by brick stamps to the late third century, built on the same north northeast–south southeast orientation as the insula. The excavator, M. de' Spagnolis, suggests that these two buildings are pendents of one another[30] (*see Ill. 17*). In any case, all buildings known between the Column and the Via Lata/Flaminia are almost certainly post-Trajanic.

[29] The evidence for the building commonly shown northeast of the Templum (see below) has never been properly published. Ricci, *Via dell'Impero* 8, notes in this area of the Assicurazioni Generali "un vasto 'isolato' d'epoca imperiale . . . molti frammenti di iscrizioni, capitelli. . . ." The published finds are the following: the road and terminal travertine cippi, 1.90 by 0.75 by 0.45 meters, placed 4.15 meters from each other (*NSc*, 1902, 555, 628, *BullComm*, 1902, 285–86); water pipes from the fifth century (*NSc*, 1902, 627; *NSc*, 1903, 462, 510, *BullComm*, 1902, 286; *Bull-Comm*, 1903, 276, 365; cf. *BullComm*, 1904, 341–46); the building itself (*NSc*, 1903, 120); numerous sepulchral inscriptions (*NSc*, 1902, 628; *NSc*, 1903, 20, 120–21, 226, 461–62 [possible displacement, *NSc*, 1933, 431]); a dedicatory inscription to Caracalla, from A.D. 213 (*NSc*, 1903, 602, *BullComm*, 1904, 83); architectural fragments (e.g., of marble columns), busts, and reliefs: *NSc*, 1902, 555, 628; *NSc*, 1903, 20, 226, 460–61, 602); stamped bricks: *CIL* 15. 563i, 1563a (*NSc*, 1903, 21; the former dated by Steinby, "CronFig" p. 91: A.D. 123; the latter not included); *CIL* 15.276, no. 2 (*NSc*, 1903, 59; Steinby, p. 55: the early or pre-Hadrianic period); two examples of *CIL* 15.1007 (*NSc*, 1903, 59, and *NSc*, 1903, 461; Steinby, p. 51: beginning of the second century); *CIL* 15.1029a (*NSc*, 1903, 59; Steinby, p. 52: A.D. 123); two examples of *CIL* 15.1056 (*NSc*, 1903, 59; Steinby, p. 53: A.D.

136); *CIL* 15.1073 (*NSc*, 1903, 59; Steinby, p. 53: A.D. 134); *CIL* 15.143 (*NSc*, 1903, 226; Steinby, p. 36: A.D. 110); *CIL* 15.755 (*NSc*, 1903, 226; Steinby, p. 39: ?A.D. 193–198); *CIL* 15.882 (*NSc*, 1903, 226; not in Steinby); *CIL* 15.69 (*NSc*, 1903, 461; Steinby, p. 32: A.D. 128); *CIL* 15.288 (*NSc*, 1903, 461; Steinby, p. 59: A.D. 134); *CIL* 15.633 (*NSc*, 1903, 461; Steinby, p. 97: Vespasianic); *CIL* 15.1410a (*NSc*, 1903, 461; not in Steinby); *CIL* 15.1436 (*NSc*, 1903, 461; Steinby, p. 68 n. 4: A.D. 130); *CIL* 15.121 (*NSc*, 1904, 43; Steinby, p. 34: A.D. 123); *CIL* 15.515a (*NSc*, 1904, 43; Steinby, pp. 83, 85; A.D. 134); *CIL* 15.563a (*NSc*, 1904, 43; Steinby, p. 91: A.D. 123); *CIL* 15.1021 (*NSc*, 1904, 43; Steinby, pp. 47, 55: A.D. 123); *CIL* 15.1033 (*NSc*, 1904, 43; Steinby, pp. 47, 52: A.D. 123). The trench excavated in 1932 in Piazza Venezia was 20 meters east of the Via Lata/Flaminia and parallel to it, and ran from the main entrance of the Palazzo to the little garden near S. Maria di Loreto (*BullComm* 61 [1933] 257). Gismondi's plan does not show the curvilinear construction southwest of the Temple and outside the temenos that is indicated on pl. 28, frag. 29g of the *Forma Urbis*. That building is unidentified: *Forma Urbis*, text, p. 89 n. 3.

[30] E. Gatti and M. De' Spagnolis, "Un intervento nel centro storico di Roma: Impianto termale all'estremità della regio VII," *Quad-AEI* 5 (1981) 132–41, esp. 139.

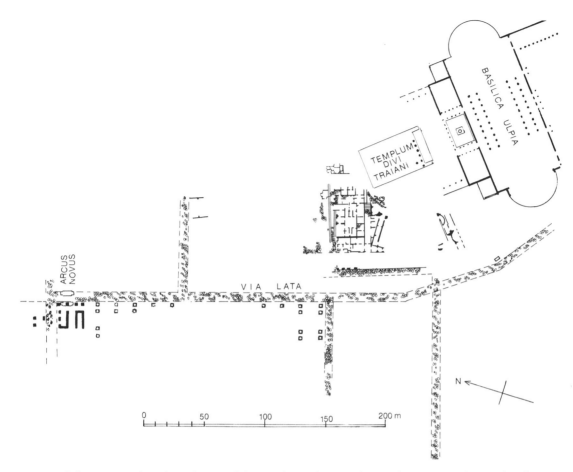

17. *The area north and northwest of the Basilica Ulpia, Column of Trajan, and Temple of the Deified Trajan and Plotina, in the late third century* A.D.

During Trajan's reign, the Column would have been highly visible from the Via Lata/Flaminia, particularly from the stretch south of the later Arcus Novus of Diocletian. The small colonnade around the Column's base would not have hidden it from the view of those in the Campus Martius or on the Via. Trajan himself had used this road when he came to Rome as princeps in 98, and he must have returned by the same route at the head of his victorious armies after the Dacian Wars.[31] The innovative spiral frieze was an immediate reminder to everyone of Trajan's military accomplishments. In topographical terms the Column functioned in three ways. It was at once the culminating

[31] Trajan's return to Rome is described by Pliny, *Pan.* 22, and envisioned by Mart. 10.6. The later Column of Marcus Aurelius, clearly modeled on that of Trajan, was given a similar location along the Via Lata/Flaminia.

element of the Forum of Trajan, to which the entire design of the Forum led, a cynosure for those coming down the Via Lata, and an important commemorative monument in its own right. This triple role of the Column underscores yet again the difference of Trajan's Forum from its imperial predecessors, for as we saw above, they were all entirely self-contained.

Thus, there is no compelling reason, either architectural or topographical, for assigning a Trajanic date to the Temple of the Deified Trajan, and we can now turn to the issue of coins from Trajan's fifth consulate that depicts an octastyle temple with colonnades. Through careful stylistic analysis of Trajan's portrait on the obverse of these coins, Hill has dated the issue to 105–107.[32] Despite the minor variations noted above, the porticoes seem to come toward the viewer tight against the flanks of the temple rather than framing a temenos or along aediculae (chapels) flanking the temple, which is the more common architectural scheme.[33]

There is no identifying legend for the temple, and our sources provide few possible candidates. In the *Panegyricus* Pliny praises Trajan for honoring Nerva with tears and then temples (*Pan.* 11.1), which indicates that Trajan built a temple for his adoptive father; Lydus (*de Mens.* 4.7) says that Trajan dedicated a temple to Fortuna; and the Fasti Ostienses date his rededication of the Temple of Venus Genetrix together with the dedication of the Column, 12 May 113 (*II*, 13.1, pp. 203, 233).[34] The deification of Trajan's sister, Marciana, in 112 and coins issued about a year later to honor Divus Traianus Pater, Trajan's natural father, whom he deified in 112, suggest that temples may have been erected to these individuals, but this is very dubious, not least be-

---

[32] The bronze coins, 105–106; the silver, 107: Hill, *D&A* 32–33; idem, "Some Architectural Types of Trajan," *NC*, ser. 7, 5 (1965) 158–59; e.g., Ward-Perkins, "Columna" 349, accepts the date. Pensa, "Architettura traianea" 267–74, well describes the issue and the problems associated with it. See also Strack, 1.149–54, pl. 6, nos. 393–94; both he and *BMC* describe only bronze coins. The gender of the seated statue is debated: Pensa, e.g., firmly calls the statue female, as does (more dubiously) Mattingly, *BMC, Emp.* III, p. cii; whereas Hill and Strack consider it male.

[33] Compare the rectangular temenos and the Temple of Jupiter Ultor on an issue of

Severus Alexander in 224 (*BMC, Emp.* VI, pp. 57, 134, nos. 207–209, pl. 8), and the representation of the curving porticoes of a nymphaeum on a coin struck in 226 by Severus Alexander (*BMC, Emp.* VI, pp. 63, 146–47, nos. 323–26, pl. 11).

[34] The *sacraria numinum vetustate collapsa* (shrines of the gods that had fallen from age), which Trajan restored in 113–114 (*ILS* 295 = Smallwood, #100), could not have been temples, although they could have been public shrines: M. van Doren, "Les *sacraria*. Une catégorie méconnue d'édifices sacrés chez les romains," *AntCl* 27 (1958) 31–75, esp. 75, and F. Castagnoli, "Il tempio Romano," *PBSR* 52 (1984) 6.

cause of the absence of any other evidence for the sacred buildings.[35] None of these attested to or alleged temples can be identified with the octastyle temple on the Trajanic coins. The Temple of Venus Genetrix is excluded on iconographical grounds; neither the Temple of the Deified Nerva nor Trajan's Temple of Fortune is otherwise known; and temples of Marciana and of Traianus Pater are only hypothetical.[36] Speculation about the identity of the temple illustrated on Trajan's coins, therefore, has ranged freely, and ever since the publication of Nibby's *Roma nell'anno 1838* various scholars have assumed that the coins show the temple later dedicated to the Deified Trajan.[37]

This association of coin and temple seems to have influenced the design of the Temple of the Deified Trajan shown on most plans of the Forum. From the scanty evidence discussed at the beginning of this chapter, it is usually re-

[35] G. Wissowa, *Religion und Kultus der Römer*, 2nd ed. (Munich 1912) 345 (hereafter cited as Wissowa, *ReKu*), notes that until the middle of the second century deified males usually had temples dedicated to them, but females hardly ever, except in conjunction with a male. For the consecration of Marciana on 29 August 112: *II*, 13.1, pp. 201–202, 230–31; coins to Divus Traianus Pater and Divus Nerva, *BMC, Emp.* III, pp. lxxxi, 100–101, nos. 498–99, pl. 17.18–19; Strack, I.199–202; to Divus Pater Traianus, *BMC, Emp.* III, p. 101, nos. 500–508, pls. 17.20, 18.1–2; *RIC* II, p. 261, nos. 251–52; p. 301, nos. 762–64. For the controversy concerning the status of Marciana and of Traianus Pater as "second-class" divi, see Chapter 2, n. 80.

[36] This issue cannot represent the Temple of Venus Genetrix because: (1) it shows a frontal staircase rather than the strikingly plain front and lateral stairs of the Temple as built; (2) the Temple as built was hexastyle, and although coins sometimes show temples with fewer columns than they actually had, the reverse is not true; and (3) the known statue of Venus Genetrix is dissimilar to the various cult statues depicted on the coins. See Pensa, "Architettura traianea" 269–71. Ward-Perkins, "Columna" 350, also notes the time lag between the coins and the Temple's completion in 113.

[37] Pensa, "Architettura traianea" 271–74, suggests that the temple with porticoes is either that later dedicated to the Deified Trajan and Plotina, but begun by Trajan for an unknown deity (here she apparently follows A. Nibby, *Roma nell'anno 1838* [Rome 1839–41] II.207–209), or the Temple of Matidia. Paribeni, *OP* II.58, concurs in the latter identification; contra, Dressel (Chapter 2, n. 74). Brown, *Temples as Coin Types* 10 n. 15; Nash, I.34, fig. 26, s.v. Appiades; F. Panvini Rosati, "Osservazioni sui tipi monetali romani raffiguranti monumenti di Roma," *RIN* 3, ser. 5, 57 (1955) 81–82; and Leon, *Bauornamentik* 41–42 n. 27, all identify the temple with the porticoes as the Temple of Venus Genetrix. (This leads Nash to identify the altar depicted on some of the variants as the Fountain of the Appiades.) Hill, "Types of Trajan" 158–60, asserts that it was a Temple of Jupiter Ultor, but his arguments are suspect on iconographical grounds, apart from the lack of support for Trajan's interest in such a temple. The identification of the temple with porticoes represented on the coins as the later Temple of the Deified Trajan and Plotina was endorsed early by T. L. Donaldson, *Architectura Numismatica* (London 1859) 33–35; it led G. Lugli to date the coin incorrectly as Hadrianic (in *Centro* 295, fig. 87). Zanker, "Trajansforum" 538 n. 152, believes that the coin has influenced the representation of the temple on Gismondi's plan.

constructed as an octastyle temple on a high podium, almost always depicted on plan flanked by colonnades that curve back to join its rear wall[38] (*see Ill. 15*). This reconstruction derives ultimately from an unpublished plan (now in the archives of the Soprintendenza alle Antichità di Roma) of the excavations from the Assicurazioni Generali supervised by Giuseppe Gatti from 1902 to their end in 1906. His grandson Guglielmo Gatti showed this plan to I. Gismondi, the architect who served as official cartographer for the excavations in connection with the creation of the Via dei Fori Imperiali, and also based a published plan of his own upon it.[39] For our purposes, the important parts of these plans (which are the basis of most reconstructions of the area) are the curved colonnades.

Guglielmo Gatti's plan, published in *BullComm* 1934, from which our Illustration 17 derives, corresponds best with what he reports to have been found in the area; for although he sketched hypothetical curving porticoes, he marks as actually excavated only a small part of a street paved with basalt blocks northwest of the presumed location of the Temple. The paving was bordered on the southeast by a stone block, and on the northwest by a slightly curving line of about eight blocks; these, in turn, define the southeast side of a triangular platea he indicates as paved in travertine. In the accompanying text Gatti summarizes the anonymous and incomplete description found with the plan among his grandfather's notes. After describing briefly the street bordered with cippi and the insula discussed above, he continues: "L'edificio era limitato a sud da una strada, con la quale comunicava per mezzo di quattro ingressi; essa ad un certo punto, verso est, si trasformava in una gradinata ascendente dalla quota 12.60 alla quota 15; a questa quota apparve un tratto di piazzale ad arco di cercio sul quale si affacciavano i resti di un edificio monumentale. Esso, . . ." He concludes from the finds and from some pencil marks sketching a curved structure behind the Temple, found on his grandfather's copy of the Kiepert-Hülsen plan of 1896, that the Temple of the Deified Trajan was originally flanked by curving porticoes.[40]

[38] Plommer, "Trajan's Forum" 126–30, gives references to earlier plans depicting the temenos as rectangular as he argues against the common reconstruction of the area.

[39] See G. Gatti, "*Saepta Iulia* e *Porticus Aemilia* nella *Forma* Severiana," *BullComm* 62 (1934) 125–26, esp. n. 11, and pl. 1. Gismondi's early plans are in *Via dell'Impero* 36; and *BullComm* 61 (1933) pl. A, between pp. 256

and 257. Leon, *Bauornamentik* 35 n. 1, lists some of the many subsequent plans (up to ca. 1971) derived from Gismondi's. I was unable to inspect the plan itself, which is in the "Archivio Gatti" currently under reorganization, but I am grateful to Dr. C. Buzzetti, in charge of the archives, for discussing it with me.

[40] "The building was bounded on the south by a street, to which it opened by means of

Although Gatti's conclusion does not violate the available archaeological evidence, it is not very plausible. First, the restricted area of the excavation did not expose the line of the southeast side of the street, so it is not clear whether or not it was curved; second, the level of the higher paved platea, 15 meters above sea level, if correct, is 1.06 meters lower than the paving around the Column in front of the Temple;[41] and third, bowed porticoes around temple precincts are very unusual, apparently found primarily with temples of Serapis.[42] Furthermore, the paving blocks of Luna marble found reused in a fifth-century context under Piazza Venezia and associated with the porticoes of the Temple show no sign of having originally belonged to a curved structure. The curving porticoes of the plan owe as much to the oddity of the porticoes shown flanking the unidentified temple on the Trajanic coins as they do to archaeological evidence in the area, and perhaps more (compare the Temple of the Deified Matidia on the Hadrianic coin, *Ill. 8*).[43]

There is also no hard evidence for the octastyle facade of the Temple, although columns of large diameter are likely to have come from an octastyle or decastyle temple. But the excavation reports published in connection with the demolition of Palazzo Torlonia in 1902–1904, Boni's investigations around the Column in 1906, and Ricci's clearing of the area of the Via dei Fori Imperiali in the 1920s and early 1930s give no basis for reconstructing an octastyle facade. Nevertheless, since the plan of the temple and temenos can be made to resemble what is shown on the Trajanic coins, the Temple has been said to have been designed, if not built, by Trajan to honor Nerva, Marciana, Traianus Pater, or Trajan himself.[44]

Apart from the lack of good archaeological support for the commonly accepted plan of the Temple of the Deified Trajan and Plotina, the assignment of the temple to Trajan is questionable on other grounds. None of the dedi-

---

four doors; at a certain point toward the east this street was transformed into a flight of stairs rising from the altitude of 12.60 to that of 15; at this height appeared an expanse of semicircular, large piazza onto which faced the remains of a monumental building. This building . . . " Gatti, "*Saepta e Porticus*" 125–26; he reproduces his grandfather's map (his fig. 1).

[41] See Boni, "Forum Ulpium" 362 fig. 1.

[42] Crema, 363, cites this and the semicircular colonnade of Palestrina as parallels. The Egyptian cult, however, had its own exotic architecture, sometimes rather more bizarre than Oriental.

[43] The relationship of the porticoes to the temple on the coin is very unusual, as can be seen by comparing the other numismatic representations of such structures listed in n. 33 of this chapter. Pensa, nevertheless, believes that the Trajanic die maker was attempting to illustrate curving porticoes ("Architettura traianea" 273).

[44] Ward-Perkins is most explicit about this theory: "Columna" 351–52.

cations so far offered is attractive or even tenable. First, although Strack argues that there was no standard iconography for cult statues of Divi and Divae, coins show that there was always a correspondence in genders between the person so honored and the cult statue. In instances of a double cult, or of two statues in a single temple, both statues are represented on the coins: on issues commemorating Antoninus Pius' restoration of the Temple of the Deified Augustus, for example, we see seated statues of Augustus and Livia (*BMC, Emp.* IV, p. 140, nos. 938–43, pl. 20.5–7).[45] The seated statue on the Trajanic coins dating to 105–107 seems to be female, but only one woman, Marciana, was deified during Trajan's rule, and her death in 112 occurs five years later than Hill's latest date for the issue and during Trajan's sixth, not fifth, consulship. We have also noted that there is no basis for presuming that she was ever honored with a temple.

If the seated statue is to be identified as male, it is possible that Trajan did begin a temple here to honor Nerva. But given the time lag between the coin issues and the actual dedication of the Temple by Hadrian,[46] and the fact that the Temple was dedicated to Trajan and Plotina without Nerva, it would be more plausible to assume that a different Trajanic series struck ca. 105–108, showing a standing male figure in an unidentified temple, depicts the otherwise unattested Temple of the Deified Nerva.[47] In addition to chronological arguments against assuming that the Temple was first destined for Trajan's deified blood father, we note again that there is no evidence that a temple ever honored this individual.

The assumption, often only implicit, that from the start the Temple must have been planned to honor Trajan, is really the important argument against a Trajanic dating for the Temple of the Deified Trajan. It does not take into consideration the intellectual and spiritual climate in the capital city during Trajan's rule. Domitian's arrogation to himself of semidivinity was still fresh in people's memories (cf. Pliny *Pan.* 52, 54).[48] More telling evidence comes

---

[45] Strack, 1.151–52, lists these types of coins and describes the figures on them.

[46] Although there are instances when an issue precedes the completion of the building it commemorates (e.g., that of the Temple of the Deified Julius and those of the Temple of Venus and Roma discussed below), they are very rare (Panvini Rosati, "Osservazioni" 79). Moreover, it seems unlikely that only this north sector of Trajan's Forum would

have been left incomplete.

[47] *BMC, Emp.* III, pp. 181–82, nos. 857–62, pl. 32.5–7; p. 79, no. 354, pl. 15.5; p. 193, nos. 915–16, pl. 35.3–4; pp. 201–202, nos. 955–58, pl. 37.7–8. Pensa, "Architettura traianea" 265–67; Strack, 1.147–49, pls. 2.152 and 6.392; cf. *BMC, Emp.* III, p. cii. Hill, "Architectural Types" 157–58, unpersuasively suggests that this is a Temple of Honos.

[48] *Pace* Zanker, "Trajansforum" 543.

from Tacitus' *Annals*, written during Trajan's second decade as princeps. In discussing the end of the Pisonian conspiracy of 65, Tacitus notes a senatorial proposal to raise a temple in the city as soon as possible to the deified Nero who, though still alive, transcended mortal bounds and deserved worship. Commenting on Nero's refusal of the honor, which he rejected as an ill omen, Tacitus remarks: *nam deum honor principi non ante habetur, quam agere inter homines desierit* (for divine honor is not considered for a princeps until he ceases to live among mankind: *Ann.* 15.74.3).[49] He would hardly have made such a remark if a temple to Trajan in Rome itself had been projected during Trajan's lifetime.

We should accept the testimony of Hadrian's biography and of the inscriptions from the temple. The Temple of the Deified Trajan was a cooperative effort of Hadrian and the senate; it is analogous to Trajan's deification, which Hadrian requested by letter and obtained from an enthusiastically compliant senate immediately after Trajan's death (*HA, Hadr.* 6.1–3).[50] The Temple was probably begun by or at the time of Trajan's posthumous triumph in 118.[51] The Column's base was then modified or adapted to accommodate his ashes there (Dio Cass. 69.2.3),[52] and coin issues of that time stress the adoption of Hadrian by Trajan, or hail Divus Traianus.[53] When Plotina

[49] Compare the Augustan refusal of divine honors: "the courteous expression of pleasure . . . coupled with deprecation of such honours as excessive and suitable to gods only": M. P. Charlesworth, "The Refusal of Divine Honours, an Augustan Formula," *PBSR* 15 (1939) 1–10, esp. 8. See, too, Hammond, *AntMon* 210–11, but note that the "divine" honors to Trajan he mentions are all outside of Rome.

[50] See Weber, 60–66; Temporini, *Frauen* 160; and Garzetti, 379–80, on Hadrian's first dealings with the senate and on the senate's responsibility for Trajan's deification; and cf. G. W. Clarke, "The Date of the *Consecratio* of Vespasian," *Historia* 15 (1966) 320.

[51] Mr. J. T. Peña has generously discussed with me his convincing association with the Temple of the Deified Trajan of the 50-foot granite column recorded in P. Giss. 69 as having been transported from Caenae to the Nile; the papyrus' date of December(?) 118 supplies a terminus post quem for the completion of

the Temple. An abstract of his paper presented at the Archaeological Institute of America annual meeting, December 1984, was published for the meeting.

[52] Zanker, "Trajansforum" 536, associates this use of the Column with hero cults in the Greek East; cf. Gauer, *Trajanssäule* 74. J.-C. Richard conflates the posthumous triumph and the funeral, in "Recherches sur certains aspects du culte impérial: Les funérailles des empereurs romains aux deux premiers siècles de notre ère," *ANRW* II.16.2 (1978) 1123–24, and "Les Funérailles de Trajan et le triomphe sur les Parthes," *REL* 44 (1966) 357–62; contra, W. den Boer, "Trajan's Deification and Hadrian's Succession," *Ancient Society* 6 (1975) 207.

[53] D. Mannsperger, "Rom. et Aug." 970–72; cf. *BMC, Emp.* III, pp. cxxvi–cxxvii; Hill, *D&A* 48–50. Recently, den Boer, "Trajan's Deification" 203–12, and J. R. Fears, *Princeps a diis electus* (Rome 1977) 238–40, have emphasized the political and religious signifi-

died in 123, her ashes may also have been placed in the chamber in the base of the Column, though no one mentions the fact. The Temple was dedicated to both Trajan and Plotina sometime before 128, the terminus ante quem for the dedicatory inscriptions.[54]

The scant archaeological evidence also supports a Hadrianic date for the Temple. The diameter of the gray granite column fragments that survive and the height of the one reasonably complete capital of Luna marble indicate that the Temple was enormous, larger than the Pantheon. The finds of rose granite column fragments that have been reported, together with the extant fragments of gray granite columns, indicate that the sacred area may have resembled the Pantheon and its temenos also in the play of color.[55]

The new Temple was similar to other Hadrianic constructions in additional ways. The framing porticoes of the temenos of the Deified Trajan and Plotina, probably with granite columns and paved with Luna marble, seem not to have completely enclosed the precinct. There were two copies of the dedicatory inscription, the larger of which originally had bronze letters and is now in the Vatican.[56] The existence of two or more identical inscriptions for an edifice often indicates that it was to be approached from more than one direction.[57] Until further excavations can be undertaken in Piazza Venezia, we cannot know whether the porticoes of Hadrian's Temple of the Deified Trajan and Plotina facilitated communication between the administrative center of the city and the Campus Martius.[58] If they did, the Hadrianic additions must have funneled and fostered the smooth flow of traffic in much the same way as contemporaneous works did in the Campus Martius. Another Hadrianic characteristic is the order that the Temple to his deified parents imposes on the design of Trajan's Forum, hitherto so incongruous in the city of Rome.

cance of P. Giss. 3 = Smallwood, #519, a papyrus of 117 that depicts Hadrian's advent to power as dependent on Apollo and the deified Trajan. Yet this papyrus comes from an Egyptian nome; as Fears notes (p. 243), in Rome Hadrian's coinage in 117–118 stresses "human institutions": Hadrian's election by the senate (or Trajan), and his adoption by the deified Trajan.

[54] Hadrian accepted the title Pater Patriae in 128, which does not appear on the inscription: see Leon, *Bauornamentik* 39.

[55] See, e.g., Ward-Perkins, "Columna" 351.

[56] The two inscriptions seem to have been of about the same size, however: the one in the Vatican (*CIL* 6.966) is 1.10 meters high for four lines of text, and the height of three lines of text preserved on the other is about two-thirds this, to judge from its description published in *CIL*.

[57] I. Calabi Limentani, *Epigrafia latina, con un appendice bibliografica di A. Degrassi*, 3rd ed. (Milan 1974) 21, 267.

[58] The design would then be similar to that of the Temple of Venus and Roma with its two flanking porticoes. For unstated reasons, H. Plommer, "Trajan's Forum: A Plea," *Pro-*

Our knowledge of the date and appearance of Hadrian's Temple of the Deified Trajan and Plotina, however imprecise and imperfect, contrasts with an almost complete dearth of information about Hadrian's restoration of the Forum Augustum (Forum of Augustus). Up until the 1960s, whenever scholars took note of the restoration cited in Hadrian's biography, it was generally assumed that much of the decoration visible today in the Forum was Hadrianic. Ward-Perkins and Strong's careful study of Augustan decoration published in 1962, however, has led to a better understanding of Augustan style,[59] and the evidence for a Hadrianic restoration of the Forum Augustum is now recognized to be meager. Only one Corinthian capital, 0.935 meters high and of Proconnesian marble, from the south part of the Forum (*see Ill. 18*), a fragment of a frieze,[60] an antefix, and possibly some lion-head spouts[61] have been identified as Hadrianic.

18. *Hadrianic capital from the south part of the Forum of Augustus.*

ceedings of the Cambridge Philosophical Society 186, N.S. 6 (1960) 61, also believes that the Forum of Trajan served as a thoroughfare, and "that the side-colonnades were quite straight."

[59] Kraus' "Ornamentfriese" appeared almost simultaneously with A. von Gerkan, "Einiges zur Aedes Castoris in Rom," *RömMitt* 60–61 (1953–54) 200, who argued that much if not all the extant work in the Forum Augustum was Hadrianic. J. B. Ward-Perkins and D. E. Strong, "The Tem-

ple of Castor in the Forum Romanum," *PBSR* 30 (1962) 1–30, have now convincingly illustrated the rich variety of Augustan ornament. For discussion of the controversy and Augustan and Hadrianic styles, see P. Zanker, *Forum Augustum. Das Bildprogramm* (Tübingen 1968) 11–12; Bertoldi, *Foro Traiano* 29–31; and Leon, *Bauornamentik* 142.

[60] Kraus, "Ornamentfriese" pl. 10.1.

[61] V. Kockel, "Beobachtungen zum Tempel des Mars Ultor und zum Forum des Augustus," *RömMitt* 80 (1983) 438–39.

Such scant evidence for the restoration indicates that Hadrian's work here was not as extensive as it was elsewhere, for instance in the Saepta Julia. No specific reason for the restoration is mentioned, and the original appearance and program of Augustus' Forum were scrupulously maintained.[62] Comparison of the Hadrianic capital with those from the original Augustan building reveals the greater linearity and schematic quality of the Hadrianic work, and underlines the point that, stylistically, such renovations did not slavishly copy the original; nevertheless, the attempt at imitation is noticeable.[63] Stylistic analysis of the capital has led Heilmeyer to attribute the work to a Pergamene-Ephesian school, and thus to the later part of Hadrian's reign.[64] If he is right, Hadrian's preoccupation with an Augustan revival and renewal may have been a constant theme thoughtout his reign.

This theme must be seen in conjunction with Hadrian's conspicuous honors to his immediate predecessor and to the imperial family as a whole. At the beginning of his rule he emphasized his attachment to and respect for his deified adoptive father, so beloved in Rome: his refusal of the senatorial decree to himself of Trajan's Parthian triumph, which was then celebrated posthumously but magnificently for Trajan (*HA, Hadr.* 6.3), marked an ostensibly selfless respect for Trajan, and the senate and Hadrian cooperated again to raise the Temple of the Deified Trajan and Plotina. Yet this Temple demonstrates that Hadrian conferred such honors to members of the imperial family rather distantly related to him and whose deification, at first sight, is unexpected and not necessarily advantageous (cf. Pliny *Pan.* 11.1).

Such actions, although foreshadowed by Trajan's consecration of Marciana in 112 and the honors to imperial consorts and daughters in the first century,[65] are remarkable for their quality and quantity. Hadrian's honors to his mother-in-law, Matidia, have already been discussed. After Plotina's death on 1 January 123, Hadrian lauded her in his funeral oration and dedicated a sumptuous building in Nimes to her (*HA, Hadr.* 12.2; cf. Dio Cass. 69.10.3 and ILS 4844 = Smallwood, #142); in Rome she shared a temple with Tra-

---

[62] For the original message of the Forum of Augustus, see Zanker, *Forum Augustum*.

[63] Heilmeyer, *Normalkapitelle* 31–32; Leon, *Bauornamentik* 283; cf. Zanker, *Forum Augustum* p. 11 and figs. 23, 24.

[64] Heilmeyer, *Normalkapitelle* 31–32, 166. Because of a misreading of *CIL* 6.207 = 30715, Anderson attributes the restoration to

the middle years of Hadrian's reign (*Hist-Top* 99).

[65] Imperial women consecrated before the second century were Livia, Drusilla (Caligula's sister), Claudia (the daughter of Nero and Poppaea), Poppaea, Domitilla (Titus' sister), and Julia (the daughter of Titus): Hammond, *AntMon* 205–209.

jan.[66] Hadrian's own wife, Sabina, was deified after her death at the end of 137 (or soon thereafter), though L. Aelius, the heir presumptive, was probably not similarly honored when he died the same year.[67]

Oliver has interpreted Hadrian's actions, particularly those at the beginning of his rule, as his way of consolidating power by allying himself more closely with Trajan's family: a senatorial decree was needed for deification, and the elevation of the women of Trajan's family to divinity symbolized both the harmonious cooperation of senate and Hadrian, and the winning over of the Trajanic faction to Hadrian's side after the inauspicious beginnings of his reign.[68] This must have been part of Hadrian's motivation, but he continued this policy throughout his principate. Coins portraying Trajan and Plotina with the legend DIVIS PARENTIBUS date as late as 137, and despite the alleged hostility between Sabina and Hadrian, she too was deified as soon as she died.[69] The evidence indicates a design to elevate the imperial family to a plane above the petty affairs of the rest of humanity, and in this context should be seen the dismissal in 121–122 of Suetonius and Septicius Clarus on grounds that they had shown themselves unacceptably familiar with Sabina

[66] Temporini, *Frauen* 161–75; on 168–69, he notes that we know of no temple dedicated to Plotina alone. He dates Hadrian's eulogy of her to 125–126, after Hadrian's return to Rome, and he associates it with Hadrian's *adlocutio* before the Temple of the Deified Julius, commemorated on coins of 128 (see Chapter 4; and Chapter 2, n. 79).

[67] For Sabina's death and deification: A. Carandini, *Vibia Sabina* (Florence 1969) 98–101, and (with new information) W. Eck, "Vibia(?) Sabina, No. 72b," *RE, Suppl.* 15 (1978) 914. Hammond, *AntMon* 207; and Garzetti, 438, doubt the deification of Aelius. The different case of Antinoos is discussed in the Appendix, yet it is significant that in Antinoopolis, the city Hadrian founded in Egypt in 130 to commemorate the youth, he named a phyle Matidia, and had the demes Marcianios and Plotinios enrolled in it: Weber, 175–78; cf. Beaujeu, 167–69.

[68] Oliver, "Divi"; Hammond, *AntMon* 204, for the cooperation of the senate and emperor in decreeing consecrations. The antagonism of the senate toward Hadrian was due

to the suspicious circumstances surrounding his adoption on Trajan's deathbed, his acclamation as Imperator by the troops, subsequent acceptance of the position before consultation with the senate, and the condemnation and death of the four consulars before Hadrian reached Rome in July 118. See, e.g., Garzetti, 379–80; R. Syme, "Ummidius Quadratus, *Capax imperii*," *HSCP* 83 (1979) 290.

[69] It is uncertain whether Hadrian's own blood relations were excluded from such honors: cf. Dio Cass. 69.11.4. Beaujeu, 418–23, wishes to explain the deification of empresses as a means for the emperors to obtain an aura of divinity while still alive. Mannsperger, "Rom. et Aug." 971–72, holds that the theme of consecration now becomes the center of the cult of the emperor. Coins: e.g., *BMC, Emp.* III, p. 318, no. 603, pl. 59.3; Temporini, *Frauen* 109 nn. 18–20, and 173–74, who also stresses the dynastic theme. Hammond, *MonAnt* 206, sees Hadrian's devotion to the family of Trajan as indicative of a dynastic concept.

(*HA, Hadr.* 11.3).[70] The attitude that later reaches full bloom in the numerous inscriptions to the *domus divina* of the late second and early third century was nurtured, if not created, by Hadrian.[71]

Hadrian's Temple of the Deified Trajan and Plotina was much more than an isolated act of filial piety. It and his restoration of the Forum of Augustus show Hadrian as the legitimate holder of dynastic imperial power ultimately deriving from Augustus himself.

---

[70] Wallace-Hadrill, *Suetonius* 6, briefly discusses this incident.

[71] References in *DizEpig*, II.3, s.v. Domus (Domus divina), 2062–66. M. T. Raepsaet-Charlier, in *ANRW* II.3 (1975) 235–55, cites such inscriptions from as early as 135. J. F. Gilliam, "On Divi under the Severi," in *Hommages . . . M. Renard* II (Brussels 1969) 284–89, discusses the Divae of the late second and third centuries. Temporini, *Frauen* 262–63, places more emphasis on Trajan's influence on this development.

# CHAPTER FOUR

# THE FORUM ROMANUM, ROME'S TRADITIONAL CENTER

Hadrianic work in the Forum Romanum, traditionally the heart of Rome—his additions to the imperial palaces overlooking the Forum from the northeastern slope of the Palatine and his Temple of Venus and Roma, covering most of the Velia next to the Arch of Titus on the Sacra Via—dates to the middle years of his reign and is proof of Hadrian's confident command of Rome and the Roman empire at that time. The various structures monumentalized and unified the southern and eastern bounds of the Forum, changing the look of the Forum far more effectively than any construction in the central space could have, but this effect has never been fully appreciated, partly because the structures all lie outside the Forum proper[1] (*see Ill. 19*).

Moreover, the character of some of the Hadrianic building is problematic: although even today the Hadrianic brickwork on the slopes of the Palatine is among the most conspicuous construction around the Forum, the last detailed archaeological investigations of it were published by R. Delbrück and by E. B. van Deman in the 1920s, and many crucial questions await clarification by the excavations now in progress.[2] The work on the Palatine, which

---

[1] Coarelli, *ForArc* 24–28, notes that the site of the Temple of Venus and Roma on the Velia was in the fourth Augustan region (Templum Pacis). The work on the Palatine is in Regio x: Palatium.

[2] R. Delbrück, "Der Südostbau am Forum Romanum," *JdI* 36 (1921) 8–33, and "Bemerkung. Nachtrag zu Seite 8ff., 'Der Südostbau am Forum Romanum,' " *JdI* 36 (1921) 186–87 (hereafter Delbrück, "Südostbau"); E. B. van Deman, "The House of Caligula," *AJA* 28 (1924) 368–98. The vexing ambiguity of the archaeological and other evidence has

been stressed in recent studies of these structures (e.g., B. Tamm, *Auditorium and Palatium* (Stockholm 1963) 79–83; and P. Castrén and H. Lilius, *Graffiti del Palatino II, Domus Tiberiana, Acta Instituti Romani Finlandiae* 4 [Helsinki 1970] 20–22). New investigations by the British School and the Soprintendenza alle Antichità (under the supervision of Dr. H. Hurst, with Dr. C. Coletti) are now under way at S. Maria Antiqua (1983–84), and the Soprintendenza and the Swiss School (under Dr. C. Krause) have worked on the Domus Tiberiana. I am grateful to Dr. Caterina Co-

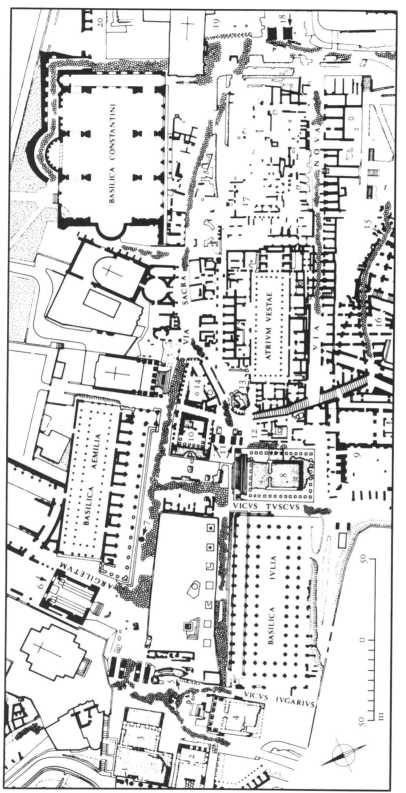

19. *The Forum Romanum during the imperial period:* (1) *Tabularium;* (2) *Temple of the Deified Vespasian and Titus;* (3) *Temple of Concord;* (4) *Temple of Saturn;* (5) *Rostra Augusti;* (6) *Curia;* (7) *Shrine of Venus Cloacina;* (8) *Temple of Castor;* (9) "*Vestibule*" *of Domitian;* (10) *Temple of the Deified Julius;* (11) *Arch of Augustus;* (12) *Lacus Juturnae;* (13) *Temple of Vesta;* (14) *Regia;* (15) *Clivus Victoriae;* (16) *Domus Tiberiana;* (17) *Porticus;* (18) *Arch of Titus;* (19) *Temple of Venus and Roma;* (20) *Clivo di Venere Felice.*

in fact belongs to two distinct buildings, is not mentioned in any ancient source, and is generally ignored and rarely associated with other Hadrianic building in Rome. It certainly has never been considered in relation to the Temple of Venus and Roma.

In contrast, the Temple of Venus and Roma, attested to by its physical remains, coins, inscriptions, and literature, has been extensively studied from many different angles. Most recently, in publications since 1973, A. Barattolo has overturned the traditional view of the Temple's architecture by distinguishing the Hadrianic design from the Maxentian rebuilding.[3] Pensa's 1978 investigation of Hadrian's architectural coins includes a careful examination of the numismatic evidence for the Temple's external appearance; and Kienast, F. E. Brown, Lugli, and G. Snidjer have calculated the significance and effect of the Temple's location on the Velia above the Forum.[4] Of equal or greater importance are Beaujeu's and Gagé's investigations into the religious importance of the Temple and its connection with Hadrian's transformation in 121 of the Parilia into the Romaia, the Natalis Urbis Romae.[5] Notwithstanding these and other studies, examination of the Temple of Venus and Roma is still profitable, specifically in respect to the relationship of the Temple to other Hadrianic construction and changes in the Forum and in the city.

The Temple and the additions to the Palatine adjacent to the Roman

---

letti and Dr. Krause for generous and patient explanations of the two sites. In a review of P. Zanker, *Forum Romanum*, Monumenta artis antiqua 5 (Tübingen 1972), R. Brilliant (*Gnomon* 46 [1974] 523–25) has stressed the importance of the "upper visual limit[s]" of the Forum.

[3] A. Barattolo, "Nuove ricerche sull'architettura del Tempio di Venere e di Roma in età Adrianea," *RömMitt* 80 (1973) 243–69, with previous bibliography on pp. 243–44; idem, "Sulla decorazione delle celle del Tempio di Venere e di Roma all'epoca di Adriano," *BullComm* 84 (1974–75) [1977] 133–48; idem, "Il Tempio di Venere e Roma: un tempio 'greco' nell'Urbe," *RömMitt* 85 (1978) 397–410. These works are hereafter referred to by author's name and their publication date. Nibby was the first to recognize that the extant parts of the cella are not Hadrianic (*Roma nel 1838*, II.738).

[4] Pensa, "Adriano" 51–59; Kienast, "Baupolitik" 399–407; F. E. Brown, "Hadrianic Architecture," in *Essays in Memory of K. Lehmann*, ed. by L. F. Sandler (New York 1964) 55–58; G. Lugli, *Monumenti minori del Foro Romano* (Rome 1947) 165–92 (hereafter Lugli, *MonMin*); idem, " 'Roma aeterna' e il suo culto sulla Velia," Accademia Nazionale dei Lincei, problemi attuali di scienza e di cultura, Quaderno 11, 8 (Rome 1949); and G.A.S. Snidjer, "Kaiser Hadrian und der Tempel der Venus und Roma," *JdI* 55 (1940) 1–11.

[5] Beaujeu, 128–61; J. Gagé, "Le *Templum urbis* et les origines de l'idée de *renovatio*," in *Mélanges F. Cumont* (Brussels 1936) 151–87; idem, *Recherches sur les Jeux Séculaires* (Paris 1934) 94–111; idem, "Le Colosse et la fortune de Rome," *MélRome* 45 (1928) 106–22; idem, "Le *sollemne urbis* du 21 avril au IIIe siècle ap. J.-C.," *Melanges . . . H.-C. Puech* (Paris 1974) 225–41.

Forum have termini post quos provided by brick stamps of 125–130,[6] and thus come later than the inception of Hadrian's work both in the Campus Martius and at the north end of Trajan's Forum. Other material dates to this time a new interest on Hadrian's part in the Forum Romanum itself. Upon his arrival in Rome in 118 as princeps, Hadrian had staged his first acts of public liberality elsewhere, although the Forum Romanum was one of the customary sites for such gestures. The burning of the debt records, so copiously celebrated on the coinage of 118, had taken place in Trajan's Forum,[7] clearly in honor of his adoptive father. Hadrian celebrated his own birthday in 119 with extravagant games in the Circus Maximus, and distributed lots for prizes there and in the theater (Dio Cass. 69.8.2). Also at the theaters aromatics and other prizes were distributed during games honoring Trajan and, later, Plotina (*HA, Hadr.* 19.5).

Our earliest knowledge of Hadrian's interest in the Roman Forum comes from a series of sestertii datable to the period ca. 125–128 (before Hadrian received the title Pater Patriae) (*see Ill. 20*). In the three variants Hadrian, togate, stands on a platform in front of a temple, and in his right hand holds a scroll. Before the temple and to the right stands a group of three to eight men, also togate, who lift their hands toward the emperor. The temple, seen obliquely, is shown as small with a pediment decorated with a single or a double crown and sometimes acroteria. It has been identified as the Temple of the Deified Julius.[8]

This coin has been interpreted in various ways. E. De Ruggiero took it as evidence for a Hadrianic restoration of the Temple of the Deified Julius, but no archaeological evidence supports this.[9] Strack has suggested that the coin

---

[6] For the brick stamps of the Palatine buildings: Bloch, *Bolli* 33–36; Blake/Bishop, 61; and below, n. 66; for those in the podium of the Temple of Venus and Roma, dating to 123 and 134, see Bloch, *Bolli* 250–53, 256; and Blake/Bishop, 40–41.

[7] This is explicitly stated by *HA, Hadr.* 7.6, and seems confirmed by the provenance in Trajan's Forum of an inscription recording the event (*CIL* 6.967 = *ILS* 309 = Smallwood, #64a). This liberal act of Hadrian was also commemorated on coins, *BMC, Emp.* III, pp. 417–18, nos. 1206–1210, pl. 79.4–6; cf. Smallwood, #64b; and cf. Dio Cass. 69.8.1.2. But the Anaglypha Traiani/Hadriani, which may be Hadrianic rather than Trajanic, show a princeps burning the debt records in the Ro-

man Forum. The controversy on the relief's date is discussed in Chapter 7, in the section entitled "Anaglypha Traiani/Hadriani."

[8] *BMC, Emp.* III, p. 433, nos. 1309–11, pl. 81.10; Hill, *D&A* 58, suggests a date of 125–126. M. Montagna Pasquinucci, "La decorazione architettonica del tempio del Divo Giulio nel Foro Romano," *Accademia Nazionale dei Lincei, Monumenti Antichi, serie miscellanea* 48 (Rome 1973) 258–59, describes in detail the coins' representations of the building.

[9] E. De Ruggiero, *Il Foro Romano* (Rome 1913) 196; and cf. Platner-Ashby, s.v. Iulius, Divus, Aedes, 287; for the archaeological evidence against this theory, see Montagna Pasquinucci, "Divo Giulio" 259.

20. *Reverse of a sestertius (ca. 125–128), depicting Hadrian, standing on the rostra in front of the Temple of the Deified Julius and addressing Roman citizens.*

commemorates the funeral oration Hadrian delivered in honor of Plotina (cf. Dio Cass. 69.10.3), which he supposes was given on Hadrian's return to Rome some three years after her death. Strack notes that the rostra regularly served in the Augustan period for the funeral laudations of particularly eminent individuals, and in support H. Temporini has added that the Forum was always the traditional location for such speeches.[10] H. Mattingly has suggested that the issue depicts Hadrian's address to the people on his return to Rome after his first great journey.[11] He stresses both that the issue dates at least three years after Plotina's death, and that none of the honors granted her posthumously is clearly attested to on Hadrian's coinage. Strack's and Temporini's interpretation seems best, although the matter cannot be settled finally without new evidence.

The coin is more than simply unusual. Only very rarely do architectural coin types show buildings that have not been constructed, completed, restored, or rededicated by the emperor issuing them, and the infrequency of architectural types in Hadrianic coinage is well known.[12] The issue seems to

[10] Strack, *Hadrian* 113–15; Temporini, *Frauen* 168–69, noting other adherents of the theory.

[11] *BMC, Emp.* III, p. clxviii; Hill, *D&A* 58, seems to accept this interpretation.

[12] See the Introduction of this book.

Brown, *Temples as Coin Types* 10–13, cites this Hadrianic issue as the "single instance" of an issue of architectural type being struck without reference to a new building or renovation.

advertise the fact that at this time, Hadrian's second stay in the capital city as princeps, he began to use the Roman Forum for public appearances.

Other evidence, unfortunately undatable, also attests to Hadrian's special interest in the Roman Forum. Dio notes that Hadrian honored many of his friends so greatly that he erected statues in the Forum to them after their deaths and to some even while still alive (69.7.4). Dio also informs us that Hadrian, attended by the senate and the foremost men of the state, often heard cases "now in the Palace, now in the Forum, or in the Pantheon, or in various other places," at which times he was always seated on a tribunal (69.7.1).[13]

A panel of the Constantinian frieze of the Arch of Constantine supports Dio's testimony.[14] The "Oratio" panel depicts the Rostra Augusti as they appeared in the early fourth century A.D., when they carried a seated statue at either end. It is generally agreed that the statue on the right, a bearded figure with a globe in his right hand and a scepter in his left, is Hadrian[15] (see Ill. 21). This statue, even more than those attested to by various bases inscribed to Hadrian found in the Forum,[16] shows the emperor's particular involvement in the Forum and its activities.

Evaluation of the Hadrianic work around the traditional center of Rome must begin with the appearance and importance of the Roman Forum at Hadrian's accession, and the ways in which earlier emperors had used it (see Ill. 19). Situated on low ground surrounded by the Capitoline, Palatine, Velia, Esquiline, and Quirinal hills, this relatively level area was the natural meeting ground of Rome's inhabitants for political and social purposes.[17]

Around the Forum's edges were located some of the oldest shrines and temples of the city: the Temples of Vesta, of Saturn, and of Castor, and the little shrines of Juturna, Janus, and Venus Cloacina. Off the northern corner

[13] Augustus, Tiberius, and Claudius are also known to have sat in judgment in the Forum: Millar, *ERW* 229, collects the evidence.

[14] For this relief, see H. P. L'Orange and A. von Gerkan, *Der spätantike Bildschmuck des Konstantinsbogens* (Berlin 1939) 82–83; and Lugli, *Centro* 140–41.

[15] The other figure is usually identified as M. Aurelius, but L. Richardson, Jr., "The Tribunals of the Praetors of Rome," *RömMitt* 80 (1973) 232–33, provocatively suggests that it might be M. Salvius Julianus, the great jurist who codified Hadrian's revision of the *edictum perpetuum*.

[16] *NSc*, 1899, 77 = *BullComm*, 1899, 59; *CIL* 6.974; and *CIL* 6.31302 = 3754.

[17] The fundamental works on the Roman Forum are: De Ruggiero, *Foro Romano*; C. Hülsen, *Das Forum Romanum*, 2nd ed. (Rome 1905); and Zanker, *Forum Romanum*, who focuses on its systemization by Caesar and Augustus. The following survey of the development of the republican Forum is based on the concise summaries of Zanker, 5–7; Platner-Ashby, s.v. Forum (Romanum s. Magnum), 230–36; and J. Russell, "The Origin and Development of Republican Forums," *Phoenix* 22 (1968) 304–26, except where noted.

21. *"Oratio" panel from the Arch of Constantine, showing the Rostra Augusti in the early fourth century* A.D. *The seated statue on the right is probably to be identified as a representation of Hadrian.*

of the early Forum the political center of the Comitium, Curia, and Rostra developed;[18] the southeastern corner, at the base of the Palatine, was associated with some of the most ancient religious traditions of Rome, including the Regia and the Temple of Vesta.[19] In time, the central area, kept free of large buildings, became dotted with small shrines and statues;[20] other temples, such as that of Concord, rose on the edges, and tabernae lined parts of the longer north and south sides. During the second century B.C. the Basilicae Porcia, Fulvia/Aemilia, Sempronia, and Opimia supplanted the tabernae and, together with the Fornix Fabianus, helped to frame the central area. Yet costly materials were conspicuously absent from the republican Forum, and the venerable antiquity of some of the shrines was felt to be underscored by

[18] E. Sjöqvist, "Pnyx and Comitium," in *Studies Presented to D. M. Robinson* 1, ed. by G. E. Mylonas (St. Louis 1951) 400–11; F. Coarelli, "Il comizio dalle origini alla fine della Repubblica. Cronologia e topografia," *PdP* 32 (1977) 166–238; idem, *ForArc* 119–60; and C. Krause, "Zur baulichen Gestalt des republikanischen Comitiums," *RömMitt* 83 (1976) 31–69.

[19] F. E. Brown, "The Regia," *MAAR* 12 (1935) 67–88; idem, "La protostoria della Regia," *RendPontAcc* 47 (1974–75) [1976] 15–36;

Coarelli, *ForArc* 56–79. The Forum proper originally extended to the Regia, for this was regarded as being "on the edges of the Forum" (Serv. *ad Aen.* 8.363), and the Temple of the Deified Julius was regarded as being within the Forum (Pliny *HN* 2.93–94). Coarelli, *ForArc* 11–118, examines the pre-Neronian Sacra Via and adjacent shrines and monuments, stressing the sanctity of the Velia.

[20] Cf. L. Richardson, Jr., "The Curia Julia and the Janus Geminus," *RömMitt* 85 (1978) 361, for statues in the Comitium.

their simple construction.[21] This urban center, though the hub of a great and growing empire, was unimpressive in its buildings and simple in its layout, particularly when compared to the great Hellenistic centers of the East.

The Forum Romanum was first systematically replanned and organized by Caesar and Augustus, at which time it lost its unsophisticated, distinctively Roman character and some of the earlier buildings disappeared. The Caesarean/Augustan Forum was more orderly and far more impressive visually than the republican one: marble buildings both beautiful and useful now enclosed a well-defined space.[22] Zanker demonstrates in his investigation of the Caesarean/Augustan Forum that by Augustus' death the political center of the republic had become essentially a showcase for the princeps and his family, proof that the new state rested on the imperial house just as firmly as on the *mos maiorum* and the republic.[23] The Forum was now bounded, proceeding clockwise from the north, by the Curia Julia, leading to Caesar's new Forum;[24] Basilica Aemilia (or Paulli)[25] and Porticus Gaii et Lucii, also known as the Porticus Julia;[26] the Temple of the Deified Julius, with its new rostra;[27]

[21] Russell, "Republican Forums" 330–31, remarks on the discordant elements of the late republican Forum, suggesting that traditional notions of sacrosanctity hindered architectural change.

[22] Russell, "Republican Forums" 330–31, dismisses the Caesarean/Augustan reorganization as an "unsatisfactory attempt . . . to integrate the Forum," yet of the work of the two leaders he cites only the new Rostra and the Temple of the Deified Julius. Much of our knowledge of the imperial Forum's edges comes from their representation on the Anaglypha Traiani/Hadriani, most recently analyzed for this purpose by Torelli, *Roman Historical Reliefs* 92–106. For the Anaglypha, see Chapter 7, the section "Anaglypha Traiani/Hadriani."

[23] The systemization was completed by Claudii as well; Tiberius was responsible for restoring both the Temple of Castor (in A.D. 6), and that of Concord (in A.D. 10) (cf. Brilliant's review of Zanker's *Forum Romanum* [above, n. 2], 524).

[24] Richardson, "Curia Julia," esp. 362–65; F. Zevi, "Il Calcidico della *Curia Iulia*," *RendLinc*, ser. 8, 26 (1971) [1972] 237–51;

T. Hastrup, "Forum Iulium as a Manifestation of Power," *AnalDan* 2 (1962) 45–61. For a general history of the site and its excavations: A. Bartoli, *Curia Senatus: lo scavo e il restauro* (Rome 1963).

[25] Financed by Caesar; Zanker, *Forum Romanum* 23, points out that Caesar's money and influence engaged others such as L. Aemilius Paullus in his undertakings.

[26] The location of this monument is disputed. Torelli, *Roman Historical Reliefs* 92–94, holds the unusual view that this structure, a porticus both Suetonius and Dio say was dedicated to the memory of Augustus' adoptive sons in A.D. 12 (*Aug.* 29.4; Cass. Dio 56.27.5), formed the entire southern facade of the Basilica Aemilia.

[27] Torelli, *Roman Historical Reliefs* 97–98, rejects without much evidence the common opinion that the new rostra formed the front wall of the first story of the podium of the Temple of the Deified Julius; he suggests instead that the rostra be identified with a long rectangular structure in tufa and travertine (originally revetted in marble) in front of the facade of the Temple.

the Arch of Augustus; Temple of Castor; Basilica Julia; Temple of Saturn;[28] Rostra Augusti; and Temple of Concord.

The area so bounded was less than the space of the old Forum Romanum.[29] This was particularly true in the southeast, where the new Temple of the Deified Julius, the Porticus Gaii et Lucii, and the Arch of Augustus effectively cut off the long gentle slope up to the Velia. The buildings and shrines along the Sacra Via on the lower Velia, although never technically within the Forum, had previously functioned as extensions of the Roman Forum.[30] Yet despite its new visual separation from the Forum, this area, sometimes called the Forum Adiectum, also benefited from the Augustan building program. Augustus restored the Regia and the Temples of the Lares and of the Penates (RG 19.5–7). The Regia, supposed to have been originally the house of Numa Pompilius, was hallowed by tradition, and the cults of the Lares and of the Penates were said to have been brought to Italy by Aeneas; the Temple of the Penates was thought to stand where the house of Tullus Hostilius had stood, and the Temple of the Lares, where the house of Ancus Marcius had been. Augustus' restoration of these emphasized the renewal of Rome's religious traditions under him.[31] Hadrian was to renew these associations again, but in his restoration Rome's traditions were to overshadow those of the Julio-Claudian dynasty.

The work of the later Julio-Claudians on the edges of the Forum continued Caesar's and Augustus' glorification of the family. Although no remains are now extant, Tiberius' arch in the Forum's northwest corner, built to honor Germanicus' German triumph of A.D. 14, balanced the Arch of Au-

---

[28] For the history and layout of the Templum Saturni, see L. Richardson, Jr., "The Approach to the Temple of Saturn," AJA 84 (1980) 51–62. M. Corbier, L'"aerarium Saturni" et l'"aerarium militare," Administration et prosopographie sénatoriale (Rome 1974) 666–67, 709, makes the interesting suggestion that soon after the establishment of the aerarium militare in A.D. 6, the new treasury was housed in the Temple of Concord, near the Temple of Saturn on the slopes of the Capitoline.

[29] Castagnoli, TRA 81; De Ruggiero, Foro Romano 29.        [30] Castagnoli, TRA 88.

[31] See, esp., Lugli, MonMin 165–92; Castagnoli, TRA 73–74; and Platner-Ashby, s.v. Sacra Via, 456–59. For the identification of the Temple of the Penates, see F. Castagnoli,

"Il tempio dei Penati e la Velia," RivFil 74 (1946) 157–65 (but see also A. Degrassi, "Frammenti inediti di calendario romano," Athenaeum 25 [1947] 134–38). These edifices were subsequently built over by various monuments, conspicuously the fourth century "Tempio di Romolo" and the Basilica of Maxentius (Constantine). Coarelli, Roma (1980) 87–90, and ForArc 11–33, points out that the term "Forum Adiectum" is modern; he also identifies the fourth-century "Temple of Romulus" as the Temple of Jupiter Stator. For the extant building, whose original attribution cannot be determined with certainty, see Il "Tempio di Romolo" al Foro Romano, Quaderni dell'istituto di storia dell'architettura, ser. 26, 157–62 (Rome 1981).

gustus in the south corner.[32] The Templum Novum divi Augusti, a still unlocated building begun by Tiberius and finished by Caligula, seems to have
risen in the Velabrum above and behind the Basilica Julia.[33] Caligula also
modified the Temple of Castor, rebuilt by his adoptive father and predecessor
in A.D. 6, to serve as a vestibule to his own residence (Suet. *Calig.* 22.2).[34] Yet
it seems to have been Nero, and not Tiberius or Caligula, who consolidated
the imperial residence or residences on the Palatine into that now called the
Domus Tiberiana, and extended it from the top of the Palatine to the line of
the Clivus Victoriae south of the Via Nova.[35]

Literary sources give Nero credit for building on the Velia the Domus
Transitoria, and then, after the fire of 64, the Vestibule of the Domus Aurea
(Suet. *Nero* 31). This second construction entailed a complete reconstruction
of everything on the Velia, and the reorganization of the Sacra Via.[36] The long

[32] D. Timpe, *Der Triumph des Germanicus.*
*Untersuchungen zu den Feldzügen der Jahre 14–*
*16 n. Chr. in Germanien* (Bonn 1968) 49–58,
discusses the historical significance of this
arch, which was voted for Germanicus in
A.D. 15 though dedicated the following year.
With new archaeological evidence, Coarelli,
*ForArc* 54–55, places the arch across the Vicus
Jugarius between the Temple of Saturn and
the Basilica Julia; cf. Brilliant's review of
Zanker's *Forum Romanum* (above, n. 2), 523–
25. Another arch may have been erected in
honor of the younger Drusus after his death
in A.D. 23 (Tac. *Ann.* 4.9.2, cf. *Ann.* 2.83.2);
if so, it may have stood at the north end of the
Augustan rostra, to balance the Arch of Tiberius at the south end (Platner-Ashby, s.v.
Arcus Drusi, 39).

[33] Torelli, *Roman Historical Reliefs* 73–74
(referring to Platner-Ashby, s.v. Augustus,
Divus, Templum, 62–65, although noting
the earlier conflation of the literary evidence
for the two temples of the Deified Augustus);
G. Lugli, "Aedes Caesarum in Palatio e Templum Novum divi Augusti," *BullComm* 69
(1941) 29–37.

[34] Caligula's transformation of the Temple
of Castor was designed to encourage imperial
worship (B. Tamm, "Ist der Castortempel
das *vestibulum* zu dem Palast des Caligula

gewesen?" *Eranos* 62 [1964] 146–69), and perhaps to show disrespect for his adoptive father who had recently restored the Temple.
For similar disrespectful acts of Caligula, see
E. Iversen, in *JEA* 51 (1965) 149–54.

[35] Tamm, *Palatium* 64–65, corrects the earlier conception that the remains of the extended palace are Tiberian; her thesis, based
partly on Jos. *AJ* 19.1.117, was tentatively accepted by Castrén and Lilius, *Domus Tiberiana*
20–21, who called for more archaeological
evidence. C. Krause, in *Domus Tiberiana.*
*Nuove ricerche—studi di restauro* (Zurich 1985)
73–77, suggests on the basis of brick stamps
that the first phase dates to the late Neronian
period. This book is hereafter referred to as
*Domus T.*

[36] E. B. van Deman's articles on the Sacra
Via ("The Neronian Sacra Via," *AJA* 27
[1923] 383–424; "The Sacra Via of Nero,"
*MAAR* 5 [1925] 115–26) attributed to Nero
most of the work along the Sacra Via, but it
should be ascribed to the Flavians (cf. F. Castagnoli, "Note sulla topografia del Palatino e
del Foro Romano," *ArchCl* 16 [1964] 195–99;
Coarelli, *ForArc* 37–49 and his fig. 12; and nn.
45 and 75 below). The Via Nova, which van
Deman also attributes to Nero, must be dated
earlier, to judge from the remains of late republican construction south and parallel to it

portico of the Domus Aurea must have loomed above the southeastern end of the Forum. Its great length along the Velia would have counteracted the relative distance from the Forum, and the impression made by it and by Caligula's nearer construction on the people in the Forum is reflected in Pliny's remark: *bis vidimus urbem totam cingi domibus principum Gai et Neronis* (twice we have seen the entire city encircled by the homes of the principes Gaius [Caligula] and Nero: *HN* 36.111).[37]

Although these constructions are generally dismissed as simply megalomanic, they were built to take advantage of the important relationship between the Forum and the higher slopes around it. In the late republic, the Tabularium had been erected on the slopes of the Capitoline as a monumental backdrop to the Forum and as the visible expression of Sullan and senatorial supremacy.[38] Individual political figures like Livius Drusus and Cicero had vied for the choice real estate on the Palatine overlooking the Forum, which would symbolize their preeminence in Roman life. Most such houses seem to have been on the lower northeast slopes of the Palatine, southeast of the Atrium Vestae.[39] The Domus Tiberiana, with a monumental facade above the Forum that was 400 Roman feet long (118.28 meters), was oriented northeast-southwest, different from most of the buildings in the Forum.[40] This and its elevation must have made it dominate everything below, just as the Co-

(pointed out to me by Dr. Krause). See MacDonald, *ARE* 20–46; and J. B. Ward-Perkins, *Roman Imperial Architecture* (Harmondsworth 1981) 57–59 (hereafter Ward-Perkins, *RIA*), for Nero's palaces. Both consider the four-armed structure in the platform of the Temple of Venus and Roma to be part of the Domus Transitoria (see n. 79 below). Tamm, *Palatium* 72–75, 102–108, discusses particularly well the effects of Nero's vestibule, but for a revisionist view, see M. T. Griffin, *Nero. The End of a Dynasty* (New Haven and London 1984) 132–42. In this context one would like to know the exact location on the Sacra Via of Nero's father's home, the Domus Domitiana, attested by the acts of the Arval Brethren (Henzen, *AFA* 61, 82; *CIL* 6.32352, 2041.25, 2042 d).

[37] Ward-Perkins, *RIA* 48, considers this to refer to urban horti and suburban villas.

[38] For the architecture of the Tabularium,

see, e.g., G. Charles-Picard, *Rome et les villes d'Italie des Gracques à la morte d'Auguste* (Paris 1978) 95–96. The building is currently under restoration (A. M. Sommella, "L'esplorazione archeologica per il restauro del Tabularium," *QuadAEI* 8 [1984] 159–64). See, too, E. B. van Deman, "The Sullan Forum," *JRS* 12 (1922) 9–10.

[39] Coarelli, *ForArc* 25, announces a forthcoming publication on the subject; for the moment, K. Ziegler, "Palatium," *RE* 18.3 (1949) 41–51, provides a convenient list of individuals known to have owned houses on the Palatine during the republic. The topography of the Palatine in that period is much debated: Tamm, *Palatium* 28–43; Castrén and Lilius, *Domus Tiberiana* 17–18.

[40] I am indebted to Dr. Krause for discussion in 1984 of this information; see his *Domus T.*

lossus of Nero in the Vestibule of the Domus Aurea dwarfed the buildings on the Velia and at that end of the Forum.

The Flavian dynasty similarly left its imprint on the Forum by works strategically and ingeniously set along its edges, and Domitian even raised a monument within the central space, a colossal equestrian statue of himself.[41] According to B. Tamm, Vespasian transformed the ostentatious Vestibule of the Domus Aurea by stripping it of the treasure with which Nero had adorned it.[42] He also replaced Nero's head on the Colossus with that of Titus (Dio Cass. 65.15.1),[43] but his greatest monument, the Templum Pacis, was distinct from and turned its back to the Forum.[44] A great porticus bounded by the Sacra Via, the ridge of the Velia, the Via Nova, and the Atrium of the Vestals, and a balancing porticus north of the Sacra Via, of which the scant remains have mostly disappeared under the enormous Basilica of Maxentius (Constantine), have both been dated to the Flavian period; these apparently utilitarian buildings helped restore to public use land Nero had taken for the Domus Aurea.[45]

Later Flavian work was more ostentatious. On the slopes of the Capitoline overlooking the Forum and below the Temple of Jupiter Optimus Maximus, restored in the 70s and again in the 80s, Titus began the Temple of the

[41] F. Castagnoli, "Note numismatiche," *ArchCl* 5 (1953) 107–109; Zanker, *Forum Romanum* 27; and R. Brilliant, *Gesture and Rank in Roman Art: The Use of Gestures to Denote Status in Roman Sculpture and Coinage* (New Haven, Conn. 1963) 96–97. C. F. Giuliani and P. Verduchi, *Foro Romano. L'area centrale* (Florence 1980) 35–49, on good archaeological grounds locate the equestrian statue just north of the area to which it is traditionally assigned. Domitian rebuilt the Curia Julia in A.D. 89 ( Jerome, *Chron.* p. 191 H.), and Richardson, "Curia Julia" 365–68, suggests that at that time he moved the building southeast. Dr. Steinby, currently excavating near the Lacus Juturnae, has generously informed me of the vast extent of Domitianic work there and in the Atrium Vestae.

[42] Tamm, *Palatium* 76–77, 94, 105–106, who also discusses the use of the residence by Galba, Otho, Vitellius, and the Flavians. I find improbable Coarelli's suggestion that Vespasian moved the Colossus (*ForArc* 42).

[43] The traditional sanctity of the Velia must

have induced Vespasian to allow the statue to stand. The substitution of Titus' image for that of Nero has been doubted: Gagé, "Colosse et fortune de Rome" 110. P. Howell, "The Colossus of Nero," *Athenaeum* 46 (1968) 292–99, has argued unconvincingly that Nero never actually put up the Colossus, which he holds was first erected in the Flavian period with the iconography of the Sun.

[44] Coarelli, *ForArc* 38–49, goes far to solve the difficulties surrounding our understanding of the ancient topography between this structure and the Forum, where the "Temple of Romulus" now stands (cf. F. Castagnoli and L. Cozza, "L'angolo meridionale del Foro della Pace," *BullComm* 76 [1956–58] {1959} 119–42; and Castagnoli, "Velia" 157–65).

[45] For example, Castagnoli, "Note sulla topografia" 195–99. S. Panciera, "Tra epigrafia e topografia," *ArchCl* 22 (1970) 135–38, concludes from epigraphical evidence that neither of these structures can be the Porticus Margaritaria, as has often been presumed.

Deified Vespasian. After Titus' death, Domitian finished the temple, dedicating it to both his father and brother (who was now deified). The location of this Temple, crowded between the Tabularium and Temple of Saturn, seems to have been chosen for its position on the slopes of the hill just below the Capitoline temple. Across the Forum at Summa Sacra Via, Domitian raised the Arch of Titus in a location well chosen for its visual and symbolic effects.[46]

Domitian drastically changed the imperial palaces on the Palatine. His great Domus August(i)ana was out of sight of the Forum, over toward the Circus Maximus, but he altered the Julio-Claudian facade of the Domus Tiberiana by bringing the eastern part of it down to the Clivus Victoriae, adding arcades to the central part, and remodeling the western part.[47] He restored the republican ramp behind the area of the Lacus Juturnae that connected the Atrium Vestae with the Palatine.[48] And at the end of his reign he began work on a structure behind the Temple of Castor that has sometimes been erroneously identified as the Temple of the Deified Augustus, but is now known as the "Vestibule" of Domitian, although its original function is still uncertain. This building, at least three high stories tall, towered over the Forum; it was later renovated by Hadrian.[49]

Indeed, Hadrian was the next princeps to alter the appearance of the Forum significantly, for Domitian's immediate successors did little work here. The Equus Domitiani was pulled down, though its base may have been used for more modest statuary in honor of Trajan.[50] Other small statues and

[46] For the Temple of the Deified Vespasian and Titus, see Leon, *Bauornamentik* 91–92; Nash, s.v. Vespasianus, Divus, Templum, II.501–504; Platner-Ashby, s.v. Divus Vespasianus, Templum, 556. For a reconstruction of the Temple of Jupiter Optimus Maximus, see A. M. Colini, "Il Campidoglio nell'antichità," *Capitolium* 40.4 (1965) 181–82; and for the Arch of Titus, see the recent work of M. Pfanner, *Der Titusbogen* (Mainz am Rhein 1983). By rehabilitating the triumphal route curtailed by Nero's residences, Domitian proclaimed his military aspirations. The symbolic balance of the Arch of Titus and the Temple of the Deified Vespasian and Titus is enhanced by the location of both on the triumphal route, for which see F. Coarelli, "La Porta Trionfale e la Via dei Trionfi," *DialArch* 2 (1968) 55–103.

[47] See Krause, *Domus T*.

[48] Dr. Steinby, who generously showed me the excavations in this area, has underlined Domitian's interest in the cult of Vesta. For the ramp, see also Coarelli, *ForArc* 237, 248.

[49] See n. 2 above. This structure may be commemorated in an issue of 96/97: E. Nash and H. A. Cahn, "Der Wohnpalast der Caesaren auf dem Palatin," *AntK* 1 (1958) 24–28, repeated in Nash's "Suggerimenti intorno ad alcuni problemi topografici del Foro e del Palatino," *ArchCl* 11 (1959) 234–36; see Nash, s.v. Domus Tiberiana, 1.371, fig. 452. Contra, Tamm, *Palatium* 81–82; and Giuliani, "Nuova lettura," 91–106, who holds that the coin represents the facade of the Domus Flavia.

[50] The pedestal of the statue may have been

sculptures were erected in the Forum itself, including the so-called Anaglypha Traiani/Hadriani (discussed in Chapter 7), depicting the Forum as the setting for gestures of imperial liberality such as the burning of public records of
debt. Although Trajan restored the Atrium Vestae, added tabernae in the area
of the Lacus Juturnae, and may have completed Domitian's remodeling of the
middle section of the Domus Tiberiana over the Clivus Victoriae,[51] he did not
erect any new buildings in or around the Forum itself.

At Hadrian's accession, therefore, the Forum was still dominated by the
Julio-Claudian and Flavian buildings along its edges. The visual boundary of
the Forum beyond the Basilica Julia was presumably provided by the still unlocated Templum Novum divi Augusti on the low saddle of the Velabrum,
and next to it, on the much steeper northwest slopes of Palatine, towered the
three-story "Vestibule" of Domitian's palace. Slightly southeast of this and
farther back from the Forum, along the Clivus Victoriae, rose the newly remodeled facade of the Domus Tiberiana. To the southeast the effective visual
limit of the Forum was less uniform, apparently consisting of the now unpre-
tentious facade of the Domus Aurea, the Colossus (transformed into a statue
of Titus), and the Arch of Titus rising above the Julio-Claudian boundary of
the Temple of the Deified Julius, the Arch of Augustus, and the Porticus Gaii
et Lucii.

These two sides of the Forum, southeast and southwest, are those to be
considered in Hadrian's constructions, begun ca. 125–130, which worked to
revive the concept of the Roman Forum as a great public space rather than a
Julio-Claudian confection and memorial. On the southwest two separate but
adjacent structures must be considered: the "Vestibule" of Domitian, which
seems to have undergone a Hadrianic remodeling, and the new multistoried
addition to the Domus Tiberiana proper, which extended the palace north
across the Clivus Victoriae to the line of the Via Nova (*see Ill. 22*).

The Domitianic "Vestibule" dates to the last decade of Domitian's reign,

---

transformed into the tribunal represented on
the Anaglypha: Blake/Bishop, 11, with earlier bibliography, including Lugli, *MonMin*
107–109; and Zanker, *Forum Romanum* 27.
Torelli, *Roman Historical Reliefs* 90, suggests
that Trajan reused the area of the base for a
statuary group depicted on the Anaglypha
and on Trajanic bronze coins. For other theories, see Giuliani and Verduchi, *Foro* 40.

[51] E. B. van Deman, *The Atrium Vestae*
(Washington, D.C. 1909) 29–34, originally
attributed the Trajanic phase of the Atrium to

Hadrian, to be refuted by Bloch's investigation of the brick stamps (*Bolli* 67–85; see
idem, "Serapeum" 225; and Blake/Bishop,
36–37, 40–41). This is discussed in Chapter 7.
Dr. Steinby has kindly discussed with me
Trajan's work in the vicinity of the Fons Juturnae. For the Domitianic structures midway along the Clivus Victoriae, see Lugli,
*Centro* 482; Blake/Bishop, 39; and Tamm,
*Palatium* 77–78. I am indebted to Dr. Krause
for the new information.

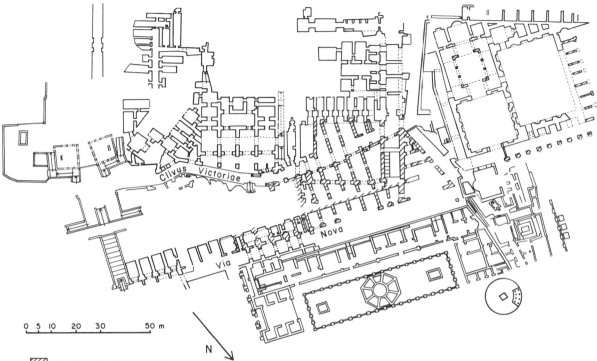

Clivus Victoriae

Via Nova

0 5 10 20 30   50 m

N

▨ Hadrianic Construction

22. *Northeast slope of the Palatine and southwest area of the Forum Romanum, as revealed by recent excavations and investigations. Hadrianic additions are indicated by hatching. Hadrianic substructures at the Clivus Victoriae and Hadrianic tabernae at the Via Nova were later reinforced (during the Severan period?).*

to judge from brick stamps found in both the superstructure and the extensive drains below it.[52] The pentagonal building on the Velabrum was bounded on the west by the Vicus Tuscus, on the north by the Via Nova, on the east by the ramp (restored by Domitian) running from the Aedicula of Juturna to the northwest angle of the Clivus Victoriae on the Palatine and also by the Clivus itself, and on the south by the Horrea Agrippiana.[53] In Hadrian's time the "Vestibule" had three main divisions, as it had earlier under Domitian; a large hall, 32.50 by 23.50 meters, on the west behind the Temple of Castor, whose east, north, and south walls are still preserved up to 28 meters; a central,

[52] Bloch, *Bolli* 33–36; above, n. 6. Although Tamm, *Palatium* 77–78, hypothesizes that the structure replaced a Neronian one destroyed by fire, the evidence shows no fire in the area (see P. Werner, *De incendiis urbis Romae aetate imperatorum* [Leipzig 1906] 23, 31–33).

[53] The following description is based on that of Delbrück, "Südostbau" 8–33, 186–87, on which subsequent discussions of the building depend, and on personal observation of the new excavations, kindly shown and explained to me by Dr. Coletti.

lower, series of rooms with a strong central axis, 19.20 by 55 meters, which
was transformed into S. Maria Antiqua in the sixth century; and farthest east,
a narrow building, 8 by 45 meters wide, now housing four sets of ramps that
rise 20 meters. A porticus ran along four-fifths of the northern side, and apparently a similar porticus faced west (*see Ill. 23*). Although fragment 75a (pl.
21) of the *Forma Urbis* shows part of the area of the north porticus, it shows
none of the Domitianic complex and may well be from a Vespasianic version
of the marble plan.[54]

Jutting out toward the Forum from the lower slopes of the Palatine, the

[54] See Coarelli, *ForArc* 252–54, and above,   of the fragment, see Rodriguez-Almeida,
Introduction, n. 18. For a detailed description   *FUM* 96–98.

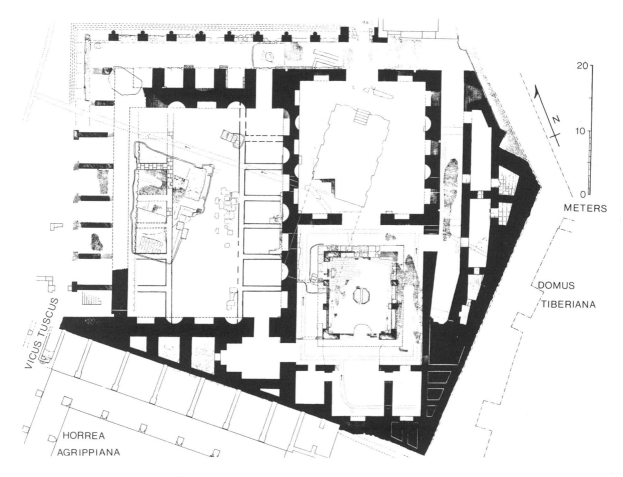

23. *"Vestibule" of Domitian, as excavated (after R. Delbrück, but incorporating later
findings).*

"Vestibule" appears physically independent of the imperial palace higher up, although the ramp building connects it to the palace. Most scholars now concur with Delbrück's rejection in 1921 of this building's earlier identification as the Templum divi Augusti, although great uncertainty surrounds its original plan and purpose and the distinction of its Domitianic phase or phases from the Hadrianic one.

The excavations in this building now being conducted by the British School in Rome and the Soprintendenza alle Antichità di Roma promise to clarify at least some of the puzzling history of this area. Here we shall consider only the Domitianic and Hadrianic periods and the main characteristics of the building.[55] The "Vestibule" seems to have undergone a radical change of plan soon after construction began in the second half of Domitian's reign. In the westernmost room an original series of large niches alternately curved and rectangular, 3 meters above the floor on the three remaining walls, and the size of the room itself imply a ceremonial function for it. And the central arched niche of the east wall suggests a monumental axial entrance across from it in the west wall of the room, which no longer survives. Yet the north entrance, that from the Via Nova, is not axially located, but at the northeast corner of the room, and the complete lack on the walls of evidence of revetment, frescoes, or architectural embellishment indicates strongly that the room never served a ceremonial purpose.[56] It looks as though the series of short perpendicular walls, now demolished, that abutted the long east and west sides to make fourteen to sixteen small rooms per story were added to the original structure while it was still under construction. The rooms thus formed (approximately 4.50 by 3.90 meters) faced onto a central courtyard paved with great travertine blocks, and the floors of the rooms themselves, paved with *opus spicatum* (brick laid in a herringbone pattern), were raised by a hypocaust system. The current working hypothesis is that this part of the "Vestibule" functioned as a horreum.

The destruction of most of the walls on the west side leaves the entrance from this direction uncertain.[57] A small door leads through the south wall of

[55] The pre-Domitianic history of the site is discussed by van Deman, "Caligula" 393–96, though her reconstruction has since been superseded: Krause, *Domus T.* 73–76. See, too, Delbrück, "Südostbau," 28–31. For the later reuse of the building, Delbrück, 27, and R. Krautheimer, W. Fränkl, and S. Corbett, *Corpus Basilicarum Christianarum Romae. The Early Christian Basilicas of Rome (IV–XI Centuries)* II.3 (Vatican City 1962) 251–70.

[56] The current investigations have disproved Delbrück's theory of pilasters or applied columns for the outermost walls (and cf. Tamm, *Palatium* 80–82).

[57] Delbrück, "Südostbau" 187, 15, notes marble paving in the area of the exterior taberna opposite the central niche of the eastern wall.

the "Vestibule" to a room that also connects east to the quadriporticus of the
central suite of rooms. Similar doorways below the rectangular niches flanking the larger central one in the eastern wall cut through to the courtyard and
quadriporticus of the central suite of rooms. The relative lightness of the main
walls of this western division of the "Vestibule" shows that it was not
vaulted.[58]

The central suite also underwent transformation early.[59] The northernmost room opens to the colonnade on the exterior by a central door 6.20 meters wide, the beginning of a central axis for the rooms opening south. In this
courtyard again a scheme of alternating rectangular and bowed niches deco-
rates the long walls, and rectangular niches flank the north and south doorways.[60] In the east wall a door opens to the ramp complex. Through a side
door in the south wall one entered to an open area surrounded by a quadriporticus; this space was slightly longer than the courtyard to its north (19.20
by 21.30 meters; cf. 19.20 by 20.35). The four porticoes of the quadriporticus
are barrel-vaulted, and surround an impluvium with remains of a fountain;
their floors were paved in opus spicatum. Doors at the south end of the east
and west walls connected the quadriporticus to the complexes to either side.

The door in the south wall from the quadriporticus area to the last main
axial element, the 7-meter deep final room, often termed the "tablinum," was
enlarged to its present width of 6 meters before its marble revetment was applied to the quadriporticus' walls.[61] The tablinum and the two small rooms
that flank it were also revetted with marble to a height of 1.31 meters, above
which the walls and the vaulting were frescoed. In the back room of the tablinum was an axial rectangular niche.[62]

The ramp division of the "Vestibule" farthest east and built into the slope
of the Palatine now rises in four sloping corridors with intermittent landings
about 3.5 meters wide within a structure whose maximum thickness and
length are 8 and 45 meters, respectively. A fifth stage, to complete the ascent

[58] Giuliani, "Nuova lettura" 94–97, has
corrected Delbrück's original hypothesis, endorsed by Lugli, "Aedes Caesarum" 30–31.

[59] The description found in Krautheimer,
Corpus Basilicarum II.3, 254–56, here supple-
ments that of Delbrück. See also A. Bongiorno, "Rilievo planimetrico dell'antico
edificio di S. Maria Antiqua," QuadIstTopAnt
5 (1968) 89–90.

[60] Delbrück, "Südostbau" 13, holds that
the courtyard was vaulted; contra, Kraut-

heimer, Corpus Basilicarum II.3, 254–56.

[61] Krautheimer, Corpus Basilicarum II.3, 254
n. 5.

[62] Krautheimer, Corpus Basilicarum II.3,
255, notes that the walls separating the tablinum from its two flanking rooms were broken through while still under construction,
and then repaired before the marble revetment was installed. There was frescoeing in
red and white above the marble revetment.

from the Forum to the imperial residences 30 meters above, can be assumed with reasonable certainty. There were occasional steps along the ascent; otherwise the ramps were paved in opus spicatum. Behind a small flight of steps on the second landing was a latrine, accessible from both the ramp and the quadriporticus.

In addition to the doorways connecting the lowest ramp and the central suite of rooms, a small hall led back from the colonnade on the exterior around the northeastern corner of the central section of the "Vestibule" to the foot of the ramp. This hall was also paved with opus spicatum.

The northern porticus on the exterior of the "Vestibule" is better preserved than the western one. The northern porticus was about 10.50 meters high and just over 4 meters wide, raised on Luna marble steps. Parts of ten of the original eleven brick-faced pillars (1.50 meters wide, 1.10 meters deep) are still in place, 3 meters from one another; these were once revetted with marble. Again, opus spicatum paves the porticus. Finally, although the western porticus is no longer extant, in Hadrian's day it was divided into tabernae by cross walls running from the western wall to the pillars.

None of this work has been dated very reliably. Relying primarily on brick stamps and construction technique, Delbrück assigned to two post-Domitianic periods—one with a terminus post quem of 123, the other slightly before—the short east-west walls in the western division, which once made three barrel-vaulted stories 7, 14, and 21 meters high; the transformation of the western porticus into a series of tabernae; the opus spicatum in the western room and quadriporticus; some vaulting work at the entrance and the barrel vaulting on piers of the quadriporticus in the central suite of rooms; the hypocaust system; the latrine in the ramp area, together with some alterations in the communications between the ramp building and the adjacent series of rooms; and the marble veneer and frescoeing. Bloch redated to Domitian the floor of the western room and, more tentatively, the northern porticus. No Trajanic brick stamps have been recorded,[63] but none of the brick stamps so far used for dating was found in situ. Corroboration of these chronologies must await the results of the current excavation.

Furthermore, only further excavation can clarify the purpose of the building. The combination of monumental design and opulent decor with utilitarian opus spicatum and unadorned walls is very odd. Earlier identifications of

[63] Delbrück, "Südostbau" 23–27, 186–87; cf. Bloch, Bolli 34–35. Van Deman, "Caligula" 397, attributes the north and west porticoes to Hadrian. Delbrück well discusses the ambiguous archaeological evidence on pp. 18–19.

the building as a monumental vestibule, a guardhouse, or Hadrian's Athenaeum[64] cannot stand.

The numerous Hadrianic brick stamps found in the area and the proximity of Hadrianic work just east of the "Vestibule" make it tempting to assign to Hadrian redesigning and completion of the "Vestibule." It was a large structure, and even now its lofty east and north walls are still imposing. If it can be proved that Hadrian was responsible for extensive changes in the construction, we must consider this in conjunction with the other work around the Forum that is more certainly his.

Domitian had extended the northeastern front of the Domus Tiberiana to the Clivus Victoriae, although Trajan may have finished the work. Hadrian brought the Domus Tiberiana all the way to the very edge of the Forum by multistoried, stepped tabernae along the Via Nova that spanned the western stretch of the Clivus Victoriae. Since members of the Swiss School in Rome and the Soprintendenza di Roma have now published the first thorough investigation of these structures, only a brief description of them can be made here.[65] In the middle of Hadrian's rule, a series of tabernae was added south of and perpendicular to the Via Nova;[66] these rose to a probable height of four stories for almost the whole length of the Atrium Vestae (*see Ill. 22*). At their west end they were carried over the Clivus Victoriae on high vaults two stories tall (some of *opus mixtum*, alternating brick-faced and reticulate-faced construction), on which were built brick-faced concrete structures (including an access ramp) in a rectangular block about 150 meters wide on the same northeast-southwest axis as the original Domus Tiberiana. This upper superstructure seems to have supported a garden. The facade of the palace's substructure in this sector, however, with its north northeast–south southwest orientation that followed the alignment of the Via Nova,[67] rose almost to the top edge of the superstructure and thus concealed the change made to the older alignment. Farther east, south of the western part of the Atrium Vestae,

[64] Delbrück concluded that Domitian's vestibule was transformed by Hadrian into a guard house ("Südostbau" 22, 26), and many scholars are in agreement; see, e.g., Tamm, *Palatium* 80–83. The Athenaeum is suggested by Coarelli, *Roma* (1980) 74. Other earlier theories are listed by Krause, *Domus T.* 73–75. We may presume that what was stored here was destined for the imperial residence.

[65] See n. 35 above; the following description is based primarily on information sup-plied me by Dr. Krause during two visits on 22 and 24 October 1984. See his *Domus T.*, esp. 126–27.

[66] E. Monaco, "Laterizi bollati dalla *Domus Tiberiana*," *RendPontAcc* 48 (1975–76)[1977] 309–13; Krause, *Domus T.* 24, 126–27; Lugli, *Centro* 480–86; Blake/Bishop, 61; Castrén and Lilius, "*Domus Tiberiana* 87; and see Coarelli, *Roma* (1980) 136.

[67] Krause, *Domus T.* 24. Cf. van Deman, "Caligula" 371; Tamm, *Palatium* 70.

the area between the Clivus Victoriae and the Via Nova was deeper, and the four levels of the new construction seem never to have been completed. The two stories of finished tabernae along the southeastern stretch of the Via Nova have not yet been properly excavated, but are almost certainly Hadrianic.[68]

In sum, the Hadrianic construction filled the 20-meter difference in height between the Via Nova and the Clivus Victoriae, and in its westernmost part covered the approximately 35-meter drop between the top of the Palatine and the Via Nova. In effect it brought the imperial residence down to the Forum.[69] Although we have no information about the tabernae's external decoration, their basic architectural scheme is utilitarian,[70] and in their repetition they bound together the south side of the Forum. Furthermore, their orientation, which followed that of the Forum's buildings just below them, indicated that the Forum was more important than the imperial house.

At the same time, to the east of the Forum Hadrian erected a building of a still larger size: the Temple of Venus and Roma. According to a strange and improbable story related by Dio Cassius (69.4.4), Hadrian, whose ideas about architecture Apollodorus had made light of during Trajan's reign, later sent the architect his plans for the Temple of Venus and Roma, asking Apollodorus' opinion of them. The architect replied that it ought to have been set high and hollowed out underneath so that the building might be more conspicuous from the Sacra Via and so its substructures might accommodate the machines for the Flavian Amphitheater; furthermore, he said, the cult statues were too tall for the building. Thereupon Hadrian became incensed "because he had fallen into a mistake that could not be righted" and had Apollodorus put to death.[71]

Although the story is well known and often repeated, it is immediately puzzling because the aedes even in ruin does dominate the Sacra Via, and its substructures toward the Colosseum do contain chambers.[72] The Temple

[68] This may have been the site of the Lucus Vestalium. For the tabernae, see also Krause, *Domus T.* 55.

[69] Van Deman, "Caligula" 395, 398; Tamm, *Palatium*, p. 87, fig. 16; Castrén and Lilius, *Domus Tiberiana*, pl. B.

[70] Castrén and Lilius, *Domus Tiberiana* 86–105, nos. 129–327, discuss the graffiti on the innermost western rooms, which suggest that under Trajan the space was used for the fiscus. They also note, on pp. 100–101, that some of the drawings there are of construction work and appropriate tools. Krause

showed me more purely ornamental frescoes in the eastern sector of the tabernae; cf. Lugli, *Centro* 482; and Krause, *Domus T.* 55.

[71] MacDonald, *ARE* 131–37, discusses this anecdote and its historicity.

[72] MacDonald, *ARE* 136, suggests that Hadrian modified his original plans to accord with Apollodorus' criticisms. Gullini, "Adriano" 73–74, also speculates on Apollodorus' criticisms. This account of Apollodorus' death is not trustworthy: see above, Introduction, n. 30. For the chambers, which are post-Hadrianic, see below, n. 108.

stood inside a precinct supported on a large platform extending from the
Summa Sacra Via almost to the Flavian Amphitheater (145 by 100 meters:
about 500 by 300 Roman feet).[73] Dio's anecdote thus refers to the two areas
bridged by the sacred area. This topographical information, however, is incidental to the anecdote, for the main thrust of Apollodorus' criticisms (if
true) was directed against the unusually Greek appearance of the Temple. The
criticism of the statues' size suggests that Hadrian was working with the proportions of classical Greece, where the cult statues were always enormous in
relationship to their cellae. The temple plan also deviated from conventional
Roman temples in being amphiprostyle, facing in both directions within a
peripteral colonnade, and being raised on all four sides on a continuous crepis
of seven steps (including the stylobate) instead of on a podium.[74]

More topographical information about the Temple comes from the reports that it was built over the Vestibule of Nero's Golden House, and that
the Colossus of Nero was moved to accommodate it (*HA, Hadr.* 19.12; cf. Pliny
*NH* 34.45). Nero's rehandling of the Summa Sacra Via and the Velia after the
fire of 64 had changed the course of the republican Sacra Via, and under the
Flavians it seems that its course may have been altered again; most important
for our purposes is that after Nero the branch of the road now called the Clivo
di Venere Felice ran south of a structure cut into the slope of the Velia.[75] The
excavations for the Via dei Fori Imperiali exposed the back of the Neronian
construction, whose south side is about 8 meters outside and parallel to the
western half of the north flank of the Temple of Venus and Roma (*see Ills. 19
and 26*). The Neronian terrace wall seems to have been part of the work for
the Vestibule of the Golden House.[76]

Hadrian extended the platform east toward the Flavian Amphitheater,
first laying down a thick bed of concrete (*opus caementicium*).[77] The few Hadrianic brick stamps that come from the Temple of Venus and Roma are from
drains to the north and west of this platform, and from the southwest side of
the platform; all date to 123, except one from the vicinity of the Arch of Titus
that dates to 134.[78] In addition to the foundations of Nero's Vestibule, the

[73] Barattolo (1978) 399 n. 12; Coarelli,
*Roma* (1980) 95.

[74] Barattolo (1978) 399, also gives further
refinements of the "Greek" plan.

[75] For the complicated modifications of the
Sacra Via, see Coarelli, *ForArc* 42–43.

[76] A. M. Colini, "Considerazioni su la Velia da Nerone in poi," in *Città e architettura*
129–45, with earlier bibiography, including

his "Compitum Acili," *BullComm* 78 (1961–
62) [1964] 148–50. For the topography of the
Golden House in this area, see n. 36 above.

[77] Lugli, *Edilizia* II, pl. C, 2, for the concrete
with aggregate of travertine and lava cae-
menta; Blake/Bishop, 40. The concrete is not
homogeneous: in some places it includes
brick, in others, tufa and harder materials.

[78] Bloch, *Bolli* 250–53.

Hadrianic platform incorporates remains of houses of late republican date and an interesting octagonal room, formed by the intersection of two corridors and associated with Nero's Domus Transitoria.[79] Thus, although the Temple of Venus and Roma made use of an existing artificial platform, it extended the platform to possibly twice its original length. A natural slope from the Arch of Titus to the Flavian Amphitheater makes the top of the platform's eastern edge stand almost 8 meters above the platea between it and the Amphitheater; to the west, where the slope toward the Forum Romanum was gentler, the top of the platform was only 2.50 meters above the paving of the Sacra Via.[80]

The date of the Temple of Venus and Roma is problematic. Bloch emphasizes how little brick stamps contribute to dating the monument; few have been recorded, and most of these come from drains.[81] The earliest stamps, however, provide a terminus post quem of 123, and a likely date of 125–126 for the beginning of construction. These dates can be reconciled with the literary and numismatic evidence, which suggests that the precinct was consecrated in 121, and a date early in the Hadrianic principate for the Temple is implied by the story about Apollodorus.

In the *Deipnosophistae*, Athenaeus remarks on the joyful and crowded celebrations of the Parilia, called "Romaia" after it was made a festival of the Fortuna of the City of Rome when the "wisest ruler," Hadrian, consecrated the Temple to the City (8.361 f).[82] Athenaeus repeats twice in the passage that all who lived or happened to be in Rome took part in the festivities every year. The traditional date of the Parilia was 21 April, and from a series of Hadrianic coins we know the year of the festival's transformation. Aurei and sestertii, with obverses showing a bust of Hadrian, laureate, and the legend IMP CAES HADRIANUS AUG COS III or IMP CAESAR TRAIANUS HADRIANUS AUG P M TR P COS III, have reverses depicting the Genius of the Circus, seated by the triple *metae* (turning posts) of the Circus and holding a wheel, with the legend ANN(IS) DCCCLXXIIII NAT(ALI) URB(IS) P(ARILIBUS) CIR(CENSES) CON(STITUTI).[83] The Varronian date of the coins' legend is A.D. 121.

[79] See, e.g., the original report by M. Barosso, "Le costruzioni sottostanti la Basilica massenziana e Velia," in *Atti del 5° congresso di studi romani*, II (Rome 1940) 58–62, plates XII–XV. See also Crema, 267 and figs. 306, 307; and MacDonald, *ARE* 21–23.

[80] Barattolo (1978) 399, gives these figures as 9 and 2.70 meters, respectively; my figures are based on the earlier ones in V. Reina et al., *Media pars urbis* (Roma 1910) fol. 6.

[81] Bloch, *Bolli* 252–53.

[82] For the interpretation "consecrate" [the ground and foundations] rather than "build": R. Turcan, "La 'Fondation' du Temple de Venus et de Roma," *Latomus* 23 (1964) 44–48.

[83] *BMC, Emp.* III, p. 282, no. 333, pl. 53.5; pp. 422–23, nos. 1242–43: the sestertii carry an additional SC in the exergue of the reverse. See, too, Hill, *D&A* 54; and Strack, *Hadrian* 102–105, who notes other possible completions for P.

In this same year, on the evidence of its obverse legend and the portrait of Hadrian, an issue of aurei showed on its reverse the legend SAEC(ULUM) AUR(EUM) P M TR P COS III and a representation of Aion, the embodiment of the golden age: a youth half draped in an oval frame, the zodiac circle in his right hand and a ball mounted with a phoenix in his left.[84] Since 121 does not co-incide with either cycle of Roman secular games, Gagé, Beaujeu, and others have associated this proclamation of a new golden age with the transforma-tion of the Parilia into the Romaia, the Natalis Urbis Romae, and with the consecration of the Temple of Venus and Roma.[85] This date coincides with Hadrian's restoration of the pomerium, another link with Rome's origins.[86] The brick stamps imply that the actual construction of the Temple was begun only five years after the dedication of the precinct.

This date for the Temple's consecration, however, has been called into question primarily by R. Turcan and M. Grant. Different coins struck during Severus Alexander's seventh year of tribunician power, 10 December 227 to 9 December 228, show Roma Aeterna, a seated statue of Roma, Roma and Romulus, or the emperor sacrificing before the Temple of Venus and Roma. The issues have been thought to mark the hundredth anniversary of the Tem-ple's consecration.[87] But the Temple and Roma Aeterna appear with increas-ing frequency on imperial coinage beginning in the time of Septimius Se-verus,[88] and so the coins of Severus Alexander seem meant to emphasize the primacy of Rome and a return to religious respect for national traditions after the sacrileges of Elagabalus, rather than the anniversary of the Temple's ded-

[84] Strack, *Hadrian* 100–102, pl. 1.78; *BMC, Emp.* III, p. 278, no. 312, pl. 52.10; Beaujeu, 153; Gagé, "Templum urbis" 176–80.

[85] Beaujeu, 131–32; Gagé, *Jeux Séculaires* 94–97. Hadrian's interest in the "true" chro-nology of the secular games may have come only later: cf. Phlegon's *peri makrobion* 37.5.2–4 (of ca. A.D. 137), reproduced in G.B. Pighi, *De ludis saecularibus populi Romani Quiritium, libri sex*, 2nd ed. (Amsterdam 1965) 56–58.

[86] A medallion of 121 that represents the sow and her piglets must be another allusion to Rome's origins: Strack, *Hadrian* 104; and J.M.C. Toynbee, *Roman Medallions* (New York 1944) 143. Strack also dates to 121 the issue of Hadrian as ROMULUS CONDITOR, al-though it is actually much later (cf. *BMC, Emp.* III, p. cxli). The year 121 also marked the fifth anniversary of Hadrian's accession;

for the increasing importance in the second century of such milestones, see J.W.E. Pearce, "The *Vota* Legends on the Roman Coinage," *NC*, ser. 5, 17 (1937) 117; and M. Grant, *Roman Anniversary Issues* (Cambridge 1950) 98–99.

[87] Turcan, "Temple de Venus et de Rome" 43; Grant, *Anniversary* 126–28. Turcan then supposes a double consecration, a consecra-tion (*inauguratio*) of the ground in 121, and the foundation proper in 128; Leon, *Bauornamen-tik* 213 n. 10, seems to accept only the date of 128. See also Toynbee, *Roman Medallions* 103.

[88] The vast majority of the 200 different is-sues showing Venus and Roma were struck from Septimius Severus on; D. F. Brown, "Architectura Numismatica" (Ph.D. diss., New York University 1941) 223–48, 334; Gagé, "Templum urbis" 158–69.

ication.[89] There is no real reason to suppose that the Temple was consecrated in 128; 121 is preferable.

The date of the Temple's completion is also problematic. The chronicles give relatively late dates for it: Cassiodorus writes under the year 135 *Templum Romae et Veneris sub Hadriano in urbe factum* (under Hadrian the Temple of Roma and Venus was made in the city [of Rome]: Mommsen, *Chron. Min.* ii, p. 142), and the same is repeated by Jerome for 131 (Jerome, *Chron.* p. 200 H.). Jerome's date is unlikely, as Hadrian was out of Rome that year,[90] and even Cassiodorus' seems too early, given the brick stamp of 134 found in the Temple's substructures near the Arch of Titus.

Again, however, the numismatic evidence is of help. Hadrianic sestertii and medallions, all datable after 132, show on the reverse a decastyle temple, unidentified but usually with SC or EX SC in the field and SPQR in the exergue (*see Ill. 24*). The variations in the representation are numerous: D. F. Brown has identified two main types with six variations, as well as a variant on a silver medallion.[91] But since the Temple of Venus and Roma is the only decastyle temple reliably attested to in Rome, and coins struck under Antoninus Pius from 141 to 143 represent a similar decastyle temple and carry in addition the explanatory legend ROMAE AETERNAE or VENERI FELICI (*see Ill. 25*), the identification of the temple on the Hadrianic coins as the Temple of Venus and Roma seems all but certain.[92] As we shall see below, the types of the cult images that were eventually housed in the temple appear on late Hadrianic coins, but it is only on Antonine coins that we find identifiable cult images represented in the cella of the temple.[93] It therefore seems likely that the Temple was actually completed in every detail only under Antoninus Pius,[94] which will also account for the late brick stamp found in situ in the substructures.

[89] Cf. Gagé, "Templum urbis" 159.

[90] Cf., e.g., Strong, "Late Ornament" 122 n. 21.

[91] Brown, "Architectura Numismatica" 223–25; Pensa, "Adriano" 51–59; Hill, *D&A* 76. For the coins see: *BMC, Emp.* III, p. 467, no. 1490, pl. 87.6; p. 476, no. 1554, pl. 89.5 and n. 1554; Gnecchi, III, p. 19, no. 88; *RIC* II, p. 440, nos. 783–84; Magnaguti, III, p. 81, no. 501, pl. 16, and p. 73, no. 43; Mazzini, II, p. 150, nos. 1421–22, pl. 52, and p. 96, no. 593, pl. 34.

[92] ROMAE AETERNAE: *BMC, Emp.* IV, pp. 205–206, nos. 1279–85, pls. 29.10–13, 30.1–3; VENERI FELICI: *BMC, Emp.* IV, pp. 211–12, nos. 1322–25, pls. 31.3, 31.8–9.

[93] *BMC, Emp.* IV, p. 206, nos. 1284–85, pls. 29.12, 30.2; cf. Strack, *Hadrian* 176–77. Other Antonine coins show no statue within the Temple (e.g., *BMC, Emp.* IV, p. 205, nos. 1279–80, pls. 29.10–11, and p. 206, no. 1282, pl. 30.1); or an indistinguishable form (e.g., *BMC, Emp.* IV, pp. 205–206, nos. 1281, 1283, pls. 29.13, 30.3; Mazzini, II, no. 699).

[94] Many scholars propose that it was dedicated in the period 135 to 137, but accept that the work was completed only under Antoninus Pius: e.g., Blake/Bishop, 41; Bloch, *Bolli* 252 n. 192; Mattingly, *BMC, Emp.* IV, p. lxxxii; Platner-Ashby, s.v. Venus et Roma, Templum, 553; and Strack, *Hadrian* 174–76, but see idem, III.69.

24. *Reverse of Hadrianic sestertius (after 132) with decastyle temple probably to be identified as the Temple of Venus and Roma. Left and right of the Temple are freestanding columns surmounted by statues, and both the legends* SC *and* SPQR *appear.*

25. *Reverse of Antonine sestertius (141–143) with the Temple of Venus and Roma, showing seated cult statue of Roma.*

Furthermore, the similarities with late Hadrianic and early Antonine decoration shown by some of the relatively rare architectural fragments from the Temple strengthen the presumption that the Temple was finished only after Hadrian's death.[95] If the Temple took better than eighteen years to complete, that is not surprising in light of its size and complexity.

Our knowledge of the original appearance of the Temple of Venus and Roma is confused not only by the variations in representations of the Temple on coins, but also by the destruction of the Temple by fire in 307 and its subsequent rebuilding by Maxentius. The only certain remains of the original Temple are the temple platform, some foundations of the aedes, a few architectural fragments, and parts of the lateral porticoes of gray granite columns that framed the long sides of the precinct. Barattolo's recent investigations of the extant remains; of the plans, elevations, and sketches of the Temple made in the early nineteenth century; and of photographs and plans taken at the beginning of the twentieth century both before and during the Temple's resto-

[95] Strong, "Late Ornament," esp. 122, 127–29.

ration have resulted in a clearer understanding of the Temple's design,[96] although many details, especially with respect to the Temple's decoration, must remain elusive.

The Hadrianic Temple of Venus and Roma, raised from the surrounding platform on a continuous crepis of seven steps, had twenty columns on the long sides and was decastyle, pseudodipteral, and with an interior pronaos at either end tetrastyle in antis.[97] (see Ill. 26). The base diameter of the fluted white marble columns (which may be Maxentian) is 1.87 meters.[98] The two cellae, back to back and separated by a straight wall, were almost square, approximately 25.70 meters on a side. Most of the cella walls survived the fire, to be used as an exterior shell for Maxentius' concrete apses and walls, and from the impression of the blocks on the concrete and the few fragments that escaped later depredations, Barattolo concludes that the Hadrianic walls were in ashlar masonry of peperino tufa, probably revetted with marble. Their maximum thickness, 2.30 meters, makes the hypothesis of vaulted roofs untenable. The cellae must have been covered by trussed roofs of timber, at least 26 meters high,[99] the collapse of which during the fire of 307 may have destroyed much of the Hadrianic floors.

Each of the twin cellae was flanked by continuous plinths about 0.19 meters high, which carried six columns, almost certainly with a second order above.[100] The side aisles, paved in Proconnesian marble, were 4.2–4.3 meters wide, and the central naves, paved in polychrome *opus sectile* (decorative work made of shaped tiles of colored marble), about 17.2 meters wide. It is generally assumed that the eastern cella was that of Venus, and the western one facing the Forum that of Roma.[101]

The few extant fragments of entablature believed to come from the Hadrianic temple are of Luna and of Proconnesian marble. Although there is a

[96] Barattolo (1973), 247–48. Two fragments of a historical relief showing a decastyle temple facade (now housed in the Museo Nazionale delle Terme and the Vatican Museo Paolino in Rome) have been held to depict the facade of Venus and Roma (e.g., Platner-Ashby, s.v. Venus et Roma, Templum, 554), but the relief is more likely Julio-Claudian and antedates the Temple: Koeppel, "Official State Reliefs" 488E. Pensa, "Adriano" 55, dates the relief as Trajanic.

[97] This description is based on that of Barattolo (1973) 245–69, except where noted.

[98] Barattolo (1978) 398; A. Muñoz, *La sistemazione del Tempio di Venere e Roma* (Rome 1935) 16, reproduces Nibby's 1838 description.          [99] Barattolo (1973) 257–60.

[100] The description of the interior is from Barattolo (1974–75), except where noted. The porphyry columns now visible in the interior belong to the Maxentian rebuilding (A. Muñoz, *Via dei Monti e Via del Mare* [Rome 1932] 17).

[101] Gagé, "Templum Urbis" 155 n. 4. Though he cites no evidence, subsequent scholars concur.

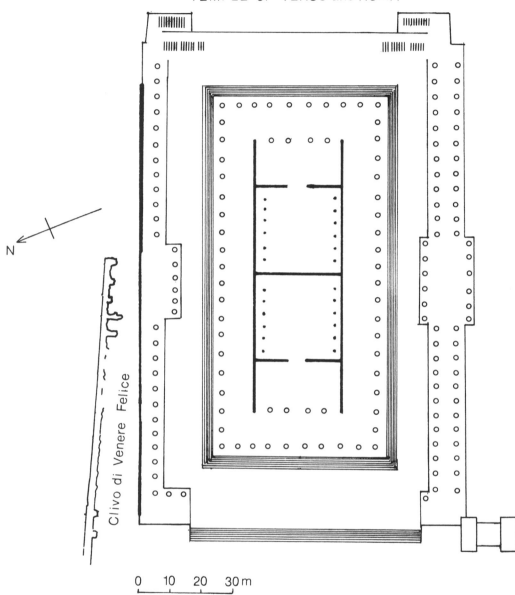

TEMPLE of VENUS and ROMA

N

Clivo di Venere Felice

0  10  20  30 m

26. *Temple of Venus and Roma, Hadrianic period. At the western corner of the podium is the Arch of Titus, and north of the Clivo di Venere Felice is Neronian construction.*

marked Pergamene character in some parts that strongly resemble the decoration of the Hadrianic Traianeum at Pergamum, Leon has pointed out other more Roman elements and suggests that two teams of carvers—one using more eastern forms and the other, more Roman ones—worked on the Temple's decoration.[102]

Although the aedes was set axially on its basement platform, 19 meters from either long side, the flanks of the temenos were not treated alike. To the north, where the platform fell short of the high Neronian terracing that was cut into the slope of the Esquiline, the lateral porticus (5.90 meters deep) was closed behind by a wall, a single row of gray granite columns with white marble Corinthian capitals responding to pilasters on the back wall. The distance from this portico to the aedes was 13.00 meters. On the south, where the platform ran along the Sacra Via from the Arch of Titus to the platea around the Meta Sudans, the portico, on a wider foundation (7.60 meters), had two rows of gray granite columns and was probably an open colonnade of Corinthian order. Here the portico was only 11.00 meters distant from the aedes. All the columns in both colonnades seem to have been four Roman feet (1.18 meters) in base diameter.[103]

A pavilion of five bays resembling a propylaeum and projecting a little from the lateral porticoes interrupts each at the middle. Since these were not true passageways, their purpose seems to have been simply ornamental, to mask the disparity of the two spaces flanking the aedes.[104] Their columns seem to have been cipollino, a striking change of color.[105]

Less is known about the treatment of the east and west ends of the temenos. A wide staircase on the west running nearly the full width of the platform seems to have had no colonnade across it, and no evidence has been

[102] Leon, *Bauornamentik* 224, 231; and see Strong, "Late Ornament" 127–29, 136–38.

[103] Barattolo (1978) 400 nn. 15, 16, gives these measurements and description, correcting the commonly accepted symmetrical plan; cf. Blake/Bishop, 40. For the size of the columns, see Nibby, in Muñoz, *Sistemazione* 14. The earlier topography of the north side can be deduced from the imprints of the wooden scaffolding for the concrete foundations, and from the prints of the blocks of *opus quadratum* at the northeast extremity. Pensa, "Adriano" 56–57, conjectures that the two isolated columns to either side of the temple

depicted on some Hadrianic coin issues (e.g., *BMC, Emp.* III, p. 467, no. 1490, pl. 87.6) symbolize these lateral colonnades.

[104] Barattolo (1978) 400 n. 16. Blake/Bishop, 41, less persuasively hold that the blind propylaea were to break the "monotony" of the long porticoes of gray granite columns.

[105] In addition to the cipollino fragments visible in the temenos, another similar fragment was found in a propylon area during the excavations in the 1930s: Muñoz, *Sistemazione* 20.

found for a colonnade on the east where the platform rose almost eight meters above the platea below. We can safely assume that there was a fence or balustrade here.[106] At the platform's northeast and southeast corners staircases in two flights gave access to the temenos. Between the northeast stair and the Flavian Amphitheater stood the Neronian Colossus which Hadrian had altered to represent Sol. Hadrian is said to have planned to erect a similar colossus of Luna, perhaps symmetrically on the axis of the Temple (cf. *HA, Hadr.* 19.13). Sol and Luna were symbols of eternity for the Romans.[107] The cavities visible in the platform's eastern edge toward the Flavian Amphitheater postdate the Hadrianic construction, and this face of the concrete substructure, like the exposed faces elsewhere, was originally covered with opus quadratum, probably of peperino.[108]

The Temple of Venus and Roma is an architectural anomaly and this fact, taken together with the anecdote of Dio, raises the question of its motivation. The coupling of Venus with Roma must strike us as surprising,[109] and will be discussed further. The Temple was not only the largest in Rome, but strongly Greek in its general appearance.[110] Most architectural historians have credited

[106] Blake/Bishop, 41, note that a colonnade on the east side would have obstructed the view to and from the amphitheater.

[107] According to Hadrian's biography, the statue of Luna was to be made with Apollodorus' aid. The *Chronicon Paschale* dates the removal of the Colossus to 130, which can be adjusted to 128: cf. Howell, "Colossus" 297. See also Gagé, "Colosse et fortune de Rome" 110–16; Strack, *Hadrian* 177; and Pensa, "Adriano" 56, for the associations with eternity.

[108] Personal inspection convinces me that the cavities were cut into the structure only later; see, too, Blake/Bishop, 40–41. The two scholars also conjecture, but without evidence, that marble revetted the north side, and that the two ramp staircases on the east were of marble steps. Instead, the relatively numerous blocks and fragments of peperino tufa found in the area indicate that peperino was used (cf. Barattolo [1973] 249), and on analogy to the fire walls of the Fora of Augustus and of Trajan, this would not have been covered.

[109] Until the time of Hadrian, it was very rare, although Venus and Roma had appeared together earlier on an issue struck in 75 B.C. by the moneyer C. Egnatius Cn. f. Cn. n. Maxsumus, in what seems to be *popularis* propaganda: M. H. Crawford, *Roman Republican Coinage*, I and II (London and New York 1974) 405–406, #391/3. Here, however, the two deities were represented standing side by side, with a rudder on top of a prow to either side of them. See below for the Hadrianic representations.

[110] Barattolo (1978) 397–99, stressing the Greek derivation of the Temple, explains its few deviations from the canons of Hermogenes of Alabanda for pseudodipteral temples. For dipteral and pseudodipteral temples in Rome, see Gros, *Aurea Templa* 115–22. Barattolo (1978) 402–403, lists the four Greek temples named by Pausanias that may have influenced the plan of Venus and Roma (at Sicyon, Argos, Olympia, and Mantineia). Snidjer, "Tempel der Venus und Roma" 3–4, mentions only the temples at Argos and Mantineia. Barattolo, (1978) 407, stresses the similarity of Venus and Roma to the Temple of Artemis Leukophryene at Magnesia on the Meander. See also n. 102 above.

Hadrian with the Temple's design and conception, and they may well be right. We should note, however, that like other temples in Rome, the new Temple, and therefore the cult it was to house, would have had to be approved by the senate. As evidence of such cooperation, Gagé has pointed to the senatorial *duodecimviri urbis Romae*, board of twelve men of the City of Rome, associated with the Temple;[111] this priesthood, however, was created only after the Temple was completed. More direct collaboration is suggested by the double legend on most of the Hadrianic coins depicting the Temple: EX SC, SPQR. Strack notes that this twofold legend emphasizes the inclusion of all Rome in the new cult,[112] an idea echoed a century later in what Athenaeus has to say about the Romaia (Parilia). The cult of Venus and Roma, although new, was calculated to appeal to Rome.

The real innovation of the Hadrianic cult of Venus and Roma was the worship of Roma in Rome itself.[113] Yet the time was right for it. From the late third and early second centuries B.C. Roma was worshiped in the Greek East as an act of political homage, and the cult had developed significantly after the establishment of the principate, when the worship of the princeps was joined to that of Roma. The double cult of Roma and Augustus spread throughout the east and, to a lesser extent, in the west, and helped promote loyalty and solidarity.[114]

Roma as a divinity made her appearance in Rome relatively late, but she had been represented in the art of the imperial city with increasing frequency. Although Ennius speaks of Roma as a semidivine personification (*Scipio* 6), it is only in Augustan and Flavian literature that she appears frequently.[115] Mar-

---

[111] Gagé, "Templum urbis" 158–59. Gagé later doubted that this priestly board dealt with the Temple: "Sollemne urbis" 227.

[112] Strack, *Hadrian* 175, who also takes the legend to exclude Hadrian's responsibility for the Temple, noting that *HA, Hadr.* does not include the Temple among Hadrian's works. Yet given the vast number of Hadrianic works omitted from the biography, this last argument cannot hold. Cf. Snidjer, "Tempel der Venus und Roma" 1, 7; and Gagé, "Templum urbis" 154–55.

[113] For example, Beaujeu, 133–36. Wissowa, *ReKu*, 2nd ed., 340–41, suggests that the worship of the Dea Roma (whom he considers the divine symbol of the city) reveals the growing importance of the city itself to

provincials and Roman citizens in the provinces. Beaujeu sees the new cult as part of Hadrian's policy of the provincialization of Rome; cf. Gagé, "Sollemne urbis" 227.

[114] See, esp., R. Mellor, *"Thea Rhome." The Worship of the Goddess Roma in the Greek World* (Göttingen 1975) 13–26; idem, "The Goddess Roma," *ANRW* II.17.2 (1981) 956–72; and C. Fayer, *Il culto della Dea Roma. Origine e diffusione nell'Impero* (Pescara 1976) 9–28.

[115] C. Koch, "Roma Aeterna," *Gymnasium* 59 (1952) 128–43, 196–209; U. Knoche, "Die augusteische Ausprägung der *Dea Roma*," *Gymnasium* 59 (1952) 324–49; Mellor, "Goddess Roma" 1004–1010.

tial, for example, attributing the words to Trajan, glorifies the deity (Mart. 12.8.1–2).[116] Similarly, although the head or figure of Roma begins to appear on Roman coins arguably from soon after the war with Pyrrhus,[117] representations of Roma on coins become rare after the beginning of the first century B.C. and are resumed only in late Neronian times.[118]

In the major arts in Rome an image of Roma was shown on the hand of Jupiter Capitolinus in the restoration of the temple by Q. Lutatius Catulus in 78 B.C. (Dio Cass. 45.2.3), but her appearance becomes common only after the Julio-Claudian period. Well-known representations of Roma on state reliefs are found on the Ara Pacis, the Cancelleria reliefs, the Arch of Titus, and the great Trajanic frieze now incorporated into the Arch of Constantine.[119] The creation in Rome of a cult for the goddess Roma was anticipated by the ever more insistent representation of her, and prior to Hadrian Roma appeared in imperial art and literature most closely associated with Augustus, the three emperors of 69, and the Flavians. She was an easily intelligible claim of legitimacy for a Roman princeps.

The Hadrianic cult of Roma transcended specific ties: the representations of the cult statue on coins carry the legend ROMAE AETERNAE or ROMA AETERNA,[120] and this concept is extended by the transformation of the Parilia into the Romaia, celebrating the birthday of the city, and association of the festival with the Temple on the Velia. The location of the new Temple near the early shrines of the Penates, the Lares, and others linked to Rome's foundation and formation reinforced the concept of a renewal of eternal Rome, a concept additionally expressed in other late Hadrianic issues with ROMULO CONDITORI.[121] The coins of ROMAE AETERNAE are matched by contemporaneous (A.D. 138) issues in gold and silver depicting Venus Felix, the other deity worshiped in the double Temple.[122] Here we can see even more clearly the universal appeal of the new cult in Rome.

---

[116] Mellor, "Goddess Roma" 1010.

[117] Crawford, *Roman Republican Coinage* 721–25, with bibliography; contra, Mellor, "Goddess Roma" 974–75.

[118] C. C. Vermeule, *The Goddess Roma in the Art of the Roman Empire* (Cambridge, Mass. 1959) 29–42.

[119] Vermeule, *Goddess Roma* 83–114, has many examples; for a different interpretation of some of these figures as representations of Virtus, see J.M.C. Toynbee, in *JRS* 36 (1946) 180–81.

[120] ROMAE AETERNAE: *BMC, Emp.* III, p. 329, no. 707, pl. 60.20 = Smallwood, #380a (denarius); ROMA AETERNA: *BMC, Emp.* III, pp. 328–29, nos. 700–703, pl. 60.17–18 (aurei); ROMA AETERNA SC: *BMC, Emp.* III, p. 474, no. 1541, pl. 88.12 (sestertius).

[121] Dated to 138 by Hill, *D&A* 69; to 137 by Mattingly, *BMC, Emp.* III, p. cxli; and above, n. 86, for the coins.

[122] *BMC, Emp.* III, p. 334, nos. 750–56, pl. 61.15–16, cf. Smallwood, #380b; R. Pera, "Venere sulle monete da Vespasiano agli An-

Venus had long been venerated in Rome under many guises.[123] She had begun to have shrines and temples in Rome by the early third century B.C., but toward the end of the republic she became especially the patroness of triumphatores, because she was thought to confer military success. Sulla ascribed his rise to power to Venus, and Pompey dedicated the temple that crowned his theater to Venus Victrix. The cult of Venus Genetrix went farther and made her ancestor and protectress of the Roman dictator, the Julian house, and the Roman people.[124] Despite the Julio-Claudian promotion of Venus as the *genetrix Aeneadum* (the ancestress of the Romans, the race sprung from Aeneas), during the first century of the principate Venus Genetrix became more of a personal patroness of the emperor than a national one.[125]

The Hadrianic cult of Venus Felix reversed this specialization. Although the Hadrianic epithet Felix is not found used with Venus' name before Hadrian, it then becomes common in the second century.[126] It indicates that this Venus is especially a goddess of fecundity and prosperity, and her popular appeal is reflected in the altar erected in the Temple's precinct in 176, on which all newly married couples were to offer sacrifice (Dio Cass. 71.31.1).

The Hadrianic coins depicting the statues of Venus Felix and Roma Aeterna show an interesting similarity between these divinities. Venus Felix sits in a high-backed throne facing left, wearing a long robe and a diadem; in her raised left hand she holds a spear and in her outstretched right, a winged Amor. The type is new. Roma sits, like Venus, but on a curule chair; she wears a long robe and a helmet. In her raised left hand she holds a spear and in her right, the Palladium, the symbol of the eternal city, a Victoria, or the sun and the moon. The issues date to 138. On analogy with the VENERIS FELICIS legend the inscription ROMAE AETERNAE must be construed as genitive, thus

tonini: aspetti storico-politici," *RIN* 80 (1978) 84–88. For the date of both sestertii and aurei: Hill, *D&A* 69–70.

[123] See, e.g., Beaujeu, 136; and R. Schilling, *La religion romaine de Vénus depuis les origines jusqu'au temps d'Auguste*, 2nd ed. (Paris 1982) 65–266.

[124] Beaujeu, 137; Schilling, *Religion de Vénus* 272–324; C. Koch, "Venus," *RE* 8 A.1 (1955) 858–68; idem, "Untersuchungen zur Geschichte der römischen Venus-Verehrung," *Hermes* 83 (1955) 35–48; and (for Sulla) Crawford, *Roman Republican Coinage* 373, on nos. 359/1 and 2.

[125] See, e.g., Koch, "Venus-Verehrung" 47–50.

[126] Koch, "Venus" 871; and idem, "Venus-Verehrung" 48–49. In 138 Hadrian also struck aurei and a medallion labeled VENERI GENETRICI (*BMC, Emp.* III, pp. 307, 334, 360, 538, nos. 529, ★, 944–49, 1883–84, pls. 57.12, 65.19–20, 99.4), and denarii slightly earlier, with ROMA FELIX (*BMC, Emp.* III, p. 329, nos. 704–706, pl. 60.19), or ROMA FELIX COS III P P (*BMC, Emp.* III, p. 313, nos. 566–69, pl. 58.11); cf. Hill, *D&A* 69; and Strack, *Hadrian* 177–80. Hadrian's new cult on the Velia united all these aspects.

marking the images as those belonging to the Temple then under way.[127] The two seated statues, back to back in the Temple, expressed complementary concepts: Rome's perennial might rests on the Roman people.

Hadrian's new Temple (and cult) of Venus and Roma was more national than dynastic, breaking precedent with earlier imperial temples in and around the Forum by exalting the strength and origins of Rome and the Roman people above those of an individual family. The Temple's enormous foundation runs alongside the Arch of Titus and the upper portion of the Sacred Way, thus stressing the association of Roman triumphs with the divine origins of Rome and with the very strength of the city. The substructures incorporated the remains of Nero's Vestibule and other domiciles of Roman dynasts, and the relocation and transfiguration of Nero's colossal statue manifested the reappropriation of the area as public. Kienast has justly said that the monumental whole towered over the buildings of the Roman Forum below it, superseding the earlier limits of the area established by the Temple of the Deified Julius; it documented that for Hadrian, Rome was materially and ideally the center of the Roman world, and substantiated Hadrian's claims to be a new founder of the city, another "Romulus Conditor."[128] Yet the Temple of Venus and Roma also marks a broader conception of Rome.

The new national temple epitomizes the Roman empire of Hadrian's day. It was unmistakably Greek in general appearance: F. E. Brown has called it "a Greek mass set in a Roman space," and notes the analogy of its site across from the Capitoline to that of Athen's Olympieion, which Hadrian finally completed across from the Acropolis.[129] Barattolo goes a step farther and believes that this Greek temple in Rome advertised Hadrian's hopes of a new panhellenism.[130] Despite the Greek appearance of Hadrian's Temple of Venus and Roma, however, it is important to recall that the building was begun by a princeps with a Spanish background, and its appeal was to Romans at home. It was linked to some of the earliest shrines of Rome, and to a new annual celebration of Rome's founding date. The Hadrianic Temple of Venus and Roma was to unite all Romans in a new state cult that reflected their glory and

---

[127] Strack, *Hadrian* 176–77. The similar images marked ROMA AETERNA (see n. 120 above) must also be representations of the cult statue. Vermeule, *Goddess Roma* 35–38, discusses Roma Aeterna. This scholar rather implausibly concludes from the variants in the numismatic depictions of the cult statue that the attribute in its right hand was detach-able. Toynbee, *Hadrianic School* 135–37, remarks on the novelty in Roman art of Roma's long chiton, which associates the representation closely with the Greek Athena type.

[128] Kienast, "Baupolitik" 402–407, citing the coins mentioned in n. 86 above.

[129] F. E. Brown, "Hadrianic Architecture" 56.    [130] Barattolo (1978) 410.

their origins, much as Hadrian's Olympieion and Panhellenion served to unite the Greek East.[131] The new concept and cult were extremely popular, although the cult of Roma seems to have eclipsed that of Venus by the third century. Gagé has shown that the Temple and the worship of Roma were among the longest-lived survivors of pagan Rome, significant even for Christians of the fifth century.[132] The associated festival of the Natalis Urbis Romae was also famous and durable, and had constant official favor: the Feriale Duranum records its celebration by the army in the early third century in Dura Europus out on the banks of the Euphrates.[133]

With Greek architectural ambiguity reinforced by the double apses back to back, Hadrian's Temple looked both to the ancestral center of the city and out to the larger Roman world. Its physical mass did indeed dominate the Forum below, but this mass, strategically located, extolled Rome's traditions rather than an individual dynasty. Similarly, Hadrian's additions to the Palatine residences were oriented in accordance to the major buildings of the Forum below them. Through his work at and near the Forum Romanum, Hadrian evinced imperial submission to the state rather than imperial domination of the Roman people; his constructions reiterated the public claims he made at the beginning of his principate: that he would govern the state so that all would know it belonged to the people, not to him alone (*populi rem esse, non propriam*: *HA, Hadr.* 8.3). These constructions reflect the harmony that must have characterized the middle years of Hadrian's principate, when there were no provincial or foreign disturbances, the government was running smoothly, and all Romans could unite in celebrating Hadrian's assumption of the title Pater Patriae in 128.[134]

---

[131] Olympieion and Panhellion: A. S. Benjamin, "The Altars of Hadrian in Athens and Hadrian's Panhellenic Program," *Hesperia* 32 (1963) 57–86.

[132] Beaujeu, 133, 161; Gagé, "Sollemne urbis" 225–41; idem, "Templum urbis" 169–72. Wissowa, *ReKu*, 2nd ed., 340 n. 6, notes Maxentius' dedication of a base on 21 April 308: *Marti invicto patri et aeternae urbis suae conditoribus* [To the invincible Father Mars and the founders of his eternal city] (*CIL* 6.33856).

[133] R. O. Fink, A. S. Hoey, and W. F. Snyder, "The Feriale Duranum," *YCS* 7 (1940) 102–12, who argue, however, that the cult of Urbs Roma Aeterna was not very popular in the provinces, particularly not in the Greek East.

[134] For the date: Jerome, *Chron.* p. 199 H.; L. Perret, *La Titulature impériale d'Hadrien* (Paris 1929) 62–73, suggests that Hadrian assumed the title on 21 April 128, on the occasion of the Natalis Urbis; Weber, 200 n. 710, on 11 August 128, on the *dies natalis imperii*. The earlier date suggested by W. Eck, "Vibia(?) Sabina, No. 72b," *RE, Suppl.* 15 (1978) 910, does not affect my argument. Garzetti, 395, notes the frequency of the legend CONCORDIA on the first coins struck after 128.

# CHAPTER FIVE

# IMPERIAL RESIDENCES

Hadrian inherited a strong tradition regarding imperial residences. Excessive exclusiveness and acquisitiveness were insufferable in a princeps, yet a certain splendor was not only desirable but necessary.[1] In 117 Hadrian's personal property, such as his house on the Aventine, and the property of Sabina, possibly including a villa in Tibur, became part of the imperial fiscus, which already included in Rome most if not all of the Palatine, the Horti Maecenatis and Sallustiani, and other gardens in the city, and vast holdings in peninsular Italy, with special concentration around the Bay of Naples.[2] Although the new princeps probably visited and may have stayed some time at many of these estates,[3] those that he remodeled to his taste are significant for an understanding of his principate. These are his palace at Tivoli (ancient Tibur) known as Villa Adriana, work on which was begun in his first years of power, the Palatine palace, and the Horti Sallustiani.

Hadrian's residences in and near Rome molded his interactions with the upper classes, and also helped shape his public image among Rome's populace. Such roles are particularly important in light of Hadrian's unusual division of time, for he spent more than half his rule outside the capital city. Acclaimed princeps in Syria on 11 August 117, he reached Rome only in 118 after passing through Illyricum; in 119 or 120 he went to Campania for a short visit; and from 121 to 125 (less plausibly 126) his travels included Gaul, Germany, Britain, Spain, Mauretania, Greece and the Greek East, Sicily, and

---

[1] See, briefly, C. F. Giuliani, "Note sulle architettura delle residenze imperiali dal I al III secolo d.Cr.," *ANRW* II.12.1 (1982) 233–42; intimated by A. G. McKay, *Houses, Villas and Palaces in the Roman World* (Ithaca, N.Y. 1975) 72–77.

[2] O. Hirschfeld, "Der Grundbesitz der römischen Kaiser in den ersten drei Jahrhunderten," in *Kleine Schriften* (Berlin 1913) 526–44, provides the basic list of imperial proper-

ties in Rome and Italy; cf. Millar, *ERW* 175–89; and D. J. Crawford, "Imperial Estates," in *Studies in Roman Property* 35–70.

[3] For example, some Hadrianic restorations, whose extent is unknown, were undertaken in Centumcellae, and Hadrian also seems to have been responsible for restorations in the imperial villas at Albanum, Antium, and perhaps Praeneste: Blake/Bishop, 237, 256–58.

perhaps Raetia, Noricum, and Pannonia. After returning to Rome, he set out again in 127 for a brief tour of Italy, and then an equally short visit to Africa in 128. Following a few weeks in Rome in late summer and early fall that year (128), he embarked on his second great trip, which brought him to Greece, Asia, Caria, Lycia, Pamphylia, Cilicia, Syria, Arabia, Egypt, Judaea, Cappadocia, Crete, Pontus, and possibly Bithynia, Cyrene, and the Balkans, with perhaps a short visit to Rome in 132, to return finally to the capital city only in 134.[4] In sum, more than twelve years of Hadrian's twenty-one-year rule were passed outside of Rome, an unprecedented proportion, given that the voyages were undertaken for predominantly nonbelligerent purposes.[5]

The manifold benefits of these trips—increased discipline and readiness of the army; encouragement of provincial urbanization and Romanization through imperial donations of aqueducts, games, and the like as well as through grants of privileges and rights; direct supervision of the law and the imperial bureaucracy; and personal acquaintance with local notables—are obvious and acknowledged even in the literary tradition generally hostile to Hadrian (cf., e.g., Dio Cass. 69.5.2, 9.1; *HA, Hadr.* 5.10, *Epit. de Caes.* 14.4–5; Dio Cass. 69.10.1, 16.2; *HA, Hadr.* 9.6, 13.10, 22.11).[6] Yet Hadrian's absences from Rome were quite unusual in their frequency and length and potentially troublesome, if only because they separated Hadrian from the individuals accustomed to personal interaction with the emperor. Saller argues that during the empire "all senatorial [and equestrian] magistracies, offices and honors were at the disposal of the emperor," depending on access to him or to one close to him, and that the imperial distribution of these *beneficia* and the corresponding accrual of *gratia* (grateful obligation) among the upper

---

[4] Garzetti, 386–401, noting the many difficulties in the itinerary and the chronology, such as the exact date of departure in 121.

[5] Thorton, "Hadrian" 451–53 (referring to D. Magie, *Roman Rule in Asia Minor to the End of the Third Century after Christ*, 2 vols. [Princeton 1950] 1.612 [hereafter Magie *RRAM*]), notes that, except for Nero's tour in Greece, Hadrian was the first reigning emperor after Augustus to depart from Italy for a purpose other than making war or seeing a conquest. M. Wegner, *Hadrian, Plotina, Marciana, Matidia, Sabina*, Das römische Herrscherbild II.3 (Berlin 1956) 33–44, reconstructing a hypothetical general itinerary for Hadrian's voyages from the types and provenances of his likenesses found in the prov-

inces, notes that provincial portraits of Hadrian are more numerous than for any other emperor.

[6] Another reason for his travels was simple curiosity: *HA, Hadr.* 17.8, and cf. 13.3; 14.3; Tert. *Apol.* 5.7. For the trips, see (in general) Weber; Garzetti, 386–401; Thorton, "Hadrian" 445–53; Z. Yavetz, "Hadrianus the 'Wanderer,' " in *Commentationes ad antiquitatem classicam pertinentes in memoriam B. Katz*, ed. by M. Rozelaar and B. Shimron (Tel Aviv 1970) 67–77. F. Grelle, *L'autonomia cittadina fra Traiano e Adriano. Teoria e prassi dell'organizzazione municipale* (Naples 1972) 153–54, discusses briefly the importance of the concept of law in Hadrian's policy.

classes in Rome were essential for the maintenance of social cohesion among these classes.[7] Furthermore, by this time the tradition of the *consilium principis* was well established: the emperor was expected to make decisions of every sort in consultation with his eminent friends.[8] A different but equally important consideration was the emperor's visibility for the Roman masses. Tiberius' disappearance and secession to Capri had been deeply resented as well as actually harmful to Rome,[9] and Nero's extended tour of Greece may have been one cause of his loss of support in the city.[10] Given this background, we might expect Hadrian's frequent and long absences from the city to have had similar repercussions.

Yet this was not the case, at least so far as can be judged from the extant literary tradition. Only Aelius Aristides' praise of Antoninus Pius' ability to pass far-reaching judgments despite remaining in Rome has been construed as a criticism of Hadrian's travels (Aristid. *Or.* 26.33).[11] Other evidence of senatorial disquiet at Hadrian's voyages may be reflected in the mission of P. Cluvius Maximus Paullinus, whom the senate sent (probably to Campania) to meet Hadrian upon his return from Africa in August 128 (Smallwood, #200).[12] The only known analogy for this mission is the much larger embassy that met Augustus in 19 B.C. upon the latter's return from Spain and Gaul.

In the earlier instance, the circumstances are fairly clear. Although Augustus marked the embassy as a signal honor (*RG* 12.1), Dio Cassius explains it as having been sent to inform Augustus of the disorders accompanying the election of his co-consul for the coming year, and one of the ambassadors, Q. Lucretius, was then nominated to that post by Augustus (Dio Cass. 54.10.2).[13] In contrast, the specific motivations for the senatorial embassy to Hadrian in 128 are unknown, and Hadrian's assumption of the title Pater Patriae in that same year and the legends of CONCORDIA on the contemporaneous

[7] Saller, *Patronage* 41–78.

[8] In general, Crook, *Consilium Principis* 1–65, who denies that Hadrian effected a radical reform of the *consilium*; Millar, *ERW* 110–22, discusses the various roles the *amici* played throughout the imperial period.

[9] See, e.g., R. Syme, *Tacitus* (Oxford 1958) 402, 427–28, 695. Suetonius, *Tib.* 41ff., collocates notice of reluctance on Tiberius' part to receive embassies with reports of his debauchery.

[10] K. R. Bradley, "Nero's Retinue in Greece, A.D. 66/67," *Illinois Classical Studies* 4 (1979) 152–57.

[11] K. F. Stroheker, "Die Aussenpolitik des Antoninus Pius nach der *Historia Augusta*," *HAC* 1964/1965 (Bonn 1966) 251–52; but see J. H. Oliver, *The Ruling Power* (Philadelphia 1953) 919.

[12] A. Degrassi, "P. Cluvius Maximus Paullinus," *Epigraphica* 1 (1939) 307–21, originally published and discussed the inscription.

[13] Degrassi, "Cluvius" 314 n. 2, for the circumstances of Augustus' embassy.

coinage proclaim the harmony of the time.[14] Yet Cluvius' subsequent outstanding career[15] indicates what could be gained from personal meetings with the princeps (cf. Q. Lucretius' co-consulship with Augustus), and such considerations may have underlain the embassy to Hadrian.

The interaction between the princeps and the elite that was essential for the smooth functioning of government could occur anywhere, although the ideal setting was the imperial residence, or the house of an *amicus principis*. Ostensibly at leisure and in surroundings befitting their political and social status, the princeps and his friends could discuss politics, law, and aesthetic matters, and make decisions about careers.[16] Both Dio and the biography put Hadrian repeatedly in such settings. One great social activity of the Hadrianic court was hunting (cf., e.g., Dio Cass. 69.7.3, *HA, Hadr.* 26.3), which will be discussed in the investigation of the Tondi Adrianei; another was discussion and disputation about literary matters (cf., e.g., *HA, Hadr.* 15.12–13), which will be considered in the examination of Hadrian's Athenaeum (both in Chapter 7). Hadrian seems to have taken special care to ensure good communications with the aristocracy throughout his principate.

Despite Fronto's criticism that Hadrian was cold and standoffish (*Ep.* 2.1), Dio and the biography record that Hadrian repeatedly publicly honored the consuls and his friends (Dio Cass. 69.7.1, 4), surrounded himself with outstanding men in the law courts,[17] in his carriage, and at dinner, and went to visit them when they were ill (Dio Cass. 69.7.3–4; *HA, Hadr.* 8.9–10, 9.7, 17.3, 18.1, 20.11, 22.4, 22.11, 23.4, cf. 4.2, 8.1, 26.4). Hadrian's palace was constantly open both for official purposes—the praetorian prefect, Q. Marcius Turbo, for example, is said to have spent most of his time there (Dio Cass. 69.18)—and for consultations, as when from his sick bed Hadrian an-

[14] See above, Chapter 4 n. 134; and Garzetti, 395; one could always argue, of course, that the coin legends mask a lack of concord.

[15] He was governor of Sicily in 133 or shortly thereafter; consul in 138; and governor of Asia in 155–156. He held other posts as well after his embassy: he was prefect in charge of grain distribution; on the board of six of the three squadrons of Roman knights; governor of the province of A . . . ; deputy governor of Asia; commander of the fourteenth Gemina legion; supervisor of the Via Flaminia; governor of Moesia Superior; on the board of fifteen overseeing sacred rites;

and on the board of seven overseeing public banquets.

[16] Cf. Millar, *ERW* 18–28, with references. It was important, however that both imperial and private residences be not too luxurious, as indicated by Augustus' razing of Vedius Pollio's house in Rome (Dio Cass. 54.23.6; Ovid *Fast.* 6.637–648).

[17] See, e.g., Crook, *Consilium Principis*, 60–61, on Hadrian's use of this consilium in settling quarrels between the Alexandrian Jews and Greeks (as described in the *Acts of the Pagan Martyrs*, P. Oxy. XVIII.2177, col. II, 59–63).

nounced his adoption of Antoninus Pius (Dio Cass. 69.20). In the version of Zonarus, Dio mentions a banquet at which Hadrian asked for the names of ten men capable to rule, only to correct the number to nine, saying that he knew one already, Servianus (Dio Cass. 69.17.3). The anecdote indicates that at imperial dinners discussion included matters of the gravest political import.[18] Both sources mention that Hadrian donated to members of the aristocracy the means necessary for a public career, which he would give even unasked (Dio Cass. 69.5.1–2; *HA, Hadr.* 7.9–11, 15.1, and cf. 17.3). Hadrian was deliberately modest (Dio Cass. 69.6.3, 7.2; *HA, Hadr.* 8.11, 9.8, 20.1, 22.4). Finally, our sources furnish the names of many of Hadrian's friends, a heterogeneous collection of military and political men (e.g., Q. Marcius Turbo and C. Avidius Heliodorus, also a philosopher), jurisconsults (e.g., M. Salvius Julianus), rhetoricians and philosophers (e.g., Valerius Eudaemon), and poets (e.g., Florus); the list reflects Hadrian's own varied interests.[19]

The setting for many of these exchanges must have been the imperial palaces, as is clear from the biography's remarks on Hadrian's hunting parties and banquets leading up to the description of the villa at Tibur (*HA, Hadr.* 26.2–5), and from Aurelius Victor's defamatory notice that in this villa Hadrian piled up *palatia* and wasted his time on banquets, statues, and paintings, finally dedicating himself to luxury and debauchery (*Caes.* 14.6). Knowledge of the location and character of Hadrian's favorite residences illuminates the Hadrianic city in the wider sense. The following discussion, arranged chronologically, turns first but only briefly to Villa Adriana, then to Hadrian's modifications of the Palatine palace, and finally to the Horti Sallustiani.

Twenty-eight kilometers (about 16 miles) northeast of Rome below Tivoli lies Hadrian's most famous residence, called in antiquity Villa Tiburs (*CIL* 14.3635–3637), Villa Tiburtina (*HA, Hadr.* 26.5), and Aelia Vil⟨l⟩a (*CIL* 14.3911), and now known as Villa Adriana. Spreading over 120 hectares (about half a square mile) (*see Ill. 27*), it is so large that it was known in the

---

[18] Xiphilinus has Trajan, which R. Syme prefers (*HSCP* 83 [1979] 309 n. 95); in any case, the scene is probably a *topos*. See the similar notes of Tacitus about Augustus and Nero (*Ann.* 1.13.2 and 14.47.1).

[19] For Hadrian's friends and political alliances in his early years, see now R. Syme, "Hadrian and the Senate," *Athenaeum* 62.1 (1984) 31–60, who stresses that Hadrian combined "personal tastes or affinities with obli-gations towards government nexus." For Hadrian's later years: H.-G. Pflaum, "Le Règlement successoral d'Hadrien," *HAC* 1963 (Bonn 1964) 98–99, 109–22. See also Crook, *Consilium Principis* 56–65; and R. Etienne, "Les Sénateurs espagnols sous Trajan et Hadrien," in *Empereurs d'Espagne* 79–82. Literary acquaintances will be discussed in more detail in Chapter 7, in the section entitled "Athenaeum."

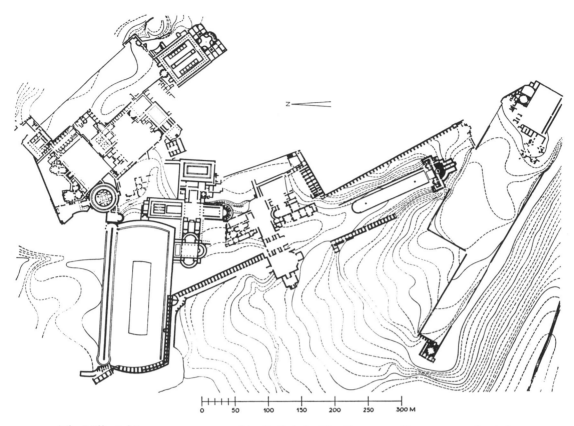

27. *The Villa Adriana, as reconstructed by F. Rakob. The Serapeum-Canopus complex is in the southern central sector.*

Middle Ages as Vecchia Tivoli. In the sixteenth century F. di Giorgio Martini and Giuliano da Sangallo sketched parts of the ruins, and Pope Alessandro VI began excavations. Exploration became more systematic when Cardinal Ippolyto d'Este, then *governatore perpetuo di Tivoli*, commissioned Pirro Ligorio to study it and mine it for material for d'Este's own palace, which Ligorio was building higher up the hill. For the next three centuries Villa Adriana was ransacked for sculpture, marble, and mosaics, although the decoration that remains is still impressive.[20]

At first sight one is struck by the Villa's distance from Rome and by the biography's notice that Hadrian named various parts of the Villa for the most famous places in the world, and even for the underworld (*Tiburtinam villam mire exaedificavit, ita ut in ea et provinciarum et locorum celeberrima nomina inscri-*

[20] For the history of the site in Tivoli, see W. Winnefeld, *Die Villa des Hadrian bei Tivoli* (Berlin 1895) 150–68; P. Gusman, *La Villa im-* *périale de Tibur* (Paris 1904) 219–321; S. Aurigemma, *Villa Adriana* (Rome 1961) passim.

*beret, velut Lyceum, Academian, Prytanium, Canopum, P⟨o⟩ecilen, Tempe vocaret. et, ut nihil praetermitteret, etiam inferos finxit* [and he built up the Tiber villa wonderfully, in such a way that he could apply to it the names of provinces and places most renowned and could call (parts of it), for example, the Lycaeum, the Academy, the Prytany, the Canopus, the Poecile, Tempe. And so that he might omit nothing, he even fashioned a Hades]: *HA, Hadr.* 26.5).[21] The impression that the Villa was a retreat is strengthened by Aurelius Victor's remarks (noted earlier), by the splendor of the works of art that have been found there, and by the architectural finesse of the plan.[22] Yet the Villa's location is in accord with the fifth Cyrenean edict that assumes for Roman senators a residence in Rome or within a twenty-mile radius of the city,[23] and both Augustus and Claudius had made extended stays in their holdings at Tivoli without incurring criticism.[24]

Close to Rome, with spectacular views and well-watered orchards, Tibur was one of the choicest sites for luxury villas from the second century B.C. on.[25] And by the first century B.C. at the latest, owners had been giving the peristyles, *oeci*, and watercourses in their villas exotic and pretentious names, such as Academia, Nili, and Euripi.[26] Yet Hadrian's Villa is known to have

[21] This seems also to echo Hadrian's vision of the empire as a unity, a concept that can also be seen in his great *provincia* coin series: Toynbee, *Hadrianic School* 152, notes in this connection the reliefs of the provinces found on the Hadrianeum.

[22] Yet Hadrian differed from other wealthy and powerful Romans of the late republic and later only in the extent of the wealth expended on his Villa; see, e.g., X. La Fon, "A propos des *villae* républicaines, quelques notes sur les programmes décoratifs et les commanditaires," in *L'Art décoratif à Rome à la fin de la république et au début du principat* (Rome 1981) 151–72. Among many others, R. Duncan-Jones, *The Economy of the Roman Empire*, 2nd ed. (Cambridge 1982) 17–24 (hereafter Duncan-Jones, *ERE*), notes Pliny's delight in his houses, villas, and their appointments (cf. Sherwin-White, *Pliny*, 186–99). Fronto is more modest: E. Champlin, *Fronto and Antonine Rome* (Cambridge, Mass. 1980) 25.

[23] *FIRA*[2] I, n. 68, vv. 107–110, noted by I. Shatzman, *Senatorial Wealth and Roman Pol-*

*itics* (Brussels 1975) 22 and n. 40, who also discusses the suggestion that senators were bound by law to own a house in Rome. He concludes that at the time of Augustus there existed no legal requirement, but only the matter of custom and convenience. See, too, A. Chastagnol, "Le Problème du domicile légal des sénateurs romains à l'époque imperiale," *Mélanges . . . Senghor* (Dakar 1977) 43–54.

[24] Hirschfeld, "Grundbesitz" 542, collects the literary references, remarking that Caesar, too, had a villa there.

[25] N. Neuerburg, "The Other Villas of Tivoli," *Archeology* 21 (1968) 288–97, illustrates the archaeological remains and the history of villas there; cf. Shatzman, *Senatorial Wealth* 13, 19, 29, and passim.

[26] Crema, 112–17; A. Hoffmann, *Das Gartenstadion in der Villa Hadriana* (Mainz 1980) 64–65; and P. Grimal, *Les Jardins romains*, 2nd ed. (Paris 1969) 247–49, 296–99; all referring to Vitruv. *De Arch.* 6.7.3; Cic. *Leg.* 2.1.2; and Varro, *Rust.* 2.*praef.* 2. Cf. Sen. *Ep.* 90.15.

been used as an official residence. An inscription found at Delphi is a copy of a letter Hadrian addressed to that city from the Villa in August/September 125, thus after his return from his second great voyage.[27] Another inscription, on a base dedicated to Hadrian on 29 December 135 by the cities of Hispania Baetica *ob liberalitates*, was found in the town of Tivoli, which suggests that the imperial benefactions it commemorates were granted in the Villa (*CIL* 14.4235 = *ILS* 318 = Smallwood, #117).[28] The scale of all the important rooms in the Villa is too grand for anything less than a public appearance and assembly.[29] In addition, the Villa had its own staff of accountants (cf. *CIL* 14.3635–3637: two *tabularii* and a *comme(ntariensis) Villae Tiburtis*). This was a working imperial court, no mere retreat.

The Villa has been studied only sporadically and in bits and pieces. No scientific map of it was made before 1906, when the School of Engineering of the Università di Roma undertook one. The early studies of H. Winnefeld (1895) and P. Gusman (1904), though still useful, have been superseded by more recent investigations, particularly those since World War II under the direction of S. Aurigemma, who also helped complete Gismondi's model of a reconstruction of the Villa now on display at the modern entrance to the site.[30] Following the important books of H. Kähler (1950) and Aurigemma (1961), excellent brief studies of isolated parts of the Villa have appeared that have corrected many of the inaccuracies and misunderstandings of those who tried to treat the Villa as a whole though without new excavation, yet there is no work that takes account of all these investigations available.[31]

One of the remarkable characteristics of Villa Adriana is that, despite its physical extent, it is arranged in a series of complexes, each more or less self-contained. In part this may be due to the sequence of campaigns of construction in the Villa, which is known from brick stamps found in the buildings

[27] E. Bourguet, *De rebus Delphicis imperatoriae aetatis capita duo* (Montepessulano 1905) 82–84 (late August, early September); cf. Bloch, *Bolli* 158–59.

[28] This would allow us to conclude that Hadrian went to Baiae only in 136.

[29] Such features in the imperial villas are receiving increasing attention: e.g., F. L. Rakob, "Der Bauplan einer kaiserlichen Villa," in *Festschrift K. Lankheit* (Cologne 1973) 122–24; idem, in *PropKg* 2.157.

[30] V. Reina and U. Barbieri, "Rilievo planimetrico ed altimetrico di Villa Adriana

. . . ," *NSc*, ser. 5, 3 (1906) 314–17; and n. 20 above.

[31] Kähler, *Villa*; for Aurigemma, see above, n. 20. Blake/Bishop, 237–56, rely primarily on these two works and on Winnefeld. The various nymphaea and triclinia receive special treatment in Neuerburg, *Fontane*. F. Coarelli, *Lazio*, Guide archeologiche Laterza 5 (Bari 1982) 394, provides a good general bibliography for the Villa. William L. MacDonald and John Pinto are now collaborating on a book on the Villa.

(except the two stone theaters in the north and another near the Accademia). The first comprehensive interpretation of the stamps, that by Bloch, distinguished three building periods coinciding more or less with Hadrian's sojourns in Rome (beginning in 118, 125, 133/135), but Smith's recent reevaluation of the stamps shows that most of the work belongs to only two periods, and that little was done in the last years of Hadrian's life. The earliest complex, apparently begun even before Hadrian arrived in Rome, was built around an already existing villa in what is now the northeast quadrant.[32] This complex is of a more private character than the later pavilions and rooms, which seem designed to accommodate the Villa to more official uses.[33]

The initial campaign of construction (117–125, especially 117–121), begun at Hadrian's accession, comprised a remodeling of the site's earlier villa with much new construction. The complexes are as follows: Biblioteche-Ospitali-Tempe (built over the republican villa); Peristilio di Palazzo (Great Court) and surroundings; Sala a Pilastri Dorici (throne room) complex; Teatro Marittimo, Sala dei Filosofi, and Poecile, with the remodeling and addition of the Cento Camerelle and garden; Garden Stadium complex, including the Winter Palace and the trilobate Cenatio; the Heliocaminus baths; Caserma dei Vigili; and Terme Grandi.

During the second building campaign, from 125 to 133 (with work significantly diminishing after ca. 130), the more traditional embellishments of villas were added: pavilions, groves, exedrae, and the like. These also can be grouped in complexes: Piazza d'Oro; Terme Piccole; Serapeum-Canopus; Pretorio and Vestibule complex; Accademia; Roccabruna and adjacent terraces; and the Nymphaeum and Villa Fea, theaters and palestrae. As Rakob and others have shown, the various complexes of both phases should be discussed individually, although in a general plan of the whole they seem to be obedient to six main axes[34] (see Ill. 27).

Since our main concern is to determine the purpose and effect of the representational spaces and the organization of Hadrian's residences, only one

---

[32] Bloch, *Bolli* 117–83, esp. 158–59, for the original hypothesis about chronology; see now Smith, "Grandi Terme" 73–93; followed by Coarelli, *Lazio* 49–52; and Hoffmann, *Gartenstadion* 3 (without attribution), among others. Coarelli gives an interesting, intelligible, and succinct description of the Villa, although he inexplicably dates to 118 Hadrian's letter to Delphi. Kähler, *Villa* 170 n. 109, implausibly suggests that Hadrian be-

gan building at the site before 114, when he went east to the Parthian wars.

[33] Rakob, "Der Bauplan einer kaiserlichen Villa" 122–23.

[34] Rakob, in *PropKg* 2.190–92; idem, "Der Bauplan einer kaiserlichen Villa" 116–24 (although both works antedate Smith's redating of the Villa's phases); cf. Coarelli, *Lazio* 51–52.

such complex, the Serapeum-Canopus, will be described, and a few words added on the Villa's maintenance. The Serapeum-Canopus area is one of the most interesting of the Villa at Tivoli; its apparent similarities to the Alexandrian Canopus and Serapeum seem to confirm the biography's observation that Hadrian named various sectors of his Villa for different parts of the Roman world. Its ribbed half dome is a tremendous feat of Hadrianic engineering; the use of water is brilliant; and its eclectic and unusual decoration is characteristic of Hadrianic taste. Moreover, the purpose of the whole has excited much discussion. Once considered a garden, since the excavations of the 1950s the Serapeum-Canopus has been held to be a nymphaeum-triclinium, yet a new interpretation would see the area as dedicated to a cult of Antinoos.[35] As I shall show in the Appendix, this last is implausible.

In a valley in the southern part of the Villa is a basin about 120 meters long, 19 meters wide, and 1.60 meters deep[36] (*see Ill. 28*). Its overall dimensions correspond with the Euripus of the Canopus in Alexandria. At its southern end is a complex dominated by a large half-domed apse. To the east the basin was flanked by a colonnaded walk believed to have carried a gable roof, the columns of Corinthian order. This extended beyond the curved northern end of the basin, and between the columns of the outer row were plantings, perhaps of flowers.[37] Farther east at a slight angle to the basin runs a wall with buttresses projecting at regular intervals to support the hillside.[38] To the west the valley is bounded toward its north end by a retaining wall buttressed by two stories of barrel-vaulted rooms, the lower one now used as the site's Museum.[39]

---

[35] For the nymphaeum-triclinium concept, see in detail J. Raeder, *Die statuarische Ausstattung der Villa Hadriana bei Tivoli* (Frankfurt am Main and Bern 1983) 300–14; also L. Bek, "*Questiones Convivales*. The Idea of the Triclinium and the Staging of Convivial Ceremony from Rome to Byzantium," *AnalDan* 12 (1983) 91–92; Blake/Bishop, 251 n. 98; Coarelli, *Lazio* 69. A reaffirmation of the theory with even more detail is now awaited from E. Salza Prina Ricotti. For the theory that the area was used for a cult in honor of Antinoos, see below.

[36] N. Hannestad, "Über das Grabmal des Antinoos," *AnalDan* 11 (1983) 72, gives the more exact measurements of 121.40 by 18.60, depth 1.60 meters. He also provides a general bibliography on this pavilion, including Au-

rigemma, *Villa Adriana* 100–33, who found the statues in the excavations of the Canopus in 1950–55. The following description is taken from both sources. For convenience sake I discuss the plan as though it were oriented to the cardinal points of the compass, although the main axis actually runs north northwest–south southeast.

[37] Hannestad, "Grabmal" 74.

[38] Blake/Bishop, 250, opine that most of the buttressing is Antonine.

[39] For a full description of this structure, see Blake/Bishop, 249–50, who note that the lower level of rooms was very high and divided by wooden mezzanine floors supported on travertine consoles. This is similar to the contemporary structures on the Palatine's slopes.

Set up along the western side of the basin are reproductions of the four Caryatids flanked by two figures resembling Bes or Silenus (which also functioned as telamons) that were found in the basin when it was excavated in the 1950s (*see Ill. 29*). All the statues are larger than life. The Caryatids are copies of two belonging to the Erechtheum in Athens, and the two male figures, which will be discussed below, have been said to be Egyptianizing.[40] The six figures must have carried some sort of entablature, now lost. The two columns reerected at the north of this side of the basin may never have stood there.

The curved north end of the basin was embellished with a freestanding colonnade, its architrave alternately flat and arched in a very Roman arrangement (*see Ill. 29*). Around this were arranged two copies of Amazons (one of a statue attributed to Kresilas, one by Pheidias), a statue of Hermes, one of a warrior (Ares? Theseus?), one of Athena (of the Ince type), all larger than life, and a reclining figure of the Nile and another of the Tiber. Near the east end within the basin was a pedestal that seems destined for the large fountain figure of a crocodile found in the excavations of 1950–55, and on the east side of the basin was another pedestal that apparently once carried a Hellenistic group showing Scylla with victims.[41] The sixteen Corinthian columns, their marble entablature, and the statues were spaced widely enough around the northern edge of the basin not to obstruct the view to the north, where the Vestibule rose about 100 meters away. Along the east side of this visual avenue rose the facade of the Terme Grandi (*see Ill. 27*). Thus the Serapeum-Ca-

[40] Hannestad, "Grabmal" 80, who characterizes them as Bes figures. A. Schmidt-Colinet, *Antike Stützfiguren. Untersuchungen zu Typus und Bedeutung der menschengestaltigen Architekturstütze in der griechischen und römischen Kunst* (Frankfurt 1977) 117–18, calls them Egyptianizing Sileni. P. Zanker, in Helbig, IV.3195, pp. 158–59, sees them derived from decorations found in Hellenistic theaters (tempering the remarks of K. Schefold, "Aphrodite von Knidos, Isis und Serapis," *AntK* 7 [1964] 57–58, who refers them to an Alexandrian sanctuary). Raeder, *Statuarische Ausstattung* 85, considers them Sileni derived from late Hellenistic precedents. On iconographical grounds only, Schmidt-Colinet, 120, holds that the two Osiris telamons of rose granite found in Tivoli before the six-

teenth century (now in the Vatican) are from the Canopus and depict Antinoos (for a different interpretation of the figures, see Helbig, I.30, pp. 25–26). This theory makes reconstructing the western porticus even more problematic; it is almost certain, however, that the colonnade did not extend its entire length (Hannestad, "Grabmal" 73–77).

[41] Aurigemma, *Villa Adriana* 110–11; Helbig, IV.3196–98, 3200–3202, pp. 159–66. B. Kapossy, "Zwei Anlagen der Villa Hadriana," *Gymnasium* 74 (1967) 38–40, stresses the difficulty of reconstructing the original layout. Coarelli, *Lazio* 70, notes that a similar but larger pair of statues depicting the Nile and the Tiber were found in the Isaeum Campense.

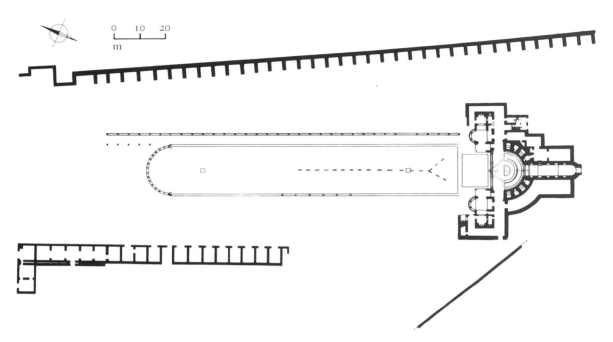

28. *Villa Adriana: Serapeum-Canopus complex, sited between retaining walls and rooms (to the west, southwest, and east).*

29. *Villa Adriana: Serapeum-Canopus complex as reconstructed in situ, viewed on axis from the north from the Canopus to the Serapeum. Note Caryatids and male telamons in the middle distance.*

nopus area was an entity clearly defined by the domed structure at its south end and the freestanding curved colonnade at its north, and simultaneously part of a larger unit.

The most impressive buildings of this complex are those at the south end, commonly grouped together and called the Serapeum because of the similarity of the semicircular room, its curved wall lined with deep niches, and the overall plan to other known Serapeum complexes.[42] A large hemicycle faces north, and between it and the long "Canopus" is a separate rectangular pool (13.40 by 10.20 meters), flanked by two virtually symmetrical sets of small rooms, pavilions of highly playful architecture (*see Ill. 28*). Stairs to either side also provided access to an upper story of some sort. Abundant traces of frescoeing have been found on vaults and upper walls; the two barrel vaults flanking the half dome were covered in mosaic; and the lower walls were revetted with marble.[43] The semicircular apse (16.75 meters across the front) is covered by a half dome of segments alternately strongly concave and essentially flat, seven in all in a pattern somewhat similar to the domes of the vestibule of the Piazza d'Oro in the Villa and the Palazzo of the Horti Sallustiani.[44] Here, however, the three wider curved segments rise over the high central opening to the back and brick-faced lunettes over two central niches on either side. The half dome was decorated with blue and green mosaic, and the walls revetted with marble up to the springing of the dome. This is one of the earliest known examples of a dome decorated with mosaic.[45]

The central axis of the complex, continuing the axis of the Canopus, was developed as a long barrel-vaulted room, its walls revetted with marble and its vault encrusted with green, yellow, and blue mosaic. This extended back to a rounded apse into which opened an aqueduct. Three semicircular niches alternating with two rectangular ones interrupt each side wall. The barrel-vaulted room was lit from its far end by concealed windows high in the wall.

[42] For a comparison of this plan to those of Serapea, see Roullet, 27, and figs. 348–51.

[43] F. B. Sear, *Roman Wall and Vault Mosaics* (Heidelberg 1977) 111–12, for the barrel vaults covered in tesserae of colors similar to those of the half dome; for details of the layout, see C. Tiberi, "L'esedra di Erode Attico a Olympia e il Canopo della Villa di Adriano presso Tivoli," in *Studi in onore . . . V. Fasolo* (Rome 1961) 38–42 (unfortunately, with an untenable interpretation of the structures); and Hannstad, "Grabmal" 105 n. 76.

[44] Aurigemma, *Villa Adriana* 102–104; Neuerburg, *Fontane* 240–41, no. 201; G. de Angelis d'Ossat, *RivRom* 14 (1936) 339; idem, "La forma e la costruzione delle cupole nell'architettura romana," in *Atti del 3° convegno nazionale di storia dell'architettura, Roma 9–13 Ottobre 1938* (Rome 1940) 227, 238; idem, *Romanità delle cupole paleocristiane* (Rome 1946) 10, 13–14.

[45] Sear, *Mosaics* 111–12, 35; and see Rakob, in *PropKg* 2.191–92; the holes for the revetment are still visible.

Along the curved wall of the half dome itself, symmetrically deposed, are eight niches, also alternately rectangular and bowed. The rectangular ones contain steps for cascading water, and the rounded niches, with half domes decorated with mosaic, held statues.[46] The radiating walls of the eight niches supported a second story of barrel-vaulted rooms, which served to carry the weight of the dome in a system like that of the Pantheon.[47] Under the half dome was a semicircular inclined couch of masonry for reclining at dining parties, a *sigma*.[48] The long view over the rectangular basin and down the Canopus was artistically framed by four large cippolino columns carrying Ionic capitals and an arcuated architrave.[49]

Interpretation of the vista that confronted the symposiasts from the sigma under the half dome is controversial, because it is tied to the larger question of the meaning of the whole complex. In addition to the sculptures listed above, in the excavations of the 1950s archaeologists discovered a small statue of Demeter and some other pieces, including four marble heads, that probably did not decorate the Canopus. The heads are of Julia Domna, possibly Dionysos, a beardless athlete (probably not a portrait), and one usually (though somewhat dubiously) identified as L. Aelius Caesar, which N. Hannestad has recently and unconvincingly proposed represents "Hadrianus Renatus," a supposed representation of Hadrian idealized as reborn and youthful.[50] Several Egyptianizing statues found in the Villa during the Renaissance have also been associated with this complex.[51]

Until recently the common interpretation of the decorative program of the Serapeum-Canopus was that it reflected Hadrian's interests and travels: B. Kapossy and Zanker support this theory, pointing to the diversity among

[46] For a comparison of this type of water display, see F. L. Rakob, "Ein Grottentriklinium in Pompeji," *RömMitt* 71 (1964) 182–94.

[47] The mosaic was apparently patterned with acanthus scrolls. In the area of the barrel vault in the rear passageway Sear also found red tesserae, and he notes a very few other traces of mosaic work in the complex (*Mosaics*, 111–12). For the complicated water system, see A. Del Caldo, in Aurigemma, *Villa Adriana* 127–33. Here, as in the Pantheon, there is no correspondence between the articulation of the dome and the wall immediately below it.

[48] Rakob, "Der Bauplan einer kaiserlichen Villa" 124, reports that the central area of the couch is raised for the princeps; the modern reconstruction of the *sigma* on site, however, does not reproduce this aspect.

[49] Aurigemma, *Villa Adriana* 102–107.

[50] Helbig, IV.3203 (Demeter), 3208 (Julia Domna), 3205 (athlete), 3204 (youth, here tentatively identified as L. Verus), pp. 166–72; and Aurigemma, *Villa Adriana* 110. Hannestad's arguments for the identity of this head as Hadrianus Renatus, which he uses to support his theory that the Canopus served in a Dionysus-Osiris mystery cult ("Grabmal" 97–101), are not convincing on iconographical grounds. See Raeder, *Statuarische Ausstattung* 89–92.

[51] See n. 40 above, and Roullet, 49–51.

the sculptures and the evocation of sea voyages.[52] But a new emphasis on the figures along the west bank of the Canopus has led Hannestad, A. Schmidt-Colinet, and others to propose that somewhere in the area stood the tomb or cenotaph and the obelisk of Antinoos, and that the complex was a memorial to Hadrian's deified favorite.[53] Kähler, Hannestad, and Schmidt-Colinet adduce the inscription of Antinoos' obelisk as support for this hypothesis, but as we shall see in the Appendix, they rely on a misreading of the text. Hannestad also maintains that the two male telamons are statues of Bes, an Egyptian chthonic deity, and that they and the four copies of the Caryatids, the originals of which were created for the tomb of Cecrops in Athens, mark the probable position of Antinoos' obelisk.[54]

Hannestad has made probes in the slope of the hill west of the six figures and found the base of a Hadrianic wall in front of a line of amphora bottoms presumably used as flowerpots. Although he admits that on technical grounds it is not now possible to prove or disprove that the obelisk stood here, he sees his findings as support for his theory.[55] But the argument that the Caryatids and two male telamons are sepulchral and provide a suitable setting for Antinoos' obelisk and tomb overlook other associations of the types. It is also not certain that the two male figures represent Bes rather than Silenus.[56] No independent evidence warrants supposing that the Canopus was a cult area.[57] Hannestad's archaeological evidence does not corroborate his presumptions. Moreover, he assumes that the design of the whole Canopus was devised to commemorate Antinoos' death, therefore dating it to after 130. This ignores the brick stamps of the structure, predominantly dated to 123, that suggest the Canopus was built ca. 125–128.[58]

[52] Kapossy, "Anlagen der Villa Hadriana" 40–44; Zanker, in Helbig, IV, pp. 155–59.

[53] H. Kähler, "Zur Herkunft des Antinousobelisken," *Acta ad archaeologiam et artium historiam pertinentia* 6 (1975) 37–44 (hereafter Kähler, "Antinousobelisk"; Schmidt-Colinet, *Stützfiguren* 118–21, and n. 460; Hannestad, "Grabmal"; and C. S. Sweet, "The Dedication of the Canopus at Hadrian's Villa," *AJA* 77 (1973) 229, among others.

[54] Hannestad, "Grabmal" 80.

[55] Hannestad, "Grabmal" 74–97, who does maintain convincingly, however, that in the modern reconstruction the statues are more closely set than they were originally.

[56] Kähler's iconographical arguments ("Antinousobelisk" 42–44) are expanded by

Hannestad, "Grabmal" 80. Contra, n. 41 above. Zanker, *Forum Augustum* 12–13; and Raeder, *Statuarische Ausstattung* 311–12, note various meanings of Caryatids (also found in the Forum of Augustus). M. Malaise, *Les Conditions de pénétration et de diffusion des cultes égyptiens en Italie* (Leiden 1972) 214–15 (hereafter Malaise, *Cultes égyptiens*); and Roullet, 28, discuss the differing meanings of Bes.

[57] See, e.g., Malaise, *Cultes égyptiens* 426–27; and Raeder, *Statuarische Ausstattung* 307. On similarly flimsy grounds Kähler has elsewhere proposed that the Biblioteca Latina of the Villa was transformed into a shrine to Antinoos (*Villa* 156: a bust of Antinoos as Bacchus was found there).

[58] Bloch, *Bolli* 141–44, 169; with Smith,

The most plausible interpretation of the program of the Serapeum-Canopus is that it exemplifies the eclectic tastes of the time. The pieces of Egyptian flavor were particularly well suited to a design that evokes the Canopus of Alexandria, and may have assumed some poignancy after Antinoos' death. But Egyptian art and the Egyptian taste had had a certain vogue in Rome at least since the time of Augustus, and Egyptian pieces are found in other villas of this period, as well as in temples of Isis and Serapis.[59] More significant is the heterogeneity and lavishness of the overall decoration and layout. The "Egyptian" statues stood with copies of fifth-century Greek masterpieces, copies of the Erechtheum Caryatids, and of Hellenistic sculptures, in places framed by a very Roman colonnade of alternating flat and curved lintels. Walls of the "Serapeum" were articulated with niches and embellished with colored mosaic, marble revetment, stucco, and fresco. Although attention is focused on interior spaces, the architectural design sets up splendid vistas.[60] Liberal use of water and clever exploitation of light enlivened interior rooms, which, although distinct units, were combined by axes and symmetries. Statuary furnished and counterbalanced a highly sculptural architecture.

Of very different design are the utilitarian parts of the Villa, such as the horreum commonly called "Caserma dei Vigili." Although these were an integral part of the Villa, E. Salza Prina Ricotti's investigations have shown that such buildings were carefully concealed in a variety of ways from the ceremonial and state apartments.[61] Furthermore, the extensive system of tunnels and cryptoportici running throughout the whole Villa that she has also called to our attention makes it quite clear that the Villa's plan as a whole was worked out in considerable detail in advance. Some of the tunnels are large enough to accommodate carts drawn by oxen.[62]

The use of water and the orientation of the Serapeum-Canopus, the open, airy architecture of most of the state apartments, and the Villa's location in the foothills of Tivoli suggest that the court used the Villa Adriana primarily dur-

---

"Grandi Terme" 93; cf. Aurigemma, *Villa Adriana* 127. There is also insufficient room for a tomb or cenotaph behind the place Hannestad presumes for the obelisk.

[59] For Egyptian material from the Horti Sallustiani, see Roullet, 48, with references to her catalogue; for the general taste, 45–51.

[60] H. Kähler, *The Art of Rome and Her Empire*, trans. by J. R. Foster (London 1962) 152; Ward-Perkins, *RIA* 204–206; Hoffmann, *Gartenstadion* 67–68; and K. Lehmann-Hartleben and J. Lindros, "Il palazzo degli Orti Sal-

lustiani," *OpusArch* 1 (1935) 225 (hereafter Lehman-Hartleben and Lindros).

[61] E. Salza Prina Ricotti, "Cucine e quartieri servili in epoca romana," *RendPontAcc* 51–52 (1978–80) [1982] 291–94, who also analyzes the various phases of the "Caserma" (cf. Coarelli, *Lazio* 59–60; Blake/Bishop, 244).

[62] E. Salza Prina Ricotti, "Criptoportici e gallerie sotterranee di Villa Adriana nella loro tipologia e nelle loro funzioni," in *Les cryptoportiques dans l'architecture romaine* (Rome 1973) 219–59.

ing the summer months. Hadrian's letter to Delphi from the Villa in Tibur is dated to August/September 125. And Salza Prina Ricotti has tentatively identified one cryptoportico as intended for storage of snow to cool wine in summer.[63] When he was in Italy, Hadrian probably resided in Rome during the winter in the imperial palace on the Palatine.[64]

Hadrian refurbished and renovated the Domitianic palace, adapting it for greater comfort in winter and altering its exterior. Domitian's massive construction covering most of the top of the Palatine was characterized by monumental facades and rigidly axial state rooms (cf. Ill. 31); and Giuliani, MacDonald, P. H. von Blanckenhagen, and others have called attention to various architectural and decorative elements that enhanced the presentation of Domitian as *dominus et deus*.[65] Giuliani's recent examination of the northwest block of the palace, which includes the Lararium, Aula Regia, Basilica, and supposedly the main entrance, reconstructs on the basis of a Domitianic coin (see Ill. 30) its appearance as a rectangular unit rising some 30 meters in three successively smaller stories. The top story is a four-sided colonnade open to the sky. The lowest story presents a rather plain facade to the north, broken only by a projecting central portal for the Aula Regia and two smaller entrances, similar to aediculae, to either side for the Lararium and the Basilica. In front of the lowest story on the west was a long, high Corinthian colonnade in travertine, the columns about 8.20 meters high (including base and capital), the ceiling a barrel vault. Giuliani emphasizes that everything here was so imposing that any ordinary man would have been made ill at ease.[66]

Similarly, in the interior spaces such as the Aula Regia, the Basilica, and the Cenatio Jovis (see Ill. 31), the sheer size of the rooms (31.44 by 32.10,

[63] Ricotti, "Criptoportici" 246–48.

[64] See, too, *IGRR* 4.1156 (corrected by L. Robert, in *Hellenica* 6 [1948] 80–84) = Smallwood, #453, copies of letters from Hadrian to the city of Stratoniceia-Hadrianopolis sent from Rome in February and March 127. See also n. 70 below.

[65] Platner-Ashby, s.v. Domus Augustiana, 158–66, have the sources for the palace. The palace has been recently restudied by MacDonald, *ARE* 47–74, and with a more archaeological approach, by H. Finsen, *Domus Flavia sur le Palatin: Aula Regia—Basilica*, *AnalDan*, Supplement 2 (Copenhagen 1962); idem, *La Résidence de Domitien sur le Palatin*, *AnalDan*, Supplement 5 (Copenhagen 1969);

G. Wataghin Cantino, *Domus Augustana* (Turin 1966); and cf. F. Rakob, *Gnomon* 40 (1968) 186–87. For the decor: P. H. von Blanckenhagen, *Flavische Architektur und ihre Dekoration, Untersucht am Nervaforum* (Berlin 1940) 64–76, 109–16, 160–62. I am indebted to Dr. I. Jacobi for permission to inspect part of the site in November 1984.

[66] Giuliani, "Nuova lettura" 91–106; idem, "Residenze imperiali" 251–53. The reconstruction starts from Giuliani's objections to accepting vaulted roofs for the three rooms. Although Finsen, *Domus Flavia* 31, says that the original colonnade was Ionic, on the site there are only Corinthian capitals of the appropriate size and material.

30. *Reverse of Domitianic sestertius possibly depicting the northwest block of Domitian's palace on the Palatine.*

20.19 by 30.30, and 29.05 by 31.64 meters); their height, which must have been proportionate; the enrichment of the walls with marble revetment, addorsed and engaged colonnades, and alternating curved and rectangular niches; together with the axial emphasis on a raised apse—all must have combined to seem awesome.[67] Pliny underlines the forbiddingness of Domitian's palace and the emperor's inaccessibility (*Pan.* 47, 49, 83; cf. Suet. *Dom.* 21), and Domitian's superiority to ordinary humanity is a theme of Flavian poets.[68] Although Pliny praises Nerva and Trajan for having restored to the Roman people the "stronghold of tyranny," Domitian's residence on the Palatine (*Pan.* 47.4–5), neither Trajan nor Nerva seems to have used the Palatine residence much. Nerva preferred the Horti Sallustiani, and Pliny speaks of calling on Trajan at his new villa at Centumcellae and conducting judicial business there at pleasure (*Ep.* 6.31). The intimate association of the Domus Augustiana and Flavia with the "tyrant" Domitian may have discouraged his immediate successors from residing there.

[67] See, e.g., MacDonald, *ARE* 53–55, 71; for the apses, see, e.g., Tamm, *Palatium* 165–68, 181–82; and cf. Rakob, in *PropKg* 2.158. G. Hornsbostel-Huttner, *Studien zur römischen Nischenarchitektur* (Leiden 1979) 122–27, discusses in detail the use and derivation of the niches in the Domus Augustiana. The figures come from MacDonald, *ARE* 57.

[68] In specific connection to the palace: Stat. *Silv.* 4.2.18–31; Mart. 7.56, 8.36.

The Hadrianic modifications to Domitian's palace are dated by brick stamps to ca. 126–132.[69] A hypocaust system was added in the Cenatio Jovis, the state room that seems to have been a banquet hall. A new floor, supported on pillars of brick 60 centimeters high installed over the original floors, let hot air circulate underneath. (The opus sectile floor preserved in the east part of the room belongs to a Maxentian redecoration.) The heating system was not extended to the walls or to the raised apse, perhaps because the decoration with engaged granite columns would have been difficult to adapt, but four vents at the junction of floor and wall allowed heated air to enter the room.[70]

More difficult to assess are the modifications to the northern rooms of the Domus Flavia (*see Ill. 31*). Rectangular buttressing, measuring about 3.1 by 2.5 meters, was added inside the Basilica's northwesternmost pier, and more buttressing inside the semicircular apse. Although perhaps Domitianic, the buttressing seems Hadrianic, and a number of alterations to the exterior are definitely Hadrianic. A door in the west wall of the Basilica was closed, and two series of Hadrianic spur walls were built between the columns of the northwestern porticus of Domitian's palace and the wall of the building. Each of these spur walls, except the fifth from the north, was broken by a central doorway to make a continuous passage, 2.40 meters wide, which the fifth spur wall interrupted for reasons that are not clear. The brick stamps of these walls give a terminus post quem of 126.[71]

The spur walls of the second set, which are outside the peristyle, differ in appearance, and their brick stamps give them a terminus post quem of 129. Bloch takes them to indicate that Hadrian undertook modifications first in the area of the Basilica.[72] Yet the two sets seem to have been planned simultaneously, for in the lower-lying ground just west of the terracing for the palace

[69] Bloch, *Bolli* 211–18; his latest brick stamp dates to 126, but it is one described by Dressel and not seen by Bloch. Bloch shows also that although the large eastern exedra of the Hippodrome is sometimes attributed to Hadrian, the brick stamps prove it Domitianic, with some Severan modification.

[70] G. Carettoni, *NSc*, ser. 8, 3 (1949) [1950] 73–76, 79; Bloch, *Bolli* 216. It is uncertain how the Domitianic wall revetment was altered to compensate for the elevation of the floor level. Coarelli, *Lazio* 65, also notes the modifications of the floor as indicative that Hadrian used the Palatine residence in winter.

[71] Bloch dates the reinforcement of the Basilica's northwest pier and southern apse to a second Domitianic phase: this accords well with Giuliani's new evidence for various Domitianic modifications in the Aula Regia ("Residenze imperiali" 246–51). Bloch was unable to find the brick stamp of 126 reported by Dressel, and his latest confirmed stamp from these walls dates to 123 (*Bolli* 217–18). The measurements in this description were taken by the author in November 1984.

[72] Bloch, *Bolli* 217–18, citing a need for buttressing along the Basilica.

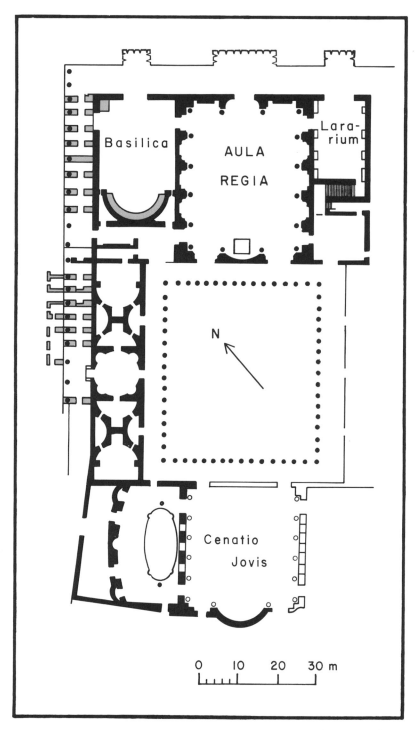

31. *Northwest block of the palace of Domitian on the Palatine. Hadrianic work, except stairs in the Lararium and the hypocaust system added to the Cenatio Jovis, is lightly shaded.*

in the area of the peristyle, and aligned with the later set of Hadrianic spur walls just above them, are Hadrianic walls that form a series of small rooms, about 4.5 meters deep, 3.5 meters wide (*see Ill. 31*). Bloch notes that the technique and bricks of these tabernae are similar to those of the spur walls in the area of the Basilica, that is, the earlier of Hadrian's modifications to this area of the palace.[73]

All these brick-faced walls, although presumably once covered with stucco, effectively changed the aesthetic of the earlier travertine porticus uniting the west side of the Basilica and part of the western peristyle. It is generally assumed that the northern series of spur walls was necessitated by the weight of the roof of the Basilica, yet since the original roofing of this (and of the Aula Regia and Lararium as well) is still in question, there is room for doubt.[74] H. Finsen has suggested that the spur walls here provided support for a gallery that was reached by a stairway built over the fifth wall;[75] if so, this may have been associated with the addition of what appear to be Hadrianic stairs in the Lararium.[76] Such a gallery would have drastically changed the external appearance of the palace.[77]

Even more perplexing are the changes worked by the Hadrianic tabernae along the peristyle. Most scholars believe that the central room west of the peristyle was one of the main entrances to the palace.[78] The added Hadrianic rooms must have made the approach, if not confusing, certainly less impressive.

Hadrianic construction on the northwest and northeast slopes of the Palatine was also changing the way the imperial palace appeared from the Velabrum and the Forum. His transformation of the western porticoed facade of the Domitianic "Vestibule" into a series of tabernae is similar to the changes of the western portico of the Domus Flavia, in that these made monumental

---

[73] Bloch, *Bolli* 217.

[74] Giuliani, "Nuova lettura" 94–106, with review of the earlier controversy.

[75] Finsen, *Domus Flavia* 30–31, rejects the idea that the spur walls were buttresses, maintaining that their foundations are too shallow; he suggests instead that they formed a Domitianic (sic) gallery.

[76] Wataghin Cantino, *Domus Augustana* 66–67; and Bloch, *Bolli* 216, for the stairs of the Lararium. Blake/Bishop, 60, speak of five Hadrianic piers "inserted on the inside of each of the long walls obviously to support a barrel vault."

[77] It is difficult to envisage how this gallery could have been added to the Domitianic palace as Giuliani reconstructs it.

[78] For example, MacDonald, *ARE* 54–55; Wataghin Cantino, *Domus Augustana* 69. Finsen, *Domus Flavia* 33, speculates that it was east of the Lararium. Only new excavations can solve the question of the entrances to the palace: Wataghin Cantino, *Domus Augustana* 69, suggests that the main entrance was from the west, and also notes that the south part of the palace could be entered only from the upper story and was completely closed toward the Circus Maximus (pp. 40–41).

facades less impressive. Moreover, as we saw above, Hadrian brought the facade of the Domus Tiberiana closer to the Forum by stories of tabernae aligned to the other buildings here. The coincidence of Hadrian's massive building program at Tivoli with his first lengthy sojourn abroad (ca. 121–125) may have raised suspicions that he was deliberately slighting the capital city.[79] Both the changes on the Palatine that brought the imperial residences closer to, and in better communication with, the Forum, and the alterations to the Domitianic facade at the top of the hill, contradict this.

At the same time, Hadrian gave other evidence of a personal interest in the city by the construction of a monumental garden building in the Horti Sallustiani. These gardens originally belonged to Caesar, who bequeathed them to C. Sallustius Crispus; during the reign of Tiberius the property passed by testament into the imperial fiscus. The gardens seldom figure in the literary sources prior to the Flavian period. They were situated toward the high, northeastern edge of the city, and were bordered on the east by the Via Salaria, on the north by the line of the Aurelian walls between Porta Pinciana and Porta Salaria, and on the west and south by (possibly) the modern Via Vittorio Veneto, Vicolo S. Nicolo da Tolentino, and the Alta Semita to the Porta Collina.[80] They thus covered the entire eastern portion of the Pincian Hill, the northwest slope of the Quirinal, and the head and much of a deepening valley between the two hills. In the valley ran a stream, now known as the Acqua Sallustiana, whose source is probably under the pavilion built by Hadrian.

Far from the heart of the city, the Sallustian gardens had been the scene of major fighting between the Flavian forces and the Vitellians in A.D. 70 (Tac. Hist. 3.82). Afterward, however, Vespasian made a point of living there rather than on the Palatine, and of opening his house to the public (Dio Cass. 65.10.4–5). Later Nerva lived in the gardens, dying there peacefully in 98 (Jerome, Chron. p. 193 H.). At least in the literary sources, therefore, the gardens are associated with popular emperors; furthermore, they differ from many of the other imperial *horti* acquired in the first century in that they were not confiscated and were one of the older properties of the fiscus.[81]

---

[79] Cf. Coarelli, *Lazio* 48. Yet *HA, Hadr.* 8.6 notes that Hadrian always attended regular meetings of the senate when he was in Rome or close to the city (*iuxta urbem*)—which could be a reference to Tivoli.

[80] Platner-Ashby, s.v. Horti Sallustiani, 271–72; Grimal, *Jardins* 129–31 (who incorrectly gives as the eastern border of the gardens Via Salaria Vetus rather than Via Salaria); M. Santangelo, "Il Quirinale nell'antichità classica," *MemPontAcc*, ser. 3, 5 (1941) 177–91; and Coarelli, *Roma* (1980) 247–49. I omit discussion of post-Hadrianic modifications of the gardens.

[81] See, e.g., Millar, *ERW* 163–74, for con-

Comparatively few buildings have been excavated in these gardens,[82] and by far the largest and most complex is the Hadrianic Palazzo (*see Ills. 32 and 33*). This building, sometimes known as the Nymphaeum, is a large brick-faced concrete edifice still some four stories high, nestling in the narrow head of the valley between the Quirinal and Pincian hills. The surviving structures, which once supported buildings higher on the Quirinal, began to attract the notice of architects and antiquarians in the sixteenth century,[83] but it was only in 1935 that proper scientific investigation was undertaken, and the meticulous illustrated analysis by K. Lehmann-Hartleben and J. Lindros still remains fundamental.[84] They have identified the Palazzo as an elaborate banquet hall of circular plan partly open to the sky and flanked by dependencies on the north, east, and south.

The central apartment is a lofty circular hall (about 11.20 meters in diameter, 13.25 meters high) covered with an umbrella dome of alternating flat and concave segments. It rests on massive rectangular foundations and is flanked by rectangular rooms. The unusual construction[85] may be due to the building's location above or near the source of the Acqua Sallustiana. A projecting rectangular vestibule with a great door just over 4 meters wide opens west-southwest to look down the valley toward the upper reaches of the Campus Martius, and a symmetrical antechamber of the same size and proportions as the vestibule leads east to a barrel-vaulted rectangular back room, about 5.60 by 8.00 meters. Large round-headed windows about 4 meters up in the walls of the rotunda to either side of the vestibule let light enter from the northwest and southwest, and at the same height semicircular niches decorate the vestibule, antechamber, and rear wall of the rectangular back room cut into the hillside. There are also four niches in the wall of the rotunda, two semicircular and two rectangular symmetrically disposed. All the niches had small travertine consoles projecting under them to support a shelf of some sort.[86]

demnation and confiscation as means of acquiring imperial property.

[82] Santangelo, "Quirinale" 178–94 (not including the description of the Palazzo); and for the area, *CAR* II-F, pp. 119–49, II-I, pp. 238–88.

[83] See Lehmann-Hartleben and Lindros, 196 n. 3.

[84] Lehmann-Hartleben and Lindros' work is cited in all discussions of the complex, and I rely on their measurements (pp. 212–13). New excavations under the direction of Dr. E.

Gatti, to whom I am indebted for a visit to the site, promise to add much to our knowledge.

[85] Blake/Bishop, 61. Compare the circular substructures of the Pantheon and the Mausoleum.

[86] Rakob, "Litus aureum" 138–39, compares the similar use of such consoles in the Canopus and Roccabruna of Villa Adriana, in the "Temple of Venus" at Baiae, and on house fronts in Ostia; Blake/Bishop, 63, implausibly see the consoles as adapting the niches for use as shrines.

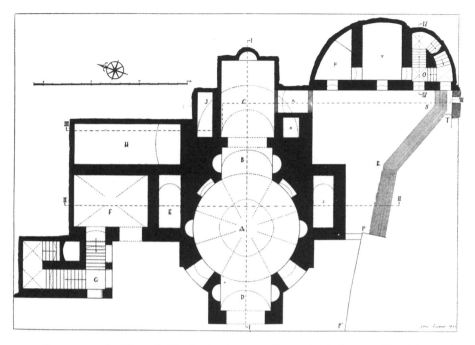

32. *Palazzo of the Horti Sallustiani, plan according to K. Lehmann-Hartleben and J. Lindros.*

33. *Palazzo of the Horti Sallustiani, as reconstructed by K. Lehmann-Hartleben and J. Lindros.*

The interior was simple yet elegant. Six smaller niches, closely grouped at ground level around the cross axis of the rotunda, were altered during Hadrian's reign. Two were made into doors to the flanking rooms, and two were filled in with masonry covered with the marble revetment that rose over 6 meters to the height of the springing of the arches over the rounded niches. The same type of marble revetment, and to the same height, decorated the vestibule, antechamber, rear rectangular room, and four side rooms (those marked E, F, L, and K in *Ill. 32*).[87] The upper part of the walls and the dome were finished with stucco,[88] and the floor paved with opus sectile in a geometric pattern.

Two annexes complement the central complex of the rotunda and its immediate dependencies, both giving access to upper stories that no longer survive (*see Ill. 33*). To the north is a rectangular hall covered with a groin vault and leading to a building that housed a massive staircase rising in flights around a central air shaft; this is still preserved to the height of two stories. Here, too, marble covered the steps and walls; the platforms between flights were paved with mosaic in black and white geometric design. To the southeast was another building of roughly semicircular ground plan cut into the slope; its facade, preserved to a height of three stories, is liberally provided with windows and doors arranged one above another. At the south end are a latrine and a stairwell. The rooms at ground level were not intercommunicating, although doorways connected those in the upper floors. The upper stories had wooden floors carried on consoles, like the Hadrianic tabernae on the northeastern slope of the Palatine.

The lower rooms in the south building are equipped with pipes and drains and may have been a nymphaeum.[89] They were richly painted and had black and white mosaic pavements. A small drain runs west from them under a forecourt or garden of irregular shape bounded to the south by the hillside, which is faced with a retaining wall of odd design.

Although the various buildings and rooms were luxuriously appointed in-

[87] Santangelo, "Quirinale" 185–86. The decoration is similar to that in the central suite of rooms of the "Vestibule" of Domitian.

[88] Dottoressa Tommasi, one of the restorers working in the building, informs me that within the cupola were found two layers of stucco of the type normally painted, but no trace of paint between the two. Here may be evidence for a change of plans for the decoration similar to the alteration of the niches. Santangelo, "Quirinale" 185, says that there may have been mosaic applied to the upper walls.

[89] Lehmann-Hartleben and Lindros, 220–21; Neuerburg, *Fontane* 66, and others stress that the rotunda itself was never a nymphaeum.

side,[90] the exterior was less splendid. Pilasters once framed the entrance to the rotunda, and this doorway may have been faced with marble.[91] The rest of the exterior was stuccoed. The central complex and north building had a thick coat of plain stucco, and above the second story was a balcony supported on huge travertine consoles cut to fit the line of the buildings. This continuous balcony unified the two separate structures in much the way that the cornices of the Pantheon work. The south building's facade was faced with stucco molded to resemble rusticated opus quadratum; here, too, was a shallow hanging balcony, supported on consoles smaller than those of the north buildings.[92] These balconies make the facade of the Palazzo seem not unlike that of an insula.

The numerous Hadrianic brick stamps show that the Palazzo has a terminus post quem of 126, and that it was built from the same brickyards as the contemporaneous (second) phase of the Villa Adriana; a few structural alterations show a redecoration of the Palazzo's interior that took place late in Hadrian's reign.[93] The architectural design, as Lehmann-Hartleben and Lindros have emphasized, also closely resembles work in the imperial villa at Tivoli: the dome of the rotunda is similar to that of the Roccabruna, and the comparable half dome of the Serapeum differs primarily in having lunettes below the concave segments.[94] Coarelli has also stressed the parallel with the Serapeum of Villa Adriana, and suggests that the circular hall functioned as a summer dining room.[95] Its west-southwest orientation, however, which is apparently dictated by the desire to command the view down the valley, suggests it might have served better in the fall.[96]

Hadrian's imperial residences illuminate the contradictory literary references to Hadrian's social relations, which mention both modest behavior toward his friends and luxurious and frivolous self-indulgence in his palatia in Tivoli. Though the Palazzo of the Horti Sallustiani is obviously a pavilion in

[90] In addition to the wall revetment and painting, we should note that Egyptianizing statues are said to have come from here: see n. 59 above.

[91] Santangelo, "Quirinale" 184, notes the possibility of marble revetment; nevertheless, it would be reminiscent of Ostian doorways (cf. Blake/Bishop, 63).

[92] This type of decoration, too, appears utilitarian; compare the Markets of Trajan.

[93] Bloch, *Bolli* 184–85, enumerates thirty-five different Hadrianic types; Lehmann-Har-tleben and Lindros, 216–17, list only twenty-three legible stamps. Bloch also notes some Flavian stamps and a Severan one from the area of the structure.

[94] Lehmann-Hartleben and Lindros, 221–25, although their plan of the Canopus is out of date. See, too, Rakob, "Litus aureum" 139.          [95] Coarelli, *Roma* (1980) 249.

[96] Here we might note Vitruvius' general indication that meeting rooms and winter dining rooms should face southwest: *De Arch.* 6.4.1, 5.1.4.

the tradition of those associated with luxury villas, and in plan is similar to other Hadrianic pavilions, the modesty of its exterior is striking. This accords well with the contemporaneous diminution of the ostentation of the Palatine palace. And even the Villa in Tivoli, impressive as it is in terms of its complexity and infinite variety, lacks the dominating architecture of the Domitianic stamp.

CHAPTER SIX

# HADRIAN'S MAUSOLEUM AND
# THE PONS AELIUS

IFFERING VASTLY in purpose and impression from his imperial residences is Hadrian's funerary complex, consisting of the Mausoleum and
Pons Aelius and begun in the later 120s, though unfinished at his death.[1] Although one of the most conspicuous buildings of ancient Rome, Hadrian's
Mausoleum is still poorly understood. The solid ancient cores of the structure
remain, after having been reused successively as bridgehead in the fortifica-
tions of Rome, prison, papal palace, and now museum and park.[2] Yet the reconstruction of the Mausoleum's original appearance, particularly in the
upper stories, is notoriously difficult, as is the general chronology of the funerary complex, notwithstanding a terminus post quem of 123 given by the
brick stamps and a terminus ante quem of 134 provided by the bridge's dedicatory inscription (*CIL* 6.973 = Smallwood, #379). These problems, perhaps insoluble with the evidence available, and the location of the complex in
the Vatican plain on the right bank of the Tiber (*see Ill. 1*), have focused previous scholarly discussion of Hadrian's Mausoleum and Pons Aelius on problems of construction and architecture.[3]

[1] For the brick stamps dating the Mausoleum, Bloch, *Bolli* 253–56; and J. R. Pierce,
"The Mausoleum of Hadrian and the Pons
Aelius," *JRS* 15 (1925) 83 n. 4, 97 n. 2. Bloch
notes that the provenance of the bricks from
the Mausoleum now in the Castel museum is
unknown, and he emphasizes the difficulty of
determining from the few brick stamps we
now have the date of the beginning of construction.

[2] M. Borgatti, *Castel Sant'Angelo in Roma*
(Rome 1931), an exhaustive study, covers in
detail the history of the Mausoleum up to the
present time, but he is untrustworthy for the

archaeology of the original structure. Pierce,
"Mausoleum and Pons" 75–103, provides an
excellent short discussion of the construction
and history of the Mausoleum and bridge.
For the most recent examination of the buildings, see M. De' Spagnolis, "Contributi per
una nuova lettura del Mausoleo di Adriano,"
*BdA* 61 (1976) 62–68.

[3] The monument was indicated on the
*Forma Urbis* by (at least) the abbreviation
MA(USOLEUM) HA(DRIANI): *Forma Urbis*, pl. 32,
frags. 41 a–c, and text, p. 107. For discussions
of the architectural typology of the Mausoleum, see M. Eisner, "Zur Typologie der

The archaeological remains enveloped in the medieval structure, ambiguous numismatic evidence, and scant references in literature are periodically reexamined. Recently both T. Squadrilli and M. De' Spagnolis have revived an unconvincing reconstruction of the Mausoleum as a four-tiered structure.[4] The bridge, whose completion some medallions seem to commemorate, was fully excavated at the end of the last century. Since it presents fewer archaeological problems, it is usually treated briefly or mainly as the appendage of the Mausoleum, as in J. R. Pierce's and M. Borgatti's works.[5] So far no one has satisfactorily explained the unusual location of the Mausoleum, nor related Hadrian's tomb and bridge to the rest of the Hadrianic city.[6]

Comparison with the location of other important Roman sepulchers of the republic and early empire, particularly that of Augustus, shows the eccentricity of Hadrian's choice of location. A well-known Roman funerary practice put tombs along the main routes leading out of a city or town, thus keeping the memory of the deceased alive and in view while simultaneously respecting the prohibition against burial within the pomerium, the city's sacred boundary. An early and famous example is the tomb of the Scipios of the third century B.C. on the Via Appia.[7]

By the end of the republic two other, much less frequent, burial places were granted at Rome. In very rare cases, by a vote of the Roman people *monumenta virtutis causa* were permitted inside the pomerium for especially prominent individuals; a case in point is the burial of Poplicola below the Velia. And in the last century of the republic, burial in the Campus Martius (outside the pomerium) became a mark of singular distinction.[8] This rare mark of

<hr />

Mausoleen des Augustus und des Hadrian," *RömMitt* 86 (1979) 319–24; Crema, 484; and J.M.C. Toynbee, *Death and Burial in the Roman World* (Ithaca, N.Y. 1971) 157, 184. The latter two wrongly believe that the square base is Antonine. For the bridge, see Le Gall, *Tibre* 211–15; and P. Gazzola, *Ponti romani. Contributo ad un indice sistematico con studio critico bibliografico* (Florence 1963) 131–32. In general for the construction technique of both structures, see Blake/Bishop, 53–59. For the architectural ornament, Strong, "Late Ornament" 142–47. For discussion of the Mausoleum as religious architecture, see, e.g., H. Windfeld-Hansen, "Les Couloirs annulaires dans l'architecture funéraire antique," *Acta Instituti Romani Norvegiae* 2 (1962) 35–39, 42–

43, 58–63.

[4] T. Squadrilli, "Il Mausoleo di Adriano," *Capitolium* 50.7–8 (1975) 20–31; De' Spagnolis, "Lettura del Mausoleo" 62–68.

[5] In addition to n. 2 above, see Pierce, "Mausoleum and Pons" 95–98; and Borgatti, *Sant'Angelo* 61–67. For the numismatic evidence, see n. 51.

[6] Kienast, "Baupolitik" 407–10, considers the monument briefly, but primarily as evidence for Hadrian's dynastic policy; see below.

[7] See Toynbee, *Death and Burial* 103–13, and passim; and F. Coarelli, "Il sepolcro degli Scipioni," *DialAr* 6 (1972) 36–106.

[8] B. Frischer, "Monumenta et Arae Honoris Virtutisque Causa," *BullComm* 98 (1982–

eminence was granted only by decree of the senate (Dio Cass. 39.64; cf. App. *BCiv.* 1.106; Strabo 5.3.8). Sulla and Caesar's daughter, Julia, are both known to have had tumuli there, Agrippa a tomb he built himself, all still unlocated, and Caesar had planned to be buried there.[9] The most important of these monuments in the Campus, however, still stands: the Mausoleum of Augustus (*see Ill. 34*).

---

83) [1984] 51–86, examines the first type; for the second type of honor, see Castagnoli, "Campo Marzio" 94; and E. La Rocca, *La riva a mezzaluna* (Rome 1984) (*non vidi*).

9 Sulla: Livy *Epit.* 90; Plut. *Sulla* 38.4; App. *BCiv.* 1.106; Lucan 2.222; Julia, whose tumulus was perhaps intended for Julius Caesar as well: Livy *Epit.* 106; Plut. *Pomp.* 53.4,

*Caes.* 23.4; Dio Cass. 39.64; Agrippa: Dio Cass. 54.28.5. Others so honored include A. Hirtius, whose burial there is attested in our literary sources (Livy *Epit.* 119; Vell. Pat. 2.62.4–5) and has been discovered under the Palazzo: F. Magi, *I rilievi Flavi del Palazzo della Cancelleria* (Rome 1945) 37–54; and Nash, s.v. Sepulcrum A. Hirtii, II.341–43.

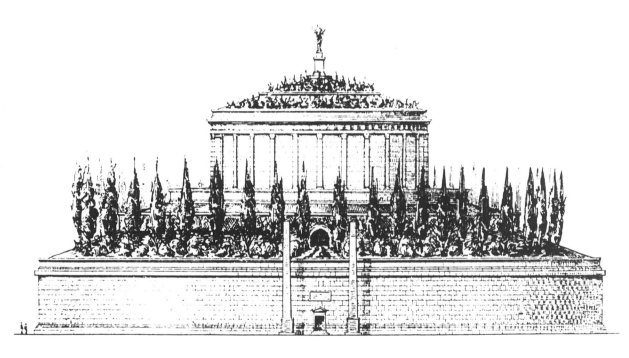

34. *Mausoleum of Augustus from the south, as reconstructed by G. Gatti. The bronze tablets inscribed with Augustus'* Res Gestae *and flanking the entrance are not depicted, and the two obelisks are post-Augustan.*

This is often thought to have been the prototype for the tomb of Hadrian.[10] Augustus' tomb was circular, about 87 meters in diameter, and rose some 45 meters.[11] Although large, it was fairly simple: the lowest element, a circular base about 12 meters high faced with travertine and possibly crowned by a Doric frieze, was surmounted by a smaller cylinder on which was a hill of earth planted with cypress trees topped by a bronze statue of Augustus (Strabo 5.3.8). The sole entrance in the southern side was flanked after Augustus' death by bronze tablets inscribed with Augustus' *Res Gestae*.

This grandiose monument, begun in the 30s and largely completed by 28 B.C. when Octavian was only thirty-five (Suet. *Aug.* 100.4), even during the princeps' lifetime received the ashes of many of Augustus' family. The subsequent Julio-Claudian emperors and their families (with a few notable exceptions) found their final resting place there. Possibly the remains of Vespasian (only temporarily) and certainly those of Nerva were put in Augustus' sepulcher.[12] With Nerva the tomb seems to have been closed for further use (cf. Dio Cass. 69.23.1). Augustus' Mausoleum combines two funerary traditions by being situated in the Campus Martius, yet close to the heavily traveled Via Flaminia (*see Ill. 1*). Its size and character made it especially conspicuous.

The locations for the tombs of the Flavians and of Trajan conform to the traditions just described. The Flavians found their final resting place on the Alta Semita, in the *aedes gentis Flaviae* that Domitian had built on the site of or near his family's house on the Quirinal.[13] Trajan, although unique in being

[10] For example, Toynbee, *Death and Burial* 157; Ward-Perkins, *RIA* 123.

[11] Nash, s.v. Mausoleum Augusti, II.38, with earlier bibliography; Eisner, "Typologie" 319–20, with additional bibliography as well as notes of variations in the measurements and reconstructions. Recent archaeological work in the Mausoleum has finally established that there were two stories below the crowning tumulus: see P. Virgili, "A proposito del Mausoleo di Augusto: Baldassare Peruzzi aveva ragione," *QuadAEI* 8 (1984) 194–98. The first interment was of Marcellus, in 23 B.C. Although the sepulcher was probably begun in the 30s as a personal monument (K. Kraft, "Der Sinn des Mausoleums des Augustus," *Historia* 16 [1967] 189–206), it was transformed into a dynastic tomb in the 20s (cf., e.g., J.-C. Richard, "'Mausoleum':

d'Halicarnasse à Rome, puis à Alexandrie," *Latomus* 29 [1970] 370–88, though dating the construction of the tomb too late [p. 376]; and G. Waurick, in *Jahrbuch des römisch–germanischen Zentralmuseums (Mainz)* 20 [1973] 110ff.).

[12] For the Julio-Claudian burials, see Platner-Ashby, s.v. Mausoleum Augusti, 332–35; for Vespasian and Nerva, see A. M. Colini and C. Q. Giglioli, "Relazione della prima campagna di scavo nel Mausoleo d'Augusto," *BullComm* 54 (1926) [1927] 202, 222; and *Epit. de Caes.* 12.12.

[13] For the aedes gentis Flaviae, see Coarelli, *Roma* (1980) 244–45; and O. Fea, *Miscellanea filologica, critica e antiquaria* I (Rome 1790) 72, cited by J.-C. Richard, "Tombeaux des empereurs et temples des 'divi': notes sur la signification religieuse des sépultures impériales

the first and probably sole emperor to be buried within Rome's pomerium, was given as a monument his Column, adjacent to his forum. In addition, this sepulcher is not far from the beginning of the Via Lata/Flaminia, and was at least partly visible from it.[14]

In contrast to the location of earlier imperial tombs, Hadrian's Mausoleum is on the right bank of the Tiber, in an area relatively desolate and inaccessible when he came to power (*see Ill. 35*). The *Historia Augusta*'s specification that Hadrian was buried in the Horti Domitiae (*HA, Pii* 5.1, cf. *Hadr.* 19.11 and Dio Cass. 69.23) informs us that the tomb was on imperial property in the Ager Vaticanus. Yet other evidence that the Vatican plain was frequently flooded by the Tiber makes Hadrian's choice somewhat odd. The low-lying plain was considered unhealthy, and Martial and Juvenal scorn it as producing only inferior wine and pottery (Mart. 6.92.3; Juv. 6.344; cf. Tac. *Hist.* 2.93). Horti and sumptuous buildings were rare in the area, and even burials were scarce.[15] Caesar had planned, by diverting the course of the Tiber, to unite this plain with the Campus Martius as a way of increasing the urban area of Rome (Cic. *Att.* 13.33.4), but the scheme came to nothing upon his death. The Ager Vaticanus later became the northern reaches of the fourteenth region of the Augustan city (Transtiberim), but remained largely undeveloped.

During the first century A.D. most of the plain along the river was in the possession of members of the imperial family, although by Trajan's day some parts were public. The Horti Domitiae of Hadrian's period (probably incorporating the Horti Drusi attested earlier in the region) seem to have belonged to Nero's aunt Domitia Lepida, whose property passed to Nero and thus into the imperial fiscus.[16] The earliest phase of the only extensive luxury villa excavated in the region dates to the first half of the first century A.D., and has been plausibly identified as the Villa of Agrippina, part of the Horti Agrippinae south of the Horti Domitiae.[17] In the vicinity Agrippina's son Caligula

---

à Rome," *RHR* 170 (1966) 133–34. I do not find convincing the suggestion of K. Lehmann-Hartleben, "L'Arco di Tito," *Bull-Comm* 62 (1934) 107–15, that Domitian put the ashes of Titus at least temporarily in the Arch of Titus.

[14] See Chapter 3.

[15] For the poor reputation of the area during the late republic and early empire, see J. Toynbee and J. Ward-Perkins, *The Shrine of St. Peter and the Vatican Excavations* (London 1956) 5; and Grimal, *Jardins* 139–42.

[16] Grimal, *Jardins* 141–42, convincingly assigns the Horti Domitiae to Domitia Lepida, an attribution shared tentatively by Toynbee and Ward-Perkins, *Shrine of St. Peter* 5; contra, Castagnoli, *TRA* 118, and *HJ* 662–63, who assign them to Domitia Longina, the wife of Domitian. In either case, the gardens were imperial property by the second century A.D.

[17] For the Villa and gardens of Agrippina, see Coarelli, *Roma* (1980) 360; W. von Sydow, "Archäologische Funde und Forschun-

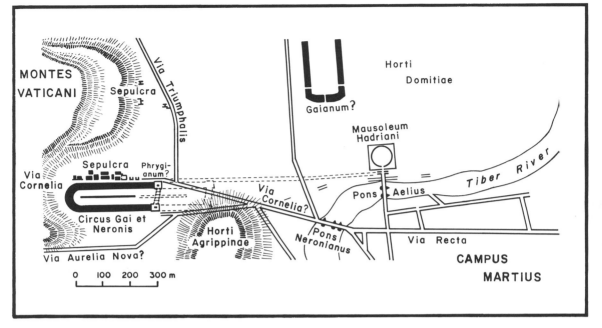

35. *The Ager Vaticanus in the second century* A.D.

built the Circus (Gaii et Neronis), which served Nero first as a private race course, and then was used for the public punishment of the Christians after the fire of 64 (Tac. *Ann.* 15.44.4–5). Nero probably built the bridge, called Pons Neronianus in the Middle Ages, that prolonged the Via Recta across the Tiber to the vicinity of the Circus. This bridge seems to have been basically private and closely associated with the horti of the imperial family. As early as Nero's day, however, one road, the Via Aurelia Nova, may have run a little south of the Circus. Beginning in the late Augustan period another street, the Via Triumphalis on the slopes of modern Monte Mario, was lined with modest burials.[18]

gen, Rom," *AA* 88 (1973) 614; and Platner-Ashby, s.v. Horti Agrippinae, 264–65.

[18] The exact location of the Circus, long debated, was determined only recently: see F. Castagnoli, "Il circo di Nerone in Vaticano," *RendPontAcc* 32 (1959–60) [1960] 97–121; and F. Magi, "Il circo vaticano in base alle più recenti scoperte. Il suo obelisco e i suoi *carceres*," *RendPontAcc* 45 (1972–73) [1974] 37–73. For the private character of the bridge, see Grimal, *Jardins* 140. For the Via Triumphalis under the modern Via del Pelle-

grino, see Jordan, 1.1, pp. 376–78. Grimal, *Jardins* 140 n. 6, implausibly dating the road to Hadrian, connects the name to Trajan's posthumous triumph. The road must antedate Trajan's Aqua Traiana, which runs along it in part (cf. T. Ashby, in *Studi Etruschi* 3 [1929] 176 n. 2), and a group of late Trajanic and Hadrianic bricks carry the name of the road (M. Steinby, "Ziegelstempel von Rom und Umgebung," *RE, Suppl.* 15 [1978] 1507). See also Platner-Ashby, s.v. Via Triumphalis (1), 569. For the sepulchers, see

The fire of 64 marks the transition of the Vatican plain from private to public domain, although it remained underutilized for another half century. The earliest evidence of the Via Cornelia, which ran just north of the Circus, is Vespasianic. Scattered, relatively poor burials, probably including that of Saint Peter, were made along the Cornelia by the late first century.[19] Northeast, and slightly northwest of the later Mausoleum of Hadrian, the remains of a stadium garden have been found; C. Buzzetti plausibly identifies them as the Gaianum created by Caligula, which has been poorly attested. A secondary road, also poorly documented, ran parallel to it to the west.[20]

It is only beginning with Hadrian's Mausoleum and Pons Aelius that the lower Ager Vaticanus began to be properly developed. In conjunction with Hadrian's works an embankment road was built, carried on a quay between the Mausoleum and the river. To the east this continued along the Tiber's bank; to the west it ran to link up with and become the Via Cornelia, the line of which reflects the orientation of the whole Hadrianic complex.[21] Thus the Pons Aelius tied the western Campus Martius into the road system in the Ager Vaticanus as well as to the Mausoleum itself. And at this time the outlying districts served by the Viae Cornelia, Aurelia Vetus, Aurelia Nova, and Triumphalis may have gained in importance, to judge from an inscription at-

F. Magi, "Relazione preliminare sui ritrovamenti archeologici nell'area dell'autoparco Vaticano," in *Triplice omaggio a sua Santità Pio XII* (Vatican City 1968) 87–99; and V. Väänanen, ed., "Le iscrizioni della necropoli dell'autoparco Vaticano," *Acta Instituti Romani Finlandiae* 6 (1973) 17–18, 157, 195. This area, however, is rather far from the city, about 400 meters north of the later Basilica of St. Peter.

[19] The Via Cornelia is assigned to Vespasian by Grimal, *Jardins* 140, 160, who suggests that it is another instance of the Flavian conversion of Nero's private holdings to public use; Toynbee and Ward-Perkins, *Shrine of St. Peter* 7, assign a Julio-Claudian date to a highway along the southern foot of the Vatican hill, and follow the initial excavators in calling it the Via Cornelia. The Vespasianic date comes from an inscription, originally published in *CRAI*, 1925, 227–37, that records L. Antistius Rusticus, who was the *curator viarum Aureliae et Corneliae* under Vespasian. For the first-century burials in the area

of St. Peter's, see M. Guarducci, *The Tomb of St. Peter*, trans. by J. McLellan (Rome 1960) 55–59; idem, "Documenti del I° secolo nella necropoli Vaticana," *RendPontAcc* 29 (1956–57) [1958] 111–37.

[20] C. Buzzetti, "Nota sulla topografia dell'Ager Vaticanus," *QuadIstTopAnt* 5 (1968) 105–11, argues that this structure cannot be the Naumachia begun by Domitian and finished by Trajan in 109 (*II*, 13.1, pp. 200–201), which he tentatively places farther south. On his map on p. 359, Coarelli, *Roma* (1980), mistakenly labels the secondary road Via Triumphalis.

[21] This quay was discovered only in Borsari's excavations for the Tiber embankments in 1892–94: Le Gall, *Tibre* 215. For the embankment road, ibid., 212–14 (referring to the original report by L. Borsari, in *NSc*, 1892, 231–33, 412–28); Pierce, "Mausoleum and Pons" 96–98, gives more detail about the quay's construction. The Gaianum indicates that there was a roughly orthogonal layout to the area: Buzzetti, "Ager Vaticanus" 109–11.

testing to a procurator responsible for their upkeep in 142/143.[22] The Phry-
gianum, an important shrine to Magna Mater amply attested to in the fourth
century and probably located south of the Circus, may date as early as 160.[23]
If so, it also shows the growing use of the Ager Vaticanus from the Hadrianic
period.

The area became popular at this time for other reasons. After ca. 125–130
richer burials and sumptuous private mausolea began to be located along the
Via Aurelia and Via Cornelia, and by 150 at the latest the Circus Gaii et Neronis had fallen into disuse, with burials invading the arena.[24] The poorer,
Christian, burials of the first and second century have been associated with
the tomb of Saint Peter, but the development along the Via Cornelia of a pres-
tigious cemetery for predominantly pagan Romans of the second century
seems due to the location there of Hadrian's Mausoleum and Pons Aelius.[25]
The bridge, strategically linked to the earlier road systems on both banks of
the river, seems to have promoted communication between the two banks,
and ultimately between Rome and the northwest. By the prestige of his own
tomb, Hadrian encouraged Romans, at least wealthy freedmen, to build their
own sepulchers on the nearby and hitherto underutilized land in the Ager Vaticanus.

Yet the proximity of the Campus Martius, with its tombs of the great
men of the past, must also have been a deciding factor in Hadrian's location

[22] This procurator, C. Popilius C.f. Carus
Pedo, also oversaw repairs on the Aurelia Ve-
tus: *ILS* 1071 = *CIL* 14.3610 = Smallwood,
#234. The inscription is dated by H. E. Her-
zig, "Namen und Daten der Via Aurelia,"
*Epigraphica* 32 (1970) 54–60. T. P. Wiseman,
"Via Aurelia Nova and Via Aemilia Scauri,'
*Epigraphica* 33 (1971) 28, suggests that the
Aurelia Vetus was included in the procurator-
ship because it led to Antoninus Pius' estates
at Alsium, bypassed by the Aurelia Nova.
Earlier controversy over the two Viae Aure-
liae is summarized by G. M. de Rossi, "La
Via Aurelia dal Marta al Fiora," *QuadIst-
TopAnt* 4 (1968) 154–55.

[23] For the shrine, see Toynbee and Ward-
Perkins, *Shrine of St. Peter* 6, who cite eleven
inscriptions documenting it (the dated ones
falling into the period 305–390), which were
found in the vicinity: *CIL* 6.1.497–503, 504;
6.4.2.30780; B. M. Apollonj-Ghetti et al., *Esplorazioni sotto la confessione di S. Pietro in Va-*

*ticano eseguite negli anni 1940–1941*, 1 (Vatican
City 1951) figs. 2, 3; and *CIL* 6.1.512. Two
others have been found farther afield: *CIL*
13.1.1.1751, found at Lyon and dating to 160;
and *CIL* 13.2.1.7281, found at Kastel am
Mainz and dating to 236.

[24] Toynbee and Ward-Perkins, *Shrine of St.
Peter* 30; Castagnoli, "Circo" 105, 120. See
now also H. Mielsch, "Hadrianische Malereien der Vatikannekropole *ad circum*,"
*RendPontAcc* 46 (1973–74) [1975] 79–87.

[25] The tombs in the area of the basilica are
predominantly pagan, and the presumed memorial to Saint Peter dates at the earliest to ca.
150: Guarducci, *Tomb of St. Peter* 64, 80–93;
and Toynbee and Ward-Perkins, *Shrine of St.
Peter* 127–67. Only cautiously can we assume
that the Petrine tradition was responsible for
attracting other burials. See, however, Guarducci, 25–43; and idem, "Nuove iscrizioni
nella zona del Circo di Nerone in Vaticano,"
*RendPontAcc* 32 (1959–60) [1960] 123–32.

of his tomb. The Mausoleum, oriented to the cardinal points of the compass on the right bank of the Tiber just above its bend, rose about 50 meters high and rests on a footing of rough concrete about 2 meters thick[26] (*see Ill. 36*). Still visible and impressive are its square base, a circular drum of smaller diameter inserted in this and rising above it, and a central tower, which is the core of the medieval structure crowning it today. Originally, a fence of panels of metal grillwork, about 115 meters long on a side and with its travertine cippi supporting bronze peacocks, surrounded the square base.[27]

[26] De' Spagnolis, "Lettura del Mausoleo" 62. Except where noted, the following description of the Mausoleum is based on that of De' Spagnolis, the most recent investigation of the monument. The height is variously estimated: e.g., De' Spagnolis (p. 64) gives it as 48 meters, and Blake/Bishop (p. 59) as 54 meters.

[27] Two peacocks can still be seen in the Cortile della Pigna. The grille and decoration are described in the *Mirabilia Romae* (reproduced and discussed by Pierce, "Mausoleum and Pons" 76–77, 97); they may have stood 15.60 meters out from the square base: Borgatti, *Sant'Angelo* 60. Richard, "Tombeaux" 132, notes that the peacock is one of the symbols of apotheosis for an empress.

36. *Mausoleum of Hadrian and the southern section of the Pons Aelius. Model of remains shows construction; the metal grillwork fence and other decorations are not represented. (Model now in the Museo della Civiltà Romana, Rome.)*

The base itself was composed of a double wall on a low socle, brick within and marble-faced travertine without; the marble-faced wall stood 10 to 12 meters high and ran 85 meters on a side.[28] On the south or entrance side a lower zone was reserved for the epitaphs of those buried within,[29] while in the upper portion a series of pilasters punctuated a revetment of Parian or Luna marble that simulated rusticated ashlar. Marble pilasters with beautifully carved capitals finished each corner, and the entablature seems to have carried a frieze of garlands and bulls' heads, with paterae carved over the garlands. This was surmounted by a classical cornice. The architectural decoration is of a type common in late Hadrianic and Antonine buildings.[30] In the center of the south side opened a large bronze door in a marble frame, over which apparently was the inscription to Hadrian and the deified Sabina that was installed by Antoninus Pius in 139 (*CIL* 6.984 = *ILS* 322 = Smallwood, #124, our terminus ante quem for the completion of the tomb).[31]

Inside the ornate external wall was a utilitarian one of brick-faced concrete into which were bonded the walls of sixty-seven barrel-vaulted chambers radiating from the central drum.[32] These communicated with one another and

[28] De' Spagnolis, "Lettura del Mausoleo" 62; Pierce, "Mausoleum and Pons" 81–82. Scholars vary as much as 10 meters in their figures.

[29] Pierce, "Mausoleum and Pons" 77–78, offers a reconstruction of the placing of the inscriptions, and lists (with references to his sources) the individuals known to have been buried in the Mausoleum: Hadrian; Sabina; L. Aelius; Antoninus Pius; Faustina the Elder; the three children of Antoninus Pius: M. Aurelius Fulvus; M. Galerius Aurelius Antoninus; Aurelia Fadilla; Marcus Aurelius and his children: T. Aurelius Antoninus, T. Aelius Aurelius, and Domitia Faustina; L. Verus; Commodus; Julia Domna; Septimius Severus; Caracalla; and Geta. Not all of these eighteen are attested in the inscriptions recorded from the Mausoleum (*CIL* 6.984–95). Pierce's reconstruction is based on that of Hülsen, in *RömMitt* 6 (1891) 142–43, though it is rejected by Borgatti, *Sant'Angelo* 56, 34–36. Although *HA, Ver.* 11.1 says that L. Aelius Verus, who died before Hadrian did, was buried in the Mausoleum, the inscription describing him as *divi Hadriani Aug. filius* found

here shows his entombment occurred sometime after Hadrian's own in 139 (*CIL* 6.985).

[30] Strong, "Late Ornament" 129, 142–47 (who believes that the surviving angle pilaster attributed to the Mausoleum "may well be considerably pre-Hadrianic"); and Blake/Bishop, 56.

[31] De' Spagnolis, "Lettura del Mausoleo" 62, says that there were doors in all four sides of the fence, but that only one door, in the south side, gave access to the interior of the Mausoleum. For the bronze door of three leaves described in the *Mirabilia*, see, e.g., Blake/Bishop, 56.

[32] Blake/Bishop, 56–57; and Pierce, "Mausoleum and Pons" 84–85, consider that the square base represents the change of an originally circular plan; Pierce further notes that the center of radiation for the rooms does not coincide with the center of the drum. The coarseness of the brickwork and the sequence of construction have led some to suggest (implausibly) that the barrel-vaulted rooms are Antonine (e.g., Toynbee, *Death and Burial* 157; and Crema, 484). But the brick stamps of 123 come from this base, and the rapidity of

with the entrance corridor; and the brick stamps of 123, mentioned earlier, were found on bipedales in their walls. The use of these rooms is disputed, but they made the top of the square base level and capable of supporting considerable weight.[33] The four corners of the upper platform were surmounted by marble groups of men and horses.[34]

This square base, of no apparent utilitarian function, is surprising in combination with a tomb of essentially circular form; it clearly differentiates it from the nearby Mausoleum of Augustus, which rose as a cylinder of two stories capped with a tumulus.[35] The square base also oriented Hadrian's tomb on the lines of most of the buildings in the central Campus Martius, an alignment emphasized by the Pons Aelius leading straight toward the Mausoleum on axis at approximately a right angle to the Via Recta, the major east-west artery of the Campus (*see Ill. 1*).

The square base, still discernible in the medieval castle, encases the foot of the central drum, the second main element of the Mausoleum. It is here that controversy begins, for this drum and the central tower it carries have been reworked so often that much of the original structure has disappeared. The following description first enumerates the well-documented remains and then considers briefly various reconstructions that have been proposed.

The central drum is faced with opus quadratum of tufa (with some travertine blocks) within the square base, where the radiating chambers abut and conceal it. Up to the height of the square base (about 12 meters), the diameter of the drum measures 74 meters, but immediately above this it diminishes to 68 meters. Its summit is 21 meters higher, over 31 meters above ground level.[36] This drum was originally almost a solid mass of concrete. Inside it were only an entrance corridor and vestibule, a ramp spiraling up counter-

most construction during the Hadrianic period makes it unlikely that the bricks' manufacture would antedate their use by more than about fifteen years.

[33] De' Spagnolis, "Lettura del Mausoleo" 62, rejects the theory that these rooms had a funerary destination and argues for a structural purpose.

[34] These marble groups were described by Procopius, *Goth.* 1.22.14. Although the *Mirabilia* says the statuary was of gilded bronze, (Pierce, "Mausoleum and Pons" 77), according to Blake/Bishop, 56, the archaeological evidence suggests that they were of marble.

[35] Eisner, "Typologie" 321, who notes that the plain tumulus type is more frequent. For illustration and discussion of the various funerary types, see Crema, 242–61, and J.-C. Richard, "Les Funérailles de Trajan et le triomphe sur les Parthes," *REL* 44 (1966) 353–54.

[36] De' Spagnolis, "Lettura del Mausoleo" 63, 66; Pierce, "Mausoleum and Pons" 83–86; Blake/Bishop, 57–58, who give the diameter of the upper drum as 64 meters, as does Squadrilli, "Mausoleo" 20–21. The description by Blake/Bishop of the interior is the basis of the following.

clockwise from the vestibule to a central burial chamber located directly over it, a second chamber over the first, four apertures with splayed openings admitting light and air to the ramp, and perhaps two apertures for light and air to the lower burial chamber. Brick faces all the Hadrianic internal walls except the entrance vestibule, where there is travertine. Marble or stucco originally revetted all the interior surfaces. A simple black and white mosaic, still visible in places, paved the floor of the ramp. The top of the cylindrical drum, slightly domed and impermeable due to its *opus signinum* (waterproofing cement), comes to the level of the modern Cortili dell'Angelo (or delle Palle) and di Alessandro VI (or dell'Olio).

The entrance corridor had openings to either side to the adjacent barrel-vaulted rooms around the central drum, and ended in a vestibule with a large axial niche, which seems to have held a statue of Hadrian.[37] The floor and travertine walls of the vestibule were once revetted with marble. Opposite a rectangular niche on the left, the spiral ramp, about 6 meters high and 3 meters wide, leads from the vestibule upward at a slope of 10 degrees. After making a complete circle, it debouches into a corridor leading to the central burial chamber lying north and south over the vestibule 12 meters below it.[38]

The burial chamber is a large square room with a vaulted ceiling in the center of the drum; it measures about 10.20 meters high, 8 meters a side.[39] In its north, east, and west walls are rectangular recesses with arched and rectangular tops that must have held the ash urns. At the base of the walls all around the chamber the lowest course of travertine projects a foot or so from the wall in a low bench. At the springing of the vault on the east and west sides openings for light were apparently later cut through to the Cortili above.[40]

Above this central burial chamber is another room, similar to that below but without niches. We have no clear evidence for the access to or the function of this room. It rose to the top of the drum, and above it rose the central tower.[41]

Only the core of this tower has survived, built into the papal palace.[42] Pre-

---

[37] Pierce, "Mausoleum and Pons" 85, gives this niche a span of nearly 12 feet (3.66 meters). The head of the statue may be one now in the Vatican; see De' Spagnolis, "Lettura del Mausoleo" 63.

[38] De' Spagnolis, "Lettura del Mausoleo" 63, 67 n. 10 (length of the ramp, 125.50 meters); Pierce, "Mausoleum and Pons" 87; Borgatti, *Sant'Angelo* 19–20.

[39] Dimensions: De' Spagnolis, "Lettura del Mausoleo" 67 n. 12 with Blake/Bishop, 58. The former's measurement of 2.20 meters a side must be incorrect. A fragment of the giallo antico revetment of the room still survives (Blake/Bishop, 58; De' Spagnolis, 63).

[40] Pierce, "Mausoleum and Pons" 87; Borgatti, *Sant'Angelo* 22; and Blake/Bishop, 58.

[41] Blake/Bishop, 58; see n. 47 below.

[42] Blake/Bishop, 58; De' Spagnolis, "Lettura del Mausoleo" 63–64.

sumably circular on the exterior, the lofty tower contained a domed cylindrical room now divided horizontally into two. This chamber was accessible by an external staircase rising from the slightly domed crown of the main drum (the level of the present Cortili). It seems to have had a crowning sculpture, perhaps the quadriga group described in a fragment of Dio Cassius as incredibly large but seen from such a distance that its proportions seemed normal. The height of the whole has been estimated as some 50 meters.[43]

The interior arrangements of the Mausoleum, which are clear enough in Castel Sant'Angelo, leave some puzzles. The allegedly modest size of Hadrian's central burial chamber, the only one clearly intended for this purpose, has perplexed some scholars. Some conjecture, without any evidence, that the barrel-vaulted rooms around the base were used for burials.[44] Squadrilli has gone as far as to imagine that sumptuous burial chambers lined a continuation of the ramp in a hypothetical arc beyond its present course,[45] although the burial chamber that exists would have been quite spacious enough to hold a large number of ash urns.[46] Nevertheless, her suggestion touches on another vexing problem: the access to the chamber directly above the central one, and for this there is simply no evidence at all.[47]

[43] For the quadriga, see Dio Cass. Exc. Salm. frag. 114 Muell (p. 396, 23–27 Cram = Loeb ed., vol. 8, pp. 466–67); and Pierce, "Mausoleum and Pons" 78, 93. For the height, see n. 26 above.

[44] But see Borgatti, Sant'Angelo 27–28; De' Spagnolis, "Lettura del Mausoleo" 64–65; and Pierce, "Mausoleum and Pons" 84 n. 2.

[45] Squadrilli, "Mausoleo" 23–27; her main evidence is her belief that Alexander VI could not have dug out Hadrianic concrete, and that much more room was needed to house the imperial urns and sarcophagi (by her count at least twenty-one) than was provided in the main burial chamber. But see the following note.

[46] Borgatti, Sant'Angelo 27, says that there is room for at least twenty cinerary urns in the central cella. J.-C. Richard, "Recherches sur certains aspects du culte impérial: Les Funérailles des empereurs romains aux deux premiers siècles de notre ère," ANRW II.16.2 (1978) 1125–27, stresses that cremation was still de rigueur for Roman imperial burials in Hadrian's day, and holds that cremation of at

least a mannequin was necessary for the apotheosis of the deceased. For imperial funeral rites, see also E. Bickerman, "Consecratio," in Le Culte des souverains dans l'empire romain 19–25; P. Gros, "Apothéose impériale et rites funéraires au second siècle de notre ère," RHR 171 (1967) 117–20; and Chapter 7, the section on the "Ustrinum" of Hadrian. For the "gradual supersession of cremation by inhumation during the second century," see Toynbee, Death and Burial 39–41; and R. Turcan, "Origines et sens de l'inhumation à l'époque impériale," REA 60 (1958) 332–47 (although his discussion of imperial burials, pp. 323–32, is not so convincing).

[47] Pierce, "Mausoleum and Pons" 87–90, saw evidence for the opening of a ramp in the north-south corridor leading to the burial chamber; and C. Hülsen, "Il Mausoleo di Adriano," BullComm 3 (1913) 31, and De' Spagnolis, "Lettura del Mauseleo," 63, also think that a vaulted ramp led upward to the level of the superior chamber. Borgatti, Sant'Angelo 53–54, categorically denied any continuation of the ramp.

The external appearance of the upper stories has also excited controversy. Three theories have been advanced: that Hadrian's tomb consisted only of the three elements just described, perhaps with a kind of gentle tumulus formed by earth between the outer wall of the large cylinder and the base of the topmost element; that it resembled a large and steep tumulus from the second to the topmost element; and that it originally had four distinct stories—the squared base, the central drum, a smaller drum above that, and the crowning tower.

The first and most conservative of these theories limits itself to the incontrovertible ancient evidence so far discovered in the fortress, although the outward appearance of the topmost story is variously reconstructed by its adherents.[48] Other scholars are more venturesome. Borgatti, the former director of Castel Sant'Angelo, is the main proponent of the tumulus theory, for he believed that fine earth found between the outer wall of the central drum and the central tower during his investigations at the beginning of this century was laid on in the Roman period. Although his conclusion—that a large tumulus rose over the central drum to terminate in a square support for a sculptural group—is dubious, the attraction of the analogy with Augustus' tomb has led most others to suppose that some sort of garden planted with trees graced the top of the central drum.[49] Finally, De' Spagnolis has combined the results of her recent study of Castel Sant'Angelo's construction with a reinvestigation of some debatable numismatic evidence, and reaffirms the hypothesis more recently revived by Squadrilli: that the Mausoleum was originally four-storied. De' Spagnolis mentions archaeological evidence for a prolongation of the ramp, but at a steeper slope and with a smaller radius as it climbed, in order not to interfere with the light shafts leading to the central (lower) burial chamber. Furthermore, she believes that the curved line of the east side of the Cortile di Alessandro VI (or dell'Olio) is due to reuse of a Roman element.[50]

[48] For example, Pierce; Blake/Bishop; Eisner; and Coarelli, *Roma* (1980) 365–68; Coarelli believes the topmost element was rectangular, Pierce and Eisner, cylindrical.

[49] Borgatti, *Sant'Angelo* 46–47, 57–59, repeating his theories advanced earlier but then rejected by C. Hülsen, *RömMitt* 8 (1893) 27; and by Pierce, "Mausoleum and Pons" 84 n. 2, 91–92; and now also by Eisner, "Typologie" 320–21; and De' Spagnolis, "Lettura del Mausoleo" 64–65, on structural grounds. They, and Blake/Bishop, 59, envision a shallow garden. Toynbee, *Death and Burial* 157. accepts the tumulus theory on typological grounds.

[50] De' Spagnolis, "Lettura del Mausoleo" 63–67, venturing the hypothesis that the circuit of the upper ramp was complete (360 degrees) but on a shorter radius and with steeper slope to allow for the air shafts to the central burial chamber; Squadrilli, "Mausoleo" 27–31. The theory about the reuse of Roman structural elements under the Cortile di Alessandro VI (or dell'Olio) originated with C. Hülsen, "Il Mausoleo di Adriano," *BullComm* 3 (1913) 31.

Yet in her publication she presents no solid evidence to support her theories, and most of her and Squadrilli's argument for a four-storied Mausoleum is based on questionable numismatic evidence.

An enigmatic structure appears on the reverses of medallions commemorating the consecration of emperors and empresses from Faustina the Elder to Constantius Chlorus[51] (*see Ill. 37*). This is a building of four stories (five, in the case of Septimius Severus and Constantius Chlorus), each successive story receding in respect to that below it. The lowest (and often the highest) story is covered with drapery and hung with garlands. The intervening stories are colonnaded or arcuated and embellished with a wealth of figural sculpture. On occasion the whole is surmounted by a quadriga or a biga, apparently vehicles of apotheosis.

[51] For these coins, see most recently P. N. Schulten, *Die Typologie der römische Konsekrationsprägungen* (Frankfurt 1979) 21–22; and A. Frazer, "A Numismatic Source for Michelangelo's First Design for the Tomb of Julius II," *Art Bulletin* 57 (1975) 53–57, who argues that the edifice depicted is a funeral pyre. Toynbee, *Death and Burial* 295 nn. 244–52, gives a list of the most important consecration issues of this type; the first of her list, the coin honoring L. Aelius Caesar (d. 138), is a forgery (and see Frazer, 53 n. 6).

37. *Examples of consecration coins showing funeral pyres erroneously considered to represent the Mausoleum of Hadrian.*

Although these structures are commonly identified as imperial funeral pyres, the similarity of these to one another, and their fundamental difference from the excavated structures in Rome identified as ustrina, recently have led Squadrilli and De' Spagnolis to propose that these issues do not show the funeral pyres on which the persons so honored were burnt, but rather the Mausoleum of Hadrian, in which they were buried.[52] Thus the Mausoleum would have had four stepped stories, and a wealth of architectural and sculptural embellishment in the intermediate levels. Yet this is all pure speculation and based on erroneous premises, such as the identification of the "Ustrina" of Antoninus Pius and of Marcus Aurelius as functioning ustrina (see Chapter 7).

Consideration of the extant remains and of the three proposed reconstructions of Hadrian's tomb, discussed earlier, shows how imperfectly we understand the architectural form and its traditions. The lowest story—the square base, with its marble statuary at the four corners and white marble revetment—dominated the impression Hadrian's tomb made on those at all close to it. This huge and ornate podium distinguished it from most of the other tombs in and around Rome, including that of Augustus. Its total height of at least 50 meters above the alluvial plain on either side of the Tiber raised Hadrian's Mausoleum above even the Pantheon and Column of Trajan, as well as Augustus' Mausoleum upstream. Looming up from the surrounding plain and the river, Hadrian's tomb must have been one of the first distinguishable signs of Rome for travelers from the north, much as the dome of Saint Peter's was until this century.[53]

Although it was located on the right, noncity, bank of the Tiber, Hadrian's Mausoleum was not isolated from the rest of Rome. Not only is its orientation the same as that of the buildings in the central Campus Martius, but the Pons Aelius on its axis connected it to the Campus. This bridge, completed in 134 and an integral part of the complex, was constructed on the same principles as other Roman bridges.[54] Two large piers sunk into the riverbed

---

[52] De' Spagnolis, "Lettura del Mausoleo" 65–66; Squadrilli, "Mausoleo" 22–31, who also asserts incorrectly that these medallions all honor individuals known to have been buried in the Mausoleum. For earlier bibliography on the question, and conclusions that what is represented is a funeral pyre, see Platner-Ashby, s.v. Mausoleum Hadriani, 336 n. 1.

[53] The other monuments mentioned rose 43.20 meters, 38 meters, and just less than 50 meters, respectively. For a good description of the impression made by the dome of St. Peter's on travelers coming to Rome by the Via Flaminia, see A.J.C. Hare, *Walks in Rome*, 17th ed. (London 1905) 6–8.

[54] Le Gall, *Tibre* 211–15, who convincingly rejects Lanciani's hypothesis of an ancient

supported three main arches of peperino tufa faced with travertine. The spans of the arches are 18 meters wide, and their keystones were 9 meters above the normal level of the Tiber. A steep ramp led down from this elevated central part to either bank.

Three arches on the left bank carry a ramp 33 meters long down to an embankment road[55] (*see Ill. 38*). The street leading south from the bridge, after crossing the embankment road, crossed the Via Recta, the main artery through this part of the Campus Martius, and ran to join the street later called the Porticus Maximae. This was a long street running from the Capitoline west and then northwest to the Pons Neronianus, on a route roughly parallel to the course of the Tiber[56] (*see Ill. 1*).

---

channeling and regulation of the river (first published in *BullComm* 21 [1893] 15–16, ill. 1, and followed by many, including Blake/Bishop, 55, and Borgatti, *Sant'Angelo* 61–67). Le Gall's conclusions are supported by recent investigations: cf. C. Mocchegiani Carpano, "Indagini archeologiche nel Tevere," *QuadAEI* 5 (1981) 144. For more detail on the bridge: Pierce, "Mausoleum and Pons" 96–97; Gazzola, *Ponti* 131–32; and Nash, s.v. Pons Aelius, II.178. The following details are from Pierce and Le Gall, except where noted. Most ancient references to the bridge link it intimately with the Mausoleum (e.g., *HA, Hadr.* 19.11).

[55] Gazzola, *Ponti* 132, gives the span of the two arches flanking the central one as 7.50 meters, and that of the five smaller ones as ca. 3.50 meters. Pierce, "Mausoleum and Pons" 97, notes that Borsari originally measured the ramp as 26.40 meters.

[56] Pierce, "Mausoleum and Pons" 95, conjectures that Hadrian or Antoninus was responsible for this long street on the left bank linking the bridge to the other long street traversing the southwest Campus Martius.

38. *Pons Aelius. Left bank in 1892, during excavations for the modern river embankments.*

On the right bank a ramp 22 meters long was supported by only two arches; its shorter length is explained by the fact that the embankment road it met perpendicularly was elevated on a quay.[57] Eight meters north of the ramp's end lay the entrance through the fence surrounding the Mausoleum. Thus the Pons Aelius served to connect the Mausoleum to the major streets of the Campus Martius.

The importance of this connection is underscored by the medallions commemorating the bridge, one of the few architectural types of Hadrian's coinage[58] (*see Ill. 39*). Although each of the two known variants is of dubious accuracy in details, the type is apparently generally trustworthy and is confirmed by the physical remains, including those along the right bank discovered only in excavations at the end of the nineteenth century. On the medallions, eight plinths over the main piers support columns surmounted by statues. Portions of the balustrading of the bridge and of the southernmost pair of plinths were found in the excavations of 1892–1894. To judge from the medallions, the Pons Aelius was unusually richly embellished for a Roman bridge, and possibly unique; in some sense its program anticipates Bernini's scheme for the Ponte Sant'Angelo, and possibly remains of the ancient plinths suggested the plan to Bernini.[59] The decorative program must have reinforced the intimate association of the bridge with Hadrian's tomb, but there is no way of telling whom the statues represented. The medallions, which depict the bridge without the Mausoleum, seem intended to emphasize primarily the connection between the two banks. In fact, the Pons Aelius had a dual purpose: at the same time as it provided a route between the Campus Martius and another part of the Ager Vaticanus, it was unthinkable without the Mausoleum of Hadrian at its northern end.

Thus Hadrian's Mausoleum, sited on the right bank of the Tiber and tied to the city by the Pons Aelius, encouraged the growth of Rome west into a

[57] This was discovered in 1892–94, by Borsari.

[58] Pensa, "Adriano" 66–69, offers an excellent discussion of these medallions, four of which are known, with illustrations and earlier bibliography. She and Le Gall, *Tibre* 214–15, accept them as genuine; others, e.g., Toynbee, *Roman Medallions* 146 n. 196, 232 (identifying the bridge as the Pons Aelius over the River Tyne in Great Britain), and Blake/Bishop, 55, doubt their authenticity.

[59] Pensa, "Adriano" 67, suggests that the statues may actually be herms, and observes how unusual any such embellishment was for a Roman bridge. C. C. Vermeule, *Greek Sculpture and Roman Taste* (Ann Arbor, Mich. 1977) 104, hypothesizes that they were statues of provinces and regions throughout the empire, or of members of the imperial family from Nerva to Lucius Verus. For balustrading and plinths: Pierce, "Mausoleum and Pons" 96; and Blake/Bishop, 56.

39. *Hadrianic medallion illustrating the Pons Aelius. (Venice exemplar, from the Museo Correr.)*

region that had only recently been endowed with roads and now with prestige; simultaneously, its visibility and orientation, emphasized in its squared base and the axial siting of the bridge, must have made it appear as the westernmost delineation of the similarly oriented Campus Martius across the river. Hadrian's Mausoleum served as a reminder of his extensive renovation of the central Campus much as Augustus' Mausoleum marked the farthest limits north of the area's original monumentalization under the earlier princeps. Furthermore, by placing his own tomb where he did, Hadrian ensured that it would be compared to that of Augustus, only 800 meters upstream.

Obvious similarities link Hadrian's Mausoleum with Augustus', both huge and of a main cylindrical mass, although their dissimilarity is just as striking. The large square base of Hadrian's tomb must have caught the eye; the tomb itself was no professed tumulus; and the central cylinders almost certainly were finished differently. Hadrian's tomb and bridge were decidedly more ornate than Augustus' Mausoleum. A fourth distinction, less significant architecturally but perhaps more significant in other ways, was that Hadrian did not display his *res gestae* at his tomb as had Augustus.[60]

[60] But he did put his *res gestae* on his Pantheon in Athens: Paus. 1.5.5. For the similarity of both Hadrian's and Augustus' Mausolea to such triumphal monuments as those of

These differences reflect some important distinctions in the political implications of and background to the two tombs. Kienast has perceived the dynastic character of Hadrian's tomb, relating it to Hadrian's establishment of a new Aelian dynasty of principes arranged through adoption; he rightly points to Augustus as Hadrian's predecessor and model for this.[61] Yet Hadrian deviated from Augustus' pattern notably. One of the most striking facts about Augustus' Mausoleum is that it was among the first constructions of his principate. Suetonius dates it to his sixth consulate (28 B.C.; Suet. *Aug.* 100.4). In contrast, the completion of Hadrian's Mausoleum dates to the latter part of his reign. Though there are brick stamps of 123 in its square base, it was first used only in 139; the bridge was finished only in 134. Work on it is therefore not likely to have begun before 125 and may not have begun until 132.[62] Similarly, Hadrian's official arrangements for the succession, although notoriously complex, were officially undertaken only in 136, when Hadrian had been in power for nineteen years and was a sixty-year old invalid.[63]

The hostility of the Roman senate to Hadrian, which had marred his accession to power and may have embittered him, was renewed and reinforced at the end of his reign when in 138, after two years of suffering and occasional savagery, he died in Baiae and was buried in Puteoli.[64] The senate,

---

La Turbie and Adamklissi, see, e.g., Pierce, "Mausoleum and Pons" 94–95. Influence could have gone in either or both directions.

[61] Kienast, "Baupolitik" 407–410.

[62] Pierce, "Mausoleum and Pons" 83 n. 5, conjectures A.D. 132; De' Spagnolis, "Lettura del Mausoleo" 67 n. 2, a few years earlier than 130; Grimal, *Jardins* 140, n. 6, suggests that as early as 118 a temporary bridge was built in the place of the Pons Aelius, which would indicate that Hadrian had plans for the Ager Vaticanus very early. Yet there is no evidence. The Mausoleum was probably begun while Hadrian was in Rome, either in 126–127 or after 131.

[63] Although E. Champlin, "Hadrian's Heir," *ZPE* 21 (1976) 79–89, has argued that from an early date Hadrian groomed his blood relative Pedanius Fuscus as the heir presumptive, the emperor made no formal arrangements until 136. The problem of Hadrian's succession is discussed also by R. Syme, "Ummidius Quadratus, *Capax imperii*," *HSCP* 83 (1979) 300–310, with earlier

bibliography including Pflaum, "Règlement" 95–122; A. R. Birley, *Marcus Aurelius* (Boston 1966) 44–47; T. D. Barnes, "Hadrian and Lucius Verus," *JRS* 57 (1967) 74–79; and R. Syme, "The Ummidii," *Historia* 17 (1968) 93–94. We can discount the unverifiable and implausible theory, advocated by J. Carcopino and P. Gerade, that L. Aelius Caesar was Hadrian's illegitimate son (in *Passion et politique chez les Césars* [Paris 1958] 143–222, and "Le règlement successoral d'Hadrien," *REA* 52 [1950] 258–77, respectively); compare, e.g., Garzetti, 437, 699–700. Augustus made clear arrangements as early as 25 B.C., when his nephew Marcellus was engaged to Julia: M. Hammond, *The Augustan Principate in Theory and Practice during the Julio-Claudian Period* (Cambridge, Mass. 1933) 66–74. For general remarks on the transmission of the imperial power in the second century, see Hammond, *AntMon* 1–24.

[64] Syme, "Ummidius, *Capax imperii*" 302–10; Garzetti, 435–40. C. P. Jones, "Aelius Aristides, *Eis Basilea*," *JRS* 62 (1972) 151–52,

angered at the deaths for which Hadrian was responsible in his final years, including those of his brother-in-law, L. Julius Servianus, and his distant relation Cn. Pedianus Fuscus Salinator, refused to vote him any honors and may even have threatened *damnatio memoriae* (condemnation of memory); only with great difficulty did his successor, Antoninus Pius, persuade them to change their minds. Hadrian was interred in Rome in 139, not yet deified even then, and Antoninus' dedicatory inscription (*CIL* 6.984 = *ILS* 322 = Smallwood, #124) honors both Hadrian and his wife, Sabina, who had died and been deified slightly earlier.[65] It is commonly assumed that the Mausoleum was incomplete in 138. Yet it is significant that the first use of Hadrian's Mausoleum was not so much as his own tomb, but as an imperial sepulcher, the resting place of the adoptive parents of Antoninus.

Idiosyncratic in placement and details of appearance, Hadrian's Mausoleum and Pons Aelius nonetheless effected both pragmatic and political aims. The funerary complex encouraged the development of Rome westward, yet gave the impression of belonging to the Campus Martius, one of the most important parts of the city. By this latter effect Hadrian ensured his association with Augustus, the first princeps whose prototypical Mausoleum lay in the northern Campus; additionally, he partook of the traditional prestige associated with burial within the Campus without having to ask the senate for a special decree to build his tomb there. Finally, the timing of this construction also reveals his deference to the senate. Overall, Hadrian's Mausoleum and Pons Aelius, two of his latest constructions in Rome, exemplify his work in the capital city.

---

discusses the transferral of this hostility to the literary tradition.

[65] For the date of Sabina's death and deification, see Eck, "Vibia(?) Sabina" 914. Richard, "Tombeaux" 135–36, goes as far as to suggest that Antoninus Pius had Hadrian's ashes put into the Mausoleum as a means of obtaining his deification despite senatorial opposition; that is, deposition within an imperial mausoleum indicated divinity.

## CHAPTER SEVEN

# MISSING AND MISIDENTIFIED

# BUILDINGS

VARIOUS BUILDINGS and monuments in Rome ascribed to Hadrian by ancient sources or modern scholarship are so poorly attested to or so controversial in date or form that little can be said about them. We shall probably never be able to identify most of the *sacrae aedes plurimae* (many sacred temples) that the biography gives Hadrian credit for (*HA, Hadr.* 19.10), the aedes destroyed by fire that he restored (*CIL* 6.979), and the buildings (*stationes?*) ruined by age that he reconstructed (*CIL* 6.981). Nevertheless, the examination of other Hadrianic buildings now missing and buildings assigned to Hadrian on dubious grounds illuminates aspects of Hadrian's principate overshadowed by more conspicuous works. In this chapter the following are treated in the chronological order commonly assigned them, although some may not be Hadrianic: the Anaglypha Traiani/Hadriani; the Tondi Adrianei; the Athenaeum and other manifestations in Rome of Hadrian's philhellenism; the Aedes Bonae Deae and the Auguratorium; and the "Ustrinum" of Hadrian. His minor repairs of buildings and fragments of historical reliefs assigned to his reign are grouped together in a final section.

### The Anaglypha Traiani/Hadriani

Two marble reliefs, the so-called Anaglypha, have been assigned to both Trajan and Hadrian since their discovery in 1872 between the Column of Phocas and the Rostra on the west side of the Forum Romanum.[1] The original purpose and location of the reliefs is as uncertain as their date; carved on both

[1] The reliefs are also called *plutei*, e.g., by Nash, s.v. Plutei Traiani, II.176–77, who provides a full bibliography. A Flavian date was also proposed earlier. For a report of the controversies over date, location, and form up to the 1940s, see Lugli, *Centro* 160–64; for additional bibliography, Koeppel, "Official State Reliefs" 495–96. I thank Dr. I. Jacobi for permission to inspect the reliefs, now in the Curia.

long faces and with an ornamental finish on the three surviving short ends, it is conjectured that they once served as balustrades of some sort, each being about 5.5 meters long, 2 meters high, and possibly once crowned with bronzework (see Ills. 40 and 41). The slabs that make up the two Anaglypha were reused in the foundations of the medieval Torre del Campanero in the Forum; reassembled, they show on one face apparently historical scenes and on the other a parade of the three victims of a *suovetaurilia* (purifacatory sacrifice consisting of a boar, a ram, and a bull). Before their reuse in the tower, almost every human head in high relief they carried was destroyed, with the result that identification of individual figures is not possible and we are thrown back on stylistic considerations that lend themselves to dating as both Hadrianic and Trajanic.[2] Finally and most important, the interpretation of the historical scenes remains controversial: within the last few years U. Rüdiger has identified them with known Hadrianic events, and M. Torelli with Trajanic ones.[3] Without new evidence, the questions of the original location, purpose, and date of the Anaglypha must remain unanswered, and the following discussion only recapitulates the main problems they pose.

The reuse of the Anaglypha has made positive determination of their original location impossible, although most scholars propose that in antiquity they stood not far from their later resting place in the Torre del Campanero.[4] It is often suggested, for example, that they stood atop the Rostra,[5] notwithstanding their height, which would have hidden speakers on the platform at least from some directions. Torelli has recently revived the supposition that they bordered the sacred area around the statue of Marsyas, but that would leave at least two sides unprotected; and this theory overlooks the fact that the reliefs would have dwarfed the statue, which was apparently just over two meters high.[6]

[2] U. Rüdiger, "Die Anaglypha Hadriani," *Antike Plastik* 12 (1973) 165, attributes the damage to Christian iconoclasts; on pp. 170–71, he provides a thorough discussion of the reliefs' style. The reliefs seem best described as "late Trajanic–early Hadrianic."

[3] Rüdiger, "Anaglypha" 171–73; Torelli, *Roman Historical Reliefs*, Chap. 4: "The *Anaglypha Traiani* and the Chatsworth Relief" 89–118. Rüdiger first noted the evidence for bronzework above the marble (p. 161); Torelli has interpreted it as the remains of a fence (p. 89). One reviewer of Torelli's book, J. Pollini (in *AJA* 87 [1983] 573), agrees with

Torelli that the reliefs are Trajanic; another (R.R.R. Smith, in *JRS* 73 [1983] 228) argues that the date must be left open.

[4] Torelli, *Roman Historical Reliefs* 89; C. F. Giuliani and P. Verduchi, *Foro Romano. L'area centrale* (Florence 1980) 21 and fig. 8.

[5] See Lugli, *Centro* 164, for various suggestions, and Rüdiger, "Anaglypha" 162–63.

[6] Torelli, *Roman Historical Reliefs* 108; earlier suggested by W. Seston, "Les 'Anaglypha Traiani' du Forum Romain et la politique d'Hadrien en 118," *MélRome* 44 (1927) 175–79. In reviews of Torelli's work, Pollini (see n. 3) 573, points out that this leaves uncertain

The composition of the Anaglypha is itself unusual. The walls on which the reliefs are cut are composed of blocks of Pentelic marble of different sizes and shapes, but with one wall almost the mirror image of the other. Although a composite format is found in other large historical reliefs, notably the Ara Pacis screens, nowhere else is it so peculiar. The piecing together of the Anaglypha suggests that the blocks were originally meant for some other use, and perhaps, as Rüdiger and Hammond think, that the reliefs were hastily worked from readily available material.[7]

The two composite slabs mirror one another not only in their piecing, but also in one of the reliefs. Each presents a suovetaurilia on one side; the two almost identical representations show the boar, ram, and bull adorned with *dorsualia* (covers for animals' backs used in sacrifices), woolen bands, and laurel branches as they march calmly to sacrifice.[8] The main difference is that the victims move in opposite directions on the two reliefs, indicating that these scenes were to be seen in relation to one another. The reiterated tableau of the major sacrifice also suggests religious associations for the Anaglypha.[9]

On its other side each of the Anaglypha presents a historical scene (*see Ills. 40 and 41*). The architectural background of both is now generally accepted to be the south side and the southern parts of the east and west sides of the Forum Romanum, seen continuously with a small overlap from one relief to the other in the reiterated representation of the statue of Marsyas next to a fig tree (probably the Ficus Ruminalis).[10] The events depicted on the two reliefs, however, are more problematic.

---

the other two sides of the enclosure, and Smith (see n. 3) 227, notes problems with the height.

[7] M. Hammond, "A Statue of Trajan Represented on the *Anaglypha Traiani*," *MAAR* 21 (1953) 129–31; Rüdiger, "Anaglypha" 162. Hammond, 135, remarks that the general execution of the historical sides of the reliefs seems hurried.

[8] See, e.g., Torelli, *Roman Historical Reliefs* 89; and M. J. Vermaseren, "The *Suovetaurilia* in Roman Art," *Bulletin Antieke Beschaving* 32 (1957) 1–12, esp. 5–6. I. S. Ryberg, *Rites of the State Religion in Roman Art* (Rome 1955) 104–19, discusses this theme in Roman historical relief without mentioning these reliefs specifically.

[9] These religious implications have been interpreted in quite different ways: e.g., To-

relli, *Roman Historical Reliefs* 105–106, understands a double lustration, and that both the Marsyas statue and the Ficus tree were purified; Rüdiger, "Anaglypha" 173, thinks only that the suovetauralia underline the importance of the emperor's acts; and Seston, "Anaglypha" 173–75, 179, associates the sacrifice, depicted twice, with a restoration by Hadrian of the sacred enclosure of Marsyas.

[10] Chapter 4. See also Hammond, "Statue of Trajan" 136–41; Rüdiger, "Anaglypha" 163–65; and Torelli, *Roman Historical Reliefs*, 92–102. Torelli's location of the Marsyas and fig tree too far north in the Forum, though implausible (cf. Smith's review of Torelli [above, n. 3], 227), points to the topographical difficulties of assuming the juxtaposition of the statue and fig tree.

40. *Anaglypha Traiani/Hadriani: adlocutio (or alimenta) relief. From left to right: princeps attended by six lictors on the rostra in front of the Temple of the Deified Julius; thirteen senators, equestrians, and plebeians; statue group with standing woman, two children, and seated magistrate; four plebeians; and fig tree and statue of Marsyas.*

41. *Anaglypha Traiani/Hadriani: debt-burning relief. From left to right: fig tree and statue of Marsyas; soldiers carrying account books to pile; plebeian, two lictors and senator or equestrian; and princeps (?) enthroned on the Rostra Augusti.*

One relief is commonly referred to as the *adlocutio* or *alimenta* relief, because at the left we see on the rostra in front of the Temple of the Deified Julius a princeps, attended by six lictors;[11] the princeps addresses a crowd of thirteen *togati* and *paenulati*. Those wearing the Roman toga must represent senators and equestrians, while the figures wearing the humbler *paenula*, a close-fitting hooded cloak, are the common *plebs*.[12] Farther right, near the center of the relief, is a platform on which stands a woman carrying a child on her left arm and resting her right hand on the head of another (both now hardly identifiable from the remains); she is facing a magistrate seated on a curule chair carved with drapery that hangs low.[13] Four more paenulati stand between this platform and the fig tree and statue of Marsyas, the final element on the relief.[14]

The other relief, the debt-burning relief, lacks one of its crowning blocks and a small part of the right end. What remains is fairly straightforward. The fig tree and statue of Marsyas appear again, now at the left end. Moving right from them, nine soldiers of ambiguous rank bring large account books tied in bundles to a pile to which two more soldiers contribute from the right.[15] There follows a group of four men: a paenulatus, two lictors, and a togatus; the first and last must again represent the plebs and the higher orders.[16] Finally, we see traces of a person enthroned on the Rostra Augusti, presumably the princeps.

The historical scenes are not self-explanatory; to the difficulties caused by lacunae are added the representation of the Marsyas statue and the fig tree in both scenes, possibly indicating continuity of narrative, and the abnormal garb of the soldiers.[17] The most difficult question, however, is the identification of the event or events represented.

W. Henzen originally identified the adlocutio relief as a commemoration of Trajan's institution of the alimenta, the state provision of the cost of maintenance for children: he based his argument on the figures on the platform

---

[11] It may be that only the four central ones of these figures are lictors: Hammond, "Statue of Trajan" 144 n. 45.

[12] Torelli, *Roman Historical Reliefs* 90–91.

[13] See Hammond, "Statue of Trajan" 155, for more detail on the group.

[14] Although Smith (see n. 3) 227, asserts that the rectangular structure around the fig tree is a statue base, which would indicate that this is a bronze tree rather than the Ficus Ruminalis, the structure represented is so much simpler than the base of the statue of

Marsyas that it surely must be a parapet or screen to protect the tree.

[15] Torelli, *Roman Historical Reliefs* 91, identifies the soldiers as from the praetorian or urban cohorts; Rüdiger, "Anaglypha" 168–69, as legionaries, with the one farthest right carrying a basket; Hammond, "Statue of Trajan" 145, as praetorians.

[16] Torelli, *Roman Historical Reliefs* 91.

[17] See, e.g., Hammond, "Statue of Trajan" 146 n. 49.

near the center of the relief, which he interpreted as a statuary group depicting Italia and her children before Trajan, erected to commemorate the alimenta and probably occupying the area in the Forum Romanum commonly assigned to the Equus Domitiani[18] (*see Ill. 42*). One problem with this interpretation is that Trajan would then appear twice on this relief: once in person, announcing the alimenta to the Roman people, and once in a statue group commemorating the institution.[19]

Observing this difficulty, other scholars have proposed that the relief commemorates Hadrian's extension of the alimenta in 118 (*HA, Hadr.* 7.8). The statuary group would then have been included to identify the subject of the address and to show Hadrian's *pietas*, his respect for Trajan, whose policies he was continuing.[20] This identification of the subject of the relief would necessarily require a Hadrianic date for the subject of the debt-burning relief, however, and as we shall see, there is little evidence to support one.

A second problem with the alimenta interpretation recently raised by Torelli, who favors a Trajanic date, is that representations of the alimenta customarily include children. Since no children are shown in the crowd listening to the adlocutio, Torelli concludes that the adlocutio represents the announcement of a *congiarium*—largesse in money—of 103 or 107, rather than the alimenta.[21] The relief would then commemorate two important events in Trajan's reign, which is an attractive solution of the difficulties. Unfortunately, Torelli's arguments for a Trajanic date for the other relief are less convincing.

The debt-burning relief is puzzling. By far the most famous public debt burning was that ordered by Hadrian in 118. The biography records it as part of Hadrian's campaign to make himself popular with the Roman senate and people (*HA, Hadr.* 7.6), and an inscription heralds him as the first and only princeps to concern himself with the security of future citizens as well as present ones, by remitting tax debts of 900 million sesterces (*CIL* 6.967 = *ILS* 309 = Smallwood, #64a).[22] Yet the relief's architectural background of the

---

[18] The statuary group appears on coins of 103 to 111: *BMC, Emp.* III, p. 184, nos. 870–72, pl. 33.2. Hammond, "Statue of Trajan" 155–76, discusses the group and its numismatic parallels most fully.

[19] Hammond, "Statue of Trajan" 178–79, addresses this problem, with review of the different solutions proposed; Seston, for example ("Anaglypha" 164), offers the unconvincing theory that the Italia group is not statuary, but rather simply a symbolic representation.

[20] For example, Rüdiger, "Anaglypha" 173.

[21] Torelli, *Roman Historical Reliefs* 91. At this early date in the history of the *alimenta*, however, the iconography may not yet have been set.

[22] *S.p.q.R./ imp. Caesari divi Traiani/ Parthici f. divi Nervae nepoti/ Traiano Hadriano Aug. pont./ max. tr[ib.] pot II cos. II/ qui primus omnium principum et/ solus remittendo sestertium novies/ milies centena milia n. debitum fiscis/*

42. *Anaglypha Traiani/Hadriani: detail of adlocutio relief. Statue group of woman, with right hand on head of standing child (no longer extant) and left arm cradling second child, standing before a togate magistrate seated on a curule chair.*

Forum Romanum is at variance with the biography's unequivocal statement that the records were burnt in the Forum Traiani. Torelli, citing the *Chronicon Paschale, ad ann.* 106, proposes that Trajan canceled debts in 106, and that the relief commemorates this earlier occasion.[23]

As R.R.R. Smith points out in his review of Torelli's *Typology and Structure of Roman Historical Reliefs*, this hypothesis is untenable.[24] The *Chronicon Paschale* reports only a "dubious temporary remission of taxes," and the inscription recording Hadrian's debt burning states explicitly that he was the first to do this. It is difficult to believe the inscription could ignore a similar event that occurred only twelve years earlier.

Yet attempts to interpret the relief as showing the Hadrianic debt burning by dismissing the Forum Romanum background are equally unsatisfactory. The inscription commemorating the debt burning, *CIL* 6.967, was found in the Forum of Trajan itself, which supports the statement of Hadrian's biography.[25] Additional corroboration is provided by the Chatsworth relief (*see Ill. 43*). This large marble fragment also represents a debt burning, but here in the background a portico is suggested by a single unfluted column raised on three steps. The heads of two figures on the relief are well preserved, and their short full beards indicate a Hadrianic date; the portico has been identified as one of the lateral colonnades of the Forum of Trajan.[26] It is therefore almost certain that the Forum Traiani was the site of Hadrian's debt burning.

Taking a different position, Rüdiger proposes that Hadrian held his debt burning in the Forum Traiani, but for ideological reasons set the representation of it in the Forum Romanum on the Anaglypha. By including the statuary group of Trajan and Italia on the adlocutio relief, Rüdiger holds, Hadrian wished to emphasize his perpetuation of Trajan's social program for the wel-

---

*non praesentes tantum cives suos sed/ et posteros eorum praestitit hac/ liberalitate securos* (The senate and the people of Rome, to [the emperor Hadrian], son of the deified [emperor Trajan], grandson of the deified Nerva, pontifex maximus, with tribunician power for the second time, consul for the second time, who first and solely of all the principes, by remitting 900,000,000 sesterces owed to the treasury, by this generosity was responsible for making secure his citizens, both those living now and their offspring). See, e.g., Hammond, "Statue of Trajan" 141–46. The coin issue commemorating this is shown in *BMC,*

*Emp.* III, pp. 417–18, nos. 1206–1210, pl. 79.4–6 = Smallwood, #64b.

[23] Torelli, *Roman Historical Reliefs* 107.

[24] Smith (see n. 3) 227–28.

[25] See, e.g., Smith (see n. 3) 228. The inscription was actually found near the Temple of the Deified Trajan and Plotina.

[26] Torelli, *Roman Historical Reliefs* 109, citing E. Petersen, "Hadrians Steuererlass," *RömMitt* 14 (1899) 222–29. Hammond, "Statue of Trajan" 145–46, noting the stylistic differences between the Chatsworth relief and the Anaglypha, maintains that "styles cannot be assumed necessarily to be successive."

43. *Chatsworth relief. Soldiers carry account books to a debt burning in the Forum of Trajan.*

fare of Rome and Italy.[27] This argument is hardly convincing. Hadrian must have chosen to stage his debt burning in Trajan's Forum precisely to remind people of his connection with Trajan. An architectural setting of the Forum Traiani would be not only correct for the relief but also a more effective reminder of Trajan.

In sum, the problems the Anaglypha present are insoluble at present. The reliefs, with their combination of historical narrative and symbolism, may well be Hadrianic, but until acceptable answers are discovered for at least some of the questions they pose we cannot assume that they are. The case against it seems equally strong.

### The Tondi Adrianei

Eight large tondo reliefs of the Hadrianic period, known collectively as the Tondi Adrianei, now decorate the Arch of Constantine (*see Ill. 44*). Their unusual shape, uniform diameter of about 2.40 meters, and common theme indicate that they originally belonged to a single monument, whose location in Rome seems assured by the way in which the Arch was decorated with reliefs and statues taken from a number of other buildings.[28] The present arrange-

[27] Rüdiger, "Anaglypha" 173.
[28] A plausible explanation for their shape is that it was influenced by the bronze medallions cited below: E. Condurachi, "La Genèse

ment of the Tondi in four pairs—two above each of the side arches on each
face of the arch—as well as a suggestion of sequence in the eight scenes and
the composition of the figures within each tondo, led E. Buschor in 1923–24
to hazard that the Tondi were appropriated from a four-sided monument on
which they had been disposed two to each outer side.[29] It has also been proposed that this structure was a rectangular precinct like the Ara Pacis,[30] but
the shape of the eight reliefs seems more appropriate to a tetrapylon, where
the medallions would have been inserted in the eight spandrels.[31]

The eight Tondi depict a series of hunts and sacrifices (*see Ills. 45–52*). On

des sujets de chasse des *tondi adrianei* de l'arc
de Constantin," in *Atti VII° Congr. internaz.
di archeol. class., Roma-Napoli, sett. 1958*, II
(Rome 1961) 451–59, arguing against
H. Bulle's derivation of the Tondi from metal
shields depicting glorious deeds, laudatory
memorials akin to *imagines clipeatae* (in "Ein
Jagddenkmal des Kaisers Hadrian," *JdI* 34
[1919] 161–63). Without supporting argu-
mentation, I. Maull, "Hadrians Jagddenkmal," *ÖJh* 42 (1955) 57, suggests a derivation
from the *clipeus votivus*. Condurachi's theory
has been accepted by later scholars such as
J. Ruysschaert, "Essai d'interprétation
synthétique de l'arc de Constantin," *Rend-
PontAcc* 35 (1962–63) [1964] 91; and apparently by A. Bonanno, *Portraits and Other
Heads on Roman Historical Relief up to the Age
of Septimius Severus* (Oxford 1976) 201 n. 493.
For the size of the Tondi, see R. Bianchi Bandinelli and M. Torelli, *L'arte dell'antichità classica*, II (Turin 1976) #132. For the fourth-century arch, see L'Orange and von Gerkan,
*Konstantinsbogen*. Personal inspection reveals
that the Tondi are not completely round, but
have a base roughly under the ground line of
the various scenes. I am indebted to Dr. G.
Martines for permission to visit the monument.

[29] E. Buschor, "Die hadrianischen Jagdbilder," *RömMitt* 38/39 (1923–24) 52–54. Earlier scholars did not know what to make of
the reliefs: e.g., in *HJ* I.3, 25 n. 57, it is suggested that the "Trajanic" reliefs were used as
decoration for a room in the Palatine palace.
Bulle, "Jagddenkmal" 166, convincingly rejects a structural connection of the Tondi

with the Temple of Venus and Roma or with
the Temple of Apollo on the Palatine. Buschor arranges the reliefs counterclockwise
from a main entrance: the departure, bear sacrifice, bear hunt, boar sacrifice, boar hunt,
lion sacrifice, lion hunt, and homecoming.
This order is generally accepted, although
some, noting a small relief head of Antoninus
Pius in the Antiquario del Foro Romano that
is the same size and seems to be of the same
hand as that on the arch, suggest that the original Hadrianic monument had more than
eight reliefs. See L'Orange and von Gerkan,
*Konstantinsbogen* 166 n. 1; J. Aymard, *Essai sur
les chasses romaines* (Paris 1951) 529, with legitimate doubts about Buschor's reconstruction; and H. von Heintze, in Helbig II.2055,
pp. 826–27. For an explanation of the different order of the Tondi on the Arch of Constantine, see Ruysschaert, "Interprétation de
l'arc de Constantin" 90.

[30] For example, Bulle, "Jagddenkmal"
166–68; Maull, "Hadrians Jagddenkmal" 56;
and Condurachi, "Genèse des *tondi*" 452.

[31] G. Becatti, *La colonna coclide istoriata*
(Rome 1960) 67 n. 122, who cites the analogy
of the Tetrapylon of Marcus Aurelius in Trip-
oli. A better parallel would be the Arch of
Augustus at Rimini, or perhaps the triumphal
arch in Trajan's Forum that had medallions
above each niche and the central passage, to
judge from numismatic evidence (Anderson,
*HistTop* 143). The religious associations of
the imagines clipeatae of the Arch of Rimini
are underlined by G. Gualandi, in *Studi
sull'arco onorario romano* (Rome 1979) 113.

44. *Arch of Constantine, north side, with four Tondi Adrianei—boar hunt, sacrifice to Apollo, lion hunt, and sacrifice to Hercules—reused above the lateral arches.*

the first tondo, a group of hunters with a horse and a large dog moves forward from an arched gateway, evidently setting out for a day of sport; this is followed by three scenes of the chase, each paired with a scene of sacrifice, and a concluding tondo shows a sacrifice to Apollo at the return from the hunt. In each of the three pairs we see first the hunt of a wild animal—a bear, a boar, and a lion—and then, presumably after the successful kill, sacrifices to Silvanus, Diana, and Hercules, respectively.

45. *Tondi Adrianei: departure tondo. From left to right: Antinoos, princeps (Hadrian), attendant, amicus principis.*

46. *Tondi Adrianei: bear-hunt tondo. From left to right: amicus principis (M. Aurelius ?), princeps (Hadrian), T. Caesernius Macedo Quinctianus.*

New portraits were added to the main figures when the reliefs were installed on the Arch of Constantine.[32] The surviving heads of the main figure
in the boar- and lion-hunting panels are now identifiable as the young Constantine.[33] In the sacrificial scenes, the main figure standing before Diana was
altered to represent Constantine; the chief figure in the scene with Silvanus is
unidentifiable, due to damage, and in the sacrifices to Hercules and Apollo the
main figure was reworked to resemble Constantius Chlorus, Constantine's
father.[34]

Arguments for the dating of the Tondi on the basis of style were for a long
time inconclusive, due to both the altering of the main figures and the classicizing style common to both the late first and the early second century. It was
only in the 1920s, when certain secondary figures were identified as Antinoos
and attention was drawn to the beards of other background figures, that the
scholarly world settled on a Hadrianic date, with a terminus post quem of
Antinoos' death in 130.[35]

The Hadrianic date also suits our knowledge of the tastes and amusements
of the princeps. Not only do the usual literary sources attest to Hadrian's passion for hunting with his friends (e.g., *HA, Hadr.* 26.3, cf. 2.1, 20.12–13; Dio
Cass. 69.10.2, and cf. 69.2.5), but a host of incidental documents confirms
this.[36] An inscription from Apt in France, *CIL* 12.1122 = Smallwood, #520,
contains part of the epitaph Hadrian is reported to have written ca. 121 for his
horse Borysthenes (cf. *Poet. Lat. Min.*, ed. Bahrens, 4, 126 = *Anthol. Lat.*, ed.
Riese, 903 = Buecheler, *Carm. Epig.* 1522).[37] A city in Mysia, named Hadrianoutherae, was founded in commemoration of the success Hadrian met

[32] L'Orange and von Gerkan, *Konstantinsbogen* 161–83, the fundamental discussion of
the Tondi as they appear on the Arch of Constantine, here also treating the two tondi created in the Constantinian period to match the
Hadrianic ones and to continue the scheme
around the two ends of the arch (Sol Invictus
in a quadriga, on the east side; Luna in a biga,
on the west). Early identifications as Licinius
have now been corrected to identifications as
Constantius Chlorus: see n. 34 below.

[33] The heads of the main figure of the reliefs
of the setting out and of the sacrifice to Silvanus are now lost.

[34] R. Calza, "Un problema di iconografia
imperiale sull'arco di Costantino," *Rend-
PontAcc* 32 (1959–60) [1960] 133–61; accepted
by Ruysschaert, "Interprétation de l'arc de

Constantin" 91–92.

[35] C. Blümel, "Ein Porträt des Antoninus
Pius," *JdI* 47 (1932) 92–93, gives a good review of the controversy over the date up to
that time, as does Toynbee, *Hadrianic School*
245–46; for later bibliography, see Koeppel,
"Official State Reliefs" 496–97 B.

[36] Aymard, *Chasses romaines* 523–27. Coarelli, *Lazio* 40–42, also associates with Hadrian and hunting *CIL* 14.3911, an elegiac dedication to the healing deity of a spring in
Tibur, purportedly written by a horse in
thanks for renewed health after a hunting accident.

[37] H. Bardon, *Les Empereurs et les lettres latines d'Auguste à Hadrien*, 2nd ed. (Paris 1968)
419–20, discusses its authenticity.

47.  *Tondi Adrianei: sacrifice to Silvanus tondo. From left to right: amicus principis, attendant, princeps (Hadrian), attendants.*

48.  *Tondi Adrianei: boar-hunt tondo. From left to right: T. Caesernius Macedo Quinctianus, attendant, princeps (Hadrian, recut to resemble the young Constantine).*

49. *Tondi Adrianei: sacrifice to Diana tondo. From left to right: attendant, T. Caesernius Statianus, princeps (Hadrian, recut to resemble Constantine), attendant.*

50. *Tondi Adrianei: lion-hunt tondo. From left to right: attendant, princeps (Hadrian, recut to resemble the young Constantine), L. Aelius Verus, T. Caesernius Macedo Quinctianus, attendant.*

51. *Tondi Adrianei: sacrifice to Hercules tondo. From left to right: attendant, Antoninus Pius (head now in Berlin), princeps (Hadrian, recut to resemble Constantius Chlorus), T. Caesernius Statianus.*

52. *Tondi Adrianei: sacrifice to Apollo tondo. From left to right: Antoninus Pius, princeps (Hadrian, recut to resemble Constantius Chlorus), T. Caesernius Statianus.*

while hunting there ca. 123 (*HA, Hadr.* 20.13; Dio Cass. 69.10.1).[38] An inscription from the Temple of Eros in Thespiae, Greece (*IG* 7.1828 = Kaibel, *Epig. Gr.* 811) records Hadrian's dedication to Eros of the spoils of a she bear that he himself killed ca. 125.[39] A papyrus from Oxyrhynchus preserves a long fragment of a poem the Alexandrian poet Pankrates wrote to celebrate a lion hunt by Hadrian and Antinoos in the Libyan desert in 130 (P. Oxy. VIII.1085; cf. Athenaeus 15.677 d–e).[40] Finally, medallions struck after Hadrian assumed the title of Pater Patriae in 128 show Hadrian galloping on horseback, sometimes in pursuit of a lion or a bear, and carry the legend VIRTUTI AUGUSTI[41] (*see Ills. 53a and b*).

[38] Some coins of the city carried a likeness of Antinoos, and represented the emperor on horseback about to cast his spear at a bear in flight: Magie, *RRAM* 617, 1476 n. 20. See Bürchner, "Hadrianothera," *RE* 7.2 (1912) 2177.

[39] Aymard, *Chasses romaines* 180–81. Weber, 157, also gives the text; cf. Bardon, *Empereurs et lettres* 423–24.

[40] This poem prompted Hadrian to have Pankrates entered in the Museum in Alexandria: Aymard, *Chasses romaines* 181–82. See also A. S. Hunt, ed., *The Oxyrhynchus Papyri*, part 8 (London 1911) #1085, pp. 73–76.

[41] Toynbee, *Roman Medallions* 219, who dates two of the four lion-hunt types to ca. 129, and the other two lion-hunt types, and all three boar-hunt types, to 130–138. Gnecchi, III.17, 20, nos. 69, 95–96, pls. 144.12, 146.3–4, 146.7; and Condurachi, "Genèse des tondi" 453–57.

53a and b. *Medallions (after 128) depicting Hadrian hunting a lion, with the legend* VIRTUTI AUGUSTI.

Once the date of the Tondi was settled, attention focused on their content. Some, but not all the figures can be identified. Although many of the beautiful young pages who accompany Hadrian on the reliefs have been held to be Antinoos, on iconographical grounds the only one that could represent Hadrian's lover is the heroically nude youth who leads Hadrian's horse in the departure Tondo.[42] (*See Ill. 45.*) In 1919 H. Bulle identified two almost identical figures, appearing in six reliefs in all, as the brothers T. Caesernius Statianus and T. Caesernius Macedo Quinctianus, members of Hadrian's group of *amici* and each identified in his epitaph as a *comes (imp. Hadriani) per Orientem* (companion [of the emperor Hadrian] through the East: *ILS* 1068, 1069). Bulle divided the rest of Hadrian's company into attendants portrayed generically (*famuli*) but including Antinoos, and unidentifiable companions of the *princeps* (cf. *HA, Hadr.* 26.3), including the bearded figure standing behind Hadrian in the sacrifice to Apollo.[43]

In 1932 C. Blümel identified this bearded figure as Antoninus Pius, and the bearded youth to the right of Hadrian in the lion-hunt panel as L. Aelius Verus. This, if correct, gives a date for the Tondi in the last year of Hadrian's rule.[44] Though F. von Lorentz's quick rebuttal of Blümel on iconographical and chronological grounds was then accepted by many scholars, including

[42] The observations of S. Reinach against identifying other figures as Antinoos ("Les Têtes des médaillons de l'arc de Constantin à Rome," *RA*, ser. 4, 15 [1910] 126–28) are still valid, although he also suggests that the youth, turned left, who rides behind Hadrian in the boar hunt is Antinoos. Identifications of Antinoos have ranged wildly: e.g., Kähler, *Villa* 154, 177–79 n. 151, identifies Antinoos in the lion hunt and the sacrifice to Hercules as well as in the two figures Reinach accepts. He explains the vast differences in the likenesses as changes in Antinoos' age. C. W. Clairmont, *Die Bildnisse des Antinous* (Bern 1966) no. 57, pp. 56–57, accepts only the youth in the boar hunt, though noting that his hair corresponds to none of the known prototypes; Bonanno, *Portraits* 96, 100, on facial features, hair style, and head, only this youth; and F. de la Maza, *Antinoo, el último dios del mundo clásico* (Mexico City 1966) 273–74, refuses any identifications. See also G. Koeppel, "Profectio und Adventus" *BJb* 169 (1969) 133, and n. 57 below.

[43] Bulle, "Jagddenkmal" 156–59: Statianus appears in the sacrifice to Diana, to the left of the altar; in the sacrifice to Hercules, to the right of the altar; and in the sacrifice to Apollo, to the right of the statue. Quinctianus appears in the bear hunt, to the right of Hadrian; in the boar hunt, as the figure farthest to the left; and in the lion hunt, as the figure to the right of the tree. For these brothers, see *PIR*, 2nd ed., II, pp. 36–37, nos. 182–83. The identifications are accepted by Condurachi, "Genèse des *tondi*" 452, and by Bonanno, *Portraits* 97–106, but rejected by Aymard, *Chasses romaines* 533.

[44] Blümel, "Porträt des Antoninus Pius" 90–92 (Antoninus Pius), pp. 94–95 (Aelius Verus). Part of his argument for the identification of Antoninus Pius is a head, now found in the Berlin Museum but originally from the man behind Hadrian in the sacrifice to Hercules, which is almost identical to that of the individual attending Hadrian in the sacrifice to Apollo.

M. Wegner, opinion has now swung back and Blümel's identifications are widely believed to be correct.[45] J. Aymard's more recent and tentative identification of the young horseman in the bear hunt as Marcus Aurelius[46] is less convincing.

These identifications of figures in the Tondi contrast with the failure to reach any agreement about the incidents represented. Bulle linked the hunting scenes with known events of Hadrian's life, and postulated other episodes to correspond with the sacrifices. He associated the boar hunt and sacrifice to Diana with hunts in Asia Minor and Greece; the bear hunt and sacrifice to Silvanus with the hunt at Hadrianoutherae and one in south Italy; and the lion hunt and sacrifice to Hercules with Hadrian's and Antinoos' hunt in the Libyan desert and a sacrifice in Africa to Hercules Gaditanus.[47] At best, the lion-hunt Tondo could be only a general reference to the celebrated exploits of Hadrian and his favorite in Libya, since Antinoos is not portrayed. This contrasts his role as one of the protagonists of Pankrates' poem.[48] The identifications of the other hunting scenes are even less satisfying, and those of the sacrificial scenes are pure speculation.[49]

Historical interpretation of the eight Tondi should not be carried too far: the reliefs seem clearly intended to be allegorical rather than documentary. One clue to their meaning comes from comparison of them to the bronze medallions with the legend VIRTUTI AUGUSTI, which represent Hadrian hunting. On the reliefs and the medallions we see the princeps informally, almost in private, indulging in a favorite avocation. Hunting was the most rigorous and violent of all sports. Although Sallust had dismissed it as servile in comparison to politics and war (Sall. *Cat.* 4.1), later Romans such as Trajan enjoyed it not only as a diversion, but also as a means of keeping in physical shape to meet the demands of government and warfare (Pliny *Pan.* 81.1–3).[50] Hadrian appears on the Tondi in a costume midway between military and civilian dress.[51] He is firmly in command of things; we may see here a reflection of

[45] F. von Lorentz, "Ein Bildnis des Antoninus Pius?" *RömMitt* 48 (1933) 308–11. Although L'Orange and von Gerkan, *Konstantinsbogen* 166 n. 1, accepted the identification of Antoninus Pius, M. Wegner, *Die Herrscherbildnisse in antoninischer Zeit*, Das römische Herrscherbild II.4 (Berlin 1939) 125, rejected it, and Bonanno, *Portraits* 101–103, 106, rejects both of Blümel's identifications, though offering no specific ones of his own. Contra, Aymard, *Chasses romaines* 534; and N. Hannestad, "The Portraits of Aelius Caesar," *AnalDan* 7 (1974) 75–77, 91, no. 12.

[46] Aymard, *Chasses romaines* 534–35.

[47] Bulle, "Jagddenkmal" 148–51.

[48] Kähler, *Villa* 178 n. 151, accepts this identification of the lion-hunt Tondo, but he is not convincing that in this scene Antinoos is the bearded youth to Hadrian's left.

[49] See Aymard, *Chasses romaines* 530–32.

[50] Aymard, *Chasses romaines* 43–196, 469–502, for this development.

[51] Toynbee, *Hadrianic School* 4 n. 1.

Dio's remark that Hadrian's passion for hunting did not distract him from affairs of state (Dio Cass. 69.10.2). The hunting Tondi, like the bronze medallions, speak for a new evaluation of the sport. Not only was it a way for a man to keep fit, but the courageous pursuit of ferocious and dangerous animals makes Hadrian one with Theseus and Heracles. Like them, Hadrian rid the world of violence and encouraged the peaceful growth of civilization and art.[52]

The sacrifice scenes of the Tondi emphasize the last point. The princeps is shown paying homage to four of the traditional gods of the Roman West.[53] The detailed representations of the statues of the gods have led scholars to identify these with particular images, such as the Hercules of Gades.[54] We should also note that the number of sacrifice panels is one more than that of the hunt panels. If these eight Tondi were the only ones in antiquity, it would appear that Hadrian's piety was being stressed even more than his intrepidity.[55]

Finally, the presence of other historical figures on the relief symbolizes the transmission of these qualities to both the new generation and other members of Hadrian's court.[56] Many of the figures now appear idealized and barely distinguishable from one another, and may have been so even when the reliefs were first carved. The heroized Antinoos appears alongside the heirs designate and friends of the princeps;[57] in each of the reliefs the figures aesthetically

[52] For Hadrian's passion for hunting, see, e.g., P. A. Stadter, *Arrian of Nicomedia* (Chapel Hill, N.C. 1980) 50–52; and Kähler, *Villa* 145–46, who further associates the reliefs with Hadrian's vicennalia (in 137); Condurachi, "Genèse des *tondi*" 454–56. Ruysschaert sees the Tondi as expressing primarily military virtue ("Interprétation de l'arc de Constantin" 91, 93); contra, Syme, "Hadrian and the Senate" *Athenaeum* 62.1 (1984) 48, who notes Hadrian's aversion to such bellicose displays. Maull, "Hadrians Jagddenkmal" 56, 58–66, notes the resemblance of the hunting Tondi to such earlier monuments as Hellenistic sarcophagi.

[53] For Hadrian's devotion to these traditional rustic gods, see Beaujeu, 161–63, and cf. Maull, "Hadrians Jagddenkmal" 57–58.

[54] See, for example, Bulle, "Jagddenkmal" 148–51; and Calza, "Iconografia sull'arco di Costantino" 144–45, who suggests that the Hercules is the type of Hercules Invictus near the Ara Maxima in Rome, and that the Apollo has affinities to the Antinoos-Apollo type represented by a statue in Berlin.

[55] Aymard, *Chasses romaines* 535–37. The inequality of the numbers strengthens the suggestion of the extra head of Antoninus Pius now in the Antiquario of the Foro Romano (see n. 29) that there were originally more than eight panels. Condurachi, "Genèse des *tondi*," though noting the religious and political implications of the Tondi, considers the monument primarily a hunting memorial. Bonanno, *Portraits* 95, marks it as "a monument of personal significance to the Emperor rather than of state importance."

[56] Aymard, *Chasses romaines* 535–37, sees the monument as primarily dynastic.

[57] Kähler, *Villa* 154, 179 n. 151, though assuming too many portraits of Antinoos in the Tondi and overlooking the heroic nudity of the figure in the departure Tondo, stresses the peculiarity of depicting Antinoos as a man rather than a god.

harmonize as they devote themselves to the hunt or the sacrifice. The effect is one of concord and dedication.

Hadrian's monument, whatever it was, unifies both private and public aspects of his reign and must have been impressive. The unusual shape of the reliefs and their superior sculptural quality would have called attention to the Tondi. The repetition of the shape eight times and the reiteration of subject matter stress the aspirations that prevailed toward the end of Hadrian's rule: peace, civilization, and respect for the gods after the violence of the Jewish and other rebellions, harmony within the imperial court, and a smooth transfer of power to Hadrian's successors.

### The Athenaeum and Other Manifestations in Rome of Hadrian's Philhellenism

A number of late and not very reliable sources attest to the existence of an "Athenaeum" that Hadrian founded in Rome after his return from the Jewish rebellion in 134. The most explicit testimony is that of Aurelius Victor:

> Igitur Aelius Hadrianus eloquio togaeque studiis accommodatior pace ad orientem composita Romam regreditur. Ibi Graecorum more seu Pompilii Numae caerimonias leges gymnasia doctoresque curare occepit, adeo quidem, ut etiam ludum ingenuarum artium, quod Athenaeum vocant, constitueret atque initia Cereris Liberaeque, quae Eleusina dicitur, Atheniensium modo Roma percoleret (Therefore Aelius Hadrian, more favorably disposed to eloquence and civilized activities now that peace had been settled in the East, returned to Rome. Here, in the Greek way or that of Numa Pompilius, he began to attend to religious rites, laws, the gymnasia, and teachers, so much so that he even established a place of instruction actually for the liberal arts, which they call the Athenaeum, and devoted himself at Rome in the manner of the Athenians to the mysteries of Ceres and Libera, which are called the Eleusinian mysteries: Aur. Vict. *Caes.* 14.1–4).

No remains of this building have ever been identified for certain, although scholars have long made efforts to determine its character and general location.[58] Since the Athenaeum was an emphatically Greek cultural center, it has

[58] The sources, conveniently reproduced by both H. Braunert, "Das Athenaeum zu Rom bei den *Scriptores Historiae Augustae*," *HAC* 1963 (Bonn 1964) 10–12; and E. Harleman, "Questions sur l'Athenaeum de l'empereur Hadrien," *Eranos* 79 (1981) 58–59, in-

also been introduced in discussions of the intellectual history of the Hadrianic period.[59] Yet, as we shall see, it was only one element in a broad and diversified program to promote civilization and peace by combining and unifying the cultural heritages of Greece and Rome.

In his high appraisal of the importance of Greek culture to Rome and the empire, Hadrian was continuing a well-established trend, as well as expressing his own admiration of Greek rhetoric and civilization. After the uncomfortable and sometimes invidious relationships of the Greeks and Romans that prevailed during the republic, Caesar and Augustus had encouraged teachers of the liberal arts, especially Greeks, to emigrate to Rome by granting them citizenship and immunities, and Vespasian had endowed chairs of Greek and Latin rhetoric at Rome. Vespasian's exemption of orators, experts on linguistics and literary questions (*grammatici*), and doctors from taxes and liturgies, and Trajan's similar exemption of philosophers, were reaffirmed by Hadrian (*Dig.* 27.1.6.8). One aim of this imperial policy must have been to facilitate and improve the training of the young in the art of rhetoric, which was the foundation of all higher education and political life in Rome (cf. Quint. *I.O.* 1.*praef.*10; 12.1.26–28).[60]

At the same time, through the first century of the principate Rome had begun to accept Greeks and Greek culture with increasing ease and even enthusiasm. Hadrian's encouragement in Rome of the cult of the Eleusinian

---

clude in addition to Aur. Vict. *Caes.* 14.2–3: *HA, Pert.* 11.3, *SevAlex.* 35.2, *Gord.* 3.4; Porph. ad Hor. *Epod.* 2.2.94; Philostr. *VS*, p. 589; Dio Cass. 51.22.1, 73.17.4; Symm. *ep.* 9.89.2; Hieron. *Ep.* 66.9 (*PL* 22.644), in *Gal.* 3.*praef.* (*PL* 26.427); Sid. Apoll. *Epist.* 2.9.4, 4.8.5, 9.9.13, 9.14.2; and Zonar. 12.7 (p. 604 D). Aurelius Victor is our source for the date. Other works focusing on the Athenaeum include: B. Tamm-Fahlström, "Remarques sur les odéons de Rome," *Eranos* 57 (1959) 67–71 (basically a topographical investigation); and F. Schemmel, in *Philol. Wochenschr.* 36 (1919) 91ff., and in *Philol. Wochenschr.* 41 (1921) 982ff. (neither of which I was able to obtain). For other bibliography, see Braunert, passim.

[59] For example, in Bardon, *Empereurs et lettres* 426–28; Carandini, *Sabina* 43.

[60] S. F. Bonner, *Education in Ancient Rome* (Berkeley and Los Angeles 1977) 159–62 and passim, and M.S.A. Woodside, "Vespasian's Patronage of Education and the Arts," *TAPA* 73 (1942) 126–29; more general comments on the same subject are found in H. I. Marrou, *A History of Education in Antiquity*, trans. by G. Lamb (New York 1954) 255–64 (though he underestimates the importance and vigor of Greek in imperial Rome), and in M. W. Clarke, *Higher Education in the Ancient World* (Albuquerque, N.M. 1971). The whole subject of Greco-Roman interplay, which far exceeded the purely cultural sphere, is too vast to be entered into here: see the brief surveys of R. Syme, *Greeks Invading the Roman Government* (Brookline, Mass. 1982); Wallace-Hadrill, *Suetonius* 30–39, esp. 33–38; and G. W. Williams, *Change and Decline. Roman Literature in the Early Empire* (Berkeley 1978) 102–52, whose general survey from the earliest times into the second century A.D., however, underplays the contributions of the Romans.

mysteries, noted by Aurelius Victor, was anticipated by the signal respect that both Augustus and Claudius accorded the cult (Suet. *Aug.* 93, *Claud.* 25.5).[61] The philhellenism of Nero and Domitian, despite the hatred of the emperors themselves, had a profound effect upon Rome. The xenophobia that even Cicero was not entirely immune to still surfaced occasionally, as in the reaction to Nero's extravagant adulation of the Greeks and Greek culture or in the prejudices of Juvenal's Umbricius. There was no denying, however, that by the second decade of the second century A.D. Rome was the center of an increasingly Greco-Roman world. By then Greeks had begun to appear in the Roman senate and in other important political and military posts, and Romans were traveling in ever larger numbers to the east on public as well as private missions. Fluent knowledge of Greek was essential in any but the humblest careers.[62] And Greek rhetoric and culture were attractive for less pragmatic reasons. The Second Sophistic was now rapidly developing into an intellectual revival of astonishing vigor in the Roman world.[63]

Hadrian is representative of, but transcends, the culture of Rome at this time. He was fluent enough in both Latin and Greek to write prose and poetry in both languages.[64] His proficiency in Greek may have been a comfort and source of pride for him, for his childhood years in Spain tinged his Latin with an accent that once provoked laughter in the senate. He made a special effort to correct this early in his career in Rome (*HA, Hadr.* 3.1), and he was so successful in this endeavor that he recited speeches for Trajan (*HA, Hadr.* 3.11). His immense knowledge of Latin literature and his seemingly perverse predilection for the archaic (*HA, Hadr.* 16.5–6) show an idiosyncratic taste,

[61] Beaujeu, 165–70, overemphasizes the importance of Hadrian's interest in the Eleusinian mysteries, overlooking the initiation of other "traditional" Romans in the cult.

[62] See, e.g., the recent work of H. Halfmann, *Die Senatoren aus dem östlichen Teil des Imperium Romanum bis zum Ende des 2. Jahrhunderts n. Chr.* (Göttingen 1979); R. Syme, "Hadrian the Intellectual," in *Empereurs d'Espagne* 247; idem, *Greeks Invading the Roman Government.* For the influence of the emperors on Roman attitudes toward Hellenic culture in the first century A.D., see Wallace-Hadrill, *Suetonius* 175–89, who discerns a reevaluation of Greek culture under the Flavians, when there was a reaction against those aspects of Greek culture considered "luxurious." Wal-

lace-Hadrill also justly remarks: "the court played its role as disseminator, but in its turn it merely responded to larger historical waves of fashion."

[63] See, e.g., G. W. Bowersock, *Greek Sophists in the Roman Empire* (Oxford 1969); idem, ed., *Approaches to the Second Sophistic* (University Park, Pa. 1974).

[64] See also Bardon, *Empereurs et lettres* 393–424. The authenticity of Hadrian's poem to his soul has been doubted, most recently (with recapitulation of the arguments) by T. D. Barnes, "Hadrian's Farewell to Life," *CQ* 18 (1968) 384–85; contra B. Baldwin, "Hadrian's Farewell to Life: Some Arguments for Authenticity," *CQ* 20 (1970) 372–74.

though also erudition and skill; and in Greek literature, too, he seems to have preferred the archaic.[65] In the intensity of his passion for the Greeks, he stood out among those in Rome who shared his literary interests and training.[66]

Hadrian's philhellenism was notorious in Rome, and a nickname given him, "Graeculus," derided him for it (*HA, Hadr.* 1.5). He visited the Greek world, and especially Athens, repeatedly, and always as a benefactor.[67] Before his accession he had been archon in Athens in 111–112, and among the first acts of his principate was the bestowal in 121 of special privileges to the Epicurean school in Athens at the urging of Plotina (*IG*, II/III, 1099 = *ILS* 7784 = Smallwood, #442). In 124–125 he returned to Athens and undertook important public works there, and seems to have been initiated into the lowest grade of the Eleusinian mysteries. On a subsequent visit in 128–129 he was raised to the highest grade, at which time he also dedicated several monuments in Athens itself. In 131–132 he returned to dedicate the Temple of Zeus Olympios and to found the sanctuary of the Panhellenion.

In Rome Hadrian consistently encouraged Greek culture and the Greek presence within the capital. Although G. B. Townend has argued that the secretariat in charge of Greek correspondence (*ab epistulis graecis*) was not finally separated from that in charge of Latin correspondence (*ab epistulis latinis*) until 166, most of those who are known to have held the ab epistulis post during the Hadrianic period were Greek literary men, and Suetonius, one of its holders and famous for his Latin works, was also fluent in Greek.[68] Moreover, Hadrian appointed L. Julius Vestinus, the *epistates* of the Museum of Alexandria, to the secretariats *a studiis* and ab epistulis in Rome.[69] Hadrian's freed-

---

[65] On Hadrian's taste for the archaic in Greek, cf. *HA, Hadr.* 16.2, 6, and Dio Cass. 69.4.6; this was, however, characteristic of the period. See n. 66.

[66] For the Hadrianic period, see Wallace-Hadrill, *Suetonius* 38–41, 203, and passim; compare the tastes and training of Fronto and his contemporaries, brilliantly recreated by Champlin, *Fronto* 29–59. For more general remarks on the archaizing movement, see Williams, *Change and Decline* 306–12; and Bowersock, *Sophists* 16.

[67] For Hadrian's stays and works in Athens: Weber, 158–78, 205–10, 268–75; P. Graindor, *Athènes sous Hadrien* (Cairo 1934; reprinted New York 1973) 1–58, 213–88; D. J. Geagan, "Roman Athens: Some Aspects of Life and

Culture, I: 86 B.C.–A.D. 267," *ANRW* II.7.1 (1979) 389–99; S. Follet, *Athènes au IIe et au IIIe siècle* (Paris 1976) 107–35; and M. T. Boatwright, "Further Thoughts on Hadrianic Athens," *Hesperia* 52 (1983) 173–76.

[68] G. B. Townend, "The Post of *ab epistulis* in the Second Century," *Historia* 10 (1961) 375–81. For the most recent list of the Hadrianic *ab epistulis*, see N. Lewis, "Literati in the Service of Roman Emperors: Politics before Culture," in *Coins, Culture and History in the Ancient World. Numismatic and Other Studies in Honor of B. L. Trell*, ed. by L. Casson and M. Price (Detroit 1981) 150–51; and cf. Bowersock, *Sophists*, 50–53; and Millar, *ERW* 88–92.

[69] H.-G. Pflaum, *Les Carrières procurato-*

man Phlegon of Tralles was a prolific scholar whose works included a history
of the Olympic festival from its beginnings down to his own time, a history
of the festivals of Rome, and a topographical study of Rome (mentioned in
Chapter 1.)[70]

Hadrian's interest in such Greek intellectuals, however, went beyond em-
ploying them in public offices and his own service in the capital. During a
visit to the Museum in Alexandria in 130 he pointedly debated with its scholars (*HA, Hadr.* 20.2). Other Greek literary men seem to have been tied to him
more personally, although it is difficult to discern precisely how. His disputes
at unknown dates with C. Avidius Heliodorus, Valerius Eudaemon, Favorinus, and Dionysius of Miletus are recorded in the ancient sources; in contrast,
our other information shows successful careers for all these men, uninter-
rupted except for the temporary exile of Favorinus.[71] The Syrian rhetorician
and philosopher Heliodorus, despite the notice of Hadrian's biography that
the princeps attacked him in a scurrilous diatribe (*HA, Hadr.* 15.5), rose during Hadrian's principate to be prefect of Egypt. The Alexandrian Eudaemon,
who was reported to have been reduced to poverty by the princeps' displeas-
ure (*HA, Hadr.* 15.3), was also ab epistulis under Hadrian, and is known to
have been prefect of Egypt in the early years of Antoninus Pius.[72] Favorinus,
the famous rhetorician and sophist from Arles, disagreed with Hadrian, "yet
lived" (Dio Cass. 69.3.4; *HA, Hadr.* 15.12–13; Philostr. *VS*, p. 489). His exile, recently revealed by a new papyrus, is tentatively dated by Bowersock to
the end of Hadrian's reign.[73] Finally, although Dio says that Hadrian tried to
overthrow Dionysius of Miletus together with Favorinus (69.3.4), Philostratus makes Dionysius a particular favorite of Hadrian, and an inscription from
Ephesus published in 1953 proves that Dionysius was procurator there,[74] providing a factual basis for Philostratus' exaggerated report that Hadrian made
the sophist "satrap of eminent peoples" (Philostr. *VS*, p. 524).

Bowersock sums up the above information by saying that in these four

*riennes équestres sous le Haut-Empire romain*
(Paris 1960–61) no. 105, pp. 245–47. For Hadrian's relationship with the Museum, see
Millar, *ERW* 504–506; and for a more objective view of the Museum's management
throughout the imperial period, Lewis, "Literati" 154–58.

[70] E. Frank, "Phlegon (2)," *RE* 20.1 (1941)
261–64; and *FGrHist*, II B, #257, 1159–96.

[71] For these individuals and incidents, see
Bowersock, *Sophists*, 50–53.

[72] See, too, Pflaum, *Carrières* no. 110, pp.
264–71, who concludes that Antoninus Pius
reinstated the sophist while repairing the
abuses of Hadrian's last years.

[73] The papyrus is published most conveniently in A. Barigazzi, *Opere: Favorino di Arelate* (Florence 1966) 375–409, with commentary on pp. 409–521 (briefly, Bowersock,
*Sophists* 36).

[74] J. Keil, "Vertreter der zweiten Sophistik
in Ephesos," in *ÖJh* 40 (1953) 6.

cases "there is reason to assume the emperor's favour *and* his hostility."[75] Yet Hadrian "ruined" the two sophists Favorinus and Dionysius chiefly by elevating their rivals (Dio Cass. 69.3.4). These disagreements are on the level of Hadrian's altercations with Latin writers and critics, such as the well-known dispute with the poet Florus (*HA, Hadr.* 16.3–4). The sources use such disputes to give us the impression of a tyrannical ruler; the same bias can be seen in the accounts of Tiberius' spirited exchanges with Greek grammarians (e.g., Suet. *Tib.* 11.3, 70.3).[76] What should not be overlooked, however, is Hadrian's interest and engagement in the intellectual controversies of the day (cf. *HA, Hadr.* 16.8).

The founding of the Athenaeum in the heart of Rome reflects both Hadrian's active interest in Greek intellectual life and its exponents, and an enlarged participation in Roman life for Greek rhetoricians, philosophers, and men of letters such as Arrian of Nicomedia, one of Hadrian's friends.[77] H. Braunert has been able to separate the sixteen testimonia for the Athenaeum into two groups. The first, including Cassius Dio, Philostratus, Porphyrio, and Aurelius Victor, testifies to the institution as it was established by Hadrian. The second, made up of the *HA* and the late authors Symmachus, Jerome, Sidonius, and Zonaras, knows the Athenaeum as it evolved in the second half of the fourth century.[78] According to Braunert, Hadrian's establishment was a school of Greek grammar and rhetoric; he interprets the name Athenaeum as a reference to the goddess Athena and maintains that Hadrian installed the school in the Atrium Minervae, an adjunct of the Curia Senatus. By the fourth century, however, after Diocletian's reconstruction of the Curia and replanning of adjacent areas, the Athenaeum was housed in a building with arrangements like an odeum or theater. It then served as a hall for public declamation in both languages and as an advanced school of Greek and Latin rhetoric and grammar.[79]

Braunert's ingenious reconstruction of the Athenaeum's history, based on an exhaustive study of the texts, agrees with earlier inquiries in stressing the

---

[75] Bowersock, *Sophists* 52.

[76] For Tiberius' interests, see Wallace-Hadrill, *Suetonius* 84–85. Yet personal dialogue with Greeks was long familiar, and it must have included such disputes: see, e.g., G. W. Bowersock, *Augustus and the Greek World* (Oxford 1965) 1–13, 30–41.

[77] Stadter, *Arrian* 13–14, 168–69, and passim, for the integration of the Greek and Ro-

man intelligentsia in this period.

[78] Braunert, "Athenaeum" 30, 36–40; for the passages, see n. 58 above. Harleman does not address Braunert's main arguments directly, and apparently accepts all of them except the location in the Atrium Minervae ("Sur l'Athenaeum" 63).

[79] Braunert, "Athenaeum" 13–36.

importance of the establishment of a center for the study of Greek in the heart of Rome. This may not have been the "state university of Rome" that some have claimed,[80] but it offered an official blessing for, and patronage of, Greek in the capital. Unfortunately, without more information than is available we cannot locate or identify the Athenaeum with any certainty.[81]

This was not the only side of Greek culture that Hadrian promoted in Rome. He apparently was also responsible for the decision to establish the headquarters of the ecumenical (i.e., international) guild of athletes and victors in Rome, and perhaps that of the ecumenical guild of actors as well.

The numerous festivals of the Greek world were very popular, and in Rome and Italy, Greek games, notwithstanding slighting references to them in some literary texts, were also admired and celebrated, especially in the second century A.D. The Sebasta in Naples, created by Augustus probably in 2 B.C., and the Capitolia in Rome, inaugurated by Domitian in A.D. 86, were longer lived than the ephemeral Neroneia of Nero and survived until the third and fourth centuries, respectively.[82] Both the Sebasta, officially called the Italica Romaea Sebasta Isolympia, and the Capitolia, in honor of Jupiter Capitolinus, were ostensibly modeled on the Olympic games, but they included elements from all four of the great Greek games and combined equestrian events, athletic competitions, and musical and dramatic contests.[83] In the principate of Hadrian, the two festivals in Rome and Naples and many others in Greek lands became an imperial interest and responsibility through imperial encouragement of the ecumenical guilds of athletes and actors who performed in them.

---

[80] For example, S. Mazzarino, "Prima Cathedra," in *Mélanges . . . A. Piganiol*, III (Paris 1966) 1663–64. Harleman's objection that it would be difficult to associate the library necessary for such an institution to what else we know about the school ("Sur l'Athenaeum" 63) overlooks the preexisting libraries of the nearby Forum of Trajan.

[81] Braunert's location of the Hadrianic Athenaeum cannot be proved, although he is probably right about the general placement; he convincingly refutes ("Athenaeum" 18, 37, 39–40) others' suggestions that the Athenaeum was at the Forum of Trajan (reference to H. I. Marrou, "La Vie intellectuelle au Forum de Trajan et au Forum d'Auguste," *MélRome* 49 [1932] 109–110), and that it was in the Graecostadium (cf. Platner-Ashby, s.v.

Athenaeum, 56). As we saw above in Chapter 4, the "Vestibule" of Domitian could not have been the Athenaeum (as suggested by Coarelli, *Roma* [1980] 74).

[82] Robert, "Deux concours" 6–9; I. R. Arnold, "Agonistic Festivals in Italy and Sicily," *AJA* 64 (1960) 245–49; E. J. Jory, "Associations of Actors in Rome," *Hermes* 98 (1970) 248–49.

[83] Robert, "Deux concours" 6–7; Arnold, "Agonistic Festivals" 246–47; and for more details on the Capitolia, *DizEpig*, I, s.v. Agon, Capitolinus, 364–65; and Wissowa, "Capitolia," *RE* 3.2 (1899) 1527–29. The games are entitled Capitolia Olympia in *CIG* add. 2810b (cited incorrectly in both works as 2180b).

By the time of the principate guilds of athletes and actors were well established in the Greek East, performing in a variety of festivals, great and small. The guilds were considered so important that they could request and receive corporate privileges from kings, cities, leagues, and Rome itself. Synods of actors were first formed in Greece in the early third century B.C. and were under the patronage of the god Dionysos.[84] Regional guilds of actors, including some in Rome, make their appearance after the late third century B.C., but most important in the Greek world was the ecumenical guild of Dionysiac artists (actors), organized about the time of Augustus' rise to power.[85] Professional athletes, although equally necessary to the festivals, apparently were not organized into guilds before the first century B.C., when we have evidence of a worldwide guild of athletes and a separate worldwide guild of those athletes who were victors.[86] These ecumenical guilds of athletes seem to have prospered in their dealings with the Roman authorities: M. Antonius (in 41 or 32 B.C.), Claudius (in A.D. 44), and Vespasian all granted or restored to their members such privileges as exemption from military service.[87] By the mid-second century, and apparently by the reign of Hadrian, the two guilds were incorporated into a single organization of athletes and victors, which then received an even greater mark of favor: headquarters in the center of Rome.[88]

In 134 M. Ulpius Domesticus, who would become the director of the Imperial Baths in 143, addressed a petition to Hadrian for a seat in Rome for the

[84] A. W. Pickard-Cambridge, *The Dramatic Festivals of Athens*, 2nd ed., rev. by J. Gould and D. M. Lewis (Oxford 1969) 279–305.

[85] Pickard-Cambridge, *Dramatic Festivals* 297, who assigns no location to the guild seat.

[86] Magie, *RRAM* 1279 n. 4; H. W. Pleket, "Some Aspects of the History of the Athletic Guilds," *ZPE* 10 (1973) 199–203. Both scholars stress that there is no evidence for the unification of the guild of the athletes and that of the actors at this time, and again there is no evidence for the location of the guilds other than the probability that it was in Asia Minor. Pleket, 213, discusses the two dubious suggestions of Sardis and Ephesus as the seat of the ecumenical synod of the athletes. For an earlier discussion of the synod, with full bibliography and citation of pertinent Greek documents in Rome, see *IGUR* I, p. 199;

some of Moretti's conclusions, however, have to be corrected (cf. n. 88 below).

[87] Pleket, "Athletic Guilds" 200–208; C. A. Forbes, "Ancient Athletic Guilds," *CP* 50 (1955) 243. Antonius' rescript is preserved on the verso of P. Lond. 137 (= R.K. Sherk, *Roman Documents from the Greek East* [Baltimore 1969] #57, pp. 290–93); those of Claudius and Vespasian, P. Lond. 1178 (cf. M. P. Charlesworth, *Documents Illustrating the Reigns of Claudius and Nero* [Cambridge 1939] p. 11, #7).

[88] Pleket, "Athletic Guilds" 208–209; he also convincingly refutes the widely held belief that the ecumenical guild of athletes was dissolved and then reformed during the principate (pp. 214–22), and argues against its having a headquarters in Rome before Hadrian's time (pp. 225–26).

sacred guild of athletes and victors (*IG* 14.1054 = *IGUR* 1.235 = *IGRR* 1.149). For some unknown reason, though the request was granted by Hadrian on May 5, 134, this was not realized until the time of Antoninus Pius, when the headquarters of the guild was installed in a location near the Baths of Trajan, "from which the athletes could best participate in the Capitolia" (*IG* 14.1055 = *IGUR* 1.236 = *IGRR* 1.146).[89] The headquarters was thereafter used at least until the fourth century, and C. A. Forbes notes that in an administrative way the establishment made Rome the athletic capital of the world.[90] Although the actual headquarters was not brought into being until after Hadrian's death, his responsibility for it is recalled by the addition of the epithet "Hadriana" to the names of several guilds of athletes throughout the Roman empire.[91]

The headquarters of the ecumenical guild of Dionysiac artists (actors) may also have been transferred to Rome from the Greek East at this time. From the time of Trajan on, this association's ties with the emperors became stronger, and in Hadrian's day the guild's full title was the Sacred Thymelic Hadriana Synod of Those Who Compete Together for the Sake of Imperator Caesar Traianus Hadrianus Augustus, the New Dionysos (*IGRR* 1.17). The epithet Hadriana was retained and other imperial ones were subsequently added.[92]

Around 142 T. Aelius Alcibiades of Nysa gave a number of gifts to the guild of actors of Rome, including a library of books for its headquarters in a sacred temenos and an endowment, the revenues of which were to be used for the celebration of the birthday of Divus Hadrianus.[93] From this and other evi-

---

[89] This headquarters, called *curia athletarum* in an inscription (*CIL* 6.10154), has not been found; see Platner-Ashby, s.v. Curia athletarum, 142, and Lugli, *Fontes* III, pp. 171–74, for the documents. For the date, *IGUR* I, p. 199.

[90] Forbes, "Ancient Athletic Guilds" 244.

[91] See Pleket, "Athletic Guilds" 208.

[92] Cf. F. Poland, "Nachträge, technitai," *RE* 5 A.2 (1934) 2517–18, with a list of inscriptions. D. J. Geagan, "Hadrian and the Athenian Dionysiac Technitai," *TAPA* 103 (1972) 146, cites *SEG* 7, no. 825 and *IGRR* 1.18, as examples of Trajan being called the "new Dionysos" by the ecumenical synod, but in *IGRR* 1.18 the title is restored. See also Magie, *RRAM* 617, 1477–78 n. 24.

[93] The inscription is most conveniently published by Pickard-Cambridge, *Dramatic Festivals* 319, no. 15, and is exhaustively discussed by L. Robert, "Les Aelius Alcibiade de Nysa," in his *Etudes épigraphiques et philologiques* (Paris 1938) 45–53. Robert argues that this T. Aelius Alcibiades is the son of P. Aelius Alcibiades, the friend to whom Phlegon dedicated his works on the Olympiads; he suggests that these are the books donated by his son to the guild. J. Gérard's association of Juvenal's exile with his supposed mockery of T. Aelius Alcibiades in 7.84 (*Juvénal et la réalité contemporaine* [Paris 1976] 92–114) is rejected in J. Beaujeu's review of the book (*REL* 54 [1976] 458).

dence H. W. Pleket argues that Hadrian must have been responsible for the location in Rome of the ecumenical actors' guild.[94]

Hadrian's interest in these ecumenical guilds is due to both his concern for efficient organization and his philhellenism,[95] but it also has wider implications. He had established many festivals throughout the Greek East and in Egypt during his own lifetime,[96] and after Hadrian's death Antoninus Pius instituted a new festival in his honor in Italy, the Eusebia at Puteoli where he was first buried (*HA, Hadr.* 27.3). Though little is known about these later games, the inscriptions that list this festival together with the Capitolia, Sebasta, and great panhellenic festivals in Greece indicate that they were of equal splendor and included gymnastic, musical, and dramatic competitions.[97] And other games were also celebrated by cities in the East for the deified Hadrian.[98]

The significance of such games is perhaps best conveyed by Hadrian's near contemporaries, Plutarch and Aelius Aristides. These Greeks, writing in

[94] Pleket, "Athletic Guilds" 225–27. Geagan, "Dionysiac Technitai" 149 n. 26, suggests that *BGU* 4, 1074, reedited by P. Viereck, *Klio* 8 (1908) 415–17, line 3, indicates that Hadrian was concerned with a reorganization of the ecumenical actors.

[95] Pleket, "Athletic Guilds" 221–22, notes the links between the *agones* and imperial worship; philhellenism of Hadrian: Poland, "Technitai" 2517–18. Geagan, "Dionysiac Technitai" 149–51, noting Hadrian's large benefactions to the Dionysiac *technitai* in Athens, attributes them to Hadrian's philhellenism and to an alleged wish to form an Athenian mystic synod of technitai to worship Antinoos as Dionysos Choreios. All of Hadrian's acts noted in this section seem at variance with the puzzling notice of the biography that Hadrian destroyed a theater Trajan had built in the Campus Martius in the same way as he relinquished many provinces conquered by Trajan, claiming to have had instructions from Trajan (*HA, Hadr.* 9.1–2). Things are further complicated by Dio's report of an odeum built by Apollodorus for Trajan, together with a gymnasium (69.4.1). There is no other evidence for either theater or odeum (cf. Platner-Ashby, s.vv. Theatrum Traiani, 518, and Odeum, 371). Tamm-

Fahlström, "Odéons" 69–71, holds that theater and odeum were separate buildings, and that Hadrian jealously destroyed Trajan's theater to build his own Athenaeum; this ignores the chronology for these events implied by the biography and given by Aurelius Victor. Platner-Ashby, s.v. Odeum, cites Dio as evidence that Apollodorus restored Domitian's odeum; and G. Lugli, "Date de la fondation du Forum de Trajan" 236, considers Dio's report due to a confusion in the tradition about Domitian's buildings, which wrongly assigns many of them to Trajan (similarly, Blake/Bishop, 36). Lugli's suspicion should probably be extended to Trajan's theater as well; and we should note the tendentiousness of the whole passage in the biography (cf. Benario, *Commentary*, ad *HA, Hadr.* 9.1).

[96] Robert, "Deux concours" 10–11, with references.

[97] Robert, "Deux concours" 8–10, with the classical texts; idem, *RevPhil* 1930, 37–38, refuting earlier theories that Hadrianeia were established in Rome.

[98] For example, in Athens: Follett, *Athènes* 322, with thirty-four inscriptions from the beginning of Antoninus' reign to 255/256.

the context of imperial Rome, make the observation that competition at festivals replaces the competition of war, thus contributing to orderly government and a prosperous and contented society; Plutarch makes his remark in his life of Numa (Plut. *Numa* 20.4; Aristid. *Or.* 26.99). In the passage from Aurelius Victor on the Athenaeum quoted at the beginning of this discussion, this later author has similarly linked Hadrian to Numa in the emphasis on peace and the arts of civilization.[99] Establishing the Athenaeum served much the same purpose as fostering the celebrations of Greek festivals and the guilds of those who participated in them: Hadrian thus encouraged unification, peace, and civilization in Rome and throughout the Roman world. Furthermore, while demonstrating symbolically in Rome that the Roman empire was a Greco-Roman world, as he was doing with the Temple of Venus and Roma, Hadrian encouraged this integration by functional buildings for daily use.

### The Aedes Bonae Deae and the Auguratorium

Hadrian is often credited with the construction or reconstruction of a temple of the Bona Dea, although the only evidence for this is an ambiguous passage in his biography: *fecit et sui nominis pontem et sepulchrum iuxta Tiberim et aedem Bonae Deae* (*HA, Hadr.* 19.11, translated below). A fragmentary inscription (*CIL* 6.976, cited below) assigns to Hadrian the restoration of an "Augurato[rium]," but again we lack other testimony for this. These two bits of information, however, correspond to better documented interests of the emperor.

Most commentators read the passage in Hadrian's biography making *aedem* a direct object of the verb *fecit*, but Syme, without consideration of the beginning of the sentence, construes *aedem* as object of the preposition *iuxta*. Thus, instead of translating "he built the bridge with his own name, and the tomb next to the Tiber, and a Temple of the Bona Dea," Syme reads "he built . . . the tomb, next to the Tiber and (next to) the Temple of the Bona Dea."[100] As we shall see, however, there is unlikely to have been any Temple of the Bona Dea near the Mausoleum, and the usual reading of the sentence should be accepted.

[99] Cf. Oliver, *Ruling Power* 946, who stresses the imperial patronage of the festivals as "a means of keeping alive the spiritual values of Hellenism." For Hadrian's emulation of Numa, see R. Zoepffel, "Hadrian und Numa," *Chiron* 8 (1978) 391–427, esp. 398.

G. Kennedy, *The Art of Rhetoric in the Roman World* (Princeton 1972) 583, has even suggested that Aristides delivered his speech in 143 in Hadrian's Athenaeum.

[100] Syme, *Emperors and Biography* 43; see also the earlier and more speculative remarks

If we assume that the biography reflects a sound tradition crediting Hadrian with construction of a temple of Bona Dea, this may have been a new temple or reconstruction of an existing one. Despite the relative wealth of evidence of many sorts for the cult of Bona Dea in Rome, including over forty inscriptions,[101] nothing but the passage in question shows Hadrian had any outstanding interest in her cult or indicates that any new temple for her was built in Rome in the second century. So it is generally assumed that Hadrian restored a temple of the Bona Dea.[102] Though such careful scholars as Beaujeu note that *fecit* is used here rather than *instauravit* (restored), more correct if it is a question of rebuilding (cf., for example, *HA, Hadr.* 19.10), such precision in the niceties of Latin is seldom encountered in the *HA*.[103]

In addition to many small shrines, we know of two "aedes" of the Bona Dea in Rome, the famous one to Bona Dea Subsaxana, and one of imperial date in the Transtiberim region. The earlier temple, perhaps erected ca. 272 B.C., stood at the north end of the eastern hill of the Aventine, now called the Little Aventine, directly south of the east end of the Circus Maximus.[104] Bona Dea was a fertility goddess, a healing goddess, and a warrior goddess, and combined Italic elements with Greek ones.[105] Her cult was particularly popular in Rome during the republic, when even the highest-born Roman matrons participated in her annual mysteries. These were celebrated under the supervision of the Vestal Virgins in the house of a magistrate with *imperium*, and were strictly forbidden to men. The outcry at the sacrilege committed by P. Clo-

---

of A. Merlin, *L'Aventin dans l'antiquité* (Paris 1906) 362 n. 3.

[101] M. Céballac collects the inscriptions and examines them for information for the social standing and wealth of individuals associated with the cult, in "Octavia, épouse de Gamala, et la 'Bona Dea,'" *MélRome* 85 (1973) 517–53, esp. 533–45. Statuettes of the goddess, many of which are from Rome, are collected and discussed by A. Greifenhagen, "Bona Dea," *RömMitt* 52 (1937) 227–44. For the literary references, see K. Latte, *Römische Religionsgeschichte* (Munich 1960) 228–31, and G. Radke, *Die Götter Altitaliens* (Munich 1965) 73–74.

[102] B. M. Felletti-Maj, in *NSc*, ser. 8, 11 (1957) 335 n. 1, cautiously proposes that Hadrian built a new temple to Bona Dea and moved the cult from the Aventine temple, but he does not offer a location for this. F. Préchac's identification (in *RevNum* 1919,

163ff., and ibid., 1920, 205) of the temple depicted on Hadrianic coinage and usually thought to be that of Hercules Gaditanus as the aedes Bonae Deae is generally rejected: see *BMC, Emp.* III, p. cxxix n. 2; and Pensa, "Adriano" 30–31.

[103] Beaujeu, 125–26. In his review of Beaujeu's book, P. Lambrechts accepts Beaujeu's theory and notes an analogous use of *facere* in *RG* 19.11 to mean restoration (*Revue belge de philologie et d'histoire* 35 [1957] 501 n. 1). For *instaurare* used in late Latin with this sense, see Merten, *Bäder* 16.

[104] Platner-Ashby, s.v. Bona Dea Subsaxana, Aedes, 85; and Merlin, *Aventin* 107–11.

[105] See Latte and Radke (n. 101 above); J. Marouzeau, "Juppiter Optimus et Bona Dea," *Eranos* 54 (1956) 229; and G. Piccaluga, "Bona Dea," *Studi e materiali di storia delle religioni* 35 (1964) 195–237.

dius, when disguised as a female musician he intruded in the celebration of 62 B.C. held at the house of Julius Caesar, then praetor, shows the reverence, possibly even sacrosanctity, in which the cult was held at that time.[106]

The cult survived the scandal, as we can see from Livia's renovation of the aedes Bonae Deae sometime before 8 B.C. (Ov. *Fast.* 5.148–159). Ovid, who is our sole authority for this restoration, says that the temple was originally built by a Vestal Virgin named Claudia; although he is wrong about this (Cic. *Dom.* 136),[107] it provides him with an incentive for the restoration by Livia, the wife and mother of Claudii. He also gives another reason for Livia's benefaction: Livia restored the Temple so that she might imitate her husband and follow him in everything (*Fast.* 5.157–158).

The passage by Ovid builds up to his last statement. He notes specifically that the Temple stood on the place from which Remus took his auspices in his contest with Romulus to be the founder of Rome (*Fast.* 5.151–154). The connection between Bona Dea and Rome's foundation seems to have been advanced in other ways during the Augustan period, if we accept R.E.A. Palmer's reinterpretation of the pedimental sculptures of the Temple of Quirinus depicted on the Hartwig relief. Palmer holds that figure 11, usually presumed to be Faustulus, in fact represents Bona Dea Subsaxana, and that the entire pedimental group refers to the legendary foundation of Rome.[108] The Hartwig relief almost certainly shows the Temple of Quirinus as it was restored by Augustus in 16 B.C.[109]

In restoring the Temple of Bona Dea Subsaxana, Livia imitated Augustus' restoration of the Temple of Quirinus (cf. *RG* 19.2; Dio Cass. 54.19.4). Although Augustus was careful to distinguish himself from Romulus, a king and fratricide (cf. Suet. *Aug.* 7.2; Dio Cass. 53.16.7),[110] during his reign the

[106] Cicero, exploiting the incident in his attacks on Clodius, gives us much of our information about the cult: *Har. Resp.* 37, *Leg.* 2.21, *Att.* 1.13.3; and cf. Plut. *Cic.* 19.3–4; Dio Cass. 37.45.1. F. Bömer notes that even during the republic there must have been another side to the cult, which would explain its attraction to slaves (in *Untersuchungen über die Religion der Sklaven in Griechenland und Rom*, I, 2nd ed., rev. by P. Herz, *Forschungen zur antiken Sklaverei* 14.1 [Wiesbaden 1981] 154).

[107] See, e.g., F. Bömer, *P. Ovidius Naso. Die Fasten* (Heidelberg 1957–58) II.302–303.

[108] R.E.A. Palmer, "Jupiter Blaze, Gods of the Hills, and the Roman Topography of *CIL* VI 337," *AJA* 80 (1976) 54–55.

[109] The relief itself is almost certainly late Flavian: G. M. Koeppel, "Die historischen Reliefs der römischen Kaiserzeit II," *BJb* 184 (1984) 13–15; and Palmer, "Jupiter Blaze" 53. Earlier bibliography includes the detailed discussion of the pediment and its symbolism by P. Hommel, *Studien zu den römischen Figurengiebeln der Kaiserzeit* (Berlin 1954) 9–22. See, too, Gros, *Aurea Templa* 116–18, on the unusual architecture of the temple, our knowledge of which is complicated by Vitruvius' mention of a dipteral aedes Quirini (*De Arch.* 3.2.7).

[110] Cf., e.g., R. Syme, *The Roman Revolution* (Oxford 1939) 313–14.

emphasis on Rome's sacred beginnings suggested that the princeps was re-founding Rome with all its traditional strength and pristine *pax deorum*. Livia's restoration of the Temple of Bona Dea picked up the religious implications of Augustus' name by embellishing an augural *templum* (Enn. *ap.* Varro *Rust.* 3.1.2 and *ap.* Cic. *Rep.* 1.64; Suet. *Aug.* 7.2). She also associated herself and Augustus with Rome's sacred origins,[111] and restored to the cult its dignity.

Nothing much is known about this temple after the Augustan period, though since the regionary catalogues list it in the twelfth region (Piscina Publica), it must have still been standing in the fourth century.[112] There was, however, another shrine to Bona Dea in Rome, in the fourteenth region, Transtiberim. In the eighteenth century a small building, "un tempietto come un tabernacolino," with an inscription still in situ, *Bonae Deae/ Sacrum/ M. Vettius Bolanus/ restitui iussit* (sacred to the Bona Dea. M. Vettius Bolanus ordered [this] to be restored: *CIL* 6.65 = *ILS* 3500), was excavated just north of S. Cecilia in Trastevere. Two other inscriptions were found in the excavation, both of a certain Cladus, who there erected a statue (*simulacrum*) and an "aed." for the Bona Dea for the protection of the Insula Bolaniana. In one inscription the goddess seems to be called Bona Dea Restituta (*CIL* 6.66, 67 = *ILS* 3501, 3501a).[113]

Syme refers to this temple of Bona Dea in locating Hadrian's Mausoleum "next to the Tiber and the Temple of the Bona Dea."[114] Yet almost 2 kilometers (as the crow flies) and two bends of the river separate the Mausoleum

[111] M. B. Flory, "*Sic exempla parantur*: Livia's Shrine to Concordia and the Porticus Liviae," *Historia* 33 (1984) 317–19, further associates Livia's reconstruction of the Temple of Bona Dea Subsaxana with Augustus' encouragement of marriage and the birthrate. Livia, and possibly Augustus as well, was connected elsewhere with Bona Dea: there was a shrine to Bona Dea in Bovillae (Cic. *Mil.* 86), the *patria* of the gens Julia; and Livia's birthday was celebrated in A.D. 18 by the women of the Vicus ad Bonam Deam of the Forum Clodii (*CIL* 11.3303; cf. G. Grether, "Livia and the Roman Imperial Cult," *AJP* 67 [1946] 238). The latter information may give us both more corroboration and a terminus ante quem for Livia's restoration of the temple in Rome.

[112] Nordh, *Libellus* 92.14, and Valentini and Zucchetti, 1.180, 137: (*Notitia*) Aedes Bonae Deae Subsaxanae; (*Curiosum*) Aedes Bonae Deae Subsaxaneae.

[113] *ILS* 3501: *B. d. r./ Cladus/ d. d.* (To Bona Dea Restituta. Cladus gave and dedicated [this]); *ILS* 3501a: *Bon. deae restitu[t]./ simulacr. in tut. insul./ Bolan. posuit, item aed. / dedit Cladus l. m.* (side) *Bol.* (To Bona Dea Restituta. Gladly and with good cause Cladus erected a statue for the safety of the Insula Bolaniana, and likewise gave a small shrine. [side] Bol[aniana?]). The name of the insula is completed in *CIL* as Bolan(i), in *ILS* as Bolan(iana); the latter seems preferable, on analogy with other named insulae such as the insula Vitaliana (*CIL* 6.33893).

[114] Syme, *Emperors and Biography* 43 and n. 6, referring to Platner-Ashby; Syme adduces the passage in Hadrian's biography as evidence of "Ignotus' " attention to precise topographical detail.

and the "tempietto," and the shrine itself seems to have been insignificant. The little "tempietto" that was excavated had a niche for a statuette, and the "aed." of the inscription should probably be completed as "aed(icula)." Cladus' building most likely resembled the aediculae mentioned in two inscriptions recording dedications to Bona Dea elsewhere (*CIL* 6.56, and 6.62). Furthermore, in other Roman inscriptions Bona Dea frequently has epithets indicating local associations: Bona Dea Gabilla, for example, is to be connected with the Horrea Galbiana (*CIL* 6.30855 = *ILS* 1621), and Bona Dea Anneanensis with a house of the Annii (*CIL* 6.69 = *ILS* 3511).[115] These humbler cults of Bona Dea might have employed such statuettes of the goddess as those that A. Greifenhagen has identified, and we should suppose, as did the excavators, that the "tempietto" they discovered is the aedicula of Cladus, and once held the statue he dedicated.[116] It seems unlikely that Hadrian had any connection with this aedes.

Although the inscription recording M. Vettius Bolanus' order to restore the shrine gives no information other than his name, the cognate name of the insula, Bolaniana, suggests he was not unimportant, at least locally. Two M. Vettii Bolani are known, the suffect consul of A.D. 66 and his son, a *consul ordinarius* of 111.[117] We can presume a date for the shrine in the first or early second century A.D. The shrine of the Bona Dea here was supported by donations from the neighborhood,[118] but ones on a relatively humble scale. This fits the rest of the evidence attesting the worship of the Bona Dea in Rome during the imperial period. As a healing and tutelary deity, the Bona Dea was particularly attractive to the poorer inhabitants of the city (cf. *CIL* 6.68 = *ILS* 3513; *CIL* 6.72 = *ILS* 3514; *CIL* 6.73 = *ILS* 3506; *CIL* 6.75 = *ILS* 3508; *CIL* 6.57, 60, 63, 64, 36766).[119] A benefaction of Hadrian to any of these

[115] See Mommsen's note on *CIL* 6.30855; and Felletti-Maj, *NSc*, 1957, 335, for other examples.

[116] Greifenhagen, "Bona Dea" 227–44, compiles and discusses a list of eleven statuettes, averaging about 0.50 meters high and having as attributes a serpent entwined about the right arm and a cornucopia in the left hand; they date from the first and second centuries A.D. Cébeillac, "Bona Dea" 549 n. 3, considers the shrine at the insula to have been a temple.

[117] *PIR* III, p. 411, nos. 323, 324; for the son, see also the Fasti Ostienses for 111: II, 13.1, p. 200–201. E. M. Savage, "The Cults of Ancient Trastevere," *MAAR* 17 (1940) 42, dates the "modest shrine" to the Neronian period.

[118] Another undated dedication to the Bona Dea, found in the vicinity of the shrine, is reported in *NSc*, 1905, 270 (cf. *CIL* 6.36766).

[119] Cébeillac, "Bona Dea" 530–48, noting that outside of Rome, however, the cult attracted the rich. I find no evidence to substantiate her conclusion that in Rome the elite shunned the cult as a notoriously immoral religion (Juv. 3.83–116, of course, is not valid evidence).

Bonae Deae would have been too inconsequential to be noted specifically in the biography.[120]

Other evidence also recommends that if the tradition of Hadrian's "building" of a Temple of the Bona Dea is correct, this ought to refer to Bona Dea Subsaxana. An inscription of 136, now found in the floor of St. John Lateran, records Hadrian's restoration of an Auguratorium from its foundations: *Imp. Caesar divi Traiani/ Parthici f. divi Nervae n./ Traianus Hadrianus/ Aug. pontif. max. trib. pot. XX/ imp. II cos. III p. p./ Augurato[rium] dilaps(um)/ a solo pe[c. sua restitu]it* ([The emperor Hadrian], son of the deified [emperor Trajan] grandson of the deified Nerva, pontifex maximus, with tribunician power for the twentieth time, [acclaimed] imperator for the second time, consul for the third time, father of his country, with his own funds restored from the ground up the Auguratorium, which had collapsed: *CIL* 6.976). The fourth-century regionary catalogues[121] and the *Mirabilia* (28) record the existence of an Auguratorium on the Palatine, and it has been proposed that this marked the place, given suitable monumental form, from which Romulus was believed to have taken his auspices at the foundation of Rome.[122] P. Pensabene's recent excavations have disposed of G. Schneider Graziosi's identification in 1915 of the Auguratorium as the Hadrianic aedicula east of the Temple of Magna Mater, and lacking new and positive information we have little knowledge of what the Auguratorium may have been like.[123] Ovid, however, emphasizes for the Temple of Bona Dea Subsaxana the tradition of Rome's foundation that seems memorialized later in the Auguratorium.

---

[120] Perhaps an imperial gift to such a shrine would be included in such statements as: (*Hadrianus*) *instauravit . . . sacras aedes plurimas* ([Hadrian] restored . . . many sacred temples: *HA, Hadr.* 19.10).

[121] Nordh, *Libellus* 89.14, and Valentini and Zucchetti, I.130, 177, in Regio X (Palatium): (*Curiosum* and *Notitia*) Auguratorium.

[122] For example, Platner-Ashby, s.v. Auguratorium, 61; Coarelli, *ForArc* 194; and Beaujeu, 125, who refutes the theory that the Auguratorium is identical with the Curia Saliorum. Although one tradition holds that Romulus sighted the vultures from an *auguraculum* on the Palatine, another places him on the Aventine proper, and has the vultures fly over the Palatine. See O. Skutsch, *Studia Enniana* (London 1968) 62–85. The Auguratorium is probably to be distinguished from the

auguraculum of the Capitoline arx, and from that of the Latiaris hill (a part of the Quirinal), although F. Castagnoli, "Il tempio Romano: Questioni di terminologia e di tipologia," *PBSR* 52 (1984) 16, tantalizingly associates a Trajanic-Hadrianic wall near the summit of the Capitoline arx, perfectly oriented according to the cardinal points and now 14 meters long, with the location of the "auguratorium" (sic).

[123] G. Schneider Graziosi, "L'*Auguratorium* del Palatino," *Dissertazioni della Pontificia Accademia Romana di Archeologia*, ser. 2, 12 (1918) 147–78. The brick aedicula is dated by Trajanic-Hadrianic brick stamps: P. Pensabene, "*Auguratorium* e Tempio della Magna Mater," *QuadAEI* 2 (1979) 68–70, and fig. 4 on p. 72; cf. Coarelli, *Roma* (1980) 129, and Blake/Bishop, 64–65.

This link, the reference to Rome's sacred origins, is the one apparent in Livia's restoration of the Temple. It is also one that appears in other Hadrianic constructions and gestures. The elevation of the Parilia to the Natalis Urbis Romae, the Temple of Venus and Roma, the retracing of the pomerium in 121 by the college of augurs, and Hadrianic coins depicting Romulus Conditor show that Hadrian was more assiduous than Augustus or the Flavians in his propaganda proclaiming a rebirth of Rome in his principate.[124] The restoration of the Auguratorium, furthermore, dates to 136, while Hadrian's vicennalia was celebrated in 137; the theme of renovation may have been in the air.[125] Restoration of both the Temple of Bona Dea Subsaxana and the Palatine Auguratorium would be appropriate to the occasion. We can presume that Hadrian restored them both, although without further evidence this must remain simply a hypothesis.

## The "Ustrinum" of Hadrian

Recent scholarship has assigned to Hadrian a monument in the western Campus Martius supposed to be the ustrinum where the bodies of Hadrian and his family were cremated.[126] This new identification replaces an earlier one by Lanciani, who believed the architectural elements discovered at Piazza Sforza between 1886 and 1888 belonged to the Ara Ditis and published the find somewhat inaccurately as such in 1889.[127] In 1946 Castagnoli argued that this complex could not be the Ara Ditis; but at a loss for a new identification, he followed Lanciani in comparing its plan to those of other complexes in the Campus Martius identified as imperial ustrina.[128] This similarity, together

---

[124] See Chapters 2 and 4.

[125] M. Hammond, "The Tribunician Day during the Early Empire," *MAAR* 15 (1938) 45, also noting that the first definite instance of a decennalial celebration comes under Hadrian. See Strack, *Hadrian* 184–88, for the coins minted at this time with legends VOTA PUBLICA and LIBERALITAS AUG VI and VII.

[126] Coarelli, *Roma* (1980) 265, 303, 366; earlier suggested in his "Campo Marzio occidentale" 821 n. 34. Pensa, "Adriano" 69 n. 164, accepts the new identification. This section is an abridged version of "The 'Ara Ditis–*Ustrinum* of Hadrian' in the Western Campus Martius, and Other Problematic Roman Ustrina," *AJA* 89 (1985) 485–97.

[127] The earliest finds were first published by G. Gatti, in *Bull Comm* 15 (1887) 276, and cf. *NSc*, 1887, 180; those of the next year by R. Lanciani, "L'itinerario di Einsiedeln e l'ordine di Benedetto Canonico," *MonAnt* 1 (1889) 540–49 (whose interpretation was followed by C. Hülsen, in *RömMitt* 6 [1891] 127–29).

[128] Castagnoli, "Campo Marzio" 152–57. He places the altar to the chthonic deities in the Tarentum, near the modern Ponte Vittorio. Not all scholars accepted Castagnoli's location of the Ara Ditis: see, e.g., Nash, s.v. Ara Ditis Patris et Proserpina, 1.57, who follows Lanciani's interpretation of the remains and reproduces his plan of the site at Piazza

with interpretation of the relief showing the Apotheosis of Sabina, has now been developed into identification of the remains at Piazza Sforza as the "Ustrinum" of Hadrian. What was discovered, however, is really parts of at least two distinct structures, not one: the Euripus canal and, adjacent to it, what seems to have been a large altar tomb (or tombs) of the early empire. The complex cannot have been Hadrian's ustrinum.

Our knowledge of the complex is flawed by the history of its discovery, which occurred in two different excavations, both separated in time and limited in scope. In 1886 and 1887, parts of an apparently rectangular enclosure were found under Corso Vittorio Emanuele during construction of a sewer line from Palazzo Sforza Cesarini to Piazza della Chiesa Nuova[129] (*see Ill. 1*). G. Gatti reported the find briefly as three tufa walls, 0.80 meters thick, each broken by a doorway 1.90 meters wide (one still decorated with marble moldings and a marble lintel) and equidistant from one another. Between the first and second walls from the northwest were three steps of a marble staircase uniformly 5.60 meters long and 0.37 meters high, out of line with the doorways and at right angles to these leading up to the northeast. Also found were two parts of a "colonna marmorea" (marble column) that joined to make a length of 2.80 meters, about two-thirds of the original length. These are now in the entrance court of Palazzo dei Conservatori and are clearly part of a *pulvinus*, a sculpted cushionlike finishing element for the top of an altar, here of colossal scale. The other remains could be sketched and described only summarily before construction of the sewer line.

The following year Lanciani returned to Rome and began excavation immediately northeast of this discovery. He soon uncovered ancient remains, but these had little in common with what had been found nearby.[130] He found a 30-meter-long stretch of a canal, about 3.5 meters wide and over 1 meter deep, lined with opus signinum and bordered on both sides by a margin of blocks of travertine 0.75 meter wide; a stout ashlar wall of tufa with a travertine coping about 2 cubic meters large ("alcuni di due metri cubi") ran parallel to the canal on the south. He notes that except for the travertine revetment, this wall was identical with one discovered along a stretch of the canal found in 1885 farther to the northwest under the Via del Pavone.

---

Sforza. For the Ara Ditis, see now F. Coarelli, "Navalia, Tarentum e la topografia del Campo Marzio meridionale," *QuadIst-TopAnt* 5 (1968) 33–37.

[129] See n. 127 above. According to Gatti,

the need to finish the sewer line prevented proper excavation of the site.

[130] Lanciani, "Itinerario" 540–49; this stretch of the canal was found under the Palazzi (or "Case") Villa and de' Niccolo.

Surmising that his new finds adjoined those of Gatti, Lanciani drew a plan
that incorporated the finds of both excavations, including an unpublished report by A. Arieti, the inspector of Gatti's excavation, which had noted five
walls spaced 10.30 meters from one another (not three walls 13 meters apart,
as Gatti noted). Lanciani's plan, however, is markedly at variance with that
of Gatti and with the description of Arieti.[131] Lanciani based his interpretation
of the complex on the pulvinus, which he supposed was part of one of the
great altars known to have stood in the Campus Martius in antiquity, and on
the similarity of the new complex to the "Ustrinum Antoninorum," which
he also calls an "ara." Although the "Ustrinum Antoninorum" had been discovered in 1703, Bianchini's account of the excavation and identification of
the structure had just been published by Hülsen.[132] Lanciani identified his reconstruction of the monument in the western Campus Martius as the "Ara
Ditis."

Lanciani's reconstruction and identification were generally accepted until
Castagnoli convincingly proved in 1946 that the Tarentum, where certain
parts of the Secular Games were celebrated at the Ara Ditis, must have been
situated farther west, on the left bank of the Tiber just downstream of the
later Pons Neronianus (cf., e.g., Zos. 2.5.2–3) (see Ill. 1). Castagnoli turned
to the original excavation reports and sketches by Arieti and Lanciani but only
as supporting evidence to show that the excavated remains bore no real resemblance to the Ara Pacis, to which the complex had been compared typo-
logically.[133] Although Castagnoli demonstrated that Lanciani's reconstruction was incorrect, he perpetuated it when he cautiously reaffirmed a
similarity to the "Ustrinum Antoninorum," and although the scholarly
world has now accepted his conclusions about the location of the Ara Ditis, it
continues to give credence to the erroneous plan.[134]

Lanciani had noted the similarity of his discoveries to what had been
found three years earlier under the Via del Pavone, just northwest of his own
excavation: a stretch of a canal 10 meters long, with two stout walls parallel
to it on the southwest.[135] Since 1888, other stretches of what must be the same

[131] Lanciani did interview Arieti and included his report in his own publication (p.
542). For other discrepancies between the reports of Arieti and Gatti, see Castagnoli,
"Campo Marzio" 154.

[132] In "Campo Marzio" 153, Castagnoli
notes that Lanciani shows this "ara" as complete. He also notes dissimilarities, overlooked by Lanciani, between the "Ara Ditis"
and the "Ustrinum Antoninorum."

[133] Castagnoli, "Campo Marzio" 154–55,
who also notes that in FUR Lanciani gives a
reconstruction of the Ara Pacis analogous to
that of his Ara Ditis "coll'aggiunta arbitraria
di due recinzioni" around the Ara Pacis.

[134] For a reconstruction of the Tarentum
and its buildings, see Coarelli, "Navalia" 33–
37; and see above, n. 128.

[135] The original report of the finds in 1885
from BullComm 14 (1886) 282, is reproduced

canal have been discovered at Piazza di Sant'Andrea della Valle, Via dei Baul-
lari, Palazzo della Cancelleria, between the Vicoli Sora and del Governo Vecchio, and in Via Paola; their locations and similarities to the discoveries of
1888 and 1885 indicate that all seven lengths belong to the same structure, a
long canal (*see Ill. 1*).

This open canal, generally, but not universally, identified since 1938 as the
Euripus of Agrippa, and the walls bordering it, are of uncertain date and function.[136] The sections thus far excavated indicate that it traversed the western
Campus Martius, running in a northwesterly direction from the vicinity of
the southern end of the Baths of Agrippa to the Tiber at a point between the
Pons Neronianus and the Pons Aelius. The sections differ somewhat in their
states of preservation, the most complete being that found in 1938 under the
Cancelleria, southeast of Piazza Sforza, and that under Via del Pavone, just
northwest of Lanciani's excavation of 1888.[137] Because both these sections

---

by Lanciani, "Itinerario" 542; we should note
that Lanciani does not reproduce the closer
wall on his published plans. The stretch of
canal under the Vicolo del Pavone was
flanked by two walls parallel to it on the
southwest: one 2.5 meters from the canal,
faced with reticulate; the other, of heavy tufa
ashlar, 2.5 meters from its counterpart.

[136] For the canal, identified with the Euripus
of Agrippa by B. Nogara ("Campo Marzio
nell'età Augustea," in *Quaderni di Studi Romani* 8 [1941] 10–12), see Nash, s.v. Euripus
Thermarum Agrippae, I.393–94, with earlier
bibliography; add to his list of remains a
stretch discovered in Piazza di Sant'Andrea
della Valle (cf. F. Castagnoli, *BullComm* 73
[1949–50] {1952} 150), and another, 50 meters
long, between Corso Vittorio Emanuele, Via
del Pellegrino, Vicoli Sora and del Governo
Vecchio (*NSc*, 1923, 247). Coarelli, "Campo
Marzio occidentale" 819–22, 830–37, points
out that the line of the canal acts as a topographical boundary, and he suggests, rather
implausibly, that it follows the course of an
imperial pomerium. R. B. Lloyd, "The Aqua
Virgo, Euripus and Pons Agrippa," *AJA* 83
(1979) 197–98, convincingly rejects the identification of the canal with the Euripus of
Agrippa. It is uncertain how the canal was
crossed by streets.

[137] For the canal at Via del Pavone, see
G. Gatti, *BullComm* 14 (1886) 282, and S.
Quilici Gigli, "Estremo Campo Marzio," in
*Città e architettura* 51–52. For the stretch under
the Cancelleria, see Magi, *Rilievi Flavi* 36–42,
138–39, and (less exactly reported) Nogara,
"Campo Marzio nell'età Augustea" 10–12.
Magi, 138–39, reports that under the Cancelleria the reticulate wall was about 4 meters
south of the canal, and the tufa wall 2.25 farther south. The reticulate wall here rose from
a base 0.90 meters high and was revetted with
travertine, and had a marble molding at the
top and bottom facing the tomb; overall the
wall was 0.60 meters thick and 2.10 meters
high. The rusticated tufa wall here was 0.60
meters thick and 2.12 meters high; its flat
travertine coping, inclined slightly to the
south, had a series of holes cut along the
southern edge that seems to have held a grat-
ing. Nash, s.v. Euripus Thermarum Agrippae, I.394, pl. 482, has a photograph of this
stretch, incorrectly identified as the northern
embankment of the "Euripus." Nash's confusion of northern for southern is due to the
plan of the excavation reproduced on his p.
393, in which south is at the top; his sketch is
derived from that of Magi, p. 38, fig. 37,
which is without orientation.

have the walls bordering the canal on the south, although the closer reticulate wall under the Cancelleria has extra marble moldings attached to the top and base, it is reasonable to conclude that the stout tufa wall Lanciani uncovered in 1888 along the canal was a segment of the similar wall documented farther northwest and southeast of it rather than part of an independent building as Lanciani thought.[138]

The limited information available about the canal and the walls parallel to it suggests a construction date in the late republic or early empire, but allows no positive identification. The uncertainty of its date and a careful reexamination of the literary evidence for Agrippa's Euripus have led R. B. Lloyd to reject the usual identification of the canal as the Euripus of Agrippa. He tentatively proposes that since the canal runs on high rather than low ground, it may have been intended in conjunction with the two walls along it for flood control.[139] The pronounced turn to the north the canal takes at its final leg, so that its mouth at the Tiber faces upstream, suggests that it was to convey water to the Stagnum Agrippae.[140] Lanciani's travertine revetment on the tufa wall just to the north of the excavations of 1886–87, and marble moldings found attached to the reticulate wall across from the tomb of Hirtius in the Cancelleria excavations, indicate that various parts were decorated. As in the area under the Cancelleria, the decoration may always have been associated with a tomb.

The only results of the excavations of 1886–87 under the Piazza Sforza that can be verified today are the joining fragments of the pulvinus now in the entrance courtyard of Palazzo dei Conservatori. These are, as Lanciani saw, about two-thirds of a pulvinus originally approximately 3.80 meters long;[141] he was probably correct in associating this with the three steps reveted in marble. His identification of the whole as the Ara Ditis, however, perhaps because of the great size of the pulvinus, led him to neglect other comparisons

---

[138] This is now generally assumed: see, e.g., Castagnoli, "Campo Marzio" 154; and n. 136 above.

[139] Lloyd, "Aqua Virgo" 198–99. For approximate dating by levels and by materials, see also Boatwright, "Problematic *Ustrina*" 490. Yet even this "high ground" is relatively low: Lanciani, "Itinerario" 542–43, reports that the soil around the canal was so swampy that the canal had to have a concrete bedding about 8.60 meters wide and as much as 2.80 meters deep.

[140] Quilici Gigli, "Estremo Campo Marzio" 57 n. 34.

[141] A good description of the pulvinus in the Museo dei Conservatori is given by H. Stuart Jones, ed., *A Catalogue of Ancient Sculptures . . . of the Palazzo dei Conservatori* [Oxford 1926] 13, no. 20 (hereafter Jones, *Conservatori*). For this general type of pulvinus, see *DarSag* IV.1, s.v. "pulvinus," II, p. 767; and W. Hermann, *Römische Götteraltäre* (Kallmünz 1961) 12–15.

for the pulvinus and steps in Roman funerary monuments. The general configuration of the pulvinus, the height at which the three steps were found, and the series of walls and ornate doorways found under Piazza Sforza suggest a tomb or row of tombs. The pulvinus would have come from an altar tomb like those of Naevoleia Tyche and Umbricius Scaurus along Via dei Sepolcri outside Pompeii, but on a gargantuan scale.[142]

This type of altar tomb in Pompeii dates from ca. A.D. 50 to the destruction of the town, and is developed from a simpler type in which the monumental altar tomb stands by itself, not surrounded by a precinct wall, and the grave chamber, if there is one, is inaccessible. Later, tufa is often used for the enclosure wall and the base of the altar, and the grave chamber in the base is accessible by a door.[143] Its marble and the stylistic parallels for the pulvinus imply that the tomb (or tombs) under Piazza Sforza cannot have been erected before the last years of the republic.[144]

Yet this altar is distinguished from other examples by its size—at least twice that of the altar tombs in Pompeii, for example[145]—and the complex in which it stood is remarkable in having at least three doorways in succession, which suggests that there may have been more than one tomb here, and that the enclosure was more elaborate and more accessible than the ones found outside the capital. These distinctions, however, are less startling in the context of other tombs known in the Campus Martius.[146] As we saw in Chapter 6, burial in the Campus Martius was an honor voted by the senate in the late republic and early empire, and for only the most eminent Romans; one such burial, the simple yet large tomb of A. Hirtius mentioned by Livy and Vel-

[142] See Jones, *Conservatori* 13, no. 20, for a comparison with a funerary monument from Britain; for the tombs in Pompeii, dated by Kockel from the Claudian period to the eruption of Vesuvius, see Toynbee, *Death and Burial* 123–25; A. de Franciscis and R. Pane, *Mausolei romani in Campania* (Naples 1957) 30–33, figs. 4, 15, 17, 20; and V. Kockel, *Die Grabbauten vor dem Herkulaner Tor in Pompeji* (Mainz 1983) 100–109, ills. 11, 14–16, figs. 26a–b, 27–30 (Naevoleia Tyche); 70–75, ills. 5–8, figs. 5c, 15–17 (Umbricius Scaurus). On pp. 22–26 Kockel provides a detailed discussion of the development of the type.

[143] Kockel, *Grabbauten* 22–23.

[144] Boatwright, "Problematic *Ustrina*" 491–92.

[145] Kockel, *Grabbauten* 100, gives the measurements of the altar on the tomb of Naevoleia Tyche: height, 2.42 meters; width, 2.27 meters; depth, 1.84 meters. On p. 71 he notes the width of the altar on the tomb of Umbricius Scaurus as 1.67 meters. The depth of the altar at Piazza Sforza would have been at least 3.80 meters.

[146] Although the exact course of the pomerium in the Campus Martius is not known, the finds of 1886–87 lie outside the pomerium lines presumed for Claudius and for Vespasian (the latter retraced by Hadrian), to judge by findspots of pomerial cippi. See M. Labrousse, "Le *pomerium* de la Rome impériale. Notes de topographie romaine," *MélRome* 54 (1937) 193–94; and Le Gall, *Tibre* 191–93.

leius Paterculus (*Epit.* 119; 2.62), came to light in the excavations under the Cancelleria, which also uncovered a stretch of the canal just southeast of our altar tomb.[147] The extraordinary size and unusual layout of the structure under the Piazza Sforza would correspond to the importance of the other individuals known to have been entombed in the plain; for a similarly unusual funerary monument we may turn to the Mausoleum of Augustus, not far to the north.

Since most plans of the area reproduce Lanciani's erroneous reconstruction of the Ara Ditis, mistakes are easily made. Coarelli, for example, first copied the plan but added the legend "USTRINUM HADRIANI ?" In his text in *Roma* (1980) he more firmly refers to the monument as the "Ustrinum of Hadrian." Here he observes that the Pons Aelius made a direct connection between the "Ustrinum" and Hadrian's Mausoleum.[148] Others working on the topography of the western Campus Martius call attention to the similarity between Lanciani's plan and the plans of the "Ustrina of Antoninus Pius and of Marcus Aurelius,"[149] overlooking the possibility that Lanciani made it that way deliberately.

Three other monuments in Rome are commonly identified as imperial ustrina; the Ustrinum of Antoninus Pius, the Ustrinum of Marcus Aurelius, and the Ustrinum of Augustus. These identifications derive from F. Bianchini's description of the "Ustrinum Antoninorum," an ancient monument discovered lying athwart Via degli Uffici del Vicario near the Column of Antoninus Pius, west of Montecitorio. On the basis of the ancient testimonia for consecration ceremonies and imperial funerals (principally Herodian 4.2; Strabo 5.3.8; *consecratio* coins showing funeral pyres; and the relief of the Apotheosis of Sabina), Bianchini proposed that a series of ancient walls forming concentric square enclosures belonged to the "ustrinum seu bustum" of the Antonine emperors. His work was published only in 1889, when Hülsen reproduced his manuscript and endorsed the identification.[150] In the same year

[147] For the tomb of Hirtius, see Magi, *Rilievi Flavi* 37–54; Nogara, "Campo Marzio nell'età Augustea" 12–14; and Nash, s.v. Sepulcrum A. Hirtii, II.341–43.

[148] See n. 126 above.

[149] See n. 126 above. E. La Rocca, whose earlier views on the "Ara Ditis Ustrinum of Hadrian" were presented in a public lecture at the American Academy in Rome, spring 1981, has now rethought the problem, and

his monograph on the Campus Martius, *La riva a mezzaluna* (Rome 1984), has his latest conclusions.

[150] Bianchini's description (with other early descriptions of the "Ustrinum Antoninorum" or "Ustrinum of Antoninus") is reproduced by C. Hülsen, "Antichità di Monte Citorio," *RömMitt* 4 (1889) 48–64; Bianchini's incomplete description is in Codex Veronese 356. Bianchini never specifies what "nummi"

Lanciani related his "Ara Ditis" to this "ustrinum." When construction near the Column of Marcus Aurelius in 1907 for the addition to Palazzo di Montecitorio uncovered remains strongly resembling those described by Bianchini, G. Mancini identified them as the "Ustrinum of Marcus Aurelius."[151] (This then made it necessary to change "Ustrinum Antoninorum" to "Ustrinum of Antoninus Pius.") Finally, the very rare Greek term Strabo uses for the crematory of Augustus, *kaustra* (5.3.8), is usually translated as "ustrinum" to describe the crematory excavated near Augustus' Mausoleum in 1777.[152]

Of all these "ustrina," only that of Augustus could have functioned as an imperial ustrinum as elucidated by the ancient evidence. Every literary source that describes Roman funeral ceremonies for important individuals makes it clear that the spot where the cadaver or effigy was burnt had to be accessible from all sides.[153] Circling the pyre was an essential part of a public funeral. Dio, Appian, and Herodian note military exercises of various types organized as ceremonial pageants (*decursiones*) around the funeral pyres of Augustus, Pertinax, Sulla, Drusilla, Livia, and Septimius Severus. The equestrian order always partook in the parades around the pyres, and sometimes the magistrates and chariots would join in, performing complex maneuvers.[154] A decursio resembling any of the ones described would have been impossible around the "Ara Ditis—Ustrinum of Hadrian": the canal prevented circling the monument.[155]

Furthermore, as we know from the descriptions of the obsequies of Au-

---

he refers to, and he identifies the relief, then in the Capitoline Museum, as showing the apotheosis of Faustina Minor (see n. 163 below). See Hülsen, 52–55.

[151] G. Mancini, "Le recenti scoperte di antichità a Monte Citorio," *Studi Romani* 1 (1913) 3–15; and see R. Lanciani, in *RendLinc*, ser. 5, 17 (1908) 92. For more recent bibliography on both monuments, see Nash, s.v. Ustrinum Antoninorum, 11.487–89.

[152] See Platner-Ashby, s.v. Ustrinum Domus Augustae, 545, but see *BullComm* 66 (1938) [1939] 275–78. Strabo's description of the crematory is notoriously difficult to interpret.

[153] For excellent discussions of such rites, see L. Vogel, *The Column of Antoninus Pius* (Cambridge, Mass. 1973) 57–60, with earlier

bibliography; and Toynbee, *Death and Burial* 56–61. For the ancient definition of "ustrinum," see Serv. ad *Aen.* 3.22; Paul. ex Fest. 32 M.; and Boatwright, "Problematic *Ustrina*" 493.

[154] Dio Cass. 56.42.2 (Augustus' obsequies), 75.5.5 (= Xiph. 294, 30–296, 32 R. St.) (Pertinax's); App. *BCiv.* 1.106 (Sulla's); Dio Cass. 59.11.2 (those of Drusilla and of Livia); and Herodian 4.2.10 (Septimus Severus').

[155] Even if the heavy tufa wall (revetted with travertine) running parallel to the "Euripus" were abutted at some later date by the perpendicular peperino walls, the wall and the Euripus, which are almost certainly pre-Hadrianic, would have been obstacles to circumambulation.

gustus, Pertinax, and Septimius Severus, the culmination of imperial funerals
was the burning of a huge pyre containing the corpse (or effigy) of the deceased and a caged eagle, which was released to carry the emperor's soul
heavenward as the flames mounted.[156] The pyres are likened to towers (Dio
Cass. 75.5.3) and to lighthouses (Herodian 4.2.8), and towering pyres are depicted on consecration medallions and coins from A.D. 141 to 306.[157] The heat
of these huge pyres would have destroyed the marble and travertine walls of
the structures now called the "Ustrina" of Antoninus Pius and Marcus Aurelius and, of course, the marble and tufa walls of the "Ustrinum of Hadrian." Only the Ustrinum of Augustus, which consisted of a simple travertine platea near the Via Flaminia, could have been used in the imperial funeral
ceremonies as they are described.[158]

Although the ancient remains under Piazza Sforza could not have belonged to an "Ustrinum of Hadrian," we must now consider the "ustrinum"
depicted on a relief showing the apotheosis of Sabina (see Ill. 54). The relief
seems to show the ustrinum used for the cremation of Hadrian's wife, Sabina,
and, since the half-nude youth in the lower left-hand corner of the composition is often identified as a personification of the Campus Martius, it suggests
that this ustrinum was in the Campus Martius. The relief and its companion,
the "Adlocutio of Hadrian" (see Ill. 56), decorated the Arco di Portogallo,
which spanned the Via Lata/Flaminia (the modern Via del Corso) just north
of the Ara Pacis, until the arch was demolished in 1662–64 and the reliefs
transferred to the collection later housed in the Capitoline Museums.[159] The
relief, now heavily restored, depicts the apotheosis of Sabina (see Ill. 54). A

---

[156] See, e.g., Dio Cass. 56.42.3, 75.5.5; and
Toynbee, *Death and Burial* 56–61. For the particular importance of the cremation ceremony in the rite of *consecratio* in the second
century, see E. Bickerman, "Consecratio," in
*Le Culte des souverains dans l'empire romain* 19–
25, a revision of his earlier "Die römische
Kaiserapotheose," *Archiv für Religionswissen-
schaft* 27 (1929) 1–34 (criticized by E. Hohl,
"Die angebliche 'Doppelbestattung' des Antoninus Pius," *Klio* 31 [1938] 169–85). For
other bibliography on consecrations, see Vogel, *Column of Antoninus Pius* 122 n. 52.

[157] See above, Chapter 6.

[158] The two Antonine monuments may
have commemorated the temporary ustrina
of the two emperors: see R. Delbrück, in *AA*
1913, col. 140–43; Frischer, "Monumenta
Honoris" 73–75; and A. Frazer, "The Roman
Imperial Funeral Pyre," *JSAH* 27.3 (1968)
209.

[159] The Apotheosis relief is now in Palazzo
dei Conservatori, on Scala IV, no. 11; see
Jones, *Conservatori* 266–67, pl. 105, and pp.
37–38; E. Simon, in Helbig, II.1800, pp. 569–
70; Nash, s.v. Arco di Portogallo, I.86; and
Bonanno, *Portraits* 107–109. For the history of
the relief after its removal from the arch, see
A. Michaelis, "Storia della Collezione Capitolina di antichità fino all'inaugurazione del
Museo (1734)," *RömMitt* 6 (1891) 53, who
notes that the reliefs were not put into their
present position until his century.

54. *Relief of the Apotheosis of Sabina. Restored elements include the ashlar masonry construction and flames, the stone under the youth's left elbow, the head and right arm of Hadrian, and the head of the attendant. (Relief now in the Palazzo dei Conservatori, Rome.)*

female winged figure (Aeternitas?) carrying a large torch in both hands bears the empress seated on her back heavenward above flames covering a large block of ashlar masonry. At the lower left a seminude youth sits half reclining on the ground, his back to the viewer; he rests his left elbow on a stone (possibly an identifying attribute, before recutting) and lifts his right hand in admiration. At the lower right Hadrian, togate and wreathed with laurel, sits on a heavily draped stool, possibly a curule chair; he raises his right hand and is attended by a bearded man standing behind him.[160]

The evidence this relief supplies for a Hadrianic ustrinum in the Campus Martius turns out on examination to be minimal. Both H. Stuart Jones and E. Simon, who have examined the relief firsthand, report that the block of ashlar masonry and the fire appear to be entirely modern.[161] Moreover, these elements do not appear in the sixteenth-century engravings of the Arco di Portogallo, and both are without parallels in other depictions of apotheosis.[162] They may have been added when the badly damaged relief was removed from the Arco di Portogallo in the seventeenth century;[163] the area in which

[160] Vogel, *Column of Antoninus Pius* 47, identifies the winged female figure as Aeternitas; her bibliography (p. 125 n. 80) notes other suggestions. She also remarks that the heads of both male figures on the right are new, as is "Hadrian's" right hand.

[161] See n. 159 above; and cf. A. B. Wace, "Studies in Roman Historical Reliefs," *PBSR* 4 (1907) 258–59. Personal inspection corroborates their conclusions.

[162] Vogel, *Column of Antoninus Pius* 125 n. 81; for engravings, see following note.

[163] The Dosio engraving (*Urbis Romae Aedificiorum Illustrium Quae Supersunt* 1569), a sketch by the same (from 1569, now reproduced in G. A. Dosio, *Roma Antica e i disegni di architettura agli Uffizi*, ed. by F. Borsi et al. [Rome 1976] #36, 2528/A, pp. 59–60), and a later copper-plate engraving of the Arco di Portogallo by P. Schenck ("Roma Aeterna," Amsterdam 1705; both engravings reproduced in Nash, s.v. Arco di Portogallo, 1.83–84, figs. 85, 86) suggest that the relief may have been heavily damaged in the area where we now see the ustrinum and flames. P. Ligorio's engraving of the arch (dated to 1542–

68 and now in the Biblioteca Nazionale in Turin) represents the ashlar structure and flames, but Stucchi has shown that in this engraving many other details of the arch and its decoration are fanciful ("Arco di Portogallo" 112 and fig. 11). Indeed, Ligorio's fancy may have influenced the restoration of the relief: see F. Castagnoli, "Pirro Ligorio topografo di Roma antica," *Palladio* 2 (1952) 97–102. Bianchini calls the structure on the relief a pyre when he compares remains of the "Ustrinum": *nam saxa eiusdem molis disiecta iacebant, quae corona superius ornata definitionem culminis indicabant ex proiectura et sectione fastigii, qualia ferme visuntur in rogo Faustinae minoris expresso in tabula Capitolina (olim in arcu Portugalliae dicto ad Hippodromum), cum eiusdem Augustae apotheosi* (for stones of this massive building were lying scattered about that, with a cornice worked out on the upper part, denoted the feature of a room because of this projection and a section of the roof's apex, roughly just as is seen on the funeral pyre of Faustina the Younger as it is sculpted on the Capitoline relief [once on the Arco di Portogallo, also known as "ad Hippodrome"],

they now appear may have originally been blank. Furthermore, the relief itself cannot be used to prove that the cremation of Sabina occurred in the Campus Martius. Although the youth at the lower left is generally identified as a personification of the Campus, the basis for this interpretation is the analogy with a relief showing the apotheosis of Antoninus and Faustina, where the Campus figure carries the obelisk of the Horologium Solarium Augusti as attribute.[164] On the relief of Sabina's apotheosis the identifying attribute that must originally have been included is missing, but it can hardly have been an obelisk.

Although the Apotheosis of Sabina relief itself cannot be used as evidence for a monumental Hadrianic ustrinum in the Campus Martius, its use on the Arco di Portogallo may suggest a location for Sabina's cremation nearby. This would be, however, not in the western part of the Campus Martius, but along the Via Flaminia in the northern part. Despite occasional assignment of the arch and its reliefs to Marcus Aurelius and to Hadrian himself, the level at which it stood, the architectural configuration with bowed plinths and unfluted composite order, and the eclectic decoration of the arch prove it a pastiche created in the fifth century at the earliest.[165] The two reliefs decorating it, which will be discussed at the end of this chapter, must have come from elsewhere, perhaps an altar like that shown on coins commemorating Sabina's consecration.[166] Indeed, this is where we should expect her cremation to have been, for it was here that most other imperial funeral ceremonies took place. North of the Arco di Portogallo is the crematory of Augustus, and south of the arch the cremations of the Antonines seem to have occurred.

In conclusion, the remains under the Piazza Sforza in the western Campus Martius cannot have been the Ustrinum of Hadrian. Although Hadrian may

with the apotheosis of the same empress: Hülsen, "Monte Citorio" 54, and see n. 150 above).

[164] Vogel, *Column of Antoninus Pius* 117 n. 3. It also stands to reason that the earlier personification of the Campus Martius would need an identifying attribute.

[165] For the attribution of the Arco di Portogallo to Marcus Aurelius see, e.g., Platner-Ashby, s.v. Arco di Portogallo, 33. Coarelli, *Roma* (1980) 262–63, attributes it to the second half of the second century; for a date in the fifth century, see Stucchi, "Arco di Portogallo" 101–22. E. Rodriguez-Almeida, "Il

Campo Marzio settentrionale: *Solarium* e *Pomerium*," *RendPontAcc* 51–52 (1978–79, 1979–80) [1982] 203, very dubiously proposes a Hadrianic date; H. Kähler, "Triumphbogen," *RE* 7 A (1939) 388–90, is less dubious. The archaeological data are collected most conveniently in *CAR* II-G, no. 86, pp. 168–69.

[166] *BMC, Emp.* III, pp. cli, 363, nos. 960–63, pls. 66.8–10. Wace, "Historical Reliefs" 258–63, assuming that the adlocutio relief depicts Hadrian's laudatio memoriae of Sabina, suggests a monument similar to the Column of Antoninus Pius.

have built an ustrinum for Sabina's consecration, until unequivocal evidence comes to light we should not assume its existence.[167] It may be instead that Hadrian used the preexisting crematory of Augustus for the ceremony, reaffirming his ties with the first princeps.

There are a few other buildings and parts of buildings attributed to Hadrian that do not fit into any easy categories. In 1909 E. B. van Deman ascribed to Hadrian an enlargement and renovation of the Atrium Vestae by groups of rooms on the east and south, but Bloch's study of the brick stamps of the building has now made the date for this Trajanic.[168] According to Bloch's analysis, the only significant addition to the building that can be dated to the Hadrianic period is the aedicula to the right of the entrance. Here, however, the inscription of the frieze prevents our assigning the aedicula to Hadrian himself, for it explicitly states that the senate and people of Rome paid for it (*CIL* 6.31578: *Senatus populusque Romanu[s]/ pecunia publica faciendam curavit*). Some minor repair work in the upper stories of the Atrium also dates to the Hadrianic period, when a hypocaust was added to the second room behind the shops on the north, and masonry to a wall on the mezzanine level near the northeast corner.[169]

Examination of brick stamps and construction has also revealed minor Hadrianic repairs or additions to aqueducts[170] and in the Ludus Magnus.[171] Such construction was and is unremarkable, consisting mainly of extra masonry. The Hadrianic work on the Tiber banks mentioned in Chapter 2 should be listed in the same category of maintenance.[172]

[167] In connection with the proximity of the "Ustrinum of Hadrian" to the Pons Aelius and Hadrian's Mausoleum, we must remember that Sabina's ashes were deposited in the Mausoleum only in 139 (*CIL* 6.984 = Smallwood, #124). Perhaps for this ceremony, if there was one, and more plausibly for the obsequies of the Antonines (*CIL* 6.985–95), the Via Recta served to connect the actual sites of cremation to the Pons Aelius and the Mausoleum where the ashes of the deceased were deposited.

[168] E. B. van Deman, *The Atrium Vestae* (Washington, D.C. 1909) 28–34; Bloch, *Bolli* 77–85; accepted by, e.g., Nash, s.v. Atrium Vestae, I.154.

[169] Bloch, *Bolli* 84–85. Blake/Bishop, 40, overlook the inscription while attributing the aedicula to Hadrian.

[170] Blake/Bishop, 277–79, attribute to Hadrian a general overhaul of the Anio Vetus, Marcia, Claudia, and Anio Novus, and minor repairs to the Celimontana. See also G. Panimolle, *Gli acquedotti di Roma antica* (Rome 1968) 57, 93; and P. Pace, *Gli acquedotti di Roma e il "de aquaeductu" di Frontino, contexto critico, versione e commento* (Rome 1983) 36, 47, 144, 152.

[171] Blake/Bishop, 65; and A. M. Colini and L. Cozza, *Ludus Magnus* (Rome 1962) 103, 145–46.

[172] For Hadrianic work on the banks of the Tiber, see Chapter 2, n. 111. The possibility of a Hadrianic date or phase for the as yet un-

More noteworthy would be Hadrianic monuments decorated with historical reliefs, but except for those discussed earlier in this chapter, we have too little information to identify any positively; furthermore, in many cases the Hadrianic date is still debated. An *adventus Augusti* relief, for example, depicting the formal entry of the princeps into the city and now located in the Palazzo dei Conservatori, is often used as evidence for a Hadrianic arch on Via Lata at the intersection of the modern Vie di Pietra and Montecatini. Partly because the original head of the princeps no longer survives, the relief has been assigned both a late Hadrianic and an early Antonine date[173] (*see Ill. 55*). Yet Castagnoli's arguments that the relief very probably once decorated a monumental arch over the entrance to the Hadrianeum from Via Lata are convincing, and this would make an early Antonine date more suitable.[174]

A pair of reliefs in the Capitoline Museum, the imperial adlocutio and the apotheosis of Sabina (discussed in connection with the Ustrinum of Hadrian), have also been assigned both a late Hadrianic and an early Antonine date (*see Ills. 56 and 54*). Their common provenance on the Arco di Portogallo has led some scholars, such as Simon, to assume that the adlocutio relief represents Hadrian's laudatio funeris of Sabina, but this cannot be proved. Since the head of Hadrian now visible on the adlocutio relief is a restoration, the date of that relief rests on considerations of style.[175] As we saw earlier, the original prove-

---

identified structures under S. Sebastiano, mentioned by F. Castagnoli, "Su alcuni problemi topografici del Palatino," *Rend-Linc*, ser. 8, 34 (1979) 335; and by A. Bartoli, "Avanzi di fortificazioni medievali del Palatino," *Rend Linc*, ser. 5, 18 (1909) 537–39, must await the results of the new excavations currently under way under the Ecole Française and the Soprintendenza alle antichità.

[173] Late Hadrianic: Laubscher, "Arcus Novus" 85; E. Simon, Helbig II.1445, pp. 261–63; Jones, *Conservatori* 29–31, no. 12; and Koeppel, "Profectio und Adventus" 156–58. Early Antonine: F. Castagnoli, "Due archi trionfali della Via Flaminia presso Piazza Sciarra," *BullComm* 70 (1942) [1943] 57–58, 74–82, followed by V. Cianfarani, "Rilievo romano di Villa Torlonia," *BullComm* 73 (1949–50) [1952] 249–52. These scholars, as well as Bonanno, *Portraits* 107–109, deny the hypothesis that the adventus Augusti relief was originally associated with the Torlonia

relief, and that the two were once companion pieces to the two reliefs of the Arco di Portogallo. M. Wegner, "Bemerkungen zu den Ehrendenkmälern des Marcus Aurelius," *AA*, 1938, 167–68, has convincingly assigned the Torlonia relief (now unlocatable) to the reign of Lucius Verus.

[174] Castagnoli, "Archi trionfali" 74–82. Laubscher, "Arcus Novus" 85 n. 70, accepts Castagnoli's theory about the arch, but not his dating of the relief.

[175] Late Hadrianic: e.g., E. Simon, Helbig II.1447 and 1800, pp. 264–65, 569–70; and Bonanno, *Portraits* 107–109, who notes, however, the "considerable differences in the handling of the portraiture and in style here and on the Hadrianic tondi." Early Antonine: Cianfarani, "Villa Torlonia" 246–49. Jones states that the removal in 1921 of a former restoration of the head revealed a profile "almost certainly" that of Hadrian (*Conservatori* 37 n. 1), but as Bonanno points out, this can-

55. *Adventus Augusti relief. The head and hands of Hadrian and the hands of Roma are restored. Roma and the personifications of the senate and people of Rome receive Hadrian into the city. (Relief now in the Palazzo dei Conservatori, Rome.)*

56. *Adlocutio of Hadrian relief from the Arco di Portogallo. The head of Hadrian is restored. The emperor addresses the personification of the Roman people and an elderly man and young boy. (Relief now in the Palazzo dei Conservatori, Rome.)*

nance of the reliefs is unknown, but the relief of Sabina's apotheosis would be unsuitable for an arch. They may have embellished an altar; if so, probably it was in the northern reaches of the Campus Martius.[176]

Another relief, now in the Uffizi in Florence, is more securely late Hadrianic. The incomplete relief shows the sacrifice of a bull on the left and two putti lifting a shield on the right; two figures, one partially restored, flank the shield and represent the Roman senate and the *Genius populi Romani,* the tutelary deity of the Roman people *(see Ill. 57).* On analogy to coin issues, I. S. Ryberg and others have proposed that this fragment formed part of a monument commemorating the vicennalia of Hadrian in 137,[177] but its architectural form and the rest of its program of sculpture remain entirely unknown.

Similar unanswered questions surround the Chatsworth relief *(see Ill. 43),* mentioned earlier in connection with the Anaglypha. This fragmentary piece seems to have commemorated Hadrian's burning of debts in 118, in a monument of large scale, but what sort of monument must be left in doubt.[178]

Various other fragmentary reliefs have in the past been attributed to the Hadrianic period, but are now usually dated otherwise. The Extispicium relief depicting inspection of entrails for prophesying purposes and now found in the Louvre, with its dependent Victory fragment, is Trajanic, not Hadrianic.[179] Also in the Louvre are an incomplete historical relief showing what may be praetorian soldiers, and another showing a sacrifice of a bull; both of these were long considered Hadrianic, but Koeppel and Torelli have now independently redated them Julio-Claudian.[180] Finally, H. P. Laubscher has convincingly redated to the Claudian age the fragmentary relief now at the Villa Medici, which has occasionally been assigned a late Hadrianic date.[181]

---

not now be verified. Bianchi Bandinelli and Torelli, *L'arte classica* II, #140, identify the (restored) figure behind Hadrian in the apotheosis relief as M. Annius Verus, the clean-shaven figure in the adlocutio relief as L. Aelius Caesar, and in the same relief, the togate child as L. Verus and the clean-shaven figure in the background as M. Annius Verus. Since they do not find any figure identifiable as Antoninus Pius, they give the reliefs a terminus ante quem of 138. According to Simon, depicted standing next to the *genius populi* in the adlocutio relief are Lucius Verus (the young togatus) and M. Annius Verus (the older togatus), the adoptive grandfather of Marcus

Aurelius, which would date the relief to the end of Hadrian's life. These identifications, however, cannot be confirmed.

[176] See above, n. 166.

[177] Ryberg, *Rites of the State Religion* 132–33; for other bibliography, see Koeppel, "Official State Reliefs" 497 C.

[178] For the Chatsworth relief, see above, n. 3. Other bibliography is found in Koeppel, "Official State Reliefs" 498 D.

[179] Koeppel, "Official State Reliefs" 495 D.

[180] See Koeppel, "Official State Reliefs" 488 D and F.

[181] Laubscher, "Arcus Novus" 78–85, bibliography on p. 81.

57. *Vicennalia relief, probably commemorating the festival of the twentieth anniversary of Hadrian's reign held in* 137. *(Relief now in the Uffizi, Florence.)*

Most of the "missing buildings" of Hadrian are frustratingly intriguing. The Tondi and the Athenaeum allow us to discern much more clearly Hadrian as the self-driven, contradictory, and highly intellectual individual the sources depict. The Temple of Bona Dea and the Auguratorium confirm the reports of Hadrian's religious conservatism and interest in the historical topography of Rome. Finally, the difficulties in dating and placing any of the historical reliefs, from the Anaglypha to the Apotheosis of Sabina, ironically underscore Hadrian's elusiveness, one of the "shortcomings" the literary tradition criticizes. Together, however, Hadrian's "missing buildings" add much to our understanding of Hadrian and his principate.

# CHAPTER EIGHT

# CONCLUSIONS

HADRIAN'S autobiography no longer survives and the biography written by his freedman Phlegon has also perished, to the great loss of those of us who marvel at the Pantheon, Hadrian's Mausoleum, and the Temple of Venus and Roma, all of which still impress visitors in Rome. We might expect in a life of Hadrian a catalogue, even if incomplete, of his work in Rome and throughout the Roman world, possibly an account of his aims and principles, and illumination of his values, religious tenets, and pattern of life—all vital to an understanding of his plans for and effect on the capital city and the Roman empire. The loss is the more regrettable in light of the unfortunate bitterness of his first and last years as princeps, which left in the literary tradition a distinct hostility to Hadrian. In large part, Hadrianic Rome must be pieced together from coins, inscriptions, and the ruins of the buildings themselves, which only recent advances in the topographical study of ancient Rome have made available. From the evidence collected in this book, it is apparent that Hadrian's effect on Rome was profound; he permanently changed the urban landscape and touched all segments of the population.

An intense period of construction in Rome began with Hadrian's arrival in the capital city as princeps and continued steadily throughout his rule. The first large project seems to have been the renovation of the Campus Martius, including the raising of the ground level of the northern Campus and the erection and reconstruction of many buildings in the central plain. The heavy demand for bricks this entailed probably was responsible for the regulation of the brick industry in 123. The dedication in 126 of Hadrian's reconstruction of the Divorum was obviously a marker for work in this sector, for by now the Pantheon, the South Building, and the Divorum itself can be presumed complete. Yet building continued in the Campus even after 126; brick stamps reveal that the gateway of the Saepta was being built in these very years, and that the secondary structures between the Pantheon and the South Building had not yet been begun.

By the time of Hadrian's assumption of the title Pater Patriae in 128, his Temple of the Deified Trajan and Plotina was probably almost finished. By this time, however, other constructions were under way: the Palazzo of the Horti Sallustiani, the wing of tabernae on the slopes of the Palatine and other modifications to the imperial palace there, the Temple of Venus and Roma, and slightly later, the Mausoleum. There is ample evidence that Hadrian did not moderate the pace of building in Rome toward the end of his life: for example, the late date of his restoration of the Forum Augustum and of the Auguratorium, his Athenaeum, and the unidentified monument to which the Tondi Adrianei originally belonged, as well as the incomplete state of Venus and Roma at his death.

Hadrianic construction can be found throughout the city. Although much of it was close to the heart of the ancient capital—the imperial fora, the Forum Romanum, and the Palatine—his Mausoleum and, less dramatically, the Palazzo of the Horti Sallustiani helped decentralize the city by providing focal points in hitherto undeveloped regions. Moreover, in every case where we can examine it, attention was paid to providing access to or through his complexes and to ensuring good urban communication. At times we get the impression that Hadrian had a "drawing-board mentality," but the benefits of his streets and squares and porticoes to a populace used to crowded, crooked alleys and dark courtyards must have been enormous.

The scale of Hadrian's constructions is as remarkable as their number and extent. Mastery of brick-faced concrete as a material made possible the spectacular engineering feats of the Pantheon, Palazzo of the Horti Sallustiani, Villa Adriana, and tabernae along the Forum front of the Domus Tiberiana. More traditional architectural forms were not abandoned, however; on the contrary, they were reproduced in grandiose scale. The Temples of the Deified Matidia, of the Deified Trajan and Plotina, and of Venus and Roma were the largest such buildings in Rome, to judge from the sizes of the columns from their facades. The Giano accanto alla Minerva, the gateway of the Saepta, was higher and wider than any other arch in the city, and Hadrian's Mausoleum rose above even that of Augustus. In almost every building we find both concrete and fine dressed stone, rich in color, gray and rose granite, cipollino and giallo antico. Pavements and revetments were equally splendid. And though some of the decorative work, such as the Hadrianic capital from the restoration of the Forum Augustum, now appears flat and schematic in comparison to earlier architectural ornament, the fine carving of the Tondi Adrianei testifies to the ability of the schools of sculptors working on Hadrianic projects.

Not only did the imperial projects in Rome employ hundreds of workmen of every sort, an inference confirmed by the note that Hadrian organized the building industry along paramilitary lines, but they may have inspired and strengthened private construction, providing further work for the un-skilled masses and enriching the upper classes in Rome, who profited from the production of and commerce in building materials. The *SC Acilianum* of 122 testifies to intensified private building. More direct evidence of Hadrian's effect on others is the transformation of the Via Lata/Flaminia, which by the end of his principate was flanked by the market building under S. Lorenzo in Lucina, the insulae at Galleria Colonna, and the extensive horrea that seem to have stretched from the Arch of Claudius to Piazza Venezia. All these essen-tially utilitarian buildings belong to the second half of his reign, as do the im-perial tabernae above the Forum. This continuous, possibly escalated demand for building material may account for the mysterious semirevival in 134 of consular dating in brick stamps.

The significance of Hadrian's work in Rome has emerged gradually. We can discern different layers of meaning. Hadrian's principate began inauspi-ciously, and he had to conciliate the senate and win their cooperation and trust. His buildings in Rome chart his policy. His first works—the Temple of the Deified Trajan, the restorations of numerous Augustan buildings, and the Temple of the Deified Matidia—emphasized his pietas and his respect for the imperial tradition. His interest in Roman religion, attested to as early as 121 by the retracing of the pomerium and the transformation of the Parilia into the Romaia (the Natalis Urbis Romae), must have appealed to the senate, for it decreed both the work on the pomerium and the new Temple of Venus and Roma, the consecration of which seems to have coincided with the first cele-bration of the Romaia in 121. Even the most personal of Hadrian's monu-ments, his tomb, carefully alluded to Augustus' Mausoleum. Continuity and the permanence of the principate are keynotes struck from the earliest resto-rations in the Campus Martius, through to the presentation of his adoptive sons and successors on the Tondi that once embellished an unidentified struc-ture.

The emphasis on continuity legitimized Hadrian's own principate as both a renewal of Rome's original strength and the natural continuation of Roman destiny. Yet the Temple of Venus and Roma and the Athenaeum, both of which symbolize the Greco-Roman integration Hadrian himself represents, and the eclectic decoration of the Canopus underscore the fact that Hadrianic Rome was not the expression of a self-serving power structure or an anach-ronistic denial of the present. Rather it was proof that the prosperous Roman empire Hadrian directed was a Greco-Roman world at peace.

APPENDIX

# THE OBELISCUS ANTINOI

THE OBELISK of Antinoos, found outside Porta Maggiore in the sixteenth century and now standing in the gardens of the Pincian hill (*see Ill. 58*), has generally been thought to have stood originally somewhere in or near Rome.[1] A recent theory places it in the Canopus of Hadrian's Villa at Tivoli, but on examination this proves unacceptable (see Chapter 5).[2] Beaujeu's suggestion in 1955 that the obelisk was initially set up in Antinoopolis in Egypt, the city Hadrian founded near the site of his favorite's drowning in the Nile on 30 October 130, is generally ignored.[3] Although the obelisk rarely figures in discussions of Hadrian's monuments in Rome, it raises important questions for our understanding of the capital city during his principate. The uneven quality of the hieroglyphs, indications that the text is a translation from Greek, an ambiguous passage in the inscription itself, and its discovery outside Porta Maggiore have led most of those dealing with it to locate the ob-

[1] J. H. Parker, *The Twelve Egyptian Obelisks in Rome*, 2nd ed. (Oxford 1879) 58–61; A. Erman, "Der Obelisk des Antinous," *RömMitt* 11 (1896) 113–21; C. Hülsen, "Das Grab des Antinous," *RömMitt* 11 (1896) 122–30; B. Porter and R.L.B. Moss, *Topographical Bibliography of Ancient Egyptian Hieroglyphic Texts, Reliefs, and Paintings*, VII (Oxford 1951) 412; A. M. Colini, "Horti Spei Veteris, Palatium Sessorianum," *MemPontAcc*, ser. 3, 8 (1955) 137–77; E. Nash, "Obelisk und Circus," *RömMitt* 64 (1957) 250–54; C. D'Onofrio, *Gli obelischi di Roma*, 2nd ed. (Rome 1967) 295–97; Iversen, *Obelisks* 162–63; Malaise, *Cultes égyptiens* 423 n. 1; and Roullet, 82, no. 86. The article of Erman is hereafter cited as Erman (1896).

[2] Kähler, "Antinousobelisk" 35–44 (pub-

lished posthumously), retracting his earlier remarks in *Villa* (pp. 154–55, 179 n. 158); and Hannestad, "Grabmal" 69–108, most explicitly.

[3] Beaujeu, 254–55. For Antinoopolis, see the bibliography cited in the recent brief description by D. L. Thompson, "The Lost City of Antinoos," *Archaeology* 34.1 (1981) 50, including H. I. Bell, "Antinoopolis: A Hadrianic Foundation in Egypt," *JRS* 30 (1940) 133–47; and below. Of the three versions of Antinoos' death transmitted from antiquity—that he killed himself in order to save Hadrian's life by averting danger from him, that he was killed by order of Hadrian for the same purpose, or that he drowned by accident—the last is surely most plausible: Beaujeu, 243–44; Malaise, *Cultes égyptiens* 422.

58. *Obelisk of Antinoos as reerected on the Pincian hill.*

elisk in or near Rome; but there is no unanimity about where in Rome, nor is it clear from the inscription whether the obelisk marked a tomb or a cenotaph.[4]

The date of the obelisk is also uncertain. The hieroglyphs' laudatory mention of Sabina, "who lives, is safe and healthy," gives a terminus ante quem of 137, the probable date of Sabina's death,[5] but there is no evidence to show how soon after Antinoos' death and deification in October 130 the obelisk might have been erected. Those who presume an original location in Rome implicitly accept a date after Hadrian's return to the city in 132, or more likely 134, when he finally came back to Rome to stay in Italy. The chronology of the monument, however, deserves further investigation in connection with the diffusion of the cult of Antinoos and Hadrian's religious policy.

There are numerous problems. The text of the obelisk implies it marks a tomb or cenotaph for Antinoos, and it is difficult to reconcile a Roman location for this with the statement of Epiphanius that Hadrian arranged to have Antinoos' body put in a temple to him in Antinoopolis (Epiphanius *Ancorat.* 1.130 b, Holl).[6] The impact that such an exotic monument to one who once may have been a slave would have had in Hadrianic Rome has not been adequately assessed (cf. Dio Cass. 69.11.4). The place of the worship of Antinoos (who was renamed Osirantinoos in Egypt)[7] in conjunction with the imperial cult during Hadrian's rule has not been adequately examined. And finally there is the biography's statement: *sacra Romana diligentissime curavit, peregrina contempsit* (he cared for Roman religious rites most assiduously, but despised foreign ones: *HA, Hadr.* 22.10), with the implication that this was only in Rome itself.[8]

[4] Although on the basis of the inscription Kähler suggests that the body of Antinoos was mummified and brought to Rome to be entombed ("Antinousobelisk" 42), Hannestad makes no choice between a grave and a cenotaph ("Grabmal" 79, 96).

[5] Most recently, Eck, "Vibia(?) Sabina" 914.

[6] Hülsen, "Grab des Antinous" 129, citing the passage and considering Epiphanius' Egyptian remarks to be generally reliable, says that he cannot come to any conclusion on the contradiction between the passage and his theory of an original location in Rome. Beaujeu, 254, gives greater credence to the passage; A. Hermann, "Antinous infelix," in

*Mullus. Festschrift Theodor Klauser,* ed. by A. Stuiber and A. Hermann (Munich 1964) 156 n. 15, less. For the Temple, which has never been certainly identified but is thought to be the building at the northern end of the main north-south street, see E. Kühn, *Antinoopolis. Ein Beitrag zur Geschichte des Hellenismus im römischen Ägypten. Grunding und Verfassung* (Göttingen 1913) 75.

[7] A. Calderini, *Dizionario dei nomi geografici e topografici dell'egitto greco-romano,* 1.2 (Madrid 1966), s.v. Antinooupolis (*sic*), 88, on the nomenclature.

[8] Malaise, *Cultes égyptiens* 426–27; Beaujeu, 276–78, 245–46, who also stresses the distinction between the cult of Antinoos and the im-

The history of the obelisk's discovery is complicated. Our earliest information about it dates to the sixteenth century, when it was sketched by Antonio da Sangallo the Younger as it lay in three pieces near the Via Labicana, outside the Porta Maggiore near the Aqua Claudia. In 1570 the owners of the land on which it lay, the Saccoccia brothers, commemorated their restoration of it in an inscription now mounted on an arch of the Acqua Felice, built across the area in 1585. The obelisk was acquired and removed by the Barbarini family in the 1630s, and was eventually raised on the Pincio in 1822.[9]

In the 1950s A. M. Colini investigated the area around the Porta Maggiore and identified the area southwest of Via Labicana along the Aqua Claudia as the site of the Horti Spei Veteris, an estate of Elagabalus. After some scholarly debate about the place of the obelisk in the Horti, it is now generally agreed that the obelisk was discovered on the line of the spina of the Circus Varianus, a race course that was a feature of the Horti. Since all construction associated with this palace dates to the late second century or later, it seems almost certain that the obelisk was moved here by Elagabalus to ornament the spina of the Circus, following the pattern set by Augustus and Caligula in the Circus Maximus and the Circus Gaii et Neronis.[10]

This leaves open the question of the obelisk's original location, and for

---

perial cult. Those who consider the biography's statement incorrect, at least as far as the Egyptian cults are concerned (e.g., A.C. Levi, "Hadrian as King of Egypt," *NC*, ser. 6, 8 [1948] 37), presume that the obelisk and cenotaph were erected in Rome.

[9] The inscription, still on the Acqua Felice: *obelisci fragmenta diu prostrata Curtius Saccocius et Marcellus fratres ad perpetuam huius circi Solis memoriam eregi curarunt. anno salutis MDLXX* (The fragments of the obelisk, long lying on the ground, Curtius and Marcellus, the Saccocius brothers, undertook to have erected for the eternal commemoration of this Circus of the Sun. In the year 1570 of our salvation: Hülsen, "Grab des Antinous" 123). The clearest exposition of the complicated modern history of the obelisk is found in Kähler, "Antinousobelisk" 37–39. For Sangallo's 1525 engraving, see A. Bartoli, *I monumenti antichi di Roma nei disegni degli Uffizi di Firenze* (Rome 1914–22) III, pl. 282; Nash, s.v. Obeliscus Antinoi, II.132, pl. 848 (Fototeca 3053);

and Kähler, "Antinousobelisk" pl. 2. D'Onofrio, *Obelischi* 231–32, 295–97, and M. Nota, "L'obelisco di Antinoo," *Capitolium* 50.11 (1975) 62–65, discuss the history and importance of the obelisk in the modern era; D'Onofrio, fig. 3, reproduces G. B. Cipriani's 1823 measured engraving of the twelve Egyptian obelisks of Rome. The obelisk of Antinoos is the fourth smallest.

[10] Colini, "Horti Spei Veteris" 169, misreading the topographical note on Sangallo's sketch, concluded that the obelisk had been found north of the Aqua Claudia; despite correcting this error, Nash also misplaces the obelisk's location in the sixteenth century, in his article, "Obelisk und Circus" 250–54, and in *Pictorial Dictionary* II.130–33, followed by, e.g., Hermann, "Antinous infelix" 165 n. 73. The misreading has been corrected by Kähler, "Antinousobelisk" 39 n. 5, and by Iversen, *Obelisks* 164. Nash discusses in the article cited above other instances of obelisks in circuses.

this the inscription on the obelisk is our most important document. The double lines of hieroglyphs on each of the four faces have not been studied and translated in toto since the beginning of this century. In part this is due to the oddness of the inscription, which has also deteriorated with time. The following information is based on the translations of the Egyptologists A. Erman (1896, 1917, and 1934) and O. Wintermute.[11]

The illustrations and inscription on the obelisk celebrate both the deified Antinoos, called Osirantinoos the Reborn and Ever-living, and Hadrian. The side now facing north seems to be the beginning of the inscription, which departs most noticeably from other obelisk texts in being different on every side. Furthermore, the Egyptologist E. Iversen has described the orthography as "preposterous," with the signs "frequently more or less free elaborations on the old patterns."[12]

On the north pyramidion, Hadrian offers a figure of Truth to Har-achte (Ra), and the legends read: "Says Har-achte (Ra) I give you prosperity . . . ," and "The son of the Sun, the lord of the Diadems, Hadrian the ever-living, says, '[Take] you your daughter (Truth), whom your heart loves.' "

The two-line inscription below the pyramidion acknowledges Hadrian's establishment of the cult of Antinoos, and gives Hadrian's and Sabina's titles in a prayer addressed by Osirantinoos to Har-achte:

> How desirable(?) is the praise, which is made to(?) Osirantinoos, the justified. His heart rejoices greatly when he has recognized his own form, when he was reborn and saw his father Har-[achte]. He [praises him?] and says: Praise to you, Har-achte, the highest of the Gods! You who listen to the prayers of Gods, of men, of the transfigured ones and of the dead. Hear (also) the entreaties that I entrust(?) to you. Give(?) recompense for that which your beloved son has done for me, your

[11] Erman's translation of 1896 was later modified in his article of 1917 (see Erman [1917]); parts of the later translation are repeated in his *Die Religion der Ägypter*, 3rd ed. (Berlin 1934). An English translation of 1852 by Birch (in Parker, *Twelve Obelisks* 19–20) is too general and imprecise to be useful. Kähler's translation and discussion of part of the text, "Antinousobelisk" 40–42, were developed following conversations with P. Derchain, as is the discussion of the inscription by Eck, "Vibia(?) Sabina" 913. In his own article, "A propos de l'obélisque d'Antinoüs," in *Le Monde grec . . . Hommages à Claire Préaux*, ed. by J. Bingen et al. (Brussels 1975) 808–13, Derchain forces his interpretation of the topographical passage of the obelisk; see below. I am indebted to my colleague Dr. Wintermute, of the Department of Religion at Duke University, for discussing this text with me.

[12] E. Iversen, *The Myth of Egypt and Its Hieroglyphs in European Tradition* (Copenhagen 1961) 55.

son (Hadrian) the king of Upper and Lower Egypt, who founded(?) a doctrine in the temples with which the Gods are pleased for all men, [Hadrian] [the beloved] of the Nile and the Gods, the Lord of Diadems who lives, is safe and healthy, who lives forever [just like the Sun] [in] a fresh, beautiful youthful age, while he is a possessor of fortune(?), the ruler of every country, while the great ones of Egypt and the nine bends (Libya) lie under his sandals united, likewise among them he is the lord of both lands. They are daily subject to his orders(?), while his power reaches all the way to each border of this land on its four sides. Bulls and their cows join together happily (and) they produce much, which they bear for him, in order to gladden his heart and that of the great royal lady beloved by him, the queen of both countries, Sabina, who lives, is safe and healthy, Augusta, who lives forever . . . and the (Nile), the father of the Gods, impregnates the fields for them, and makes for them a great ocean at its time in order to flood both lands.

The inscriptions on the other three sides of the obelisk are more closely concerned with specific honors for Antinoos and particular features of his cult. On the pyramidion of the east side, the mystery god Thoth, the god of Hermopolis,[13] presents life and health to Antinoos (wearing the headdress of Socharis), and says "I give to you that your heart give daily. . . ." The inscription below relates to the diffusion of Antinoos' worship and to his resurrection:

Osirantinoos, the justified—he became a youth with a beautiful face that delighted the eyes, . . . strength, with clever(?) heart like one with strong arms—he received an order of the Gods at the time of his passing. All uses of the hours of Osiris were repeated in him, including all his work as a mystery; his writings circulated, while the whole land was in . . . and . . . and . . . Such a thing has not earlier been done to this day—and similarly his altars, his temples, and his titles, and he breathed the breath of life. His respect came about in the hearts of men. The lord of Hermopolis, lord of holy writings, who rejuvenates his soul like that [of] . . . in their time, by night and day, in every

[13] Thoth, the god of magic and mystery, and the chief deity at Hermopolis Magna near Antinoopolis: Beaujeu, 237–38, 243–44, and Malaise, *Cultes égyptiens* 421–22, who both also note Hadrian's initiation into magic in the Fayum and his visit to Hermopolis just before Antinoos' death. Beaujeu, 250–51, discusses the mysteries of the cult of Antinoos; and for the abilities of Antinoos as a worker of miracles, cf. A. D. Nock, "Deification and Julian," *JRS* 47 (1957) 120, citing an *ex voto* to Antinoos from Claudiopolis, Bithynia.

time, in every second—while there is love for him in the hearts of his servants, and fear [for him] [in] everyone . . . and his praise among all men, while they praise him. He takes his seat in the hall of the just, the transfigured ones, the excellent ones who are in the court of Osiris . . . in the land of Hades, while . . . the lord of eternity(?) makes him justified. They set up his words on earth, because(?) their heart is delighted by him. He goes wherever he wants. The doorkeepers of the regions of Hades say to him, Praise to you; they loose their bolts, they open their doors before him in endless many years, while his life span is that of the [sun(?)] [never] going away [forever].[14]

On the south side, the mutilated pyramidion now shows no speech, but does depict Ammon Ra and Antinoos. The inscription below speaks to Antinoos' excellence as a miraculous healer, and gives important information about the festivals established in Antinoopolis in his honor:[15]

Antinoos, who is there (i.e., deceased) . . . a festival place(?) has been made in his city in Egypt, which is named for him, for the strong (youths) who are in this land, and for the rowing crews and for the . . . of the whole country and likewise for all the persons who are(?) with(?) the God Thoth, while there are prizes for them and crowns of flowers for their heads; they reward with every good thing. They place on his altars, they bring . . . daily which as daily(?) offerings(?). Praise is spoken to him by the artisans of Thoth according to the breadth of his excellence. He goes from his city to many temples in the whole country and he hears the requests of those who pray to him, and he heals the needy ill by sending them a dream. He completes his work amongst the living. He takes on every(?) form which his heart [desires(?)] . . . the true seed of the God is in his limbs . . . body healthy . . . of his mother; he was lifted up at the place of his birth by . . .

The inscription on the west side is the one cited by Roman topographers, as well as the one that gives the most information on the foundation of Anti-

---

[14] Dr. Wintermute notes the influence here of the *Book of the Dead*.

[15] J. and L. Robert, in "Bulletin Epigraphique," *Revue des études grecques* 65, no. 304–305 (1952) 69, distinguish here the two types of games on the Greek model, gymnastic and "musical" (here, doubtless, the encomium of Antinoos), augmented by boat races. The prizes listed are wreaths and, apparently, the usual privileges accorded victors in sacred games. I was unable to obtain the work of W. Decker, "Bemerkungen zum Agon für Antinoos in Antinoupolis (Antinoeiai)," *Kölner Beitr. zur Sportwiss.* 2 (1974) 38–56.

noopolis and the appearance of the Temple of Osirantinoos there. The scene on the pyramidion is now incomplete. Still visible, however, are a notched palm branch (once held by Ammon Ra) terminating in a tadpole, the emblem for 100,000 years, and the altar and figure of Antinoos. The first line of the inscription below has been translated in various ways because certain key words are indecipherable. Antinoos' name does not appear at the beginning of the text:

> [Antinoos] who is there (i.e., deceased), and who rests in this place, which is in the field of the lands(?) of the master(?) of . . . of Rome, has been recognized as(?) a God in the divine places of Egypt. Temples have been founded for him, he has been adored as a god by the prophets and priests of Upper and Lower Egypt, and by the inhabitants of Egypt, all of them as there are. A city is named after his name, and the troops of Greeks that belong to it[16] and the . . . of the inhabitants of the temples of Egypt, who come [from] their cities; fields are given to them so that with them(?) they might make their lives very(?) good. A temple of this god, who is there called Osirantinoos the blessed, is found in it and is built of good white stone, with sphinxes around it, and statues and numerous columns, such as were made earlier by the ancestors (Egyptians), and such as were made by the Greeks. All gods and goddesses give him the breath of life and he breathes as one rejuvenated.

The first line on this side (*see Ill. 59*), although often summoned to support theories about where the obelisk originally stood in Rome, may be untranslatable. In *RömMitt* of 1896, in the earliest scholarly treatment of the text, Erman translated the first line as: "Antinous, welcher dort ist, welcher ruht in dieser Stätte die im Grenzfelde der Herrin des Genusses(?) Hrome [i.e., Rome] liegt" (Antinous, who is there [i.e., deceased], who rests in this place which is in the boundary land of the Mistress of Fortuna [?] Rome). At that time he noted that the two characters he translated as "der Herrin des Genusses" are also found on the first (north) side as an epithet for Hadrian himself. In both cases they appear in the feminine form. Erman ignored the in-

---

[16] H. Braunert, *Die Binnenwanderung: Studien zur Sozialgeschichte Ägyptens in der Ptolemäer- und Kaiserzeit* (Bonn 1964) 213–19, has ended a long controversy by demonstrating that even during the Hadrianic period Greek veterans made up a significant portion of the new settlers of Antinoopolis (rather than being enrolled only later, as, e.g., Calderini, *Dizionario* 100–101, with earlier bibliography).

59. *Obelisk of Antinoos, detail of west side relating topographical information.*

correct feminine in the epithet of Hadrian, but here on the fourth side, he translated the characters as a feminine epithet, a noun in apposition to Rome.[17]

The character for Rome, too, is abnormal, preceded by two characters Erman interpreted in 1896 as a rough breathing. He considered this a possible indication that the text was originally written in Greek.[18] In his 1917 edition of the text, however, apparently recognizing that his earlier interpretation of these two characters as a rough breathing could not be maintained (such a hieroglyphic indication for the rough breathing is never found), he takes the two signs together with the hieroglyph he earlier translated as "Genusse"—luck, prosperity, fortune. Since this word of three hieroglyphs is unknown, Erman does not attempt to translate it, rendering only "Antinous(?), welcher dort ist, welcher ruht in dieser Stätte, die im Grenzfelde der Herrin des . . . Rom ist—."[19]

Erman's 1917 corrections have been generally overlooked. Later scholars, such as Iversen and M. Malaise, using Erman's first translation, interpret the word "fortune" in close association with Rome and speak of the rough breathing of "Hrome" as indication of an original text in Greek.[20] Kähler, also relying on the 1896 translation of the text, and pointing to the first instance of the epithet translated "der Herrin des Genusses," insists that the epithet "Herrin" must refer to Hadrian in the second instance as well.[21] In this detail he is probably right, for the feminine form frequently appears incorrectly for the masculine in late hieroglyphic texts.[22] Recently P. Derchain has proposed that the two characters construed by Erman in 1896 as "Herrin des Genusses(?)" are an expression concocted by the translator of the Egyptian text (or possibly found by him in a dictionary) for *Imperator*, the possessor of imperium.[23] But there is no parallel for this translation of Imperator, which is

[17] See Erman (1896) 119 n. 5; Hadrian's epithet is found on p. 115 of the 1896 publication.

[18] In the 1896 publication (p. 119), Erman translates *Hrome* to indicate his interpretation.

[19] Erman (1917) 44–45. Dr. Wintermute suggests that although Erman does not discuss his change of opinion, his deepening knowledge of Egyptian hieroglyphs in 1917 brought him to realize his earlier error.

[20] Iversen, *Obelisks* 163; and Malaise, *Cultes égyptiens* 423 n. 1, both of whom use their incorrect translation of *Hrome* to presume that

the obelisk was inscribed in Rome from an originally Greek text or by a scribe of Greek background. See also n. 18 above, and Derchain, "Obélisque d'Antinoüs" 808.

[21] Kähler, "Antinousobelisk" 40–41, who notes the poor preservation of the inscribed text.

[22] I must thank Dr. Wintermute for this information, corroborated by Derchain, "Obélisque d'Antinoüs" 811 n. 3.

[23] Derchain, "Obélisque d'Antinoüs" 811–12.

rendered in other texts of the Roman imperial period as "Autokrator," an easily recognizable form;[24] moreover, Derchain overlooks the "rough breathing" character following "Genusses(?)" in its second appearance, on the west side (as does Kähler).

Interpretations of the two other characters in the first line that supposedly furnish a topographical reference, those translated above as "the field of the lands(?)," complicate matters. These two characters are the words for "field" or "small, demarcated unit of land," and "frontier," "large unit of land," or "nome, district, area." Erman combined the two as "Grenzfeld" (borderland), presuming a reference to one particular place.[25] Later, Iversen interpreted the two characters as "the campus of the precinct."[26] More recently, Kähler, after consultation with Derchain, translated them to mean "an area in one's possessions," "a villa," construing the second glyph very narrowly.[27] Yet Derchain is quite tentative in the publication of his theory, admittedly basing his interpretation on the hypothetical reconstruction of what was meant by someone translating into Egyptian hieroglyphs a text Hadrian had originally written in Greek.[28] He notes that only excavation can prove or disprove this theory that would place the original location of the obelisk in the Villa Adriana. Yet subsequent excavations by Hannestad, which purportedly prove this interpretation, are in fact inconclusive.

Erman's first incorrect translation and the various topographical interpretations of it discussed earlier have led to divergent theories about an original Roman location for the obelisk and a nearby tomb or cenotaph, some of which take into account the obelisk's location in the sixteenth century, some not.[29] In his joint publication with Erman in *RömMitt* 1896, Hülsen, unaware of the true location of the Circus Varianus, held that the obelisk had been found at its original site outside the pomerium of Rome, a proper location for a tomb.[30] Following Colini's discoveries in that region during the 1950s, Hül-

[24] Cf., for example, the designation on the obelisk of Domitian: Erman (1917) 25–26.

[25] Erman (1896) 119 n. 4. I am indebted to Dr. Wintermute for discussion of the translation of these two characters.

[26] Iversen, *Obelisks* 163.

[27] Kähler, "Antinousobelisk" 41; cf. Hannestad, "Grabmal" 69 and passim.

[28] Derchain, "Obélisque d'Antinoüs" 808, 812–13, who notes that the only other instance of the two characters together designates an unlocatable area, and has been com

monly translated as "limits" or "border."

[29] Birch, in Parker, *Twelve Obelisks* 58–61, despite acknowledging the place of discovery, suggests that the obelisk was first raised in the Campus Martius.

[30] Hülsen, "Grab des Antinous" 129–30. Hülsen associates Hadrian's decision to build his own tomb with the construction of Antinoos' cenotaph, and would see the two monuments as diametrically opposed across the city.

sen's theory reappeared in suggestions that the obelisk and tomb initially stood adjacent to the area of the Circus Varianus.[31] Iversen has proposed that the obelisk was erected near a temple of Fortuna Romana, perhaps the Temple of Venus and Roma on the Velia.[32] The most recent proposal, that of Kähler and Hannestad, would have it that Hadrian raised the obelisk and tomb or cenotaph in the Canopus complex of his Villa in Tivoli.[33]

These speculations, besides being based on an erroneous translation of part of the obelisk's inscription, ignore the wider significance of the monument because they disregard both the visual effect of the obelisk and the majority of the inscription.[34] The obelisk is an explicit and conspicuous advertisement of the new god Antinoos, but specifically in his Egyptian form. The unusual detail of the hieroglyphic inscription proves it was meant to be both religious and historical. The formulaic phrasing of the epithets of Hadrian and Sabina and the glorification of the resurrected Antinoos can cause no surprise; more remarkable is the attention given to the efficacy of Osirantinoos' powers, the ubiquity of his worship in Egypt, the festivals held in his honor, the establishment of Antinoopolis, and the description of its central temple of Osirantinoos. Although the temple was an important feature of the town and the festivals were famous throughout Egypt,[35] they would have had little importance elsewhere. In Rome few people would have been interested in much of the information given here, even if they could read it.[36] Furthermore, the

[31] Porter and Moss, *Hieroglyphic Texts* 412, and Clairmont, *Antinous* 19, suggest a location on the Via Labicana; contra, D'Onofrio, *Obelischi* 296.

[32] Iversen, *Obelisks* 163; contra, Malaise, *Cultes égyptiens* 423 n. 1; and cf. Beaujeu, 255, on the implausibility of its having been set up in Rome. Iversen's interpretation, apparently, influenced Roullet to assert (p. 82, cf. p. 45) that the obelisk "was erected on Antinous' tomb in the precinct of a temple of Fortuna at Rome." Such a location for Antinoos' tomb or cenotaph is unthinkable in Rome; Trajan's tomb is obviously different.

[33] See n. 2 above. Beaujeu, 255; and Derchain, "Obélisque d'Antinoüs" 812–13, dubiously consider the possibility that the obelisk rose originally in the Villa, as do, with more enthusiasm, G. Mancini, *NSc*, 1922, 137–38; and Malaise, *Cultes égyptiens* 423 n. 1.

[34] Kähler, *Villa* 155, originally discussed the full inscription in order to demonstrate Hadrian's indulgence in mysticism and Egyptology; in his later work he focuses on the topographical text. Iversen, *Myth of Egypt* 54–55, discusses the full text, but only to demonstrate the decline of the style and execution of hieroglyphic texts.

[35] Calderini, *Dizionario* 88–89, 91, collects the evidence for the Temple and tomb of Antinoos in Antinoopolis, although he is led by Erman's and Hülsen's publications of 1896 to postulate that a "tomb" was later raised in Rome as well. Beaujeu, 249 n. 3, suggests that there were two temples in the city, one Greco-Egyptian, the other Greek. Antinoos' temple has never been positively identified. For the games, Beaujeu, 249; and J. and L. Robert, "Bulletin épigraphique," 1952, 67–73.

[36] Compare the hieroglyphs on Domitian's obelisk, carved in Rome (the Obeliscus Pamphilius). Although part of the text refers to Domitian's restoration of the Iseum Cam-

peculiarly Egyptian cast of many of the features of the cult of Antinoos as it is described here speaks even more strongly against an original location of the obelisk in Rome or in its vicinity.

Hadrian had Antinoos consecrated after his drowning on 30 October 130. Although Hadrian's biography says that the Greeks consecrated Antinoos at Hadrian's wish and asserted that oracles had been given to them by the youth (*HA, Hadr.* 14.7), it seems rather that Hadrian obtained the consecration in Egypt and with Egyptian custom. Without consulting the Roman senate, Hadrian had Antinoos deified according to the ancient Egyptian tradition of consecrating those who had drowned in the sacred Nile.[37] The city of Antinoopolis, begun in 130 or soon thereafter, marked the site of Antinoos' death near the city of Hermopolis Magna and was to be the center of the new cult. The chief temple of Osirantinoos and the most famous festivals in his honor were there. The first games date to 131, and there were citizens in the city as early as 133.[38]

The new god was well received in Egypt and the Greek East. According to C. W. Clairmont's study *Die Bildnisse des Antinous*, the first official images of the deified Antinoos date to 131/132 and were created in Greece by a sculptor of the school of Aphrodisias.[39] The earliest coins with his likeness, providing a firmer terminus post quem for the cult's diffusion, were struck in Al-

---

pense in Rome, most of it is devoted to formulaic epithets for Domitian: Erman (1917) 18–28; Iversen, *Myth of Egypt* 54; Malaise, *Inventaire* #387, pp. 203–207. Yet these epithets for Domitian are idiosyncratic: see Malaise's notes, and compare the official Egyptian titles of Augustus, in P. Wendland, *Die hellenistisch-römische Kultur in ihren Beziehungen zu Judentum und Christentum. Die urchristl. Literaturformen* (Tübingen 1912) p. 410, text 10.

[37] See, e.g., Beaujeu, 242–45; Malaise, *Cultes égyptiens* 232 n. 6; T. Kraus, "Das Bildnis des Antinoos," *Heidelberger Jahrbücher* 3 (1959) 48.

[38] J. and L. Robert, "Bulletin épigraphique," 1952, 68–70; Calderini, *Dizionario* 70. For the temple specifically, see Clem. Al. *Protr.* 4.49. For the city, modeled on Greek cities but a syncretic combination of Greek and Roman elements, see H. Braunert, "Griechische und römische Komponenten im Stadtrecht von Antinoopolis," *Journal of Juristic Papyrology* 14

(1962) 88; and Weber, 248–56; for the date of 130, see J. Schwartz in *Chronique d'Egypte* 44 (1969) 164–68. U. Wilcken, *Archiv für Papyrusforschung* 6 (1921) 383, calculating that the first of the annual games in Antinoopolis was held in 131, gives evidence that the games were organized according to the prescription of Hadrian.

[39] Clairmont, *Antinous* 23–30. Although this work omits some of the known portraits of Antinoos, it replaces the earlier catalogues of P. Marconi, "Antinoo. Saggio sull'arte dell'età Adrianea," *MonAnt* 29 (1923) 161–302; and of E. Holm, *Das Bildnis des Antinous* (Würzburg 1933). On the basis of new fragments of *IG*, 2nd ed, 2.1105, a series of documents and letters concerned with the Dionysiac technitai, Geagan, "Dionysiac Technitai" 145–51, suggests that in 131/132 Hadrian caused the technitai at Athens to identify Antinoos with Dionysos Choreios in a mystic cult.

exandria in 134, and some authorities suggest that the first official portraits came from Egypt as well.[40] By the time of Hadrian's death in 138, over thirty cities in the Greek East, two-thirds of these in Asia Minor, had issued medallions and coins in Antinoos' honor. Some of these issues seem merely flattery of Hadrian; others, however, have been associated more specifically with festivals for the new god. Games are now known to have been held at Mantineia (Paus. 8.9.8), Athens, Argos, and Hadrianeia in Bithynia.[41]

More than thirty statues and reliefs of Antinoos come from the Greek East, including the well-known statue at Delphi (height: 1.80 meters). In many cases the new god is given the attributes of one of the Olympian deities, usually Dionysos, Apollo, or Hermes.[42] In Antinoopolis miracles were attributed to a statue of Osirantinoos as late as the third century (Origen *C. Celsus* 3.36).

The lineaments of the new cult in the east share common characteristics. It was public. In Greece and Asia Minor, the syncretism of Antinoos with Dionysos and other familiar gods made it easy for cities to use the cult to curry imperial favor (cf. *HA, Hadr.* 14.7), but after Hadrian's death, enthusiasm for it dissipated.[43] It was much longer lived in Egypt, where the assimilation of Antinoos to Osiris was extremely fruitful and where the prosperity of Antinoopolis and the splendor of the games served to ensure its vitality.[44]

[40] For example, H. von Heintze, in her review of Clairmont's *Antinous*, in *Gnomon* 43 (1971) 394–96.

[41] For the coins: Kraus, "Antinous" 49–55; J.M.C. Toynbee, "Greek Imperial Medallions," *JRS* 34 (1944) 65–73, esp. 65–67; and Strack, *Hadrian* 166. I was unable to obtain G. Blum, "Numismatique d'Antinous," *Journal international d'archéologie numismatique* 16 (1914) 33–70. J. and L. Robert, "Bulletin épigraphique," 1952, 68–69, give an accurate list of the known games for Antinoos, omitting those of Corinth conjectured by C. Seltman, "Greek Sculpture and Some Festival Coins," *Hesperia* 17 (1948) 83–84. Geagan, "Dionysiac Technitai" 148, postulates annual ephebic games to Antinoos also in Eleusis.

[42] Also Asclepios, Pan, Poseidon, Ganymede, Adonis, and Aristaeus, and he is sometimes shown as simply heroic: Beaujeu, 250–53; Kraus, "Antinous" 51–52, who describes the Delphi statue on p. 60.

[43] Kraus, "Antinous" 52, 60, underlines the syncretism of Antinoos in the Greek East. Although the games of Antinoos were celebrated in Athens until the second half of the third century (Beaujeu, 256, citing P. Graindor, *Athènes sous Hadrien* [Cairo 1934, reprinted New York 1973] 100–101), they were not very popular or famous: J. and L. Robert, "Bulletin epigraphique," 1952, 68 (contra Geagan, "Dionysiac Technitai" 148), and no new coins with Antinoos' image, or works of art representing him, are known to have been made after Hadrian's death (Hermann, "Antinous infelix" 157 n. 23).

[44] The games in Antinoopolis are attested into the third century, with documentation concentrating in the period from 180/192 to 212/217 (six references: Calderini, *Dizionario* 102). Eusebius' reference to the games "held in my own day" (*HE* 4.8.2) is taken from Hegesippus, writing in the second century: J. and L. Robert, "Bulletin épigraphique," 1952, 69.

On the other hand, Dio, the Christian apologists, and many modern authorities believe that the cult of Antinoos was not well received in Rome and Italy, where it is said to have provoked ridicule of Hadrian or to have been accepted out of fear.[45] But an objective evaluation of the evidence shows simply a less highly organized worship of Antinoos in the west. As one would expect, in the west there were no festivals like those in the Greek East; this accounts at least in part for the absence of the new god on coins in the west. But Antinoos' absence from the coins of Rome also denotes that Hadrian did not promote the new cult in the capital.

Yet Antinoos was worshiped in and around Rome. Although the earliest known representations of Antinoos in the west date to 133/134, about a year or so after their appearance in the Greek East, more than half the extant statues and reliefs of Antinoos come from Rome and its environs.[46] T. Kraus has argued that those that are larger than life, and those that clearly depict Antinoos as a god, were cult images. An example would be the relief, 1.45 meters high, from Lanuvium portraying Antinoos as Silvanus[47] (*see Ill. 60*).

With the exception of seven likenesses of Antinoos agreed to be from the Villa Adriana,[48] the original location of most of Antinoos' statues in the environs of Rome is impossible to ascertain. Two inscriptions to Antinoos,

[45] For example, Clem. Al. *Protr.* 4.49; Tert. *Ad nat.* 2.10.11; Prudent. *c. Symm.* 1.271–77. For the Christian reaction to the cult: Hermann, "Antinous infelix" 159–64; P. Guyot, "Antinous als Eunuch: zur christlichen Polemik gegen das Heidentum," *Historia* 30 (1981) 250–54. His remarks are applicable to Xiphilinus, who transmits to us Dio Cass. 69.11.4. Modern scholars who believe in Antinoos' unpopularity in Rome include Beaujeu, 253–57; R. MacMullen, *Paganism in the Roman Empire* (New Haven and London 1981) 102–103; Malaise, *Cultes égyptiens* 423; and J.M.C. Toynbee, in her review of Clairmont's *Antinous*, in *JRS* 57 (1967) 267. For evidence of worship of Antinoos in the west, see MacMullen, 91. A statue of Antinoos with attributes of Apollo was found in the Hadrianic Baths of Leptis Magna: G. Caputo, "Sincretismo religioso ed espressione figurativa in Tripolitania," *Quaderni di archeologia della Libia* 9 (1977) 119–24.

[46] See, e.g., von Heintze, in her review of

Clairmont's *Antinous* (above n. 40), 395; Kraus, "Antinous" 57.

[47] Kraus, "Antinous" 55–57. Now in the Banco Nazionale of Rome, this relief was originally found at a villa between Lanuvium and Antium. The only large-scale portrayal of Antinoos that is signed, it was made by Antonianos of Aphrodisias; for the sculptor, see M. Floriani Squarciapino, *La scuola di Aphrodisia* (Rome 1943) 16, 21, 29–32, who implausibly dates the relief to the period 130–133 (p. 16). Clairmont's similar contention (*Antinous* 30–32) that this Antonianos was the creator of the official portrait of Antinoos is admitted as plausible by Toynbee in her review of Clairmont's *Antinous* (above, n. 45), 286, but viewed with more suspicion by others (see n. 40 above).

[48] Roullet, 85–87, and cf. 158, lists and describes seven Eqyptianizing statues of Antinoos found in the Villa; other similar images from the region may also be from there.

60. *Relief of Antinoos as Silvanus, found in Lanuvium. Height,* 1.45 *meters. (Relief now in the Banco Nazionale, Rome.)*

"ruling jointly with the gods in Egypt" (*IG* 14.961 = *IGUR* 1.98 = *SIG* 383; and *IG* 14.960 = *IGRR* 1.31), found near the Arco di Camigliano at the Isaeum Campense in Rome and in Portus, respectively, may indicate that the new god found a suitable place in existing shrines and temples to the Egyptian gods, which were fairly numerous by this time throughout Italy.[49] The Egyptianizing statues and busts of Antinoos would be appropriate for such settings, but all those with known provenance seem to come from Villa Adriana or Egypt.[50]

The phratry of the "Antinoitae et Eunostidae" in Naples (*CIL* 6.1851a, c)[51] may have had an image of Antinoos in their headquarters, and the mention of a priest of Antinoos (*aratas Antinoou*) honored by the *Adriana sunodos*, or ecumenical guild of actors (*IG* 14.978a [add p. 695] = *IGRR* 1.55), suggests that an image of Antinoos was placed in the guild halls of such groups. Presumably most images of Antinoos in such places would depict the young god as Dionysos, his most common guise.[52]

A temple of Antinoos is mentioned in an inscription of the *collegium salutare Dianae et Antinoi* in Lanuvium. This burial club, established in 133, is well known thanks to *CIL* 14.2112 (= *ILS* 7212 = Smallwood, #165), which contains its constitution and an account of a meeting, held *[in] templo Antinoi* (in the Temple of Antinoos) in June 136, called by the president at the request of the patron of the town and of the society.[53] The inscription records the promise of the patron, L. Caesennius L.f. Quir. Rufus, to give the society 400 sesterces twice yearly, on the anniversaries of the births of Diana and Antinoos, and his desire to have the constitution inscribed *sub tetra[stylo A]ntinoi*

[49] Roullet, 23–42, assembles the evidence for shrines to the Egyptian deities or with Egyptianizing decoration in Rome and its environs, and on p. 3 suggests that Antinoos was worshiped in the Isaeum Campense or close by. L. Moretti, "Sulle iscrizione greche di Porto," *RendLinc*, ser. 8, 19 (1964) 196–97, assigns the inscription from Portus to the Serapeum at Portus (distinct from that at Ostia), and notes that the two statues of Antinoos from Ostia indicate a fairly wide diffusion of the cult there. These statues were not Egyptianizing, however.

[50] See Marconi, "Antinoo" nos. 10, 11, 12 (perhaps representing Antinoos), 27, 66, 79, 81, 84, 103, 106, and pp. 233–38; and Clairmont, *Antinous* 16 n. 3.

[51] In this case an existing phratry received the additional honorific name: Beaujeu, 256 n. 1.

[52] Such would be the Antinoos-Dionysos found near the Villa Pamphilji, Rome, and now in the British Museum: Clairmont, *Antinous* no. 37, p. 51 and ill. 27; and the Antinoos-Apollo or -Dionysos formerly in the Borghese collection in Frascati, and now in the Louvre: Clairmont, no. 58, p. 57 and ill. 33.

[53] A. E. Gordon, "The Cults of Lanuvium," *CPCA* ii.2 (1938) 44–46, discusses this inscription, the cult of Antinoos, and the collegium, citing earlier bibliography for the collegium.

*parte interiori* (under the tetrastyle of the Temple of Antinoos, in the inner part). It then continues with the constitution of the funerary collegium, which included slaves, freedmen, and probably also the freeborn.[54]

Although A. E. Gordon doubts that a public temple was dedicated to the two deities, though named after its chief guardian, Antinoos,[55] no other conclusion can easily be drawn from the inscription. In this *collegium salutare*, Antinoos is associated with Diana, a frequent patroness of burial clubs who is here identified as the chief goddess of Aricia and Rome, thus one of the oldest divinities in Latium.[56] Antinoos, in contrast, has no distinguishing epithet. Since Antinoos is frequently represented in the west as Silvanus or Vertumnus, and Diana is associated with Silvanus on the Tondi Adrianei, I suggest that the statue of Antinoos *in templo Antinoi* represented the young god as Silvanus.[57] The cult relief found in Lanuvium (*see Ill. 60*) may have been dedicated in this temple of Antinoos.

The inscription provides other information about the cult of Antinoos in the west. By its date of 133 for the founding of the collegium, it marks a terminus post quem for the cult's diffusion. Antinoos, however, is not put first: although the temple seems to be named for him alone, his name occurs second in the title of the collegium. In our earliest datable testimony from Italy, the new god appears in the company of a well-established divinity. Finally, the patron of the collegium, undocumented elsewhere,[58] was a prominent local man, the duumvir and patron of Lanuvium. And the size of the endowment and donations Caesennius gave for the club was substantial if not extravagant.[59]

The relatively numerous statues, busts, and reliefs of Antinoos that have

[54] This, our fullest documentation for such funerary collegia, indicates that these associations were legalized sometime between Caesar's lex Julia and Hadrian's day: J.-P. Waltzing, *Etude historique sur les corporations professionnelles chez les Romains depuis les origines jusqu'à la chute de l'Empire d'Occident* (Brussels 1895–1900) I.141–53.

[55] Gordon, "Cults of Lanuvium" 45, who notes that most other scholars presume the existence of a temple.

[56] Gordon, "Cults of Lanuvium" 44: the dies natalis cited for Diana allows this identification. Beaujeu, 251, says that both gods here are deities of resurrection.

[57] Sacrifices to Diana, Silvanus, Hercules, and Apollo are depicted on these Tondi Adrianei (ca. 132–138), and Antinoos as hero is found on them as well. See Chapter 7, the section entitled "Tondi Adrianei."

[58] His brother Caesennius Silvanus, also mentioned in the inscription (col. II, line 12), may be the man of that name who owed his military tribunate to Pliny and Suetonius: cf. Pliny *Ep.* 3.8; Sherwin-White, *Pliny* 230; and *PIR*, 2nd ed., II C 176, p. 35.

[59] Duncan-Jones' compilation of known foundations in the Roman world (*ERE* 171–84, 379–80) places this as seventieth out of 121 examples arranged from largest to smallest.

been found in and near Rome but are not obviously cult images may be similar manifestations of paying homage more for political than religious reasons. Hadrian's devotion to Antinoos was amply attested to in Villa Adriana,
where at least seven likenesses of the youth, almost all Egyptianizing, have
been found.[60] Members of Hadrian's court and other friends whom he is said
to have visited frequently (Dio Cass. 69.7.4; *HA, Hadr.* 9.7) probably always
had, or were presented with, some representation of the beautiful youth. But
there was no standard iconography, and the various types known seem suitable for use both as garden statuary and interior display.[61]

Indeed, in and around Rome Antinoos is an elusive god. An Egyptian
character for the deified Antinoos appears occasionally in Rome and the west,
but not always. Although most likenesses of Antinoos found in Villa Adriana
are Egyptianizing, one shows him as Vertumnus.[62] No inscription from the
west seems to refer to him as Osirantinoos. As a god of resurrection, which
is the quintessence of his Egyptian form, we find him only in the *collegium
salutare Dianae et Antinoi*, and then by implication. An elegiac distich discovered in Tibur underlines his mutability: *Antinoo et Beleno par aetas formaque si
par/ [c]ur non Antinous sit quoque qui Belenus/ Q. Siculu[s]* (if the age of Antinoos and Belenus is the same, and their features the same, why should not
Antinoos be also Belenus? Quintus Siculus [wrote this]: *CIL* 14.3535 = Buecheler, *Carm. Epigr.* 879). Belenus was a god of Gaul and Noricum similar to
Apollo.[63]

The noticeable variation in the west of the representations of Antinoos is
striking in light of the restricted area in which they were found. Although the
new deity was certainly important in and around Rome during Hadrian's life-

---

[60] See n. 48 above. Clairmont, *Antinous* 17
n. 1, notes these as evidence for a transferral
of the cult of Antinoos from Egypt to Tivoli,
but see von Heintze's review of Clairmont's
*Antinous* (above, n. 40), 394.

[61] The random display of imperial portraits
in villas and gardens in the early empire (cf.
Tac. *Ann.* 1.73.2) may have become more
formal by the second century: Vermeule, *Roman Taste* 65–70, assumes the existence of a
"caesareum" or "augusteum" in the villa at
Monte Cagnolo from which come six imperial busts (from the Antonines to Philip the
Younger).

[62] Kraus, "Antinous" 55–56; Marconi,
"Antinoo" no. 23. This famous relief is now
in the Villa Albani in Rome: cf. Clairmont,
*Antinous* 46–47, no. 25. See also Chapter 5, n.
57.

[63] Most of the testimony for Belenus comes
from Noricum and other northern provinces,
and dates to the third century. The god was at
times assimilated to Apollo. Cf. Ihm, "Belenus," *RE* 3.1 (1897) 199–201; and F. Mar-
aspin, "Il culto di Beleno-Apollo ad Aqui-
leia," *Atti Centro Studi e Documentazione
sull'Italia romana* 1 (1967–68) 145–61. Although Wissowa, in Roscher, *Lex.* 1.1.756,
says that this inscription is a forgery, other
commentators accept it.

time, the lack of standardization in the cult of Antinoos in the west makes it difficult to accept that the obelisk of Antinoos and the tomb or cenotaph mentioned in its inscription was put up by the emperor in the capital city.

Although at first sight these arguments render more attractive Kähler's and Hannestad's theory that Hadrian raised the obelisk privately in his own villa at Tibur, as we saw in Chapter 5 the archaeological and art historical evidence does not support their case. Furthermore, both scholars rely on an incorrect translation, and their understanding of "Grenzfeld" is too specific. The range of meaning Kähler himself gives to the hieroglyph he construes as "possessions" or "villa" indicates that "Hadrian's territory" can refer not only to the Villa at Tibur, but to all imperial land in and around Rome.[64]

It is much more likely that the obelisk was first set up in Antinoopolis on land belonging to the great Temple of Osirantinoos. The city and all it contained had been created by Hadrian; all the land there was at least at one time his. This might account for the reference to the "temenos of the land(s) of the master(?) . . . of Rome."[65] Furthermore, the great Temple of Osirantinoos was Antinoos' tomb; a location for the obelisk in its precinct would suit the phase "(Antinoos) who is deceased and who rests in this place." It would also much better explain the atypical inscription, which omits most of the repetitive eulogistic formulae about the ruling princeps or pharaoh and lists instead the festival, powers, worship, city, and temple of the new god. The obelisk may have been in place during or soon after the first celebration of the games in 131.[66]

The obelisk would have been transferred to Rome during the rule of Elagabalus, 218–222. This young emperor and priest of the Sun god is known to have promoted a monotheistic religion of his god, going so far as to have the icon of Juno Caelestis brought from Carthage to be "married" to the icon of the Sun in his new temple on the Palatine (Dio Cass. 80.12; Herodian 5.6.3–5).[67] Also notoriously susceptible to flattery, Elagabalus received in 220 among other manifestations of municipal homage the honor of a new and splendid festival, the Antoneineia, declared "Isantinoeia," equal to the Anti-

---

[64] Kähler, "Antinousobelisk" 41 n. 3.

[65] On the north side of the obelisk a similarly puzzling phrase is used to refer to the extent of Hadrian's power in Egypt; Erman (1917) 31, notes that what is here transcribed as "his power reaches all the way to each border of this land on its four sides" is usually expressed as either "all that the sun borders" or "the land on its four sides."

[66] If so, we could then explain the errors in the inscription as due to the hurry with which the commission was carried out.

[67] Lambertz, "Varius Avitus, No. 10," *RE* 8 A.1 (1955) 391–404; and G. H. Halsberghe, *The Cult of Sol Invictus* (Leiden 1972) 67–76, 89–100.

noeia, the famous games of Antinoopolis. This most likely came from Leo-notopolis in Egypt.[68] Antoneineia (Antoninia) are known to have been held at numerous cities in the Greek East, and in 1970 L. Robert published an inscription from Delphi that proves the establishment in Rome of a hitherto undocumented festival, the Antoninia Pythia. Despite their assimilation to the Pythian games, these games were in honor of Elagabalus and his Sun god.[69] Robert points to Herodian's accounts of the celebrations that took place after Elagabalus arrived in Rome and built a temple for his god on the Palatine and a summer residence for the god in the suburbs. The gala events involved constructing a hippodrome (circus) and theaters, and presenting chariot races, spectacles, and entertainments (Herodian 5.5.8ff.; 5.6.6–7). Robert dates the new Roman festival to 219 or 220, and he underlines how the name Antoninia Pythia linked Elagabalus with the ancient cult of Apollo Pythia, likened to his own Sun god.[70] It seems likely that the obelisk of Antinoos was sent to Rome to ornament the new Circus,[71] in which the sacred games were in all probability held, and that by this gesture, since the source and associations of the obelisk would have been advertised, Elagabalus expressed the religious "equality"—or superiority—of his new games as well as provided his Circus with a traditional embellishment.[72] This last point would be strengthened if the summer Temple of the Sun was at or near the Horti Spei Veteris.[73]

The religious policy of Hadrian, which is in the end the strongest argument against an original location for the obelisk in Rome, was a far cry from that of Elagabalus. Whatever Hadrian's personal beliefs may have been, he adapted official policy to suit the various parts of the Roman world, though

[68] J. and L. Robert, "Bulletin épigraphique," 1952, 67–73.

[69] Robert, "Deux concours" 25–27, who also points out the difficulties in separating the Antoneineia in honor of Caracalla and those for Elagabalus.

[70] Robert, "Deux concours" 26–27. Halsberghe, Sol Invictus 85–88, describes the procession in Rome pertaining to these games, associating CIL 6.323 with it. T. Optendrenk, Die Religionspolitik des Kaisers Elagabal im Spiegel der "Historia Augusta" (Bonn 1969) 93–94, less convincingly dates the procession and festivities to 221.

[71] The subsequent liberality of Severus Alexander to Antinoopolis (cf. Thompson, "City of Antinous" 46) may have been in part motivated by Elagabalus' depredation.

[72] On such imitations of Augustus and Caligula, see, e.g., Nash, "Obelisk und Circus"; Kähler, "Antinousobelisk" 35–37.

[73] Halsberghe, Sol Invictus 75; L. Pernier, DizEp, III.667 (but see C. R. Whittaker's note in his Loeb translation of Herodian 5.6.6). R.E.A. Palmer, "The Topography and Social History of Rome's Trastevere (Southern Sector)," Proceedings of the American Philosophical Society 125.5 (1981) 378–81 and fig. 2, p. 373, locates the Temple in Trastevere. Although his grounds are plausible, he ignores the possibility of a location ad Spem veterem.

consistently promoting the cult of the imperial house. Thus in Greece, where he was an initiate of the Eleusinian mysteries, he fostered a panhellenic religion unifying the Greek East in the worship of Zeus Olympios, with whom he was identified.[74] Here Antinoos may have served as an ancillary divinity. In Egypt Hadrian was patron of the Egyptian deities, to whom he made Antinoos equivalent.[75] The new *polis* of Antinoopolis was politically favored, and the new religion promoted by splendid festivals. Just as the obelisk shows Antinoos praying for Hadrian and Sabina, the new polis was closely associated with the imperial house, with many of the names of the demes and phratries taken from members of Hadrian's family. The new cult and city were a way of attaching Egypt to the imperial dynasty.[76]

In Rome, Hadrian attended to the traditional gods and the deified imperial house. In his building programs he restored older temples and shrines and fostered the imperial cult; his private grief was not transmitted into an order that others must share it as well. The biography's asseveration of Hadrian's traditionally Roman religious policies (quoted at the beginning of this Appendix) can be justifiably applied to Hadrian's actions in the capital city. The obelisk of Antinoos is too out of harmony with Hadrian's known religious policy in Rome to have been originally erected there; it must have risen in Antinoopolis to commemorate the institution of honors to Hadrian's deified lover.

---

[74] A. S. Benjamin, "The Altars of Hadrian in Athens and Hadrian's Panhellenic Program," *Hesperia* 32 (1963) 58–60; and Beaujeu, 248. On Hadrian's religious policy in general, I agree with M. Guarducci, "La religione di Adriano," in *Empereurs d'Espagne* 209–19. W. Den Boer, "Religion and Literature in Hadrian's Policy," *Mnemosyne* 8 (1955) 123–44, is overstated and uncritical of the sources.

[75] Beaujeu, 240–41, 248; and Malaise, *Cul-*

*tes égyptiens* 419–27, who contends that this favor came before Hadrian's extended visit to Egypt in 130. See Chapter 3 n. 67 for demes in Antinoopolis named for members of the imperial family, and note too that in the city a tribe was placed under the protection of Osiris, a deme under that of Isis, and another deme under that of Apis.

[76] Weber, 251–53; Beaujeu, 248, admits this as a secondary reason for the new cult.

CATALOGUE

## Legenda

I. Date (and nature of evidence for date)
II. Location
III. State of preservation
IV. Principal measurements in meters, and architectural characteristics
    A. Overall measurements
    B. Thickness of walls
    C. Height and lower diameter of columns
    D. Architectural order
    E. Roofing (usually for rooms; when possible, for the structure as a whole)
V. Distinctions and dominant decorative motifs
VI. Principal materials
VII. Ancient testimonia, if any

## Notes and abbreviations

| — | no data exist | w. | width |
|---|---|---|---|
| NA | not applicable | d. | depth |
| ht. | height | diam. | diameter |

# CATALOGUE

THIS CATALOGUE is designed to provide a general chronology of Hadrian's public buildings and urban changes, and a basis for physical and stylistic comparison of the various works that can be assigned to him. The uncertain inception and completion dates for many of the buildings and restorations, however, permit a chronology that can be only approximate. Similarly, the fragmentary state of many edifices often precludes exact measurements and determination of stylistic details. The catalogue, therefore, should be used in conjunction with the annotated text, which explains the data in greater detail and refers specifically to archaeological information such as the *CIL* numbers of individual brick stamps. References here to the Regionary Catalogues are to Nordh, *Libellus*.

At the end of the catalogue are found those parts of Hadrian's Villa in Tivoli and three large structures in Rome dating from Hadrian's reign that are discussed in the text, although these last are not, strictly speaking, public works.

## PANTHEON

I. 118–125 (brick stamps)
II. Central Campus Martius (Regio IX)
III. Hadrianic structure mostly extant, with some reworking and repair of details
IV. A. Rotunda, 43.30 internal diam., 57 external; cylinder, 30.40 exterior ht., 22.20 interior; intermediate block, 33.10 w., ca. 5–10 d.; pronaos, 33.10 w., 15.50 d.
   B. Varying; maximum thickness of rotunda walls, ca. 7.50
   C. Monolithic shafts, 11.79 ht., 1.48 diam.; 13.96 ht. overall
   D. Corinthian, external and internal
   E. Dome of concrete with oculus; half domes for niches; barrel vaults; and trussed roof of bronzed beams for pronaos
   V. Pedimental decoration of eagle and *corona civica*; intermediate block revetted with panels carved with bucrania, festoons, and sacrificial instruments; columns, gray and rose granite
VI. Rotunda, brick-faced concrete, possibly originally stuccoed externally; pronaos, gray and rose granite columns, Pentelic marble capitals, bases (and entablature?), travertine pediment; intermediate block, brick-faced concrete exterior, but internally revetted with pavonazzetto, giallo antico, porphyry, and gray granite; marble and bronze tiles on dome
VII. *HA, Hadr.* 19.10; *CIL* 6.896

## ARCUS PIETATIS

I. Contemporaneous with Pantheon (?)
II. Forecourt of Pantheon (Regio IX)

III. Some masonry reportedly built into an edifice facing Piazza della Rotonda

IV. A. —     C. —     E. —
      B. —     D. —

V. Depiction of emperor dispensing largesse

VI. Concrete and marble (?)

VII. *Mirabilia* 23; *Anon. Magliab.* 10, Merckl.; possibly Dante, *Purgatorio* 10.73ff.

## TEMENOS OF PANTHEON

I. Contemporaneous with Pantheon (?)

II. North of Pantheon (Regio IX)

III. No remains visible

IV. A. 60 w., 100 d. (?), 1.30 m. lower than Pantheon's pronaos, and demarcated by colonnades 5–6 d. raised on 6 steps
      B. —
      C. 1.0 diam.
      D. —
      E. —

V. Coloristic

VI. Paving of forecourt, travertine; colonnades' stylobates, giallo antico; paving and columns, "granitello" and gray granite

VII. —

## SAEPTA JULIA

I. 118–125 (brick stamps)

II. East of Pantheon and Baths of Agrippa, south of Aqua Virgo (Regio IX)

III. Stretch of wall visible east of Pantheon

IV. A. Overall, 120 w., 310 d., at least 10 ht.
      B. Not uniform, maximum thickness ca. 2.10
      C. —
      D. Corinthian
      E. Wooden truss

V. Niches correspond with intercolumniation of Pantheon's portico

VI. Brick-faced concrete, Luna marble revetment

VII. *HA, Hadr.* 19.10

## SOUTH BUILDING

I. 118–125 (brick stamps)

II. Immediately south of Pantheon (Regio IX)

III. North wall and northern ends of east and west walls still visible in situ, together with fallen masonry from vaulting and architectural decoration, some still in place; one capital in the Cortile della Pigna of the Vatican. Fragments of the frieze visible immured in right wall of exit of the Grotte Vaticane; also displayed in the Camposanto Monumentale of Pisa

IV. A. 45 interior w., 48.55 exterior, with projections; 19 interior d.; at least 14.50 ht.; interior frieze 1.58 ht.; interior cornice 0.80 ht.
      B. 1.75
      C. Shafts, 1.07 diam., 9.23 ht., 11.01 ht. overall
      D. Corinthian
      E. Groin vaulting

V. Dolphin and shell pattern on frieze, spacing of which varies according to placement on long or short walls; corner columns slightly inset

VI. Brick-faced concrete; architectural decoration, Luna and Proconnesian marble; columns, pavonazzetto and rose granite

VII. See Gatti, "Basilica di Nettuno," and P. Oxy. III.412, lines 63–68 (?)

## RESTORATION OF LAVACRUM AGRIPPAE (BATHS OF AGRIPPA)

I. Contemporaneous with Pantheon (?)

II. 75 m. south of South Building, 145 south of Pantheon (Regio IX)

III. No remains of Hadrianic restoration visible

IV. A. Laconicum from Severan or later reconstruction, 25 diam.; overall complex, 85–100 w., 100–125 d.
      B. —     C. —     D. —

E. Post-Hadrianic segmental vaulting perhaps reproducing earlier plan

V. Hadrianic restoration possibly done to original (Agrippan) plan

VI. Brick-faced concrete with brick ribs (post-Hadrianic)

VII. *HA, Hadr.* 19.10; possibly *Forma Urbis*, pl. 32, frag. m

## TEMPLE OF THE DEIFIED MATIDIA

I. Terminus post quem, ca. 23 December 119 (consecration of Matidia); probable ante quem, 121 (numismatic)

II. North of Saepta, east of Pantheon's forecourt (Regio IX)

III. One column fragment visible

IV. A. —  B. —
C. 1.70 diam., 13.7–17 ht.
D. Corinthian (?)
E. —

V. First temple in Rome known to have been dedicated exclusively to a deified woman

VI. Columns, cipollino

VII. *CIL* 15.7248; Regionary Catalogues (Nordh, *Libellus* 87.16–17); medallion: Gnecchi, II, p. 5, no. 25, pl. 39.5 (Vienna exemplar; Madrid exemplar unpublished)

## BASILICAE OF MATIDIA AND OF MARCIANA

I. Termini post and ante quos, same as for the Basilica of Matidia (end of 119, and 121)

II. At the Temple of the Deified Matidia (Regio IX)

III. No reliably identifiable visible remains

IV. A. —  C. —  E. —
B. —  D. —

V. Coloristic (?)

VI. Forecourt, travertine; two-story porticoes with aediculae, possibly with green granite columns

VII. Regionary Catalogues (Nordh, *Libellus* 87.16–17); medallion: Gnecchi, II, p. 5, no. 25, pl. 39.5 (Vienna exemplar; Madrid exemplar unpublished)

## GIANO ACCANTO ALLA MINERVA

I. Terminus post quem, 123 (brick stamps)

II. Quadrifrons gateway from Saepta east to Isaeum on axis with Arcus ad Isis (Regio IX)

III. No visible remains

IV. A. 26.24 w., 21.34 d.; span of central east-west arch, 11.06, of lateral east-west arches, 3.57; span of north-south arch, 11.06
B. Pilasters, 2.01 w., 5.14 d.
C. 0.80–1.0 diam.
D. —
E. Barrel vaulting

V. Largest arch known in Rome: central vault, 21 ht.

VI. Brick-faced concrete core; columns, cipollino; bases, capitals, and cornices, white marble

VII. Cf. *HA, Hadr.* 19.10

## REESTABLISHMENT OF THE POMERIUM

I. 121 (epigraphic)

II. Presumably all around Rome; cippi found in northern Campus Martius

III. Some cippi visible: *NSc*, 1933, 241, now in the Cortile of the Museo delle Terme; *CIL* 6.1233a = 31539a, in situ in basement under #18, between Pza. Sforza Cesarini and Pza. della Chiesa Nuova; *CIL* 6.31539b, in basements of some houses near S. Stefano del Cacco; *CIL* 6.1233b = 31539 c, now near St. Peter's

IV. A. NA  C. NA  E. NA
B. NA  D. NA

V. Restoration of Vespasianic pomerial boundary rather than enlargement

VI. Cippi of travertine, except *CIL* 6.31539b of serpentine (?) marble

VII. *NSc*, 1933, 241, *CIL* 6.1233a = 31539a, 31539b (= *ILS* 311), 1233b = 31539c

## URBAN LEGISLATION

I. 122, and at other unspecified times during Hadrian's reign (documentary)

II. Applicable to Rome and provincial cities

III. NA

IV. A. NA    C. NA    E. NA
   B. NA    D. NA

V. NA

VI. NA

VII. *SC Acilianum* of 122: *Dig.* 30.1.41, 43; cf. *Dig.* 18.1.52; legislation against heavy wheeled vehicles in the city: *HA, Hadr.* 22.6; increased penalties for burial within the city: *Dig.* 47.12.3.5

## INTERVENTION IN BRICK-MAKING INDUSTRY (?)

I. 123 (brick stamps)

II. Rome

III. NA

IV. A. NA    C. NA    E. NA
   B. NA    D. NA

V. NA

VI. NA

VII. See Bloch, *Bolli*; Steinby, "CronFig" and "Ziegelstempel"

## RETAINING WALL AROUND ARA PACIS

I. Terminus post quem, 123 (brick stamps)

II. At the Ara Pacis (Regio IX)

III. No visible remains

V. A. 1.80–1.88 ht.
   B. 0.60    D. NA
   C. NA    E. NA

V. Height corresponds to the level of the figured friezes on exterior of the Ara Pacis

VI. Brick-faced concrete with travertine coping, which may have once held a grille

VII. —

## RESTORATION OF THE HOROLOGIUM SOLARIUM AUGUSTI (?)

I. 120s (?)

II. Central part of Solarium (Regio IX)

III. No visible remains

IV. A. 1.1 of earth, piled to either side of basin 1.1 ht. and ca. 6 w.
   B. 0.70    D. NA
   C. NA    E. NA

V. Decorative water basin placed directly over month line

VI. Basin, brick-faced concrete veneered with opus signinum, top capped with travertine coping

VII. —

## RESTORATION OF DIVORUM

I. Probable terminus ante quem, 126 (epigraphic)

II. East of southern half of Saepta (Regio IX)

III. No visible remains

IV. A. 75 w., 190 d.
   B. —    D. —
   C. —    E. —

V. Originally a sacred precinct for the Flavian gens

VI. Possible interior structure of brick-faced concrete with travertine blocks

VII. *II*, 13.1, 202–203, 233

## TEMPLE OF THE DEIFIED TRAJAN AND PLOTINA

I. 118–128 (epigraphic)

II. West northwest of Trajan's Column and southeast of Via Lata/Flaminia (Regio VIII)

III. A few architectural fragments visible: cornice in the Villa Albani; fragmentary column shaft and capital at the Foro di Traiano

IV. A. — B. —
    C. 1.897 diam., 14.785 ht. (= 50 Roman feet)
    D. Corinthian E. —
V. Extraordinarily large: capital, 2.12 ht.
VI. Columns, gray granite; architectural decoration, Luna marble
VII. *HA, Hadr.* 19.9; *CIL* 6.966 and 31215 = *ILS* 306 = Smallwood, #141a; Dio Cass. 69.10.3.1; P. Giss. 69 (?)

### PORTICOES FLANKING THE TEMPLE OF THE DEIFIED TRAJAN AND PLOTINA

I. 118–128 (?)
II. Between the Temple and the Libraries of Trajan (Regio IX)
III. No visible remains, except possible marble paving now mounted in the cortile of the Palazzo delle Assicurazioni Generali
IV. A. — B. —
    C. 1.80 diam.
    D. — E. —
V. —
VI. Columns, gray (and rose?) granite; entablature, white marble; porticoes, white marble paving and steps (?)
VII. *Forma Urbis*, pl. 28, frag. 29 g

### REWORKING OF NORTHWEST FACADE OF DOMUS TIBERIANA

I. Terminus post quem, 125 (brick stamps)
II. North slope of Palatine (Regio X)
III. Core largely extant, though in ruins
IV. A. 150 w., 20–35 ht.
    B. Varying thicknesses
    C. — D. —
    E. Barrel vaulting
V. External appearance of utilitarian architecture; interior walls stuccoed and frescoed

VI. Brick-faced concrete, with some walls of opus mixtum
VII. —

### ALTERATIONS IN THE "VESTIBULE" OF DOMITIAN

I. Terminus post quem, 125 (brick stamps)
II. Northwest edge of Palatine (Regio X)
III. Floors and external walls mostly extant, though in ruins
IV. A. —
    B. Ca. 1.0
    C. Pillars of northern porticus, 1.50 w., 1.10 d.
    D. —
    E. Barrel vaulting for interior rooms and for porticoes (?)
V. Appearance of utilitarian building, extensive use of opus spicatum, and hypocaust added to westernmost room
VI. Brick-faced concrete; frescoeing and marble revetment
VII. —

### PALAZZO IN THE HORTI SALLUSTIANI

I. Terminus post quem, 126, remodeled in late 130s (brick stamps)
II. Northeastern Rome, at head of valley between Pincian and Quirinal hills (Regio VII)
III. Circular hall and north and south wings largely extant, though stripped of decoration; upper stories destroyed
IV. A. Circular hall, 11.20 diam., 13.20 ht.; rear room, 5.30 w., 7.60 d.
    B. Ca. 0.60–4.80
    C. — D. —
    E. Segmental dome; barrel vaulting elsewhere
V. Interior ornate; appearance of utilitarian building on exterior
VI. Brick-faced concrete; decorative consoles, travertine; frame at entrance, marble (?); exterior, stuccoed with part rus-

ticated; interior, walls revetted with opus sectile or frescoed (in the wings); some floors, black and white mosaic, others revetted with opus sectile

VII. —

## REMODELING OF PARTS OF DOMUS AUGUSTIANA

I. 126–132 (brick stamps)

II. North (?) and west facades, Lararium, Basilica, and Cenatio Jovis of Domitian's palace on the Palatine (Regio X)

III. Lower sections of walls (median ht., 1.0) on facades; stairs in Lararium; much of reinforcement of Basilica; ca. 0.1 of hypocaust system in Cenatio Jovis

IV. A. NA
    B. Median 1.15 in work on facades
    C. NA    D. NA
    E. Barrel vaulting (?)

V. External appearance of utilitarian building; internally, added strength and amenity

VI. Brick-faced concrete

VII. —

## TEMPLE OF VENUS AND ROMA

I. 121–141, with terminus post quem for construction, 123 (literary, numismatic, brick stamps)

II. Velia (Regio IV)

III. Substructures still largely extant in situ, as well as physical impressions of original walls and of opus sectile floors; some fragments of architectural decoration

IV. A. Substructures, 100 w., 145 d.; aedes, 30 w., 90 d.
    B. Cella walls, 2.30 (26 ht.)
    C. 1.87 diam.
    D. Corinthian (?)
    E. Wooden trussed roofs

V. Classical Greek proportions and Hellenistic Greek design; with substructures, largest temple in Rome

VI. Substructures, concrete with brick, marble, basalt, and tufa inclusions; substructures and walls revetted with peperino tufa; columns, white marble (perhaps from rebuilding in 307); architectural decoration, Luna and Proconnesian marble; opus sectile floor, Proconnesian marble and porphyry (?)

VII. Dio Cass. 69.4.4; *HA, Hadr.* 19.12; Dio Cass. 56.15.1; Ath. 8.361F, with *BMC, Emp.* III, p. 282, no. 333, and pp. 422–23, nos. 1242–43; Cassiod., in Mommsen, *Chron. Min.* ii, p. 142; Jerome, *Chron.* p. 200 H.

## PORTICOES OF TEMPLE OF VENUS AND ROMA

I. 121–141 (?)

II. North and south margins of platform for Temple (Regio IV)

III. Some columns reerected on substructures, and substructures mostly extant

IV. A. 145 l.; north porticus 5.90 w.; south porticus, 7.60 w.
    B. Back wall of north porticus, ca. 1.2
    C. 1.18 diam.
    D. Corinthian
    E. Wooden trussed roofs

V. Combination of Roman and Pergamene architectural ornament; porticoes asymmetrical

VI. Gray granite columns, except cipollino in propylaea; architectural decoration, white marble

VII. —

## TRANSPORTATION OF COLOSSUS OF NERO, AND ALTERATION TO REPRESENT SOL

I. 121–138 (literary, and association with Temple of Venus and Roma)

II. Northeast of Temple of Venus and Roma, between Temple, Flavian Amphitheater, and Baths of Titus (Regio IV)

III. Place of Hadrianic base marked on modern pavement

IV. A. 35.4 ht. (120 Roman feet)
    B. NA    D. NA
    C. NA    E. NA

V. Colossus moved and altered in connection with construction of the Temple of Venus and Roma; Sol symbolic of eternity

VI. Hadrianic base, brick-faced concrete revetted with marble; statue, bronze over concrete and travertine core

VII. *HA, Hadr.* 19.12–13

## STRUCTURES BETWEEN PANTHEON AND SOUTH BUILDING, AND BETWEEN SAEPTA, PANTHEON, AND SOUTH BUILDING

I. 130s (brick stamps)

II. South of Pantheon, north of South Building, and west of Saepta (Regio IX)

III. Walls, floors, and roofing largely extant in southern structures; walls largely extant for eastern ones

IV. A. East and west walls of southern structures, 20 d.; central buttressing, 1.75 d.
    B. 1.22–1.53
    C. NA    D. NA
    E. Barrel vaulting within individual rooms, wooden pitched roof overall

V. Without obvious structural purpose

VI. Brick-faced concrete; interior paved with black and white mosaic

VII. —

## RESTORATION OF FORUM AUGUSTUM

I. 130s (stylistic)

II. South part of Forum Augustum (Regio VIII)

III. A very few architectural fragments extant, including capital in Foro di Augusto

IV. A. —    B. —    C. —

D. Corinthian
E. —

V. Pergamene-Ephesian school; schematic in comparison to Augustan work

VI. Capital and architectural fragments, Proconnesian marble

VII. *HA, Hadr.* 19.10

## MAUSOLEUM OF HADRIAN

I. Terminus post quem, 123 (brick stamps); terminus ante quem, 139 (epigraphic)

II. In the Horti Domitiae in the Ager Vaticanus, right bank of Tiber (Regio XIV)

III. Central structure largely extant for two-thirds original height, though exterior revetment in ruins; some fragments of architectural decoration in museum of Castel Sant' Angelo

IV. A. 50 ht.; square base, 85 on a side and 10–12 ht.; cylindrical stepped drum, 74 and 68 diam.
    B. Varied
    C. Pilasters, 1.60 (?)
    D. Corinthian
    E. Barrel vaulting and domes

V. South (entrance) wall revetted with epitaphs and panels carved with bucrania, poppy heads, and oak leaves; rustication used on drum; and statuary on top and on the corners of the square base

VI. Brick-faced concrete core; exterior decoration, travertine and Parian or Luna marble; interior, marble revetment (including giallo antico) and stucco; paving, black and white mosaic

VII. *HA, Hadr.* 19.11; *HA, Pii* 5.1; Dio Cass. 69.23; *CIL* 6.984

## PONS AELIUS

I. Terminus ante quem, 134 (epigraphic)

II. From the western Campus Martius to the Mausoleum of Hadrian, on axis with Mausoleum (connecting Regiones IX and XIV)

III. Largely extant until the end of the nineteenth century, when piers were rebuilt and roadway demolished

IV. A. Length overall, ca. 140, over river, 97.50; 10.95 w.
    B. NA    D. NA
    C. NA    E. NA

V. Decorated with herms or statues over each pier

VI. Travertine with peperino tufa over concrete core; roadway, paved with basalt, walkways, with travertine; balustrades, travertine

VII. *HA, Hadr.* 19.11; *CIL* 6.973; Dio Cass. 69.23; Pol. Silv. 545; Gnecchi, II, p. 8, no. 51, pl. 42.2; Küthmann and Overbeck, *Bautens Roms*, p. 64, no. 123

### REGULATION OF RELIGIOUS LIFE OF VICI

I. Pre–136 (?) (epigraphic)

II. NA

III. NA

IV. A. NA    C. NA    E. NA
    B. NA    D. NA

V. Unparalleled and short-lived imperial intervention in neighborhood life

VI. NA

VII. Inscription published in *ArchCl* 22 (1970) 138–51; cf. *CIL* 6.975 with *CIL* 6.31218 = *ILS* 6073 = Smallwood, #146

### TEMPIO DI SIEPE

I. Hadrianic (?) (architectural style)

II. North of Temple of the Deified Matidia (Regio IX)

III. No visible remains

IV. A. Dome, 9.37 diam. with oculus of 1.90 diam.; imposts of vaulting, 6.20–6.50 ht.
    B. —
    C. Ca. 0.59 diam., 5–5.30 ht. (with base and capital)
    D. Corinthian (internal)

E. Segmental dome, and barrel vaulting elsewhere

V. Unusual bull's-eye windows in segmental dome; very heavy cornice, ca. 1.20 ht.

VI. Brick-faced concrete; columns, cipollino or granite (?); architectural decoration, white marble

VII. —

### GRANT OF WORLD HEADQUARTERS IN ROME TO SACRED GUILD OF ATHLETES AND VICTORS

I. 134 (epigraphic)

II. Near the Baths of Trajan (Regio III?)

III. No known remains of building

IV. A. NA    C. NA    E. NA
    B. NA    D. NA

V. Permission to build granted in 134, but not implemented until 142

VI. NA

VII. *IG* 14.1054 = *IGUR* 1.235 = *IGRR* 1.149

### GRANT OF HEADQUARTERS IN ROME TO ECUMENICAL GUILD OF ACTORS

I. 134 (?) (epigraphic)

II. NA

III. NA

IV. A. NA    C. NA    E. NA
    B. NA    D. NA

V. NA

VI. NA

VII. Pickard-Cambridge, *Dramatic Festivals*, #15

### ATHENAEUM

I. Terminus post quem, 134 (literary)

II. Near the Forum of Trajan (?) (Regio VIII)

III. No identifiable remains

IV. A. —    C. —    E. —
    B. —    D. —

v. Greek cultural center

vi. —

vii. Aur. Vict. *Caes.* 14.2–3

## RESTORATION OF THE AUGURATORIUM

i. 136 (epigraphic)

ii. Palatine (Regio x)

iii. No visible remains

iv. A. —     C. —     E. —
    B. —     D. —

v. Association with founding legends of Rome

vi. —

vii. *CIL* 6.976; Regionary Catalogues (Nordh, *Libellus* 89.14); *Mirabilia* 28

## RESTORATION OF THE AEDES BONAE DEAE (SUBSAXANA ?)

i. 117–138 (literary)

ii. Northeast Aventine (Little Aventine) (?) (Regio xii)

iii. No identifiable remains

iv. A. —     C. —     E. —
    B. —     D. —

v. Association with founding legends of Rome

vi. —

vii. *HA, Hadr.* 19.11

## MONUMENT OF THE TONDI ADRIANEI

i. 136–138 (subjects, stylistics, and iconography)

ii. —

iii. Eight decorative Tondi (possibly complete set) preserved when reused on the Arch of Constantine and heads of main figures reworked

iv. A. 2.40 diam.
    B. —     D. —
    C. —     E. —

v. Association of traditional western and rustic gods with sacrifices, and depiction of Hadrian's successors

vi. Luna marble

vii. —

## MONUMENT WITH RELIEFS OF ADLOCUTIO OF HADRIAN AND APOTHEOSIS OF SABINA

i. Terminus post quem, end 137 (death of Sabina)

ii. Northern Campus Martius (?) (Regio ix)

iii. Heavily restored after removal from (fifth century) Arco di Portogallo

iv. A. Adlocutio relief, 2.67 ht., 2.09 w. (original size); apotheosis relief, 2.68 ht., 2.10 w. (original size)
    B. —     D. —
    C. —     E. —

v. Now heavily reworked

vi. Luna marble

vii. —

## MINOR AND LOST WORKS

*Incidental Repairs to Aqueducts, Ludus Magnus, and Banks of Tiber*
*Monument of Vota Vicennalia Relief* (137)
*Monument with Chatsworth Relief*
*Monument with Anaglypha (?)*

## SERAPEUM–CANOPUS OF VILLA ADRIANA

i. Villa mostly completed, 118–133; Serapeum-Canopus, 125–128

ii. 28 km. northeast of Rome (Latium)

iii. Many structures still extant in ruins and restorations

iv. A. At least 120 hectares; Canopus: ca. 120 d., 19 w., 1.60 deep; Serapeum: semicircular apse, 16.75 diam.
    B. Varied     C. Varied
    D. Ionic and Corinthian
    E. Serapeum: barrel vaulting, segmental half dome

v. Rich, eclectic sculptural decoration (Atticizing, Egyptianizing), and early use of glass mosaic on dome

vi. Brick-faced concrete; columns, cipollino; architectural decoration, white marble; mosaics of white, black, and red glass; polychrome marble revetment; frescoeing and stucco

vi. *HA, Hadr.* 26.5; Aur. Vict. *Caes.* 14.6

## MARKET BUILDING UNDER S. LORENZO IN LUCINA

i. Late Hadrianic (construction technique)

ii. Northern Campus Martius (Regio IX)

iii. Some remains visible in situ

iv. A. 29.5 w., 59 d. (100 by 200 Roman feet)
   B. —         D. —
   C. —         E. —

v. Built over Flavian house on northeast quadrant of Horologium Solarium Augusti

vi. Brick-faced concrete, travertine

vii. —

## INSULAE UNDER GALLERIA COLONNA

i. 123–138 (brick stamps)

ii. East of Via Lata/Flaminia, opposite Via Recta (Regio VII)

iii. No visible remains

iv. A. 120 w., 220 d.; each insula 48.50 w., 62.40 d.
   B. 0.60
   C. Pilasters, 1.03 w., 0.88 d.
   D. —
   E. Barrel vaulting (?)

v. Apparently built on land previously open

vi. Brick-faced concrete; bases for decorative brick pilasters, travertine; springing of facade arches, travertine

vii. —

## ADDITIONS TO HORREA ALONG WEST SIDE OF VIA LATA/FLAMINIA, SOUTH OF ARCH OF CLAUDIUS TO MODERN PIAZZA VENEZIA

i. Terminus post quem, 123 (brick stamp), but possibly late Hadrianic (construction technique)

ii. East of Serapeum and Divorum (Regio IX)

iii. No visible remains

iv. A. At least 230 d.
   B. —      C. —      D. —
   E. Barrel vaulting

v. Remodeling of Claudian structure

vi. Brick-faced concrete

vii. —

BIBLIOGRAPHY

Listed here are only the most important works consulted and cited in the notes and not found in the list of Abbreviations at the beginning of the text. The conventions and abbreviations of ancient authors and works that are suggested in *AJA* and the *Oxford Classical Dictionary* have been adopted. For other abbreviated references below, see the list of Abbreviations.

# BIBLIOGRAPHY

AMICI, C. M. *Foro di Traiano: Basilica Ulpia e Biblioteche.* Studi e materiali dei Musei e Monumenti Comunali di Roma, X Ripartizione: antichità, belle arti e problemi di cultura. Rome 1982.

ANDERSON, J. C., Jr. "Domitian, the Argiletum and the Temple of Peace." *AJA* 86 (1982) 101–10.

—— *The Historical Topography of the Roman Imperial Fora.* Collection Latomus 182. Brussels 1984.

—— "A Topographical Tradition in Fourth Century Chronicles: Domitian's Building Program." *Historia* 32 (1983) 93–105.

APOLLONJ-GHETTI, B. M., A. FERRUA, E. JOSI, and E. KIRSCHBAUM. *Esplorazioni sotto la confessione di S. Pietro in Vaticano eseguite negli anni 1940–1941.* Vatican City 1951.

ARNOLD, I. R. "Agonistic Festivals in Italy and Sicily." *AJA* 64 (1960) 245–51.

ASHBY, T. "The Bodleian Ms. of Pirro Ligorio." *JRS* 9 (1919) 170–201.

AURIGEMMA, S. *Villa Adriana.* Rome 1961 [1962].

AYMARD, J. *Essai sur les chasses romaines, des origines à la fin du siècle des Antonins. Cynegetica.* BEFAR 171. Paris 1951.

BARATTOLO, A. "Nuove ricerche sull'architettura del Tempio di Venere e di Roma in età Adrianea." *RömMitt* 80 (1973) 243–69.

—— "Sulla decorazione delle celle del Tempio di Venere e di Roma all'epoca di Adriano." *BullComm* 84 (1974–75) [1977] 133–48.

—— "Il Tempio di Venere e Roma: un tempio 'greco' nell' Urbe." *RömMitt* 85 (1978) 397–410.

BARDON, H. *Les Empereurs et les lettres latines d'Auguste à Hadrien.* 2nd ed. Collection d'études anciennes. Paris 1968.

—— "La Naissance d'un temple." *REL* 33 (1955) 166–82.

BARIGAZZI, A. *Opere: Favorino di Arelate.* Florence 1966.

BARNES, T. D. "Hadrian and Lucius Verus." *JRS* 57 (1967) 65–79.

—— *The Sources of the "Historia Augusta."* Collection Latomus 155. Brussels 1978.

BAROSSO, M. "Le costruzioni sottostanti la Basilica Massenziana e Velia." In *Atti del 5° congresso di studi romani*, II. Rome 1940, 58–62.

BARTOLI, A. "Avanzi di fortificazioni medievali del Palatino." *RendLinc*, ser. 5, 18 (1909) 527–39.

—— *Curia Senatus: lo scavo e il restauro.* Istituto di Studi Romani. I monumenti romani 3. Rome 1963.

—— *I monumenti antichi di Roma nei disegni degli Uffizi di Firenze.* 5 vols. Rome 1914–22.

BAUER, H. "Il Foro Transitorio e il Tempio di Giano." *RendPontAcc* 49 (1976–77) [1978] 117–48.

BAYET, J. *Histoire politique et psychologique de la religion romaine.* 2nd ed. Paris 1969.

BEAUJEU, J. "Le Paganisme romain sous le Haut Empire." *ANRW* II.16.1 (1978) 3–26.

BECATTI, G. *La colonna coclide istoriata.* Studi e materiali del Museo dell'Impero Romano 6. Rome 1960.

—— "La Colonna Traiana, espressione somma del rilievo storico romano." *ANRW* II.12.1 (1982) 536–78.

BEK, L. "*Questiones Convivales.* The Idea of the Triclinium and the Staging of the Convivial Ceremony from Rome to Byzantium." *AnalDan* 12 (1983) 81–107.

BELL, H. I. "Antinoopolis: A Hadrianic Foundation in Egypt." *JRS* 30 (1940) 133–47.

BENARIO, H.W. *A Commentary on the "vita Hadriani" in the "Historia Augusta."* Chico, Calif. 1980.

—— "Rome of the Severi." *Latomus* 17 (1958) 712–22.

BENJAMIN, A. S. "The Altars of Hadrian in Athens and Hadrian's Panhellenic Program." *Hesperia* 32 (1963) 57–86.

BERTOLDI, M. E. *Ricerche sulla decorazione architettonica del Foro Traiano.* Seminario di archeologia e storia dell'arte greca e romana dell'Università di Roma, studi miscellanei 3. Rome 1962.

BIANCHI BANDINELLI, R. and M. TORELLI. *L'arte dell'antichità classica*, II. *Etruria—Roma*. Turin 1976.

BICKERMAN, E. "Consecratio." In *Le Culte des souverains dans l'empire romain*, 1–25.

BICKERMAN, E. J. "Diva Augusta Marciana." *AJP* 95 (1974) 362–76.

BIRLEY, A. R. *Marcus Aurelius*. Boston 1966.

BLOCH, H. "A New Edition of the Marble Plan of Ancient Rome." *JRS* 51 (1961) 143–52.

—— "The Serapeum of Ostia and the Brick Stamps of 123 A.D.: A New Landmark in the History of Roman Architecture." *AJA* 63 (1959) 225–40.

BLUM, G. "Numismatique d'Antinous." *Journal international d'archéologie numismatique* 16 (1914) 33–70.

BLÜMEL, C. "Ein Porträt des Antoninus Pius." *JdI* 47 (1932) 90–96.

BOATWRIGHT, M.T. "The 'Ara Ditis-*Ustrinum* of Hadrian' in the Western Campus Martius, and Other Problematic Roman *Ustrina*." *AJA* 89 (1985) 485–97.

BODEI GIGLIONI, G. *Lavori pubblici e occupazione nell'antichità classica*. Bologna 1974.

BÖMER, F. *P. Ovidius Naso. Die Fasten*. Wissenschaftliche Kommentare zu lateinischen und griechischen Schriftstellern. Heidelberg 1957–58.

—— *Untersuchungen über die Religion der Sklaven in Griechenland und Rom. Erster Teil: Die wichtigsten Kulte und Religionen in Rom und in lateinischen Westen.* 2nd ed. Revised by P. Herz. Forschungen zur antiken Sklaverei 14.1. Weisbaden 1981.

BONANNO, A. *Portraits and Other Heads on Roman Historical Relief up to the Age of Septimius Severus*. British Archaeological Reports Suppl., ser. 6. Oxford 1976.

BONGIORNO, A. "Rilievo planimetrico dell'antico edificio di S. Maria Antiqua." *QuadIstTopAnt* 5 (1968) 89–90.

BONI, G. "Esplorazione del Forum Ulpium." *NSc*, ser. 5, 4 (1907) 361–427.

BONNER, S. F. *Education in Ancient Rome: From the Elder Cato to the Younger Pliny*. Berkeley and Los Angeles 1977.

BORGATTI, M. *Castel Sant'Angelo in Roma*. Rome 1931.

BOURGUET, E. *De rebus Delphicis imperatoriae aetatis capita duo*. Montepessulano 1905.

BOWERSOCK, G. W. *Augustus and the Greek World*. Oxford 1965.

—— *Greek Sophists in the Roman Empire*. Oxford 1969.

—— "The Imperial Cult: Perceptions and Persistence." In *Jewish and Christian Self-definition*, III: *Self-definition in the Greco-Roman World*. Edited by B. F. Meyer and E. P. Sanders. Philadelphia 1982, 171–82.

—— ed. *Approaches to the Second Sophistic*. University Park, Pa. 1974.

BRADLEY, K. R. "Imperial Virtues in Suetonius' *Caesares*." *Journal of Indo-European Studies* 4 (1976) 245–53.

—— "Nero's Retinue in Greece, A.D. 66/67." *Illinois Classical Studies* 4 (1979) 152–57.

BRAUNERT, H. "Das Athenaeum zu Rom bei den *Scriptores Historiae Augustae*." *HAC* 1963. Bonn 1964, 9–42.

—— *Die Binnenwanderung: Studien zur Sozialgeschichte Ägyptens in der Ptolemäer- und Kaiserzeit.* Bonner historische Forschungen 26. Bonn 1964.

—— "Griechische und römische Komponenten im Stadtrecht von Antinoopolis." *Journal of Juristic Papyrology* 14 (1962) 73–88.

BRENDEL, O. "Rom, Kaiserfora." *AA* 48 (1933) 600–625.

BRILLIANT, R. *Gesture and Rank in Roman Art: The Use of Gestures to Denote Status in Roman Sculpture and Coinage*. Memoirs of the Connecticut Academy of Arts and Sciences 14. New Haven 1963.

—— Review of *Forum Romanum*, by P. Zanker. In *Gnomon* 46 (1974) 523–25.

BROWN, D. F. "Architectura Numismatica." Ph.D. diss., New York University, 1941.

—— *Temples of Rome as Coin Types*. American Numismatic Society, Numismatic Notes and Monographs 90. New York 1940.

BROWN, F. E. "Hadrianic Architecture." In *Essays in Memory of K. Lehmann.* Edited by L. F. Sandler. New York 1964, 55–58.

—— "The Regia." *MAAR* 12 (1935) 67–88.

—— "Vitruvius and the Liberal Art of Architecture." *Bucknell Review* 11.4 (1963) 99–107.

BRUNT, P. A. "The 'Fiscus' and Its Development." *JRS* 56 (1966) 75–91.

—— "Free Labour and Public Works at Rome." *JRS* 70 (1980) 81–100.

—— "On Historical Fragments and Epitomes." *CQ* 30 (1980) 477–94.

—— "Princeps and Equites." *JRS* 73 (1983) 42–75.

—— "The Role of the Senate in the Augustan Regime." *CQ* 34 (1984) 423–44.

BUCHNER, E. *Die Sonnenuhr des Augustus. Nachdruck aus "RM" 1976 und 1980 und Nachtrag über die Ausgrabung 1980/1981.* Mainz 1982. This contains his "Horologium Solarium Augusti. Bericht über die Ausgrabungen 1979/1980," *RömMitt* 87 (1980) 355–73; his "Solarium Augusti und Ara Pacis," *RömMitt* 83 (1976) 319–65; and a "Nachtrag."

BULLE, H. "Ein Jagddenkmal des Kaisers Hadrian." *JdI* 34 (1919) 144–72.

BUSCHOR, E. "Die hadrianischen Jagdbilder." *RömMitt* 38/39 (1923–24) 52–54.

BUZZETTI, C. "Nota sulla topografia dell'Ager Vaticanus." *QuadIstTopAnt* 5 (1968) 105–11.

CAGNAT, R. *Cours d'épigraphie latine.* 4th ed. Paris 1914.

CALABI LIMENTANI, I. *Epigrafia latina, con un appendice bibliografica di A. Degrassi.* 3rd ed. Milan 1974.

CALDERINI, A. *Dizionario dei nomi geografici e topografici dell'egitto greco-romano,* I.2. Madrid 1966. S.v. Antinooupolis, 69–114.

CALLMER, C. "Antike Bibliotheken." *OpusArch* 3 (1944) 144–93.

CALZA, R. "Un problema di iconografia imperiale sull'arco di Costantino." *Rend-*
*PontAcc* 32 (1959–60) [1960] 133–61.

CAPUTO, G. "Sincretismo religioso ed espressione figurativa in Tripolitania." *Quaderni di archeologia della Libia* 9 (1977) 119–24.

CARANDINI, A. *Vibia Sabina. Funzione politica, iconografia e il problema del classicismo adrianeo.* Accademia toscana di scienze e lettere, "La Colombaria." Studi 13. Florence 1969.

CARCOPINO, J. *Passion et politique chez les Césars.* Paris 1958.

CASTAGNOLI, F. "Il Campo Marzio nell'antichità." *MemLinc,* ser. 8, 1 (1946) 93–193.

—— "Il circo di Nerone in Vaticano." *RendPontAcc* 32 (1959–60) [1960] 97–121.

—— "Due archi trionfali della Via Flaminia presso Piazza Sciarra." *BullComm* 70 (1942) [1943] 57–82.

—— "Gli edifici rappresentati in un rilievo del sepolcro degli Haterii." *BullComm* 69 (1941) 59–69.

—— "Minerva Calcidica." *ArchCl* 12 (1960) 91–95.

—— "Note di topografia romana." *BullComm* 74 (1951–52) [1954] 49–56.

—— "Note numismatiche." *ArchCl* 5 (1953) 104–11.

—— "Note sulla topografia del Palatino e del Foro Romano." *ArchCl* 16 (1964) 173–99.

—— "Pirro Ligorio topografo di Roma antica." *Palladio* 2 (1952) 97–102.

—— "Su alcuni problemi topografici del Palatino." *RendLinc,* ser. 8, 34 (1979) 331–47.

—— "Il Tempio dei Penati e la Velia." *RivFil* 74 (1946) 157–65.

—— "Il tempio Romano: Questioni di terminologia e di tipologia." *PBSR* 52 (1984) 3–20.

CASTAGNOLI, F. and L. COZZA. "L'angolo meridionale del Foro della Pace." *BullComm* 76 (1956–58) [1959] 119–42.

CASTRÉN, P. and H. LILIUS. *Graffiti del Palatino,* II. *Domus Tiberiana. Acta Instituti Romani Finlandiae* 4. Helsinki 1970.

CÉBAILLAC, M. "Octavia, épouse de Gamala, et la 'Bona Dea.' " *MélRome* 85 (1973) 517–52.

CHAMPLIN, E. "Figlinae Marcianae." *Athenaeum* 71 (1983) 257–64.

—— *Fronto and Antonine Rome*. Cambridge, Mass. 1980.

—— "Hadrian's Heir." *ZPE* 1 (1976) 79–89.

CHARLES-PICARD, G. *Rome et les villes d'Italie des Gracques à la morte d'Auguste*. Paris 1978.

CHARLESWORTH, M. P. "The Refusal of Divine Honours, an Augustan Formula." *PBSR* 15 (1939) 1–10.

CHASTAGNOL, A. *La Préfecture urbaine à Rome sous le Bas-Empire*. Publications de la Faculté des lettres et sciences humaines d'Alger 34. Paris 1960.

CIANFARANI, V. "Rilievo romano di Villa Torlonia." *BullComm* 73 (1949–50) [1952] 235–54.

CLAIRMONT, C. W. *Die Bildnisse des Antinous*. Bibliotheca Helvetica Romana 6. Bern 1966.

CLARKE, M. W. *Higher Education in the Ancient World*. Albuquerque 1971.

—— "The Date of the *Consecratio* of Vespasian." *Historia* 15 (1966) 318–27.

COARELLI, F. "L'area sacra di Largo Argentina. Topografia e storia." In *L'area sacra di Largo Argentina*. Studi e materiali dei Musei e Monumenti Comunali di Roma, X Ripartizione: antichità, belle arti e problemi di cultura. Rome 1981, 11–49.

—— "Il Campo Marzio occidentale. Storia e topografia." *MélRome* 89 (1977) 807–46.

—— "Il comizio dalle origini alla fine della Repubblica. Cronologia e topografia." *PdP* 32 (1977) 166–238.

—— *Il Foro Romano. Periodo arcaico*. Rome 1983.

—— *Lazio*. Guide archeologiche Laterza 5. Bari 1982.

—— "Navalia, Tarentum e la topografia del Campo Marzio meridionale." *QuadIstTopAnt* 5 (1968) 27–37.

—— "Il Pantheon, l'apoteosi di Augusto e l'apoteosi di Romolo." In *Città e architettura*, 41–46.

—— "La Porta Trionfale e la Via dei Trionfi." *DialArch* 2 (1968) 55–103.

—— "Il sepolcro degli Scipioni." *DialArch* 6 (1972) 36–106.

—— "Il Tempio di Bellona." *BullComm* 80 (1965–67) [1968] 37–72.

COLINI, A. M. "Il Campidoglio nell'antichità." *Capitolium* 40.4 (1965) 175–85.

—— "Compitum Acili." *BullComm* 78 (1961–62) [1964] 147–57.

—— "Considerazioni su la Velia da Nerone in poi." In *Città e architettura*, 129–45.

—— "Forum Pacis." *BullComm* 65 (1937) [1938] 7–40.

—— "Horti Spei Veteris, Palatium Sessorianum." *MemPontAcc*, ser. 3, 8 (1955) 137–77.

—— "La sala rotonda delle Terme di Agrippa." *Capitolium* 32.9 (1957) 6–14.

—— *Stadium Domitiani*. I monumenti romani 1. Rome 1943.

COLINI, A. M. and L. COZZA. *Ludus Magnus*. Rome 1962.

COLINI, A. M. and C. Q. GIGLIOLI. "Relazione della prima campagna di scavo nel Mausoleo d'Augusto." *BullComm* 54 (1926) [1927] 191–234.

CONDURACHI, E. "La Genèse des sujets de chasse des *tondi adrianei* de l'arc de Constantin." In *Atti VII° Congr. internaz. di archeol. class., Roma-Napoli, sett. 1958*, II. Rome 1961, 451–59.

CORBIER, M. *L'"aerarium Saturni" et l'"aerarium militare." Administration et prosopographie sénatoriale*. Collection de l'Ecole française de Rome 24. Rome 1974.

COZZA, L. "Pianta marmorea severiana, nuove ricomposizioni." *QuadIstTopAnt* 5 (1968) 9–17.

—— "Le tegole di marmo del Pantheon." In *Città e architettura*, 109–18.

COZZO, G. "Una industria nella Roma imperiale. La corporazione dei figuli ed i bolli doliari." *MemLinc*, ser. 6, 5 (1936) 233–366.

CRAWFORD, D. J. "Imperial Estates." In *Studies in Roman Property*, 35–70.

CRAWFORD, M. H. "Roman Imperial Coin Types and the Formation of Public Opinion." In *Studies in Numismatic Method Pre-*

*sented to Philip Grierson.* Edited by C.N.L. Brooke, B.H.I.H. Stewart, J. G. Pollard, and T. R. Volk. Cambridge 1983, 47–64.

—— *Roman Republican Coinage.* 2 vols. London and New York 1974.

CROOK, J. *Consilium Principis. Imperial Councils and Counsellors from Augustus to Diocletian.* Cambridge 1955, reprinted New York 1975.

D'ARMS, J. H. *Commerce and Social Standing in Ancient Rome.* Cambridge, Mass. and London 1981.

DE FINE LICHT, K. *The Rotunda in Rome. A Study of Hadrian's Pantheon.* Jutland Archeological Society Publications 8. Copenhagen 1968.

DE FRANCISCIS, A. and R. PANE. *Mausolei romani in Campania.* Naples 1957.

DEGRASSI, A. "Epigrafia romana." *Doxa* 2 (1949) 84–85.

—— "Frammenti inediti di calendario romano." *Athenaeum* 25 (1947) 127–39.

—— "P. Cluvius Maximus Paullinus." *Epigraphica* 1 (1939) 307–21.

DELBRÜCK, R. "Bemerkung. Nachtrag zu Seite 8ff., 'Der Südostbau am Forum Romanum.' " *JdI* 36 (1921) 186–87.

—— "Der Südostbau am Forum Romanum." *JdI* 36 (1921) 8–33.

DEN BOER, W. "Religion and Literature in Hadrian's Policy." *Mnemosyne* 8 (1955) 123–44.

—— "Trajan's Deification and Hadrian's Succession." *Ancient Society* 6 (1975) 203–12.

DERCHAIN, P. "A propos de l'obélisque d'Antinoüs." In *Le Monde grec . . . Hommages à Claire Préaux.* Edited by J. Bingen, G. Cambier, and G. Nachtergael. Brussels 1975, 808–13.

DE ROSSI, G. M. "La Via Aurelia dal Marta al Fiora." *QuadIstTopAnt* 4 (1968) 121–55.

DE RUGGIERO, E. *Il Foro Romano.* Rome 1913.

—— *Lo stato e le opere pubbliche in Roma antica.* Piccola biblioteca di scienze moderne 317. Turin 1925.

DE' SPAGNOLIS, M. "Contributi per una nuova lettura del Mausoleo di Adriano." *BdA* 61 (1976) 62–68.

D'ONOFRIO, C. *Castel Sant'Angelo.* Rome 1971.

—— *Gli obelischi di Roma.* 2nd ed. Rome 1967.

D'ORGEVAL, B. *L'Empereur Hadrian, oeuvre législative et administrative.* Paris 1950.

DOSIO, G. A. *Roma Antica e i disegni di architettura agli Uffizi.* Edited by F. Borsi et al. Rome 1976.

DRERUP, H. "Architektur als Symbol. Zur zeitgenössischen Bewertung der römischen Architektur." *Gymnasium* 73 (1966) 181–96.

DRESSEL, H. "Der Matidiatempel auf einem Medaillon des Hadrianus." *Corolla Numismatica in Honour of Barclay Head.* Oxford 1906, 16–28.

DUNCAN-JONES, R. *The Economy of the Roman Empire. Quantitative Studies.* 2nd ed. Cambridge 1982.

DURRY, M. *Laudatio Turiae. Eloge funèbre d'une matrone romaine (Eloge dit de Turia).* Collection des universités de France. Paris 1950.

ECK, W. "Vibia(?) Sabina, No. 72b." *RE, Suppl.* 15 (1978) 909–14.

EISNER, M. "Zur Typologie der Mausoleen des Augustus und des Hadrian." *RömMitt* 86 (1979) 319–24.

ERMAN, A. "Der Obelisk des Antinous." *RömMitt* 11 (1896) 113–21.

—— *Die Religion der Ägypter.* 3rd ed. Berlin 1934.

—— "Römische Obelisken." *Abhandlungen der königlich preussischen Akademie der Wissenschaften* 4 (1917) 3–47.

ETIENNE, R. "Les Sénateurs espagnols sous Trajan et Hadrien." In *Empereurs d'Espagne,* 55–85.

FAYER, C. *Il culto della Dea Roma. Origine e diffusione nell'Impero.* Pescara 1976.

FEA, O. *Miscellanea filogica, critica e antiquaria.* Vol. I. Rome 1790.

FEARS, J. R. *"Princeps a diis electus": The Divine Election of the Emperor as a Political Concept at Rome.* PMAAR 26. Rome 1977.

FINSEN, H. *Domus Flavia sur le Palatin: Aula Regia—Basilica. AnalDan*, Supplement 2. Copenhagen 1962.

FINSEN, H. *La Résidence de Domitien sur le Palatin. AnalDan*, Supplement 5. Copenhagen 1969.

FIORANI, G. "Problemi architettonici del Foro di Cesare." *QuadIstTopAnt* 5 (1968) 91–103.

FLORIANI SQUARCIAPINO, M. *La scuola di Aphrodisia*. Studi e materiale del Museo dell'Impero Romano 3. Rome 1943.

FOLLET, S. *Athènes au II^e et au III^e siècle: études chronologiques et prosopographiques*. Collection d'études anciennes. Paris 1976.

FORBES, C. A. "Ancient Athletic Guilds." *CP* 50 (1955) 238–52.

FRANK, T. *Economic Survey of Ancient Rome*. Vol. v. Baltimore 1940.

FRAZER, A. "The Roman Imperial Funeral Pyre." *JSAH* 27.3 (1968) 209.

FRISCHER, B. "*Monumenta et Arae Honoris Virtutisque Causa*, or, The Case of the Missing Bodies." *BullComm* 98 (1982–83) [1984] 51–86.

FROTHINGHAM, A. L., Jr. "A Revised List of Roman Memorial and Triumphal Arches." *AJA* 8 (1904) 1–34.

FRUTAZ, A. P. *Le piante di Roma*. Rome 1962.

GAGÉ, J. "Le Colosse et la fortune de Rome." *MélRome* 45 (1928) 106–22.

—— *Récherches sur les Jeux Séculaires*. Collection d'études latines. Série scientifique 11. Paris 1934.

—— "Le *sollemne urbis* du 21 avril au III^e siècle ap. J.-C. Rites positifs et speculations séculaires." In *Mélanges . . . H.-C. Puech*. Paris 1974, 225–41.

—— "Le *Templum urbis* et les origines de l'idée de *renovatio*." In *Mélanges F. Cumont*. Annuaire de l'Institute de philologie et d'histoire orientales et slaves 4. Brussels 1936, 151–87.

GARNSEY, P. "Urban Property Investment." In *Studies in Roman Property*, 123–36.

GATTI, E. and M. DE' SPAGNOLIS. "Un intervento nel centro storico di Roma: Impianto termale all'estremità della regio VII." *QuadAEI* 5 (1981) 132–41.

GATTI, G. "Caratteristiche edilizie di un quartiere di Roma del II secolo d. Cr." In *Saggi di storia dell'architettura in onore del professore Vincenzo Fasolo*. Rome 1961, 49–66.

—— "Il Mausoleo di Augusto, studio di ricostruzione." *Capitolium* 10 (1934) 457–64.

—— "Il portico degli argonauti e la basilica di Nettuno." *Atti del III^o convegno nazionale di storia dell'architettura, Rome 1938*. Rome 1940, 61–73.

—— "I Saepta Julia nel Campo Marzio." *L'Urbe* 2.9 (1937) 8–23.

—— "*Saepta Julia e Porticus Aemilia* nella *Forma* Severiana." *BullComm* 62 (1934) 123–49.

—— "Topografia dell'Iseo Campense." *RendPontAcc* 20 (1943–44) [1945] 117–63.

GAUER, W. "Ein Dakerdenkmal Domitians. Die Trajanssäule und das sogenannte grosse trajanische Relief." *JdI* 88 (1973) 318–50.

—— *Untersuchungen zur Trajanssäule. Erster Teil. Darstellungsprogramm und künstlerischer Entwurf*. Monumenta artis romanae 13. Berlin 1977.

GAZZOLA, P. *Ponti romani. Contributo ad un indice sistematico con studio critico bibliografico*. Florence 1963.

GEAGAN, D. J. "Hadrian and the Athenian Dionysiac Technitai." *TAPA* 103 (1972) 133–60.

—— "Roman Athens: Some Aspects of Life and Culture, I: 86 B.C.–A.D. 267." *ANRW* II.7.1 (1979) 373–437.

GERADE, P. "Le Règlement successoral d'Hadrien." *REA* 52 (1950) 258–77.

GÉRARD, J. *Juvénal et la réalité contemporaine*. Paris 1976.

GILLIAM, J. F. "On Divi under the Severi." In *Hommages à M. Renard*, II. Collection Latomus 102. Brussels 1969, 284–89.

GIOVANNOLI, A. *Vedute degli antichi vestigi di Roma*. Rome 1619.

GIRARD, J.-L. "Domitien et Minerve: une prédilection impériale." *ANRW* II.17.1 (1981) 233–45.

GIULIANI, C. F. "Domus Flavia: una nuova lettura." *RömMitt* 84 (1977) 91–106.

—— "Il lato nord-ovest della Piazza d'Oro." *QuadIstTopAnt* 8 (1975) 3–53.

—— "Note sull'architettura delle residenze imperiali dal I al III secolo d.Cr." *ANRW* II.12.1 (1982) 233–58.

—— "Volte e cupole a doppia calotta in età adrianea." *RömMitt* 82 (1975) 329–42.

GIULIANI, C. F. and P. VERDUCHI. *Foro Romano. L'area centrale.* Florence 1980.

GJERSTAD, E. "Pales, Palilia, Parilia." In *Studia romana in honorem Petri Krarup Septuagenarii.* Edited by K. Ascani. Odense 1976, 1–5.

GORDON, A. E. "The Cults of Lanuvium." *CPCA* II.2 (1938) 21–58.

—— "Q. Veranius, Consul A.D. 49. A Study Based upon His Recently Identified Sepulchral Inscription." *CPCA* II.5 (1952) 231–314.

GÖTZE, B. "Antike Bibliotheken." *JdI* 52 (1937) 225–47.

—— *Ein römisches Rundgrab in Falerii.* Stuttgart 1939.

GRAINDOR, P. *Athènes sous Hadrien.* Cairo 1934, reprinted New York 1973.

GRANT, M. *Roman Anniversary Issues.* Cambridge 1950.

GREIFENHAGEN, A. "Bona Dea." *RömMitt* 52 (1937) 227–44.

GRELLE, F. *L'autonomia cittadina fra Traiano e Adriano. Teoria e prassi dell'organizzazione municipale.* Naples 1972.

GRETHER, G. "Livia and the Roman Imperial Cult." *AJP* 67 (1946) 222–52.

GRIMAL, P. *Les Jardins romains.* 2nd ed. Paris 1969.

GROS, P. "Apothéose impériale et rites funéraires au second siècle de notre ère." *RHR* 171 (1967) 117–20.

—— *Architecture et société à Rome et en Italie centro-méridionale aux deux derniers siècles de la République.* Collection Latomus 156. Brussels 1978.

—— "Aurea Templa." *Recherches sur l'architecture religieuse de Rome à l'époque d'Auguste.* BEFAR 231. Rome 1976.

GUARDUCCI, M. "Documenti del Iº secolo nella necropoli Vaticana." *RendPontAcc* 29 (1956–57) [1958] 111–37.

—— "Nuove iscrizioni nella zona del circo di Nerone in Vaticano." *RendPontAcc* 32 (1959–60) [1960] 123–32.

—— "La religione di Adriano." In *Empereurs d'Espagne*, 209–21.

—— *The Tomb of St. Peter. The New Discoveries in the Sacred Grottoes of the Vatican.* Translated by J. McLellan. Rome 1960.

GUEY, J. "Devrait-on dire: le Panthéon de Septime-Sévère?" *MélRome* 53 (1936) 198–249.

GULLINI, G. "Apollodoro e Adriano. Ellenismo e classicismo nell'architettura romana." *BdA* 53 (1968) [1971] 63–80.

GUSMAN, P. *La Villa impériale de Tibur.* Paris 1904.

GUYOT, P. "Antinous als Eunuch: zur christlichen Polemik gegen das Heidentum." *Historia* 30 (1981) 250–54.

HALFMANN, H. *Die Senatoren aus dem östlichen Teil des Imperium Romanum bis zum Ende des 2. Jahrhunderts n. Chr.* Hypomnemata 58. Göttingen 1979.

HALSBERGHE, G. H. *The Cult of Sol Invictus.* EPRO 23. Leiden 1972.

HAMBERG, P. G. *Studies in Roman Imperial Art, with Special Reference to the State Reliefs of the Second Century.* Uppsala 1945.

HAMMOND, M. *The Antonine Monarchy.* PMAAR 19. Rome 1959.

—— *The Augustan Principate in Theory and Practice during the Julio-Claudian Period.* Cambridge, Mass. 1933.

—— "A Statue of Trajan Represented on the Anaglypha Traiani." *MAAR* 21 (1953) 125–83.

—— "The Tribunician Day during the Early Empire." *MAAR* 15 (1938) 23–61.

HANNESTAD, N. "The Portraits of Aelius Caesar." *AnalDan* 7 (1974) 67–100.

—— "Über das Grabmal des Antinoos. Topographische und thematische Studien im Canopus-Gebiet der Villa Adriana." *AnalDan* 11 (1983) 69–108.

HANSEN, E. *La Piazza d'Oro e la sua cupola.*

*AnalDan*, Supplement 1. Copenhagen 1960.

HARE, A.J.C. *Walks in Rome*. 17th ed. London 1905.

HARLEMAN, E. "Questions sur l'Athenaeum de l'empereur Hadrien." *Eranos* 79 (1981) 57–64.

HASSEL, F. J. *Der Trajansbogen in Benevent. Ein Bauwerk des römischen Senates*. Mainz 1966.

HASTRUP, T. "Forum Iulium as a Manifestation of Power." *AnalDan* 2 (1962) 45–61.

HEILMEYER, W.-D. "Apollodorus von Damaskus, der Architekt des Pantheon." *JdI* 90 (1975) 316–47.

—— *Korinthische Normalkapitelle. Studien zur Geschichte der römischen Architekturdekoration*. *RömMitt*, Erg.-H. 16. Heidelberg 1970.

HEINZ, W. *Römische Thermen. Badewesen und Badeluxus im römischen Reich*. Munich 1983.

HELEN, T. *Organization of Roman Brick Production in the First and Second Centuries* A.D.: *An Interpretation of Roman Brick Stamps*. Annales Academiae Scientiarum Fennicae, Dissertationes Humanarum Litterarum 5. Helsinki 1975.

HENDERSON, B. W. *The Life and Principate of the Emperor Hadrian*, A.D. *76–138*. London 1923.

HENZEN, W. "Rilievi di marmo scoperti sul foro romano." *BullInst*, 1872, 274–81.

HERMANN, A. "Antinous infelix. Zur Typologie des Heiligen-Unheiligen in der Spatantike." In *Mullus. Festschrift Theodor Klauser*. Edited by A. Stuiber and A. Hermann. Jahrbuch für Antike und Christentum, Erg. 1. Munich 1964, 155–67.

HERMANN, W. *Römische Götteraltäre*. Kallmünz 1961.

HERZIG, H. E. "Namen und Daten der Via Aurelia." *Epigraphica* 32 (1970) 50–65.

HILL, P. V. "The Dating and Arrangement of Hadrian's Cos III Coins of the Mint of Rome." In *Mints, Dies and Currency: Essays Dedicated to the Memory of A. Baldwin*. Edited by R.A.G. Carson. London 1971, 35–56.

—— *The Dating and Arrangement of the Undated Coins of Rome*, A.D. *98–148*. London 1970.

—— "Some Architectural Types of Trajan." *NC*, ser. 7, 5 (1965) 155–60.

—— "The Temples of Augustus and Elagabalus and the Identity of the Temples of the Divi and of Juppiter Ultor." *NumCirc* 68 (1960) 208ff.

HIRSCHFELD, O. "Der Grundbesitz der römischen Kaiser in den ersten drei Jahrhunderten." In *Kleine Schriften*. Berlin 1913, 516–75.

—— *Die kaiserliche Verwaltungsbeamten bis auf Diocletian*. 2nd ed. Berlin 1905.

HOFFMANN, A. *Das Gartenstadion in der Villa Hadriana*. Deutsches Archäologisches Institut Rom, Sonderschriften 4. Mainz 1980.

HOHL, E. "Die angebliche 'Doppelbestattung' des Antoninus Pius." *Klio* 31 (1938) 169–85.

HOMMEL, P. *Studien zu den römischen Figurengiebeln der Kaiserzeit*. Berlin 1954.

HOMO, L. *Roma imperiale e l'urbanesimo nell'antichità*. Translated by A. Friedemann and M. Leva. Strumenti per una nuova cultura, guide e manuali 25. Milan 1976.

HOPKINS, K. *Conquerors and Slaves*. Cambridge 1978.

HORNSBOSTEL-HUTTNER, G. *Studien zur römischen Nischenarchitektur*. Studies of the Dutch Archaeological and Historical Society 9. Leiden 1979.

HOWE, L. L. *The Pretorian Prefect from Commodus to Diocletian*. Chicago 1942.

HOWELL, P. "The Colossus of Nero." *Athenaeum* 46 (1968) 292–99.

HÜLSEN, C. "Antichità di Monte Citorio." *RömMitt* 4 (1889) 41–64.

—— *Das Forum Romanum. Seine Geschichte und seine Denkmäler*. 2nd ed. Rome 1905.

—— "Das Grab des Antinous." *RömMitt* 11 (1896) 122–30.

—— "Il Mausoleo di Adriano." *BullComm* 3 (1913) 25–32.

—— "Porticus Divorum und Serapeum im Marsfelde." *RömMitt* 18 (1903) 17–57.

——— Review of *Castel Sant' Angelo in Roma*, by M. Borgatti. In *RömMitt* 6 (1891) 137–45.

——— *Die Thermen des Agrippa. Ein Beitrag zur Topographie des Marsfeldes in Rom*. Rome 1910.

——— "Trajanische und hadrianische Bauten im Marsfelde in Rom." *ÖJh* 15 (1912) 124–42.

——— ed. *Il libro di Giuliano da Sangallo*. Leipzig 1910.

HÜLSEN, C. and H. EGGER. *Die römischen Skizzenbucher von Marten van Heemskerck in königlichen Kupferstichkabinette zu Berlin*. 2 vols. Berlin 1913–16.

IVERSEN, E. *The Myth of Egypt and Its Hieroglyphs in European Tradition*. Copenhagen 1961.

——— *Obelisks in Exile*. I: *The Obelisks of Rome*. Copenhagen 1968.

JONES, C. P. "Aelius Aristides, *Eis Basilea*." *JRS* 62 (1972) 134–52.

——— *Plutarch and Rome*. Oxford 1971.

JONES, H. Stuart, ed. *A Catalogue of the Ancient Sculptures Preserved in the Municipal Collections of Rome*. I: *The Sculptures of the Museo Capitolino*. Oxford 1912. II: *The Sculptures of the Palazzo dei Conservatori*. Oxford 1926.

JORY, E. J. "Associations of Actors in Rome." *Hermes* 98 (1970) 224–53.

KÄHLER, H. "The Pantheon as Sacral Art." *Bucknell Review* 15.2 (1967) 41–48.

——— *The Art of Rome and Her Empire*. Translated by J. R. Foster. London 1962.

——— *Hadrian und seine Villa bei Tivoli*. Berlin 1950.

——— "Zur Herkunft des Antinousobelisken." *Acta ad archaeologiam et artium historiam pertinentia* 6 (1975) 35–44.

KAPOSSY, B. "Zwei Anlagen der Villa Hadriana." *Gymnasium* 74 (1967) 34–45.

KEIL, J. "Vertreter der zweiten Sophistik in Ephesos." *ÖJh* 40 (1953) 5–26.

KENNEDY, G. *The Art of Rhetoric in the Roman World*. Princeton 1972.

KIENAST, D. "Hadrian, Augustus und die eleusinischen Mysterien." *Jahrbuch für Numismatik und Geldgeschichte* 10 (1959–60) 61–69.

——— "Zur Baupolitik Hadrians in Rom." *Chiron* 10 (1980) 391–412.

KIERDORF, W. *"Laudatio funebris": Interpretationen und Untersuchungen zur Entwicklung der römischen Leichenrede*. Beitrage zur klassischen Philologie 106. Meisenheim am Glan 1980.

KLOFT, H. *Liberalitas Principis. Herkunft und Bedeutung. Studien zur Prinzipatsideologie*. Kölner historische Abhandlungen 18. Cologne 1970.

KNEISSL, P. *Die Siegestitulatur der römischen Kaiser. Untersuchungen zu d. Siegerbeinamen d. 1 u. 2 Jahrhunderts*. Hypomnemata 23. Göttingen 1969.

KNOCHE, U. "Die augusteische Ausprägung der *Dea Roma*." *Gymnasium* 59 (1952) 324–49.

KOCH, C. "Roma Aeterna." *Gymnasium* 59 (1952) 128–43, 196–209.

——— "Untersuchungen zur Geschichte der römischen Venus-Verehrung." *Hermes* 83 (1955) 1–51.

——— "Venus." *RE* 8 A.1 (1955) 828–87.

KOCKEL, V. "Beobachtungen zum Tempel des Mars Ultor und zum Forum des Augustus." *RömMitt* 80 (1983) 421–28.

——— *Die Grabbauten von dem Herkulaner Tor in Pompeji*. Mainz 1983.

KOEPPEL, G. "Official State Reliefs of the City of Rome in the Imperial Age. A Bibliography." *ANRW* II.12.1 (1982) 477–506.

——— "Profectio und Adventus." *BJb* 169 (1969) 130–94.

KOEPPEL, G. M. "Die historischen Reliefs der römischen Kaiserzeit II." *BJb* 184 (1984) 1–65.

KRAFT, K. "Der Sinn des Mausoleums des Augustus." *Historia* 16 (1967) 189–206.

KRAUS, T. "Das Bildnis des Antinoos." *Heidelberger Jahrbücher* 3 (1959) 48–67.

——— "Ornamentfriese vom Augustusforum." *Mitteilungen des deutschen archäo-*

*logischen Instituts* (Munich and Berlin) 6 (1953) 46–57.

KRAUS, T. and J. RÖDER. "Voruntersuchungen zum Mons Claudianus 1961." *AA* 18 (1962) 693–745.

KRAUSE, C. *Domus Tiberiana. Nuove ricerche—studi di restauro.* Zurich 1985.

—— "Zur baulischen Gestalt des republikanischen Comitiums." *RömMitt* 83 (1976) 31–69.

KRAUTHEIMER, R. *Rome. Profile of a City, 312–1308.* Princeton, N.J. 1980.

KRAUTHEIMER, R., W. FRÄNKL, and S. CORBETT. *Corpus Basilicarum Christianarum Romae. The Early Christian Basilicas of Rome (IV–IX Centuries).* Monumenti di antichità christiana, ser. 2, 3. Vatican City 1962.

KRENCKER, D. *Die Trierer Kaiserthermen.* Augsburg 1929.

KRILL, R. M. "Roman Paganism under the Antonines and Severans." *ANRW* II.16.1 (1978) 27–44.

KÜHN, E. *Antinoopolis. Ein Beitrag zur Geschichte des Hellenismus im römischen Ägypten. Grundung und Verfassung.* Göttingen 1913.

KÜTHMANN, H. and B. OVERBECK. *Bauten Roms auf Münzen und Medaillen.* Munich 1973.

LABROUSSE, M. "Le *pomerium* de la Rome impériale. Notes de topographie romaine." *MélRome* 54 (1937) 165–99.

LA FON, X. "A propos des *villae* républicaines, quelques notes sur les programmes décoratifs et les commanditaires." In *L'art décoratif à Rome à la fin de la république et au début du principat.* Collection de l'Ecole française de Rome 55. Rome 1981, 151–72.

LAMBRECHTS, P. Review of *Les Empereurs romains et leur politique religieuse*, by J. Beaujeu. In *Revue belge de philologie et d'histoire* 35 (1957) 495–511.

LANA, I. "I ludi capitolini di Domiziano." *RivFil*, N.S. 29 (1951) 145–60.

LANCIANI, R. "La Basilica Matidies et Marcianes dei Cataloghi." *BullComm* 11 (1883) 5–16.

—— "L'itinerario di Einsiedeln e l'ordine di Benedetto Canonico." *MonAnt* 1 (1889) 540–49.

—— *The Ruins and Excavations of Ancient Rome.* Boston and New York 1897.

—— *Storia degli scavi di Roma e notizie intorno le collezioni romane di antichità.* Rome 1902–12.

LA ROCCA, E. *Ara Pacis Augustae.* Rome 1983.

LATTE, K. *Römische Religionsgeschichte.* Handbuch der Altertumswissenschaft 5.4. Munich 1960.

LAUBSCHER, H. P. "Arcus Novus und Arcus Claudii, zwei Triumphbogen an der Via Lata im Rom." *Nachrichten Akad. Göttingen*, 1976, 65–108.

LE GALL, J. *Le Tibre, fleuve de Rome dans l'antiquité.* Publications de l'Institute d'art et d'archéologie de l'Université de Paris 1. Paris 1953.

LEHMANN-HARTLEBEN, K. "L'Arco di Tito." *BullComm* 62 (1934) 89–122.

LEHMANN-HARTLEBEN, K. and J. LINDROS. "Il palazzo degli Orti Sallustiani." *OpusArch* 1 (1935) 196–227.

LEON, C. F. *Die Bauornamentik des Trajansforum und ihre Stellung in der früh- und mittelkaiserzeitlichen Architekturdekoration Roms.* Publikationen des österreichischen Kulturinstituts in Rom 1.4. Vienna-Cologne-Graz 1971.

LEVI, A. C. "Hadrian as King of Egypt." *NC*, ser. 6, 8 (1948) 30–38.

LEWIS, N. "Literati in the Service of Roman Emperors: Politics before Culture." In *Coins, Culture and History in the Ancient World. Numismatic and Other Studies in Honor of B. L. Trell.* Edited by L. Casson and M. Price. Detroit 1981, 149–66.

LISSI CARONNA, E. "Roma. Rinvenimenti in Piazza Capranica 78." *NSc*, ser. 8, 26 (1972) [1973] 398–403.

LLOYD, R. B. "The Aqua Virgo, Euripus and Pons Agrippa." *AJA* 83 (1979) 193–204.

LOERKE, W. "Georges Chédanne and the Pantheon: A Beaux-Arts Contribution to the History of Roman Architecture." *Modulus*, 1982, 40–55.

L'ORANGE, H. P. and A. VON GERKAN. *Der spä-*

*tantike Bildschmuck des Konstantinsbogen.* Studien zur spätantiken Kunstgeschichte 10. Berlin 1939.

LORENTZ, F. "Ein Bildnis des Antoninus Pius?" *RömMitt* 48 (1933) 308–11.

LUGLI, G. "Aedes Caesarum in Palatio e Templum Novum divi Augusti." *BullComm* 69 (1941) 29–58.

—— "Come si è trasformato nei secoli il suolo di Roma." *RendLinc*, ser. 8, 6 (1951) 471–91. Republished in his *StudMin*, 229–45.

—— "Date de la fondation du Forum de Trajan." *CRAI*, 1965, 233–38.

—— "I mercati Traianei." *Dedalo*, Feb. 1930, 527–51.

—— *Monumenti minori del Foro Romano.* Rome 1947.

—— " 'Roma aeterna' e il suo culto sulla Velia." Accademia Nazionale dei Lincei, problemi attuali di scienza e di cultura. Quaderno 11, 8. Rome 1949.

—— "La Roma di Domiziano nei versi di Marziale e di Stazio." *Studi Romani* 9 (1961) 1–17.

—— *La tecnica edilizia dei romani con particolare riguardo a Roma e Lazio.* Rome 1957.

—— "La tomba di Traiano." In *Omagiu lui Constantin Daicoviciu.* Bucharest 1960, 333–38. Republished in his *StudMin*, 293–98.

MAC DONALD, W. L. *The Architecture of the Roman Empire. An Introductory Study.* Rev. ed. New Haven and London 1982.

—— *The Pantheon. Design, Meaning and Progeny.* Cambridge, Mass. 1976.

MAC MULLEN, R. *Paganism in the Roman Empire.* New Haven and London 1981.

MAGI, F. "Il circo vaticano in base alle più recenti scoperte. Il suo obelisco e i suoi *carceres.*" *RendPontAcc* 45 (1972–73) [1974] 37–73.

—— "Un nuovo mausoleo presso il circo Neroniano e altre minori scoperte." *RACrist* 42 (1966) [1968] 207–26.

—— "Relazione preliminare sui ritrovamenti archeologici nell'area dell'autoparco Vaticano." In *Triplice omaggio a sua Santità Pio XII.* Vatican City 1968, 87–99.

—— *I rilievi Flavi del Palazzo della Cancelleria.* Rome 1945.

MAGIE, D. *Roman Rule in Asia Minor to the End of the Third Century after Christ.* 2 vols. Princeton 1950.

MALAISE, M. *Les Conditions de pénétration et de diffusion des cultes égyptiens en Italie.* EPRO 22. Leiden 1972.

—— *Inventaire préliminaire des documents égyptiens découverts en Italie.* EPRO 21. Leiden 1972.

MANCINI, G. "Le recenti scoperte di antichità a Monte Citorio." *Studi Romani* 1 (1913) 3–15.

MANDOWSKY, E. and C. MITCHELL, eds. *Pirro Ligorio's Roman Antiquities. The Drawings in Ms. XIII B.7 in the National Library of Naples.* London 1963.

MANNSPERGER, D. "ROM. ET AUG. Die Darstellung des Kaisertums in der römischen Reichsprägung." *ANRW* II.1 (1974) 919–96.

MARCONI, P. "Antinoo. Saggio sull'arte dell'età Adrianea." *MonAnt* 29 (1923) 161–302.

MAROUZEAU, J. "Juppiter Optimus et Bona Dea." *Eranos* 54 (1956) 227–31.

MARROU, H. I. *A History of Education in Antiquity.* Translated by G. Lamb. New York 1954.

—— "La Vie intellectuelle au Forum de Trajan et au Forum d'Auguste." *MélRome* 49 (1932) 93–110.

MARTIN, J. P. "Hadrien et le phénix. Propagande numismatique." In *Mélanges . . . W. Seston.* Publications de la Sorbonne, série études 9. Paris 1974, 327–37.

MARTIN, R. "Agora et Forum." *MélRome* 84.2 (1972) 903–33.

MARUCCHI, O. *Gli obelischi egiziani di Roma.* Rome 1898.

MATTINGLY, H. "Some Historical Coins of Hadrian." *JRS* 15 (1925) 209–22.

MAULL, I. "Hadrians Jagddenkmal." *ÖJh* 42 (1955) 53–67.

MAZA, F. de la. *Antinoo, el último dios del mundo clásico.* Estudios de arte y estética 10. Mexico City 1966.

MEIGGS, R. *Roman Ostia.* 2nd ed. Oxford 1973.

MELLOR, R. "The Goddess Roma." *ANRW* II.17.2 (1981) 950–1030.

—— *"Thea Rhome."* The Worship of the Goddess Roma in the Greek World. Hypomnenata 42. Göttingen 1975.

MERLIN, A. *L'Aventin dans l'antiquité.* BEFAR 97. Paris 1906.

MERTEN, E. W. *Bäder und Badegepflogenheiten in der Darstellung der Historia Augusta.* Antiquitas 4.16. Bonn 1983.

METCALF, W. E. *The Cistophori of Hadrian.* ANSNS 15. New York 1980.

MIELSCH, H. "Hadrianische Malereien der Vatikannekropole *ad circum.*" *RendPontAcc* 46 (1973–74) [1975] 79–87.

MILLAR, F. *The Emperor in the Roman World.* Ithaca, N.Y. 1977.

—— *A Study of Cassius Dio.* Oxford 1964.

MOCCHEGIANI CARPANO, C. "Indagini archeologiche nel Tevere." *QuadAEI* 5 (1981) 142–55.

MOLISANI, G. "Una dedica a Giove Dolicheno nell'Isola Tiberina." *RendLinc,* ser. 8, 26 (1971) [1972] 795–811.

MOMIGLIANO, A. "Pagan and Christian Historiography in the Fourth Century A.D." In his *Essays in Ancient and Modern Historiography.* Middletown, Conn. 1977, 107–26. Reprinted from *The Conflict between Paganism and Christianity in the Fourth Century.* Edited by A. Momigliano. Oxford 1963, 79–99.

MONACO, E. "Laterizi bollati dalla *Domus Tiberiana.*" *RendPontAcc* 48 (1975–76) [1977] 309–13.

MONTAGNA PASQUINUCCI, M. "La decorazione architettonica del tempio del Divo Giulio nel Foro Romano." *Accademia Nazionale dei Lincei, Monumenti Antichi, serie miscellanea* 48 (Rome 1973) 257–81.

MORETTI, G. *Ara Pacis Augustae.* Rome 1948.

MORETTI, L. "Sulle iscrizioni greche di Porto." *RendLinc,* ser. 8, 19 (1964) 193–202.

MORGAN, M. G. "Villa Publica and Magna Mater. Two Notes on Manubial Building

at the Close of the Second Century B.C." *Klio* 55 (1973) 215–45.

MUMFORD, L. "City. Forms and Functions." In *International Encyclopedia of the Social Sciences.* Vol. 2. Edited by D. L. Sills. New York 1968, 447–55.

MUÑOZ, A. *La sistemazione del Tempio di Venere e Roma.* Rome 1935.

—— *Via dei Monti e Via del Mare.* Rome 1932.

MURGA, J. L. *Protección a la estética en la Legislación Urbanística del Alto Imperio.* Seville 1976.

NARDUCCI, P. *Sulla fognatura della città di Roma.* Rome 1889.

NASH, E. "Obelisk und Circus." *RömMitt* 64 (1957) 232–59.

—— "Suggerimenti intorno ad alcuni problemi topografici del Foro e del Palatino." *ArchCl* 11 (1959) 227–36.

NASH, E. and H. A. CAHN. "Der Wohnpalast der Casaren auf dem Palatin." *AntK* 1 (1958) 24–28.

NEUERBURG, N. *L'architettura delle fontane e dei ninfei nell'Italia antica.* Società R. di Napoli, Memorie della R. Accademia di archeologia, lettere e belle arti 5. Naples 1965.

—— "The Other Villas of Tivoli." *Archeology* 21 (1968) 288–97.

NIBBY, A. *Roma nell'anno 1838.* Vols. I–II. Rome 1839–41.

NICOLET, C. "Le Temple des Nymphes et les distributions frumentaires à Rome à l'époque républicaine." *CRAI,* 1976, 29–51.

NOCK, A. D. "Deification and Julian." *JRS* 47 (1957) 115–23.

NOGARA, B. "Campo Marzio nell'età Augustea." *Quaderni di Studi Romani* 8 (1941) 3–26.

NORDH, A. *Libellus de regionibus urbis.* Acta Instituti Romani Regni Sueciae, ser. 8, 3 (1949).

NOTA, M. "L'obelisco di Antinoo." *Capitolium* 50.11 (1975) 62–65.

OLIVER, J. H. "The Augustan Pomerium." *MAAR* 10 (1932) 145–82.

—— "The Divi of the Hadrianic Period." *HThR* 42 (1949) 35–40.

—— *The Ruling Power. A Study of the Roman Empire in the Second Century after Christ through the Roman Oration of Aelius Aristides.* Transactions of the American Philosophical Society 43. Philadelphia 1953.

OPTENDRENK, T. *Die Religionspolitik des Kaisers Elagabal im Spiegel der "Historia Augusta."* Habelts Dissertationsdrucke. Reihe alte Geschichte 6. Bonn 1969.

PACE, P. *Gli acquedotti di Roma e il "de aquaeductu" di Frontino, contesto critico, versione e commento.* Rome 1983.

PACKER, J. "La casa di Via Giulio Romano." *BullComm* 81 (1968–69) [1972] 127–48.

—— "Numismatic Evidence for the Southeast (Forum) Facade of the Basilica Ulpia." In *Coins, Culture and History in the Ancient World. Numismatic and Other Studies in Honor of B. L. Trell.* Edited by L. Casson and M. Price. Detroit 1981, 57–68.

—— "Trajan's Basilica Ulpia: Some Reconsiderations." *AJA* 86 (1982) 280.

—— Review of *Foro di Traiano,* by C. M. Amici. In *AJA* 87 (1983) 569–72.

PACKER, J., K. L. SARRING, and R. M. SHELDON. "A New Excavation in Trajan's Forum." *AJA* 87 (1983) 165–72.

PACKER, J. E. "Housing and Population in Imperial Ostia and Rome." *JRS* 57 (1967) 80–95.

PALMER, R.E.A. "The *excusatio magisteri* and the Administration of Rome under Commodus." *Athenaeum* 52 (1974) 268–88, and *Athenaeum* 53 (1975) 57–87.

—— "Jupiter Blaze, Gods of the Hills, and the Roman Topography of *CIL* VI 337." *AJA* 80 (1976) 43–56.

—— "The Topography and Social History of Rome's Trastevere (Southern Sector)." *Proceedings of the American Philosophical Society* 125.5 (1981) 368–97.

PANCIERA, S. "Tra epigrafia e topografia." *ArchCl* 22 (1970) 131–63.

PANIMOLLE, G. *Gli acquedotti di Roma antica.* Rome 1968.

PANVINI ROSATI, F. "Osservazioni sui tipi monetali romani raffiguranti monumenti di Roma." *RIN* 3, ser. 5, 57 (1955) 70–83.

PARIBENI, R. *Optimus Princeps. Saggio sulla storia e sui tempi dell'imperatore Traiano.* 2 vols. Messina 1926–27.

PARKER, J. H. *The Twelve Egyptian Obelisks in Rome.* Part 4 of *The Archaeology of Rome.* 2nd ed. Oxford 1879.

PASSERINI, A. *Le coorti pretorie.* Studi pubblicati dal R. Istituto italiano per la storia antica 1. Rome 1939.

PAVIS D'ESCURAC, H. *La Préfecture de l'annone. Service administratif impérial d'Auguste à Constantin.* BEFAR 226. Rome 1976.

PEARCE, J.W.E. "The *Vota* Legends on the Roman Coinage." *NC,* ser. 5, 17 (1937) 112–23.

PEKARY, T. "Das Grab des Pompeius." *HAC* 1970. Bonn 1972, 195–98.

PENSA, M. "L'architettura traianea attraverso le emissioni edilizie coeve." In *Atti Centro Studi e Documentazione sull'Italia romana* 2. Milan 1969–70 [1971] 237–97.

—— "Rappresentazioni di monumenti sulle monete di Adriano." *RIN* 80 (1978) 27–78.

PENSABENE, P. "*Auguratorium* e Tempio della Magna Mater." *QuadAEI* 2 (1979) 67–74.

—— "Fregia in marmo nero da Villa Adriana." *ArchCl* 28 (1976) [1978] 126–60.

PEROWNE, S. *Hadrian.* New York 1960.

PERRET, L. *La Titulature impériale d'Hadrien.* Paris 1929.

PETERSEN, E. "Hadrians Steuererlass." *RömMitt* 14 (1899) 222–29.

PETIT, P. "Le II^e siècle après J.-C. Etat des questions et problèmes." *ANRW* II.2 (1975) 354–80.

PFANNER, M. *Der Titusbogen.* Beitrage zur Erschliessung hellenistischer und kaiserzeitlicher Skulptur und Architektur 2. Mainz am Rhein 1983.

PFLAUM, H.-G. "La Carrière di C. Aufidius Victorinus, condisciple de Marc Aurèle." *CRAI,* 1956, 189–200.

—— *Les Carrières procuratoriennes équestres sous le Haut-Empire romain.* Bibliothèque archéologique et historique 57. Paris 1960–61.

—— "Le Règlement successoral d'Hadrien." *HAC* 1963. Bonn 1964, 95–122.

PHILLIPS, E. J. "The Roman Law on the Demolition of Buildings." *Latomus* 32 (1973) 86–95.

PICCALUGA, G. "Bona Dea." *Studi e materiali di storia delle religioni* 35 (1964) 195–237.

PICKARD-CAMBRIDGE, A. W. *The Dramatic Festivals of Athens.* 2nd ed. Revised by J. Gould and D. M. Lewis. Oxford 1969.

PIERCE, J. R. "The Mausoleum of Hadrian and the Pons Aelius." *JRS* 15 (1925) 75–103.

PIGHI, G. B. *De ludis saecularibus populi Romani Quiritium, libri sex.* 2nd ed. Amsterdam 1965.

PLEKET, H. W. "Some Aspects of the History of the Athletic Guilds." *ZPE* 10 (1973) 197–227.

PLOMMER, H. "Trajan's Forum." *Antiquity* 48 (1974) 126–30.

—— "Trajan's Forum: A Plea." *Proceedings of the Cambridge Philological Society* 186, N.S. 6 (1960) 54–62.

POLAND, R. "Nachträge, technitai." *RE* 5 A.2 (1934) 2473–2558.

POLLINI, J. Review of *Typology and Structure of Roman Historical Reliefs,* by M. Torelli. In *AJA* 87 (1983) 572–73.

PORTER, B. and R.L.B. MOSS. *Topographical Bibliography of Ancient Egyptian Hieroglyphic Texts, Reliefs, and Paintings.* Vol. VII. Oxford 1951.

QUILICI, L. "Il Campo Marzio occidentale." In *Città e architettura,* 59–85.

QUILICI Gigli, S. "Estremo Campo Marzio. Alcune osservazioni sulla topografia." In *Città e architettura,* 47–57.

RADKE, G. *Die Götter Altitaliens.* Fontes et Commentationes 3. Munich 1965.

RAEDER, J. *Die statuarische Ausstattung der Villa Hadriana bei Tivoli.* Europäische Hochschulschriften, ser. 38, Archaeology 4. Frankfurt am Main and Bern 1983.

RAKOB, F. L. "Der Bauplan einer kaiserlichen Villa." In *Festschrift K. Lankheit.* Cologne 1973, 113–25.

—— "Ein Grottentriklinium in Pompeji." *RömMitt* 71 (1964) 182–94.

—— "Hellenismus in Mittelitalien. Bautypen und Bautechnik." In *Hellenismus in Mittelitalien,* 366–86.

—— "Litus beatae Veneris aureum. Untersuchungen am 'Venustempel' in Baiae." *RömMitt* 68 (1961) 114–49.

RAOSS, M. "L'iscrizione della colonna Traiana e una epigrafe latina cristiana di Roma del V secolo." In *Seconda miscellanea greca e romana.* Studi pubblicati dall'Istituto italiano per la storia antica 19. Rome 1968, 399–435.

REINA, V. and U. BARBIERI. "Rilievo planimetrico ed altimetrico di Villa Adriana . . ." *NSc,* ser. 5, 3 (1906) 314–17.

REINA, V. et al. *Media pars urbis.* Rome 1910.

REINACH, S. "Les Têtes des médaillons de l'arc de Constantin à Rome." *RA,* ser. 4, 15 (1910) 118–31.

REYNOLDS, P.K.B. *The Vigiles of Imperial Rome.* London 1926.

RICCI, C., A.M. COLINI, and V. MARIANI. *Via dell'Impero.* Rome 1933.

RICHARD, J.-C. "Les Funérailles de Trajan et le triomphe sur les Parthes." *REL* 44 (1966) 351–62.

—— " 'Mausoleum': d'Halicarnasse à Rome, puis à Alexandrie." *Latomus* 29 (1970) 370–88.

—— "Recherches sur certains aspects du culte impérial: Les funérailles des empereurs romains aux deux premiers siècles de notre ère." *ANRW* II.16.2 (1978) 1121–34.

—— "Tombeaux des empereurs et temples des 'divi': notes sur la signification religieuse des sépultures impériales à Rome." *RHR* 170 (1966) 127–42.

RICHARDSON, L., Jr. "The Approach to the Temple of Saturn." *AJA* 84 (1980) 51–62.

—— "The Architecture of the Forum of Trajan." *Archaeological News* 6 (1977) 101–7.

—— "The Curia Julia and the Janus Geminus." *RömMitt* 85 (1978) 359–69.

—— "The Tribunals of the Praetors of Rome." *RömMitt* 80 (1973) 219–33.

—— "The Villa Publica and the Divorum." In *Essays in Honor . . . O. J. Brendel.* Edited by L. Bonfante and H. von Heintze. Mainz 1976, 159–63.

RICKMAN, G. "Porticus Minucia." In *Città e architettura*, 105–108.

RICOTTI, E. Salza Prina. "Criptoportici e gallerie sotterranee di Villa Adriana nella loro tipologia e nelle loro funzioni." In *Les cryptoportiques dans l'architecture romaine*. Collection de l'Ecole française de Rome 14. Rome 1973, 219–59.

—— "Cucine e quartieri servili in epoca romana." *RendPontAcc* 51–52 (1978–80) [1982] 237–94.

ROBATHAN, D. M. "A Reconsideration of Roman Topography in the *Historia Augusta*." *TAPA* 70 (1939) 515–34.

ROBERT, L. "Les Aelius Alcibiade de Nysa." In his *Etudes épigraphiques et philologiques*. Paris 1938, 45–53.

—— "Deux concours grecs à Rome." *CRAI*, 1970, 6–27.

RODDAZ, J.-M. *Marcus Agrippa*. BEFAR 253. Rome 1984.

RODENWALDT, G. Review of *Das Römerlager Vetera*, by H. Lehner. In *Gnomon* 2 (1926) 337–43.

—— "Römische Staatsarchitektur." In *Das neue Bild der Antike*. Vol. II. Edited by H. Berve. Deutsche Geisteswissenschaft. Leipzig 1942, 356–73.

RODRIGUEZ-ALMEIDA, E. "Il Campo Marzio settentrionale: *Solarium* e *Pomerium*." *RendPontAcc* 51–52 (1978–79/1979–80) [1982] 195–212.

—— *Forma urbis marmorea, aggiornamento generale 1980*. Rome 1981.

—— "*Forma Urbis Marmorea*: nuovi elementi di analisi e nuove ipotesi di lavoro." *MélRome* 89 (1977) 219–56.

ROMANELLI, P. "II.—Roma. Reg. IX—Via della Torretta.—Cippi del pomerio." *NSc*, 1933, 240–44.

RONCAIOLI, C. "L'Arco di 'Camilliano' e il 'Cacco' di S. Stefano nell'Iseo e Serapeo del Campo Marzio." *Giornale Italiano di Filologia* 66 (1979) 81–96.

RÜDIGER, U. "Die Anaglypha Hadriani." *Antike Plastik* 12 (1973) 161–74.

RUSSELL, J. "The Origin and Development of Republican Forums." *Phoenix* 22 (1968) 304–36.

RUYSSCHAERT, J. "Essai d'interprétation synthétique de l'arc de Constantin." *RendPontAcc* 35 (1962–63) [1964] 79–100.

RYBERG, I. S. *Rites of the State Religion in Roman Art*. MAAR 22. Rome 1955.

SALLER, R. P. "Anecdotes as Historical Evidence for the Principate." *G&R* 27 (1980) 69–83.

—— *Personal Patronage under the Early Empire*. Cambridge 1982.

SANTANGELO, M. "Il Quirinale nell'antichità classica." *MemPontAcc*, ser. 3, 5 (1941) 77–214.

SAVAGE, E. M. "The Cults of Ancient Trastevere." *MAAR* 17 (1940) 26–46.

SCHEFOLD, K. "Aphrodite von Knidos, Isis und Serapis." *AntK* 7 (1964) 56–59.

SCHILLING, R. *La Religion romaine de Vénus depuis les origines jusqu'au temps d'Auguste*. BEFAR 178. 2nd ed. Paris 1982.

SCHMIDT-COLINET, A. *Antike Stützfiguren. Untersuchungen zu Typus und Bedeutung der menschengestaltigen Architekturstütze in der griechischen und römischen Kunst*. Frankfurt 1977.

SCHNEIDER GRAZIOSI, G. "L'*Auguratorium* del Palatino." *Dissertazioni della Pontificia Accademia Romana di Archeologia*, ser. 2, 12 (1918) 147–78.

SCHULTEN, P. N. *Die Typologie der römische Konsekrationsprägungen*. Frankfurt 1979.

SCOTT, K. *The Imperial Cult under the Flavians*. Stuttgart and Berlin 1936.

SEAR, F. B. *Roman Wall and Vault Mosaics*. RömMitt, Erg.-H. 23. Heidelberg 1977.

SELTMAN, C. "Greek Sculpture and Some Festival Coins." *Hesperia* 17 (1948) 71–85.

SESTON, W. "Les 'Anaglypha Traiani' du Forum Romain et la politique d'Hadrien en 118." *MélRome* 44 (1927) 154–83.

SHATZMAN, I. *Senatorial Wealth and Roman Politics*. Collection Latomus 142. Brussels 1975.

SHERWIN-WHITE, A. N. *The Letters of Pliny. A Historical and Social Commentary*. Oxford 1966.

SHIPLEY, F. W. *Agrippa's Building Activities in Rome*. Washington University Studies, N.S. 4. Language and Literature. St. Louis 1933.

SIMON, E. *Ara Pacis Augustae*. Monumenta artis antiquae I. Tübingen 1967.

SJÖQVIST, E. "Studi archeologici e topografici intorno alla Piazza del Collegio Romano." *OpusArch* 4 (1946) 47–157.

SKUTSCH, O. *Studia Enniana*. London 1968.

SKYDSGAARD, J. E. "Public Building and Society in Ancient Rome." In *Città e architettura*, 223–27.

SMITH, A.C.G. "The Date of the 'Grandi Terme' of Hadrian's Villa at Tivoli." *PBSR* 46 (1978) 73–93.

SMITH, R.R.R. Review of *Typology and Structure of Roman Historical Reliefs*, by M. Torelli. In *JRS* 73 (1983) 225–28.

SNIJDER, G.A.S. "Kaiser Hadrian und der Tempel der Venus und Roma." *JdI* 55 (1940) 1–11.

SOMMELLA, A. M. "L'esplorazione archeologica per il restauro del Tabularium." *QuadAEI* 8 (1984) 159–63.

SQUADRILLI, T. "Il Mausoleo di Adriano." *Capitolium* 50.7–8 (1975) 20–31.

STADTER, P. A. *Arrian of Nicomedia*. Chapel Hill, N.C. 1980.

STEINBY, M. "I bolli laterizi e i criteri tecnici nella datazione delle cortine laterizie. Esame su un gruppo di edifici ostiensi dei primi anni di Adriano." *Miscelànea Arqueològica II (Ampurias)*. Barcelona 1974, 389–405.

—— "L'edilizia come industria pubblica e privata." In *Città e architettura*, 219–21.

—— "Ziegelstempel von Rom und Umbegung." *RE, Suppl.* 15 (1978) 1489–1531.

STROHEKER, K. F. "Die Aussenpolitik des Antoninus Pius nach der *Historia Augusta*." *HAC* 1964/1965. Bonn 1966, 241–56.

STRONG, D. E. "The Administration of Public Building during the Late Republic and Early Empire." *Bulletin of the Institute of Classical Studies of the University of London* 15 (1968) 97–103.

—— "Late Hadrianic Architectural Ornament in Rome." *PBSR* 21 (1953) 118–51.

STUCCHI, S. "L'arco detto di Portogallo sulla via Flaminia." *BullComm* 73 (1949–50) [1953] 101–22.

SWEET, C. S. "The Dedication of the Canopus at Hadrian's Villa." *AJA* 77 (1973) 229.

SYME, R. *Ammianus and the "Historia Augusta."* Oxford 1968.

—— *Emperors and Biography. Studies in the "Historia Augusta."* Oxford 1971.

—— *Greeks Invading the Roman Government*. Brookline, Mass. 1982.

—— "Hadrian and the Senate." *Athenaeum* 62.1 (1984) 31–60.

—— *The Roman Revolution*. Oxford 1939.

—— *Tacitus*. Oxford 1958.

—— "The Ummidii." *Historia* 17 (1968) 72–105.

—— "Ummidius Quadratus, *Capax imperii*." *HSCP* 83 (1979) 287–310.

TAMM, B. *Auditorium and Palatium. A Study on Assembly Rooms in Roman Palaces during the First Century B.C. and the First Century A.D.* Stockholm Studies in Classical Archaeology 2. Stockholm 1963.

—— "Ist der Castortempel das *vestibulum* zu dem Palast des Caligula gewesen?" *Eranos* 62 (1964) 146–69.

TAMM-FAHLSTRÖM, B. "Remarques sur les odéons de Rome." *Eranos* 57 (1959) 67–71.

TEDESCHI GRISANTI, G. "Il fregio con delfini e conchiglie della Basilica Neptuni: uno spoglio romano al Camposanto Monumentale di Pisa." *RendLinc*, ser. 8, 35 (1980) 181–92.

*Il "Tempio di Romolo" al Foro Romano*. Quaderni dell'Istituto di storia dell'architettura, ser. 26, 157–62. Rome 1980.

TEMPORINI, H. *Die Frauen am Hofe Trajans. Ein Beitrag zur Stellung der Augustae im Principat*. Berlin and New York 1978.

THOMPSON, D. L. "The Lost City of Antinoos." *Archaeology* 34.1 (1981) 44–50.

THORTON, M. K. "Hadrian and His Reign." *ANRW* II.2 (1975) 432–76.

TIBERI, C. "L'esedra di Erode Attico a Olympia e il Canopo della Villa di Adriano presso Tivoli." In *Saggi di Storia dell'archittetura in onore del professore Vincenzo Fasolo*. Rome 1961, 35–48.

TIMPE, D. *Der Triumph des Germanicus. Untersuchungen zu den Feldzügen der Jahre 14–16 n. Chr. in Germanien.* Antiquitas 1. Abhandlungen zur alten Geschichte 16. Bonn 1968.

TORELLI, M. *Typology and Structure of Roman Historial Reliefs.* Jerome Lectures, ser. 14. Ann Arbor, Mich. 1982.

TOWNEND, G. B. "The Post of *ab epistulis* in the Second Century." *Historia* 10 (1961) 375–81.

TOYNBEE, J.M.C. "The Ara Pacis Reconsidered: Historical Art in Roman Italy." *ProcBritAc* 39 (1953) 67–95.

—— *Death and Burial in the Roman World.* Ithaca, N.Y. 1971.

—— *The Hadrianic School. A Chapter in the History of Greek Art.* Cambridge 1934.

—— Review of *Die Bildnisse des Antinous*, by C. Clairmont. In *JRS* 57 (1967) 267–68.

—— *Roman Medallions.* Numismatic Studies 5. New York 1944.

TOYNBEE, J. and J. WARD-PERKINS. *The Shrine of St. Peter and the Vatican Excavations.* London 1956.

TRELL, B. L. "Architectura Numismatica." *NC*, ser. 7, 12 (1972) 45–59.

TURCAN, R. "La 'Fondation' du Temple de Venus et de Rome." *Latomus* 23 (1964) 42–55.

—— "Origines et sens de l'inhumation à l'époque impériale." *REA* 60 (1958) 323–47.

VÄÄNANEN, V., ed. "Le iscrizioni della necropoli dell'autoparco Vaticano." *Acta Instituti Romani Finlandiae* 6 (1973) 475–76.

VAN DEMAN, E. B. *The Atrium Vestae.* Carnegie Institution of Washington. Publications 108. Washington, D.C. 1909.

—— "The House of Caligula." *AJA* 28 (1924) 368–98.

—— "The Neronian Sacra Via." *AJA* 27 (1923) 383–424.

—— "The Sullan Forum." *JRS* 12 (1922) 1–31.

VAN DEMAN, E. B. and A. G. CLAY. "The Sacra Via of Nero." *MAAR* 5 (1925) 115–26.

VAN DOREN, M. "Les *sacraria*. Une catégorie méconnue d'édifices sacrés chez les romains." *AntCl* 27 (1958) 31–75.

VERMASEREN, M. J. "The *Suovetaurilia* in Roman Art." *Bulletin Antieke Beschaving* 32 (1957) 1–12.

VERMEULE, C. C. *The Goddess Roma in the Art of the Roman Empire.* Cambridge, Mass. 1959.

—— *Greek Sculpture and Roman Taste: The Purpose and Setting of Graeco-Roman Art in Italy and the Greek Imperial East.* Jerome Lectures, ser. 12. Ann Arbor, Mich. 1977.

VEYNE, P. *Le Pain et le cirque. Sociologie historique d'un pluralisme politique.* Paris 1976.

VIRGILI, P. "A proposito del Mausoleo di Augusto: Baldassare Peruzzi aveva ragione." *QuadAEI* 8 (1984) 194–98.

VITUCCI, G. *Ricerche sulla praefectura urbi in età imperiale (sec. I–III).* Rome 1956.

VOGEL, L. *The Column of Antoninus Pius.* Cambridge, Mass. 1973.

VON BLANCKENHAGEN, P. H. "Elemente am Beispiel des flavischen Stils." In *Das neue Bild der Antike.* Vol. II. Edited by H. Berve. Deutsche Geisteswissenschaft. Leipzig 1942, 310–41.

—— *Flavische Architektur und ihre Dekoration, Untersucht am Nervaforum.* Berlin 1940.

—— "The Imperial Fora." *JSAH* 13.4 (1954) 21–26.

VON DOMASZEWSKI, A. *Die Topographie Roms bei den "Scriptores Historiae Augustae."* Sitzungsberichte der Heidelberger Akademie der Wissenschaften, Philosophisch-historische *Klasse* 7. Heidelberg 1916.

VON GERKAN, A. "Einiges zur Aedes Castoris in Rom." *RömMitt* 60–61 (1953–54) 200–206.

VON HEINTZE, H. Review of *Die Bildnisse des Antinous*, by C. Clairmont. In *Gnomon* 43 (1971) 393–98.

VON SYDOW, W. "Archäologische Funde und Forschungen, Rom." *AA* 88 (1973) 521–683.

WALLACE-HADRILL, A. *Suetonius. The Scholar*

*and His Caesars.* New Haven and London 1983.

WALTON, F. R. "Religious Thought in the Age of Hadrian." *Numen* 4 (1957) 165–70.

WALTZING, J.-P. *Etude historique sur les corporations professionnelles chez les Romains depuis les origines jusqu'à la chute de l'Empire d'Occident.* Brussels 1895–1900.

WARD-PERKINS, J. "Tripolitania and the Marble Trade." *JRS* 41 (1951) 89–104.

WARD-PERKINS, J. B. "Columna divi Antonini." In *Mélanges . . . P. Collart.* Cahiers d'archéologie romande de la Bibliothèque historique vaudoise 5. Lausanne 1976, 345–52.

—— "The Marble Trade and Its Organization: Evidence from Nicomedia." In *The Seaborne Commerce of Ancient Rome: Studies in Archaeology and History.* Edited by J. H. D'Arms and E. C. Kopff. MAAR 36. Rome 1980, 325–36.

—— "Nicomedia and the Marble Trade." *PBSR* 48 (1980) 23–69.

—— *Roman Imperial Architecture.* Harmondsworth 1981.

WARD-PERKINS, J. B. and D. E. STRONG. "The Temple of Castor in the Forum Romanum." *PBSR* 30 (1962) 1–30.

WATAGHIN CANTINO, G. *Domus Augustana.* Turin 1966.

WEGNER, M. *Hadrian, Plotina, Marciana, Matidia, Sabina.* Das römische Herrscherbild II.3. Berlin 1956.

—— *Die Herrscherbildnisse in antoninischer Zeit.* Das römische Herrscherbild II.4. Berlin 1939.

—— *Schmuckbasen des antiken Rom.* Orbis antiquus 22. Munich 1966.

WERNER, P. *De incendiis urbis Romae aetate imperatorum.* Leipzig 1906.

WILLIAMS, G. W. *Change and Decline. Roman Literature in the Early Empire.* Sather Classical Lectures 45. Berkeley 1978.

WILLIAMS, W. "Individuality in the Imperial Constitutions: Hadrian and the Antonines." *JRS* 66 (1976) 67–83.

WINDFELD-HANSEN, H. "Les Couloirs annulaires dans l'architecture funéraire antique." *Acta Instituti Romani Norvegiae* 2 (1962) 35–63.

WINNEFELD, H. *Die Villa des Hadrian bei Tivoli.* Berlin 1895.

WISEMAN, T. P. "Via Aurelia Nova and Via Aemilia Scauri." *Epigraphica* 33 (1971) 27–32.

WISSOWA, G. "Capitolia." *RE* 3.2 (1899) 1527–29.

—— *Religion und Kultus der Römer.* 2nd ed. Handbuch der Altertumswissenschaft 5.4. Munich 1912.

WOODSIDE, M.S.A. "Vespasian's Patronage of Education and the Arts." *TAPA* 73 (1942) 123–29.

YAVETZ, Z. "Hadrianus the 'Wanderer.' " In *Commentationes ad antiquitatem classicam pertinentes in memoriam B. Katz.* Edited by M. Rozelaar and B. Shimron. Tel Aviv 1970, 67–77.

—— *Plebs and Princeps.* Oxford 1969.

ZANKER, P. *Forum Augustum. Das Bildprogramm.* Monumenta artis antiqua 2. Tübingen 1968.

—— *Forum Romanum. Die Neugestaltung durch Augustus.* Monumenta artis antiqua 5. Tübingen 1972.

—— "Das Trajansforum in Rom." *AA* 85.4 (1970) 499–544.

ZEVI, F. "Il Calcidico della *Curia Iulia.*" *RendLinc*, ser. 8, 26 (1971) [1972] 237–51.

ZIEGLER, K. "Palatium." *RE* 18 (1949) 5–81.

ZOEPFFEL, R. "Hadrian und Numa." *Chiron* 8 (1978) 391–427.

INDEXES

All place names refer to Rome unless marked with an asterisk. C preceding a page number refers to the subject's entry in the Catalogue. Figures are indicated by italic page numbers.

# GENERAL INDEX

## A

*ab epistulis graecis*, 205
*ab epistulis latinis*, 205
M. Acilius Aviola, 23. *See also SC Acilianum*
Acqua Felice, 242
Aedes gentis Flaviae, 164
Aedicula at the Atrium Vestae, 230
Aedicula of Juturna, 113
Aelius Alcibiades, T., of Nysa, 210
Aelius Aristides, 17, 211–12
Aelius Caesar, L., 97, 147
Aelius Phlegon, P., 27, 29, 205–206; biography of Hadrian, 236
Aelius Verus, L., *196*, 199
Aeneas, 107, 131
★Africa, 135, 200
Ager Vaticanus, 161, 165–68, *166*, 178–79; burials in, 167–68; Hadrianic development of, 167
Agrippa, 36, 46, 51, 56, 73, 163
Agrippina, Villa of, 165–66
★Albanum, Italy, 134 n. 3
★Alexandria, Egypt, 206, 251–52
*alimenta*, institution, 186–87, 189–90. *See also* Anaglypha Traiani/Hadriani, *adlocutio* relief
Altar tombs, 223
Alta Semita, 155
Ammon Ra, 245, 246
Anaglypha Traiani/Hadriani, 102 n.7, 106 n. 22, 112, 182–90, *185*, *188*, 235, C271; *adlocutio* (or *alimenta*) relief, *185*, 186–87, *188*; debt-burning relief, *185*, 186–89
Annii, 216
Antinoeia, 258–59. *See also* Antinoopolis, festivals of Antinoos in
★Antinoopolis, Egypt, 239, 258, 260; festivals of Antinoos in, 245, 251, 252, 258; foundation of, 245–46, 250–51; settlers of, 246, 251; Temple of Antinoos in, 241, 246, 250–51, 258
Antinoos, 143, *193*, *194*, 199–201, *254*, 255–57, 260; alleged servile origin, 241; as a mir-

acle healer, 244–45, 252; as Osirantinoos, 241, 243–46, 250–51, 257; cult of, 241–46, 252–53, 260; death and deification, 241, 251; images of, 251, 252, 253–55; in Egypt, 250–52, 260; in the Greek East, 251–52; in the Latin West, including Rome, 253, 256; syncretism of, 252; tomb or cenotaph of, 148, 241, 258. *See also* Obelisk of Antinoos
Antiquarians, value of evidence for Roman topography, 10–11
★Antium, Italy, 134 n. 3
Antoneineia (Antoninia), 258–59; Antoninia Pythia, 259
Antonius, M., 209
Antoninus Pius (emperor A.D. 138–161), 92, 123–24, 170, 181, *197*, 199, 211; head of, in Antiquario del Foro Romano, 191 n. 29
Apollo, 192, *192*, 194, *197*, 252, 257; Apollo Pythia, 259
Apollodorus of Damascus, 14, 21, 31, 78, 84, 119–21
Apotheosis of Sabina. *See* Reliefs
★Apt, France, 194
Aqueducts: Acqua Sallustiana, 155–56; Aqua Anio Novus, 230, C271; Aqua Anio Vetus, 230, C271; Aqua Celimontana, 230, C271; Aqua Claudia, 230, 242, C271; Aqua Marcia, 230, C271; Aqua Virgo, 38, 51, *57*
Aqueducts, Hadrianic repairs on Anio Novus, Anio Vetus, Celimontana, Claudia, Marcia, 230, C271
Ara Ditis, 218, 220, 224, 225
Ara Pacis, *34*, 35, 37, 40, *41*, 46, 66–67, *70*, 70–72, 130, 138, 184, 191, 220, 226, C266
Archaeology, value of as evidence, 10–11
Arch in Trajan's Forum, 81 n. 13, 191 n. 31
Architectural decoration, styles of, 12–13, 21, 95–96; Hadrianic, 21, 94, 124, 127, 237. *See also* Asiatic style; Pergamene-Ephesian school
Arch of Augustus, *100*, 107–108, 112
★Arch of Augustus in Rimini, 191 n. 31
Arch of Claudius, *34*, 58, 238

# INDEX OF SOURCE MATERIALS

*Library of Congress Cataloging-in-Publication Data*

BOATWRIGHT, MARY TALIAFERRO.
HADRIAN AND THE CITY OF ROME.

BIBLIOGRAPHY: P.
INCLUDES INDEXES.
I. HADRIAN, EMPEROR OF ROME, 76–138.
2. ROME (ITALY)—HISTORY—TO 476. 3. ROME—
HISTORY—HADRIAN, 117–138. I. TITLE.
DG295.B63 1987 937'.07 86–30440
ISBN 0–691–03588–1 (ALK. PAPER)